VICHY
AND THE
ETERNAL
FEMININE

Duke University Press

Durham and London, 2001

VICHY AND THE ETERNAL FEMININE

A CONTRIBUTION

TO A POLITICAL

SOCIOLOGY

OF GENDER

Francine Muel-Dreyfus

Translated by Kathleen A. Johnson

© 2001 Duke University Press
to English language edition
All rights reserved
Originally published as *Vichy et
l'éternel féminin* by Editions du Seuil
© 1996 Editions du Seuil
Printed in the United States
of America on acid-free paper ∞
Typeset in Monotype Garamond
by Tseng Information Systems, Inc.
Library of Congress Cataloging-in-
Publication Data appear on the last
printed page of this book. Assistance
for the translation was provided by
the French Ministry of Culture /
Centre National du Livre.

for Bruno and Julien

CONTENTS

INTRODUCTION

In all critical moments of man's social life, the rational forces that resist the rise of the old mythical conceptions are no longer sure of themselves. In these moments the time for myth has come again. For myth has not really been vanquished and subjugated. It is always there, lurking in the dark and waiting for its hour and opportunity. This moment comes as soon as the binding forces of man's social life lose their strength and are no longer able to combat the demonic mythical powers. —Ernst Cassirer, *The Myth of the State* (1946)

In 1940, France was the only occupied Western nation not to be content with merely administrating; instead, it carried out a domestic revolution in its institutions and its moral values.[1] This undertaking would bear the name of the National Revolution. In July 1940, Paul Baudouin (secretary of state to the president of the Conseil from October 1940 to January 1941) said in an interview in the *Journal de Genève* reprinted by *Le Temps:* "The total revolution of France has been prepared by twenty years of uncertainty, discontent, disgust, and latent insurrection. . . . This possibility of *doing something new* thrills men of every walk of life." And Jacques Benoist-Méchin (secretary of state to the president, then to the vice president of the Conseil from June 1994 to July 1942, and author of a book with the provocative title, given the historical context, *La Moisson de 40*) claimed: "What we need most is a *cure of purity.*" In this "revolution" announced and celebrated at the heart of the defeat as a victory, the political construction of the feminine around the notion of an "eternal feminine" occupies a central place.

Reforms were undertaken and proposed by the French State* beginning in July 1940 regarding women's work, education and schooling for girls, family and health policy, and feminine influences in the city. Here, and in the ethical, social, and political justifications that subtended these reforms and the remarks, often militant, of their numerous defenders, we find all the facets of the myth of the eternal feminine, this notion that had become commonplace and had imposed the idea of "an" "eternal" feminine "nature" and "an" "eternal" feminine "essence" that always has and always will escape history.

This book aims to measure this sexual recentering of the social world and to reconstruct the social processes of the production of this ideology, which seemed to spring forth fully armed and immediately ready for use at a moment of chaos and upheaval in the political and social order. The National Revolution constitutes a laboratory of ideas where one can analyze with clarity the processes for imposing certain symbolic representations of the male/female opposition, as well as the way these representations structure both perception and the practical and symbolic organization of social life, thereby becoming participants in the representations and the very establishment of power. This historical moment provides the opportunity to study in privileged fashion a process of repression that seeks to impose the concept of the eternal permanence of the binary representation of gender.[2] During this period of reaction and inauguration of an authoritarian state, it is the very idea of a debate, or of the prior historical existence of a debate, on the "nature" of the masculine and the feminine that is denied in favor of the concept of society's consensus from time immemorial concerning these themes. In this case, politics had a vested interest in historical forgetting and in a mythic vision of the world. To work on the construction of femininity in the social philosophy of the National Revolution is therefore also to work on the

* The French State (L'État Français) is the name the regime gave itself. See Jean-Pierre Azéma, *De Munich à la Libération 1938–1944* (Paris: Seuil, "Points Histoire," 1979), 78. — *Trans.*

social logic of the processes of resurgence of mythic reason during a period of crisis.

"We will draw our lesson from lost battles. Since the victory, the spirit of pleasure has won out over the spirit of sacrifice. People claimed more than they served. We wanted to spare the effort; today we are facing misfortune."[3] In this period of profound crisis, Marshal Pétain might appear to be a prophet as defined by Max Weber: opposed to the sacerdotal body like the extraordinary to the ordinary and deriving his authority from the correspondence between the offer of religious service and the public's religious demand, the prophet derives his charismatic legitimacy from the fact that "he brings to the level of discourse representations, feelings and aspirations that existed before him but in an implicit, semiconscious, or unconscious state." Such prophetic discourse encourages "reinterpretive perceptions that import all the expectations of the receivers into the message."[4] Women's return to motherhood and to the home as homemakers belong to these semiconscious aspirations that would find in the Marshal's words a continuous return to the sources tailor-made to fit their expectations. The relationship between the Marshal and his predestined public is a relationship of *believing expectation,* an effective force that, according to Freud, is at work in miraculous cures.[5] The opposition between the spirit of pleasure and the spirit of sacrifice is one of these prophetic enunciations in which each believer can recognize his or her rancor and invest his or her ethical-political hopes.

The Marshal's prophecies inscribe the analysis of the defeat in the *contrition/redemption* scheme and deliver the country over to a veritable "hypnosis of punishment," to use Marc Bloch's expression.[6] The founding period of the National Revolution is thus placed under the sign of expiation and redemption. For Yves Durand, "This abusive extension of the Christian notion of individual conversion to the profane fate of a collectivity stems from an apocalyptic millennialism that gives the catastrophe redemptive value."[7] Indeed, in this representation of disorder and the return to order, of social decadence and regeneration, it was the return to the "real," to "natural" communities and to "millennial" balances that organized the social philosophy of the regime. Women occupied a strategic place in this representation: the declining birthrate was seen as the symptom and the cause of the national "decadence," the family as the basic "social cell," the division of masculine and feminine "duties" as the guarantor of "organic" solidarity, the recognition of "natural" male and female aptitudes as the basis of "legitimate" social hierarchies, women's return to the home as a return to cyclical time, the time of seasons, of nature, of what is biological in opposition to the chaos engendered by "egotistic" individualism, the artificial, and the democratic "lie." The "eternal feminine" is made to serve contrition and redemption. Perceived through its attempts to reconstruct femininity, the National Revolution seems to possess numerous characteristics that make it similar to a millenary movement. A collective quest for salvation against the backdrop of catastrophe under the guidance of an inspired prophet, millenarianism combines a representation of time that is both historical (impending denouement) and mythic: cyclical and eternally repetitive time. The return to a golden age is accompanied by a process of inclusion and exclusion that designates the elect and the damned.[8] In these types of movements, the world's return to order may be based on a return to a rigid sexual division of aptitudes, of "natural" duties and places specific to each sex.[9] The hypnotic power of punishment, the anchoring in collective guilt, the messianic hope for a new order built on trial, remorse, and sacrifice are all elements of this historical situation that encouraged the return of archaic mythic conceptions.

These millenary traits did not spring forth from nothing in the French society of 1940; they were embodied and borne by social agents that had a common interest in the production of the goods of salvation. Men of letters, men of the Church, and men of science found in the eschatology of the National Revolution a fertile terrain for developing and systematizing a radicalized expression of their vision of the return to order and of the foundations of this order that included the sexual division of the social world on the basis of "natural" inequalities that are eternally established and biologically founded and not culturally or historically constructed. One of the major political impacts of the ideology of the "eternal feminine" was its rallying effect. By proposing that the country return to a sexual division of the social world founded on the idea of an eternal "natural" difference between the sexes, the National Revolution launched a request for proposals answered without delay by all those who, for ideological or strategic reasons, had long produced the "eternal feminine." The conflagration of the National Revolution, its character as successful prophetism, was due to the preexistence of multiple dispersed centers that, with the help of the crisis, joined forces. Silencing the adversaries of the past through the establishment of the authoritarian state that immediately broke with democracy permitted the harsh and unanimous expression of a vision of the social world in which feminine destiny was placed under the sign of submission and resignation. The unanimity of the National Revolution in this regard itself needs to be examined, as it is the sign of a political phenomenon of immediate, prereflective adherence, a consequence of a monopolistic situation in which the safeguards have given way and which, as a result, is ripe for any raised stakes and induration. But this unanimity must not make us forget that the processes of adherence are the product of a long history. Only a work of historical sociology will allow us to follow the thread of the political and institutional stakes involved in defending and promoting the "eternal feminine" that the Vichy government would never have succeeded in imposing with such irrepressible force by itself. This was a collective creation at an unprecedented historical moment in which the implicit could become explicit and symbolic violence and practice were given free rein. The strategic institutional uses of this vision of the world therefore succeeded in assuming forms of adherence to the regime that were not necessarily political but that had political effects, for they always further rearmed one of the central issues of the social philosophy of the National Revolution.

In fact, to speak of women is to speak of something else. Vichy is a shining example. The social philosophy of the return to "natural" communities, hierarchies, and inequalities, to "organic" solidarities, to the "real," to the earth "that does not lie," as the Marshal said, to the "little fatherlands" (*petites patries*) dear to Maurras, the condemnation of "egotistical" "sensualists," of the urban "masses," and the justification for excluding the "inassimilable" still made room in their rhetoric for the "just" place of women. Women's place could, in turn, become the metaphor of the return to the order of things and to purity or the incarnation of individualism and chaos. I am interested in showing that if this vision borrows from archaic mythic conceptions, it also owes much to a recent history of struggles in which antagonistic interests opposed each other and to its inscription in the philosophy of power. I have therefore attempted to reconstruct the *sociogenesis of these visions of the feminine* that united during the National Revolution under the banner of the "eternal feminine." It is clear that the logic of mythic reason is inscribed in conflicts that are eminently political, for the vision of women is also always a vision of the people, always caught up in a political representation of equality and inequality, and sexual racism feeds into racism. Woman was never posited alone: "Friends in emancipation or brothers in servitude, others surrounded her in the discourse: children, fools, slaves, workers, Jews, the colonized, beasts." [10] Producing the sociogenesis of the processes of production of the "eternal feminine" therefore first requires a look back at the history of the construction of cultural, social, institutional, and political interests in defense of this vision of the world, interests that invested themselves completely in the National Revolution. This history merges with the history of the competing construction from the turn of the century of a lay feminism linked to the scholarly and professional conquests of women, and of a "Christian feminism" that defended the civic advances of women while refusing to undermine the traditional feminine role of the mother at home. These conceptions are all the more antagonistic toward feminism because they disappeared into the major political oppositions of the century, particularly the opposition between the supporters and detractors of Dreyfus. It also merges with the history of the confrontations that marked the educational question and constructed it as a political question since the establishment of the Republican school. It is crisscrossed once again by Church/state opposition. Battles concerning the school took as ideological hostage the idea of educating girls, which was entirely unrelated to the "democratization" of education so deplored during the 1930s by the adversaries of the *école unique* (single school), who saw their positions triumph under the French State. Finally, it merges with the history of the biological construction of social problems and social inequalities under the sign of "degeneracy," of "natural" aptitudes and inaptitudes, a construction that provided scientific legitimacy for social and racial exclusion.

Very close by, present in all memories, was the Popular Front, which haunted the minds of the leaders, the ideologues, and the most conscious partisans of the French State. Marc Bloch writes in his analysis of the defeat: "It would be difficult to exaggerate the sense of shock felt by the comfortable classes, and even by men who had a reputation for liberal-mindedness, at the coming of the Popular Front in 1936. All those who had a few pennies to bless themselves with smelled the rising wind of disaster. . . . What an outcry there was when the authorities began to talk about the organization of leisure! The idea was greeted with mockery, and attempts were even made to bring it to nothing. . . . Yet the very people who took that attitude then are now prepared to extol to the skies similar efforts, made more or less seriously, though under a different name, by regimes after their own hearts."[11] In 1969, in the film by Marcel Ophuls, *Le Chagrin et la Pitié,* Pierre Mendès France recalls that "the attitude Hitler rather than Léon Blum" had wreaked havoc in middle-class circles. In 1935 and 1936, Marshal Pétain, the vanquisher of Verdun, had already been called the awaited savior by a vast press campaign that took on the aspect of a referendum.[12] The campaign, "It's Pétain we need," which lasted until the elections of 1936, was launched in February 1935 (the anniversary of the days of February 1934) in *La Victoire.* A heading in *Le Jour* at the end of February read "Before the threat, it is up to the leader to rise and impose his will at any cost," and in June: "Will the Leader's time come?" With the increase in the power of the leagues,* and especially the Croix de Feu, during the second half of 1935, a leftist newspaper, *Vu,* presented Pétain as a man foreign to political fights and as guarantor of the Republic: "Do we need to call on him one more time? Pétain the Republican Marshal." The author adds, prefiguring the celebratory discourse of the National Revolution: "I think I will be seconded by all who have seen this surprising thing: the gaze of Marshal Pétain." In March 1936, in *L'Ami du peuple,* a reactionary and anti-Semitic newspaper founded by the millionaire François Coty, the leagues called Pétain to the head of a national government, and *Le Figaro* saw him as the only man capable of unifying all "the healthy forces" of the nation. Between the two rounds of elections of April and May 1936, in an interview granted to the *Journal,* Pétain expressed his support for the right and commented: "We are like sailors without a pilot, without a rudder. It is against that that we must fight. It is that we must find again: a mystic." The Pétain legend and its messianic dimension were already in place before the defeat. Although they did not find their full dimension until 1940, they were

* Extreme right-wing political groups during the interwar period. — *Trans.*

born during the social and political crisis of the 1930s. The defense of the "eternal feminine" in 1940 was caught up in the heritage of political battles in which opposing views of the social world clashed. Its imposition as the only legitimate social definition of femininity was also the imposition of a conservative social philosophy that rejected and excluded "outsiders."[13]

By following the producers of the "eternal feminine" on the path of restoring order, I suggest that readers allow themselves to be struck, as I was, by the "uncanniness" of these texts so historically close to us and yet seemingly ageless.[14]

To study the symbolic and practical place allotted to women by the French State is to study the *violence of banality*. What could be more banal than this maxim, common in so many texts, and among the dignitaries and incense bearers of the regime, as among those, more obscure, who adhered from the start to the "new" order they promoted: "A woman is a woman." In reading and rereading these texts, the very object of research slips away as if there were nothing there to capture, and the research activity itself freezes and becomes paralyzed, caught in the leaden cloak of repetitive images that evoke the real-time filming of peeling potatoes — fixed frame shot from behind of a woman in front of her kitchen sink — in a film by Chantal Akerman. As Robert Paxton says, passing quickly and with an obvious grin: "Vichy preferred women barefoot and pregnant in the kitchen."[15]

However, when one persists in drawing up the inventory of these deathly flat discourses and makes oneself study them in their very repetition, it is the violence that suddenly appears. Violence first of the brutal explosion, the profound agreement, that lets surge forth suddenly without restraint visions of the social world that take advantage of the absolute gulf between masculine and feminine belonging to the world, as if this force had been contained, ready to spring forth at the opportune moment, and that one held there one of the deep motives of the social logic behind these immediate adherences — for some expected, for others more surprising — to the Vichy agenda. The explicit violence of the statements and prescriptions, of this production of identity that seemed to have existed for all time, is a vast cultural and symbolic reservoir from which one could endlessly draw images of femininity suitable for illustrating Pétain's little phrase about the spirit of pleasure and the spirit of sacrifice. Practical violence too was perpetrated against women, who were prohibited from working, divorcing, having abortions, who saw their access to education questioned and the use of their bodies channeled in favor of the sole imperative of maternity. The symbolic violence of these representations of feminine "aptitudes" and "destiny" is so profoundly internalized that reading them can make one mute. And if the violence was precisely this denial of history of which the Vichy rhetoric on the feminine offers such a striking example? In this view of the world, what became of the educational and professional advancements of women, their sports accomplishments, the gains of the feminist movements, the thin, lively bodies of *garçonnes*?* Nothing remains but the "eternal feminine." The sociogenesis of the categories of the feminine produced by and for the regime and of the institutional and political interests in defense of these categories was the most powerful weapon for fighting against the torpor created by this ideology that imposed itself (for all time?) during the National Revolution. If the "eternal feminine" of high culture and common sense is part of the social unconscious, it is also a historical object, produced and reproduced over time, particularly during periods of crisis, and its production obeys the logics of market conquest and institutional defense, strategic and political imperatives that must be assessed. When the Church and the Doctors Association, for example, defended their view of the "eternal feminine" alongside the French State, they first reassured themselves about their institutional and professional eternity, denying the crises in growth and survival that affected their recent history. To be truly effective, this fight against the amnesia of genesis had to base itself on the construction of the specifically political uses of the "eternal feminine" by a social philosophy that inscribed it in its logic, that legitimized inequalities, domination, and exclusion. This is the other face of the violence masked by banality.

As a first step, I analyze the inscription of women in the collective mea culpa to which they were called by the regime and those who were quick to serve its notion of national redress. The debacle of 1940 had

* This term, which has no real English equivalent, is defined in *Le Petit Robert* (Paris, 1992) as "a young woman leading an independent life." The French term is used throughout this book. It is the title of a famous novel by Victor Margueritte published in 1922 (see ch. 7, page 210). — *Trans.*

much in common with the social and political crisis of 1871, and many have linked these two periods in their analyses of the national "degeneration." Representations of disorder and order used in 1940 often borrowed, without always knowing it, from the schemes devised during the 1870s to account for the dangerousness of cities and crowds: the construction of "good" and "bad" femininity had its place in the corresponding social fantasies of both periods. The hypnotic power of punishment imposed a simplistic and pessimistic vision of history defended by lesser prophets of doom who denied all the military and sociopolitical analyses of the defeat to sell their soothsaying talents, finally revealed, to the new power in an unprecedented historical climate of market conquest. In the intellectual and literary realm, in the Church, in that portion of the scientific field comprising demography, medicine, and a French version of eugenics mobilized by the natalist movement, the return to the "eternal feminine" found many defenders who made it one of the central thrusts of their vision of the social world. It allowed them to defend a set of values specific to this conservative revolution that they hailed as in keeping with their wishes and to defend their specific ethical, cultural, and institutional interests.

I then undertake an analysis of what I propose to call "the culture of sacrifice," a specific form of the culture of femininity that came into its own and found a particularly consummate form of expression during the National Revolution. The culture of sacrifice developed at the intersection of the French State's profamily and pronatalist policy and the Catholic female culture, constructed over a long history, that developed new conquering forms to oppose the secular state and school from the beginning of the Third Republic. It was this cultural background, always identical and always renewed, that nurtured the ideology of the new regime, giving those men and women who defended these visions of the feminine and of the male/female opposition stemming from it the feeling that the National Revolution was invented for them, while at the same time they could invent it themselves every day. I attempt to reconstruct the major stages of the political clashes and debates at which the culture of sacrifice was challenged and sometimes checked, and to measure its vital force, its significance in the collective and individual unconscious. This is why I often include lengthy citations from texts produced by and for the

National Revolution: the rhetoric, the vocabulary, the rhythms, the images, and the metaphors alone give an idea of this force and its potential for resurgence. If the culture of female submission is expressed in all its violence between 1940 and 1944, it is nevertheless at work though dormant during the most ordinary periods of history. Reading Vichy texts on women also teaches us something about the everyday (and the most contemporary?) aspects of the symbolic violence that is at the basis of male domination and female submission.

Finally, I study the strictly political effects of this return to a biological basis for essential inequalities. The representation of an immutable, "natural," necessary biological order legitimizes the representation of an immutable, "natural," and necessary social order. The culture of sacrifice is a paradigm of the culture of submission in the broadest sense: submission of the "masses" to the elite (the "true," according to the regime), of the poor to the rich, of newcomers to old notables, of "unhealthy stocks" to "healthy stocks," of the deracinated to those firmly rooted, of outsiders to those who are established. By repositing the relationship of women to work and to the educational system, Vichy recreated an elitist educational system that denounced the ambitions of the primary school proponents and those newly come to secondary schooling, condemned a relationship between scholastic order and family order that attempted to relativize the importance of family heritage in acquiring social positions, and stigmatized the social mobility of "those without roots." Finally, by rediscovering "natural" aptitudes and "biotypology," by once again recasting doctors in the role of experts in social order and social philosophy, by founding a system for the "scientific" legitimization of social destinies on the notion of a female anatomical "destiny," Vichy definitively established a relationship between the biological order and the social order. Social exclusions and racial exclusions satisfied the same obsession to "sanitize" the social body, which must reject the "inassimilable." Following this logic, the return to the "eternal feminine" made it possible to posit a world where all inequalities were inequalities of "nature" inscribed in an "eternal" order of things.

PART ONE.
THE HYPNOTIC
POWER OF
PUNISHMENT

1. WRITERS OF THE DEFEAT
IN SEARCH OF ETERNITY

In the intellectual field, the hypnotic power of punishment produced a "literature of renunciation," whose "bucolic recommendations," Marc Bloch notes, were familiar before the war: "It lashed out against 'Americanism.' It denounced the dangers of the machine and of material progress. It contrasted these things, to their disadvantage, with the quiet pleasures of the countryside, with the grace of a civilization dominated by the small market town, with the charm as well as the hidden strength of a society which it called upon to remain increasingly loyal to the ways of life of a vanished age."[1] The rhetoric of the culture of crisis speaks the language, imposes the sound and cadence of mythic temporality. In this it is close to the *völkish* ideology whose emergence, historical developments since the nineteenth century, and role in the sociogenesis of Nazi ideology are analyzed by George L. Mosse. It recommends a return to the old virtues against the chaos and decadence introduced by the course of history, and defends the "natural" order established by putting down roots in one's native soil, by communing with the landscape of one's ancestors, by the ancient gesture of the artisan and the peasant in opposition to the disorder of anomic metropolises and the crowd of eternally deracinated individuals.[2] The myth of eternal return permeates the writing of those who served the National Revolution, and the literary production of the "eternal feminine" followed naturally, becoming one of the key elements of their particular formulation of the contrition-redemption scheme.

The ideological climate of the defeat of 1940 and the establishment of the French State are related in many aspects to the climate that developed in reaction to Sedan and during the years that followed the defeat of the Paris Commune. For writers close to the National Revolution, the Commune was viewed in the same way as the Popular Front. A propaganda journal published by the new regime stated: "It is a constant law of history that defeats result in revolutions. The French had not forgotten the bloody disturbances of the commune of 1871. . . . France was going to add even more misfortune to those that already overwhelmed it. It was to be feared that, following the bent to which odious propaganda had accustomed them, minds would turn toward a bloody, fratricidal fight. . . . The Marshal's government successfully confronted and dealt with this danger. Without any movement, without one cry of dissension, the political revolution was brought about."[3] Henri Massis, the officer responsible for press relations to General Huntziger at the time, stated plainly that the first news of the armistice had evoked the memory of 1871 and the fear of a new Commune. Thus, the primary task of the armistice army was to maintain order.[4] The defeat would appear to many intellectuals as the final blow to French decadence.[5] The themes of national decline, collective fault, and biological and political sins echoed one another in an obsessive litany during the period following June 1940, just as during the 1870s. Maurras even suggested anthologizing Renan's *La Réforme intellectuelle et morale,* which he felt might render "a great service to the French people of 1940, since those of 1870 failed to take proper note of it."[6] The precepts and maxims of the Marshal—the "guide in possession of incomparable and almost superhuman wisdom and intellectual control"—functioned like calls to self-flagellation, and many would lend their skills to an attempt at exegesis.[7] Georges Bernanos offered a gripping expression of the political bases and effects of the encounter between the message of the defeat, spoken by the prophet, and the "expectation" of those who saw the National Revolution as a national opportunity: "All that is called the Right, which ranges from the self-styled monarchists of the Action française to the self-styled national socialist radicals and includes big industry, big business, the high clergy, the Academies, and the officers' staff spontaneously united and cohered around the disaster of my country like a swarm of bees around their queen. I am not saying that they deliberately wished the disaster. They were waiting for it. This monstrous anticipation passes judgment on them."[8]

Writers against the Popular Front

A study of the reaction of intellectuals to the debacle of 1870 gave Michel Mohrt the opportunity to analyze what he calls a "collective examination of conscience" at a historic moment—1940—that was a kind of "reply" to this reaction.[9] The choice of authors he convokes to the tribunal of history and the numerous subtle references to the situation of 1940 sketch a panorama of the disaster and the means for exorcising it that are consistent with the rhetoric of the National Revolution. This fantasy meeting of intellectuals presided by Taine, with Sarcey acting as secretary, Gobineau on the right and About on the left, sets itself the task of analyzing both the causes of the defeat and the necessary remedies. They conclude, first, that "France is paying for its moral laxity"; second, that "intellectual and moral reform is imperative"; third, that the "abolishment of universal suffrage" and a "halt in the democratization of the country" are required and that a "return to a hierarchical social order" is needed; and finally, that there must be a "break with Paris" and a "return to the source, to the richness of the soil." During this meeting of great minds who, "the day after Sedan, suggested to the country moral and political reforms that would have to wait until after Dunkerque to be undertaken," Renan is presented as the unrivaled master in positing the crisis.[10] In this vast work, Mohrt exhumes a small note that makes feminine guilt one of the national culpabilities; at the same time, it points out the lucidity of women who know how to return to the "true values" in times of chaos: "Renan attributes part of the responsibility for our downfall to women: 'Women,' he says in a note, 'account for an enormous part of the social and political movement in France; in Prussia they account for much less.'" And Mohrt comments: "I believe in fact that, under the Second Empire, the 'ethics of the tart,' as they might be called, worthy ancestor of the 'ethics of the shop girl,' denounced by Montherlant, had assumed an enormous influence over social life—at least over 'Parisian life.'"[11]

Contrary to the "tarts" and far removed from evil Paris, George

Sand maintained a dialogue with Flaubert, the other great provincial. For Mohrt, she found the conditions of her "clairvoyant patriotism" (she declares herself to be against Gambetta and for an immediate armistice) in a return to the sources:

> Love of the land, the house, of work, the love of the good and simple beings who surround her, love of the fields, the flowers, the woods . . . she clings to all these *earthy values* amidst the general collapse. In attending to them daily, she, the revolutionary intoxicated by political romanticism, found a *common sense* and lucidity that never failed her during the ordeal. . . . Instinctively she went to the essential, to the one who, through his virtues of endurance and labor, his patience and his courage, is able to reconstruct and repair: to the peasant. . . . "His comprehension is not reasoned," she says, "but he has the profound, unshakable instinct of undying vitality. . . . He represents the *species* with its persistent confidence in the law of renewal." Admirable praise that helps us understand why George Sand did not lose hope in her country.

Curiously, it is in the pages of Colette's *Journal à rebours,* dating from the end of June 1940, that Mohrt recognizes the same feminine and rural tone in the return to "true values" and in her praise of the peasant she loves to contemplate "motionless, with his brave wife, his children, his flocks, against a background of modest steeples, flowing water, and a hesitant dawn." If Sand "indicated to the country a policy of meditation and wisdom," it is because she "unconsciously" took the side of the "real France." The "familiar voices" of these two women of letters, "so strangely in tune with each other, teach us great wisdom. Something needs to be written about *feminine Realism.*"

Handsome portraits of "authorized" women, who, finally mature, have returned to reason, unconsciously of course, by following their "instinct" freed from the revolutionary intoxication of their youth, and who, in their singular conversation with "the" peasant, find the path of "feminine realism" that may also be seen as a metaphor for literary realism. Between the "return to the real" espoused by the ideologues of the National Revolution and the "feminine realism" of the young writer, there is more than a homology of terms. The social philosophy of Gustave Thibon privileges the "realism of the earth": "At perhaps the blackest moment of our history, at the time we were probing the depths of our weaknesses, we heard a leader's voice that said: 'I hate the lies that have hurt you so.' And this voice that brought us back toward the truth so long forgotten added: 'The earth does not lie.' " Unlike "political charlatans," "sowers of imaginary promises," "the earth does not make vain promises." The "authentic and necessary goods" that it produces "merge with man's flesh and blood." [12] Woman and peasant form a strategic couple in the condemnation of the city, of the democratic "illusion," of the wild excitement of the Commune and of the Popular Front, and in the exaltation of redemption through natality and the return to the earth.

For Daniel Halévy, who compares three "ordeals"—1814, 1871, 1940—the voice of Marshal Pétain, the "voice of a father as well as a leader," "announced the misfortune with a dignity that was so steadfast that it was impossible for anyone listening to it not to see in the very disaster itself the dawn of hope." [13] In his inventory of "faults" and his exploration of the "tasks" to be accomplished, Halévy gives first place to the decline in the birthrate, which sums up all the degeneration, and calls for the regeneration of the "maternal instinct":

Final example: the ruin of the French population, made anemic by alcoholism, weakened by the declining birthrate, at odds with the nonnatives drawn to France by its empty interior. Three important subjects: let us consider, in order to emphasize it, the decline in the birthrate. This sums up everything. . . . What is in question is the fate of a people, who, for a long time, was brimming with ambition and life, and is suddenly perverting itself . . . and is content with a form of State, entirely new to it, that strives in principle to diminish the effort of each. . . . "When the father works and the mother keeps her house," an inspector who knows households tells me, "misery is avoided. When the mother is negligent, the family allowances melt in her hands, and misery is present." If morale is not affected, nothing effective will have been done, and the state-controlled allowances will be lost in the flood of these subsidies that the Treasury vainly distributes to the supplicant crowd. As soon as we touch on this decisive problem, we leave the realm of the political and find ourselves in the region of invisible sources, some vivifying, others debilitating, from which peoples derive greatness or degradation. Moral sources, religious sources. . . . In the end, it is charity that is always needed. Charity for the childhood snuffed out by abortionists, charity for the unborn, charity for those who will be born, like us, residents of our streams and rivers, sinuous Seine or broad Loire, which for so many centuries have inspired so many beings. . . . At the heart of the tasks of this ordeal there are those of the earth and those of maternity, major tasks, one that creates beings, the other that nourishes them. . . . Overburdened, thwarted by the demands of a new time, the maternal instinct is suffering and declining. We must go to its aid.

Raymond Aron vehemently criticized Halévy's book in which he saw a typical conservative manifesto embittered by a sort of "morose delight," "a rehashing of disappointments and of French abasement," a catalogue of "biases: preference for the peasantry, hostility toward the world of industrial workers, indifference toward industrial development, nostalgia for the France prior to the revolution of 1789."[14] It is striking to see Halévy, one of the first Dreyfusards, defend the values of the new regime in May 1941, after the promulgation of the first Jewish Statute, and thus indicate the kind of danger represented by "nonnatives" and "abortionists," even if we are familiar with his defense of *notables* and of the rural world against urban anonymity. Nevertheless, this immediate adherence to the official interpretation of the "ordeal" and to the reform of mores for which it was the occasion is less surprising if we think of the profound ambivalence of Halévy's ethicopolitical constructions. These imbue, for example, his worship of Péguy and Proudhon, whom he installs as intermediaries (just as the saints are intercessors) between the "true" France—provincial France, the France of peasants, of artisans, of Catholicism, of the "true" people—and the "notable" Parisian he is, born into the upper classes, into a family with a strong Orleanist bias (Prévost-Paradol was his uncle), Jewish on his father's side and Protestant on his mother's, ceaselessly haunted by assimilation with the "residents of our rivers." What seems to fascinate Halévy in Péguy is his continuous belonging, from the very beginning, to this archaic France of native soil and old trades that he himself will see only as a traveler. When he compares (in *Le Mariage de Proudhon,* published in 1955) Proudhon and Sorel with regard to their marital choices, he por-

Vichy and the Eternal Feminine ▸ 20

trays their respective spouses, one of whom was a domestic servant, the other a seamstress, as "simple, docile, and modest," the emblematic incarnation of these "popular virtues" capable of fostering the social theories of both men.[15] This sociopolitical fantasy is akin to the fantasy of Mohrt's feminine realism.

The affinity of these values with the values of the new regime is, in any case, in their praise of the middle-class birthrate and their suspicion of popular permissiveness, as family allowances did not suffice to make good mothers and attested to the political perversity of the Popular Front. However, in a more profound way, it is in the region of "invisible sources" that we must look for the secret of the energy of peoples, and the discourse on maternity provides an opportunity to defend eternal values, to rediscover the sources of regeneration in the immutable course of the great rivers. Women are on the side of nature, and it is probably in part to Halévy's fascination with the native soil, which is inseparably political and existential, that we need to look for the true motive behind his call to aid the maternal instinct.

In *Les murs sont bons,* Henry Bordeaux, like Halévy, begins his analysis of the defeat with Pétain's appeal of June 20, 1940—"The spirit of pleasure has won out over the spirit of sacrifice"—which he describes as an indispensable "expiatory explanation" and a "magic" formula: "It obligated each of us and the entire nation to participate in the *mea culpa* that demands contrition."[16] In the second part of his book, entitled "Nos erreurs et nos fautes," he decries the labor crisis and the responsibility of the Popular Front, which "precipitated the downfall by ruining these two supports of all social life: work and authority," the occupation of factories and a work week consisting of, "if not four Thursdays, at least two days off." He cites a report, read at the Academy of Medicine, establishing the "repercussion of so-called social laws promulgated by the government of the Popular Front concerning the development of alcoholism in Normandy." He also decries universal suffrage in the name of the "natural role of the social authorities," laments "the end of notables" and "the neglect of morality and religion." But the foremost sin in this examination of the conscience of others is the declining birthrate: "The numbers failed us during the war. Well, numbers are only provided by the family and not by the overly easy and dangerous admission of foreigners."

Next follows a portrait of family happiness on a farm in the Savoie, the author's native soil and the source of inspiration for his literary regionalism. At the end of a mountain hike, Bordeaux asks to rest and restore himself at a farm; the solitary, unkempt peasant who welcomes him is preparing to eat a cold meal at his rickety table and tells him that "this is not a home" because there is no fire and because his wife is gone. On the other hand, a bit further on, he discovers "a *real* roof," "the husband, the wife, the children around a glowing fire," and so on, where he learns that the wife of his solitary peasant ran off with a smuggler! "Thus I learned that a house is not a home without a plume of smoke. In the past, the villages were counted by counting the fires. . . . Every fire is a family. The fire is the hearth. Without a hearth, there is no family, no country, no happiness, and no duration. A nation is a collection of hearths." This is a long way from the "caravansaries" of the Porte des Lilas that he visited during the 1930s, as did Baron de Gérando a hundred years earlier, where the women work, where "the notion of marriage has been lost: they make love with each other and leave each other at the drop of a hat." He, too, finds himself in the company of Taine and Renan to meditate on the disaster of 1871 and on the moral decadence of the people seduced by "easy pleasures," and cites the Balzac of *Médecin de campagne* and *Curé de village,* those two "natural" spiritual advisors of popular and feminine souls: "Only what is natural is solid and durable, and the natural thing in politics is the Family. The Family must be the starting point for all institutions." "Balzac's politics," Bordeaux comments, "are directly linked to the politics of Joseph de Maistre and Bonald; they are not foreign to the politics of Taine, Renan, and Fustel de Coulanges, and they inspire the politics of Paul Bourget, Maurice Barrès, Charles Maurras, those that I am honored to have served." In celebrating "fires," the alliance of woman and earth, the cult of ancestors and small village cemeteries, Bordeaux continues the Barresian nationalist tradition that sought to "root individuals in the Earth and in the Dead": "An old country like ours is long sustained by the occult power of its dead, of its good women at prayer, of its laborers sweating in their fields." [17]

At the end of his essay, Bordeaux pays tribute to young Catholic women — and to legitimate female professionals — whom the great freedom of the interwar period armed for the fight: "Having experienced the fight, they are prepared for it. But it is the type of fight that too often risks taking them away from the hearth." He concludes: "The peasant woman has not changed. Eternal guardian of the earth and the house, today as yesterday, as a hundred years ago, as a thousand years ago."

These three essays on the defeat and the "opportunity" for national regeneration that it carries within it demonstrate an unconditional support for the new regime for which they prepare the arrival like an unhoped-for response to the country's decline. Intellectual and moral reform is predicated on the return to the sources, love of the earth, carnal values, the recovery of the maternal instinct, the restoration of the family and of the "fires" whose collection constitutes the "real France." "Feminine realism" is a political arm against the Popular Front and its egalitarian "delirium," just as it was an arm against the Commune and its bloody "hysteria."

The Great Cosmic and Social Continuities

Further still, for the Vichy ideologues, the return to the family, to natality, to the social philosophy of the eternal feminine would end individualism, born of the French Revolution and a veritable defect of the Republic. In the Vichy scheme of contrition, individualism was the root of all evil: "The ordeal suffered by the French people must be written in fire in its spirit and its heart. What the people need to understand so as never to forget it is that individualism, which it used to glorify as a privilege, is the source of all the ills from which it almost died. . . . The individual, if he claims to detach himself from the *maternal and nurturing society,* dries up and dies without bearing fruit. In a well-made society, the individual must accept the *law of the species.*"[18] Women must once again become the privileged intermediaries of this agreement with the eternity of things that will make it possible to escape the dangers of individualism, "political egotism," as Marshal Pétain called it, and the "egalitarian fever" that "gives birth to chaos" by perverting the play of "natural inequalities," to borrow the expressions of Gustave Thibon.[19]

Thibon is one of the most interesting intellectual figures of the National Revolution. A wine grower and self-taught philosopher, he was unknown before 1940 except in Catholic intellectual circles, where, during the 1930s, he joined the ranks of conservatives who rejected personalism, the Thomism of Maritain, and the currents of Social Catholicism. Thibon published *Diagnostics,* a collection of articles that appeared before the war, in May 1940. Indeed, this book, like the prophecies, found thousands of readers after the defeat. From that point on, Thibon became the great ideologue of the regime. He was often invited to Vichy by Marshal Pétain and became a member of the Centre français de synthèse, destined to produce the elite of the new regime. He also published a second book in the same vein, *Retour au réel, nouveaux diagnostics,* in which he developed his "social physiology" that adhered to the social philosophy of the Action française.[20] He is exemplary of the lesser prophets that suddenly appear during periods of crisis, and Henri Massis, who opened the columns of *La Revue universelle* to him, quite naturally turned to the language of the sacred to relate his encounter with this unknown become famous: "Any encounter is a kind of mystery, where something in us is *called;* but there are encounters that are inevitable. The 'encounter' with Gustave Thibon was for me one of those."[21] Massis, a Catholic intellectual and proponent of Maurras's "integral nationalism" and a great admirer of Franco and Salazar, was a very important figure in the National Revolution; he appeared as the leading intellectual of the Conseil national and inspired and directed the youth policy. In 1941, paraphrasing Taine, he published *Les idées restent,* a meditation on the defeat and the responsibilities of parliamentarianism. Instigator in 1919 of the manifesto of the Intelligence Party that wanted to organize the intellectual defense of the Christian West against Bolshevism under the leadership of France, in 1920 Massis had helped create *La Revue universelle,* an intellectual journal of the Action française. When it reappeared in 1941 in Vichy, he was its editor in chief. *La Revue universelle* supported the National Revolution until the end.[22]

The evidence witnessed by Massis was clearly prophetic, revealing to those who awaited it only what they always believed. With Thibon, the words and ideas of the Action française seemed to come from on high to guarantee the National Revolution through the innocent mouth of the "philosopher-peasant." During the Middle Ages, he said, "the biological, familial, and social frameworks of humanity were not shaken to their foundations, and nature did not take long to recover. . . . Certain questions were not asked. Men were still healthy in body and soul. . . . Carnal man and the 'carnal cities' conserved their profound equilibrium. The terms of the problem are quite different today. The flesh, nature, society are sick. It is not enough to direct them. They need to be cured." Placing the exploitation of "the current catastrophe" by "each of us" under the patronage of Thérèse of Lisieux, in his eyes the incarnation of "natural saintliness" whose path the country must find once again, Thibon in his turn depicted the declining birthrate as a deadly sin: "A millennial equilibrium—that through the very fact of its duration had every opportunity to conform to the eternal requirements of human nature—was abruptly unbalanced. Forcefully aided in their work of separation and death by the ease offered by technology, the liberal, materialistic, and democratic myths succeeded in pulling the individual away from the great cosmic and social continuities (the soil, trade, the family, the native land). . . . Lack of religion, immorality and the declining birthrate are but the various particular symptoms of the general corruption that affects a humanity thrust outside of its natural climate." [23]

Women were urged by the National Revolution to reestablish the "great continuities." Fecundity was one of those virtues that are "solid as the instinct that an era of ease and artifice had atrophied in souls." [24] It was once again peasant wives who revealed the natural course of things: "The desires, the aspirations of these women rooted in nature and without any other horizon than their hearth had virtually no other outlet than the joys of motherhood. Their granddaughters are not like that anymore. . . . They received a veneer of pseudo-culture at school, they've read *Marie-Claire* and the novels of Delly or even worse, they've seen the movie stars smile on the silver screen, they wear silk stockings and permanents." [25] Permanents, paid vacations, and all the "so-called" social laws, as Bordeaux and Halévy called them, that always risk encouraging the poor to make less of an effort, are amalgamated in this expiatory rhetoric with very political accents in which the celebration of the peasant woman, like the construction of woman/peasant affinities, is first a celebration of peasant "virtues," particularly of this "spirit of economy" that knows how to "resist the appeal of immediate attraction" and that allows one to "vanquish oneself today" in the "interest of tomorrow." [26] In "the" woman as in "the" peasant, the monotony of tasks and the instinctive knowledge of duration would develop one of the civic virtues called on by the new social order: patience, sister of resignation. "Unlike industrial workers, the peasant's labor is not always rewarded as it should be, and this reward is not always immediate. Many months separate the labor from the harvest, during which he must live on hope."[27]

As we see through these meditations on the defeat written in urgency and appearing during the first months of the regime, recognition of the National Revolution seemed self-evident. One of the hypotheses of this book is that grasping the ideology of the French State through its production of the "eternal feminine" allows us to identify and reconstruct the social logic of "believing expectation" that culminates in forms of immediate adherence that express visions of the world and value systems that amply go beyond positions that are usually qualified as political. And yet this mode of identifying with the imperatives and slogans of the National Revolution had eminently political effects. On the one hand, it tended to gloss over questions concerning the legitimacy of the new regime, concerning the constitutional upheavals that it had carried out since July 1940, and concerning the purification and the exclusionist laws that accompanied its establishment. On the other hand, it immediately mobilized a vast expiatory construction site that denied politicomilitary analyses of the debacle in favor of a messianic and millenary sensibility: "We hope that the current catastrophe, wisely exploited by each of us (for nothing is more beneficial than a misfortune from which one knows how to reap the fruit), will place men in situations in which individualism will not find any outlets and will force them to draw closer, in order to live, to the *basic realities* that have been lost."[28] The image of the return to the sources, in which the return to "true" femininity is a central element, allows us to posit the National Revolution as an outcome and as self-evident.

Women, Peasants, and Mother Nature

Writers at the end of the century opposed the figure of an imaginary peasant that symbolized "the healthy part of France, the responsible, levelheaded rustic, the one who remained closest to the earth, who suppressed the crazy, exasperated part spoiled by the Empire, unsettled by illusions and pleasures," to the unstable, nomadic, déclassé, and deracinated Communards. Just so, the writers of the defeat began the break with Paris.[29] Bohemianism, artificiality, tarts and shop girls, slums and working-class debauchery, "fête impériale" and decadence of all kinds, without its ever being clear whether it is the city of 1861 or of 1936 that is being condemned, form the repulsive background against which the enchanted tableau of the "true" France and of its potential regenerator unfolds. In any event, the prophetic tone is common to both periods; this phrase from Zola could appear in an anthology of the National Revolution: "It was the unquestionable rejuvenation of eternal nature, of eternal humanity, the renewal promised to him who hopes and labors, the tree that puts out a powerful new shoot when the rotted branch whose sap was yellowing the leaves is cut off."[30] Bordeaux expresses his disgust for the city and its crowds with a violence that echoes that of the writers against the Commune. Describing the installation of the government in Clermont on June 29, 1940, the ultimate step before Vichy, he writes: "Why was it necessary for this official debarkation to be preceded by riff-raff somehow hastily returned from Bordeaux: bare-headed girls wearing pants, bare feet in espadrilles, guys with uncombed hair, unbridled and in ragged clothing, who had broken off their military service. A whole slovenly choir that our police must once again learn how to control, just like the roads department must resign itself to disinfecting the filthy alleys that end at the quaint Romanesque church of Notre-Dame-du-Port."[31] Is the call to disinfect the "filthy" the hidden face of the idyllic portrait of the valleys of the Savoie?

For Michel Mohrt, when Flaubert and George Sand take the side of the province against Paris, they are defending "the peasant against the 'lawyer'" (read Gambetta), "the real France, laborious and simple, serious and modest, against the false France," and their proximity to "French realities" comes from their being "caught up in the provincial and rural current." It is what gives their thoughts, "heavy with a French juice," a perfect fullness: "These natives of Normandy and Berry have French soil on the soles of their country shoes."[32] When he analyzes the responsibility of Parisian intellectuals in the debacle, Mohrt uses the same vocabulary to criticize best-selling writers and journalists; his "political" critique of Paris seems inseparably linked to these forms of resentment toward the literary game in the capital that are often the source of a commitment to literary regionalism.[33]

In a manifesto of the National Revolution instigated by Henri Massis concerning "the new destinies of French intellects," Halévy calls for the "awakening of the provinces" where "literature found refuge," and salutes regionalist writers, "all Catholics," who "follow or renew familial habits with simplicity." He praises Péguy, Pourrat, Pesquidoux, and Thibon, that "steadfast man of the earth," "new to us," who "all of a sudden is finding his readers."[34]

These positions, at once political, ethical, and aesthetic, resonate in harmony with the central aspect of the propaganda of the new regime: the revitalization of regional cultures and folklores. This explains the revival of the National Commission for Propaganda through Folklore. Founded in August 1939, it "awaken[ed] to the Marshal's call." Its regional branches were directed by the newly appointed prefects who organized parades of battalions of young women in "traditional" regional costumes throughout the Occupation, thereby marking their enrollment in an old order of bodies: "Today, France is being reborn from the torment. She yearns to live again through her scattered children, through their customs . . . , henceforth drawing from the very earth her basic reasons for breathing. Oh! She will not look very far since she has but to bend down to find on her own soil her means of maternal and spiritual existence."[35]

The relationship of regionalist literature and the folklorist movement to Vichy is a complicated one that could be illustrated by the National Revolution's annexation of Maurras's Mistral, which ignored the linguistic demands of the Félibrige movement* and the local communist uses of Occitan culture during the 1930s in favor of the incessant parade of Arlesian girls in full costume.[36] This political staging beautifully incarnates a pleasant form of the traditionalism of femininity. While Alphonse de Châteaubriand lent his reputation as a regionalist writer—he had won the grand prize of the Académie française in 1923 for *La Brière*—to the Parisian collaboration by founding *La Gerbe* in July 1940, a site where a synthesis between Vichy ideology and pro-Nazism was produced, others, like Émile Guillaumin, one of the rare regionalist writers who truly belonged to the peasantry, continually refused to support the Vichy regime. Instead, the National Revolution gave particular attention to promoting cer-

---

* A literary school devoted to restoring Provençal as a literary language. — *Trans.*

tain regionalist writers as ideologues, while the regionalist culture, concrete and French, undefined and ecumenical, provided it an ideal counterpoint to the denunciation of abstract and cosmopolitan intellectualism.[37] Pierre Barral clearly shows that Vichy's "regionalism" was in fact very ambiguous and that the effective policy of reorganizing the territorial administrative entities ultimately allowed the state to maintain its power and decentralized little.[38] The encouragement of a literary and cultural regionalism can also be analyzed as a kind of "decoy" allowing an entire local cultural tradition and elite to rally around the regime at the same time it masked a political desire to centralize. Some even placed themselves in the service of a politically correct folklorist centralism; "Love of the language and respect for traditions are auxiliary virtues, faithful guardians of the trilogy: Work, Family, Nation." By denouncing the "parasites of folklore," who practiced an unorganized form of "Mistralism," they sought to construct a monopoly over legitimate folklorism.[39]

Joseph de Pesquidoux, the great Gascon vineyard owner, was a poet who celebrated the earth, rural patriarchy, and the virtues of the race. He was elected to the Académie française in 1936 and was a member of the Conseil national, where he sat alongside Charles-Brun, the father of French regionalism, and where he represented "the peasants."[40] In 1942, he published *Pour la Terre,* dedicated to Henry Bordeaux, who "throughout his life served God, Country, Family, and Soil," with this epigraph by Pétain: "The earth does not lie." He saw women as in great part responsible for the rural exodus linked to the loss of "ancestral disciplines" broken down by "twenty years of a corrupt regime, of sloppiness, of irreverence, of pleasure and egotism," linked, too, to "the crazy forty-hour work week law." The peasant women of the past, "collaborators in mind and body," "tough, relentless women," were now being sought but not found. The "woman of the soil" was "the cornerstone of the rural household"; if she is faithful to the earth, "man puts down roots." Once again, it is the "eternal temptress" who bears the guilt for the depopulation of the countryside. What was needed, therefore, was to find an attitude other than the one adopted by "these girls of the soil who are more preoccupied with entertainment, finery, 'permanents,' casualness, and freedom of action" and to return to the "fundamental things" that have "their immutable rhythm in germinations and maturations" and that blend so well with the "songs of the native soil sprung from the *millennial soul of women.*"[41] Typical of these traditionalist factions that supported the National Revolution, Pesquidoux, who played the "ancestral disciplines" against paid vacations and made tenant farming the perfect model of social relations, presents the peasant "eternal feminine" as a social and political weapon.

Henri Pourrat, a native of Auvergne and one of the most famous regional writers of his generation with *Gaspard des montagnes,* published between the two wars, became the official writer of the National Revolution. He sang the praises of an "original, universal, atemporal" rural civilization and of a rural mystique capable of fighting against all the artifices of modernity.[42] He won a virtually prescribed Goncourt prize in 1941 for *Vent de mars,* a sort of diary (September 1938 to October 1940) of Auvergne encounters propitious to meditation on the alliance between man and earth: "Life needs the opposite of ease and facility. But it also needs this powerful peace, this way of getting close to Mother Nature, of depending on her, of feeling oneself carried by this Great Work of life of seven days, of working in the same sense as the grass and as trees, in the great enterprise of Creation. This unimaginable industrial progress, can't you see where it's heading: toward the enormous folly of war, toward the desiccation in cities of races without posterity. . . . Between the laundry shed and the house the farmwife comes and goes. Farms make the country. . . . Houses, more houses. If the State now speaks in similar fashion—and this seems to be the case, Family Code, etc.—is there not great hope?"[43] The regime committed him to a whirlwind of activity as an essayist and editorialist.[44] He celebrated the Marshal's gaze, "so clear it seems to wash things and they will never again be anything other than what they are," and brings about a "return to wisdom that is a return to the nature of things": " 'It is truly a miracle like the miracle of Joan of Arc,' says a woman who follows him with her eyes in a whisper, with the low tone one uses when speaking to oneself."[45]

These hymns to the soil, to nature, and to the laws of nature in which women, guardians of the "fires," who keep others in their place and where the woman/peasant, maternity/harvest association works as a magic formula to exorcise all the specters of the disorder that led to the debacle, are very close to the thinking of the *völkisch* ideology that weaves ties between the soul of a people and its natural environment and opposes the cyclical time of return, symbol of the conservative revolution, to the linear time of the technological world. In his approach to the symbolic foundations of the German nation, George L. Mosse foregrounds the function of "guardian of continuity" that has fallen to woman as national symbol: "Even as defender and protector of her people, [woman] was assimilated to her traditional role as woman and mother, the custodian of tradition who kept nostalgia alive in the active world of men. . . . Like all symbols, the female embodiment of the nation stood for eternal forces. They look backward with their ancient armor (let those in France think of Joan of Arc) and medieval dress. Woman as a preindustrial symbol evokes innocence and chastity, a kind of moral rigor directed against modernity, the pastoral and the eternal set against the big city as the nursery of vice."[46]

The Action française and the Myth of Eternal Return

This collective construction of the return to the "real" owed much to the ideological work of the Action française and, more particularly, to the form of collective unconscious that imbued its worldview and made it much more than a simple current of ideas shared only by active members of the movement. Adherence to the myth of eternal return is, in fact, directly related to the latent content of the ideology of the Action française as analyzed by Colette Capitan Peter.[47] The desire for "intemporality," a means of denying time that "dispossesses" and of denying the great temporal fracture represented by the French Revolution, leads the ideologues of the movement to choose "the duration without a future and without a past of *nature*." For the author, the Action française's conception of time is "the core around which everything gravitates": by restoring the duration interrupted by the Revolution of 1789, one can negate time and return to this golden age, which is the Middle Ages marked by the "predominance of a spiritual power." The "irrational nature of national sentiment" that ultimately judges the nation's decline to be inevitable like the "intemporal function of 'integral nationalism'" takes on the very traits of the unconscious. Thus, the Action française and its audience were living a time "without scansions, without a past and without a future, arrested, immobilized in the pure moment of the instinct of conservation that the monarchy was charged with signifying." Against "ideas," intellectual activity that saps the "vital energy," emancipation through culture and the diffusion of knowledge, Maurras defends elitism, "instinct," and "mystery." From this perspective, women are invested with a "dual nature," "alternately a source of redemption (the mother or ancient goddess who regenerates and purifies) or of sin, orgiastic demon, 'generative power' of evil." There is both evil and good within femininity: "The 'true' woman is the one who remains in her place: the home"; every attempt to leave this "natural" condition is a transgression: work is "a crime," the woman of letters is "the most hideous monster that the earth can bear." Woman must be a comfort, a mediator, and a redemptrice. By remaining in her place she is the guardian of order. When Mme de Noailles was a candidate for election to the Académie, Vaugeois expressed the same anger against "this new monster of ugliness and absurdity" (a female member of the Académie) and Captain Dreyfus (an innocent Jew): "Is this not the same anger of twelve years ago during the time of Bernard Lazare, when we were besieged with 'the innocent Jew.' This rage comes from the insult to reason. If that were to be, his Majesty Disorder would burst forth. We must protect enclosures and guarded preserves in order to retain — if not the desire — at least the dream that in the world there are beautiful, desired and dreamed of gardens, superb family homes, shelters of honor and memory." [48] To this fantasy of an enclosed, reserved purity echoed in the Vichy metaphor of the renovation of the "house of France," the Action française opposed these evil forces, always ready to reappear, in women as in the masses, and took "an almost masochistic pleasure" in depicting the horror that would result from transgression. The fascination with barbarism merges ambivalently into the condemnation of a lack of morality and evil spectacles.

Historians concur in recognizing the influence of the Maurrasians at Vichy and the support given to the new regime by the Action française. There is a correlation between the doctrinal discourses with "the same image of eternal France and its roots, the same primacy of the family," [49] and the same rejections: rejection of parliamentary democracy, denunciation of "the Anti-France" and of the "four confederated states"—Jews, Freemasons, *métèques,** and Protestants —which for the first time found expression in institutional acts such as the first Jewish Statute of October 2, 1940.[50] Ultimately, "the government of a single man" was realized by Pétain, who took the place of the king.[51] The Maurrasian permeation of the National Revolution, like the adherence of friends of the Action française to the values of the new regime—which does not prejudice the subsequent evolution of their choices and political commitments—stemmed from the logic of prophetic encounters. The famous article by Maurras entitled "La divine surprise" can be read in this way: "A poet said that, when Poetry attains all the points of its consummate perfection, when it touches the very sublime, something is still missing if it does not produce what can be called *The Divine Surprise,* precisely that surprise that submerges all hopes of the best-disposed admiration. . . . Well, the divine part of political art has been reached by the extraordinary surprises that the Marshal has given us. We expected so much from him, we could and ought to expect everything. With this natural expectation, he has the knowledge to add anything. Afterwards, nothing more was missing."[52] It is this "natural," satisfied expectation that is expressed in the works of celebration I have cited. Belonging to different generations and having experienced sharply different intellectual itineraries, their authors share a great admiration for Maurras and their ideological proximity to the Action française is obvious. The young Maurrasian Michel Mohrt contributed to theoretical journals in which the ideology of the National Revolution was developed; Daniel Halévy participated in the banquets of the Fustel-de-Coulanges circle (spearhead of Maurrasism in the university) and testified on Maurras's behalf during the trial in January 1945. Henry Bordeaux had been one of those responsible for Maurras's election to the Académie française in June 1938; in 1965, Gustave Thibon wrote a preface to *Souvenirs de prison de Charles Maurras.*[53] Their books testify to the vitality of this current of ideas developed at the turn of the century and that imbued the generation of 1940, when many Frenchmen were "Maurrasians without knowing it," as Eugen Weber points out. One could "belong" to the Action française without ever joining the

* *Métèque* is a word coined by Maurras to refer to "a recently domiciled or naturalized guest or his children." See Curtis, *Three against the Republic* (Princeton: Princeton University Press, 1959).—*Trans.*

movement, and it was this very "vagueness of sympathy" that made the Action française such an effective transmission belt for a regime that preferred to present itself as a unification around one man and was permeated with a "strong but diffuse Maurrasism."[54]

The National Revolution was the culmination of fifty years of ideological battles led by the Action française since the Dreyfus affair. This can be seen clearly in the French State's political options and perhaps more markedly in the rhetorical kinship that united official texts and individual writings to such an extent that the intellectual traveling companions of the Action française were more than organic intellectuals of the regime, because they "invented" the National Revolution every day. Hence this "Chronique de la quinzaine" of *La Revue universelle* that used the symbolics of the political-liturgical calendar of the new French State and sounded out its cadences.[55] For the old May Day celebrations, a theater of "absurd spectacle" where "disorder mobilized its troops," where parades were merely the pretext for "outbursts of oratory" and "incitements to hate," the "new state" substituted the "celebration of union and collaboration" between the French "united under a paternal aegis." May 11, the feast day of Joan of Arc, from whom France "asks the secret of recovery," celebrated "the miracle of Pétain, who would shine in history with a light as beautiful as the miracle of Joan." "The month of May evokes another date, this one shameful and sinister: the last gasps of the Commune of 1871, its massacres and its fires. . . . Revolutionary threats were more serious on the eve of the armistice than after the fall of the Empire. Subversive propaganda had developed along with barbarism, alas, as witnessed by the crimes of the Spanish Frente popular. . . . The France of 1940 was much more afflicted than the France of 1870. The wonder is that instead of unleashing a new Commune, the defeat purified and exalted it. Again the Pétain miracle!" Finally, May 25 is Mother's Day, mothers being "natural" allies of the new state charged with "creating souls," for "the virtues of men and citizens are taught in the home." "The Republic was not capable of rising to this lofty vision," concluded the chronicler. This "lofty vision" belonged to the Action française, which employed its own feminine pantheon to restore the interrupted duration in the service of the "miracle" of the National Revolution.

While other currents of thought, other economic opinions, other conceptions of the state were at work in Vichy, which, as numerous studies have shown, was far from being a bloc,[56] the Action française remained one of the major sources of inspiration for a regime for which it had long catalyzed support. Rejecting parliamentarianism, universal suffrage, and human rights; preaching anti-Semitism and xenophobia; defending elitism and "natural" inequalities, the Action française rediscovered during the 1930s its political pugnacity and its taste for manifesto in a domestic political situation once again marked by the bipolarization of the intellectual field.[57] In October 1935, Henri Massis published the manifesto "For the Defense of the West," which justified the invasion of Ethiopia by Mussolini's Italy in the name of civilization. In 1937, "Manifesto to Spanish Intellectuals" expressed the solidarity of the signatories with the nationalist writers fighting against Republican "barbarism." The special issue of *La Revue universelle* of January 1937 celebrated the fiftieth anniversary of the start of the literary career of Maurras at the time he was imprisoned for incitement to murder some *députés* of the Popular Front, and his election to the Académie française in 1938 demonstrated the opposition of a large portion of this institution to the government of Léon Blum. Bordeaux and Goyau, who had worked so hard for the success of this election, were also among those who crafted the Action française's rapprochement with Rome, which had finally lifted any ban on the relationship of the Church of France with this movement, thereby freeing the consensus of the 1940s from any obstacles. One political observer emphasized the political effect of these commitments and this diplomatic activity around Maurras, who, as a result, in 1937 could appear as a supreme savior, like Marshal Pétain: "The way seems open for Maurras, and the idea of making him sole chief of the right-wing factions, provided he declares himself loyal to Republic and to Church, seems perfectly feasible. 'Well-informed sources' are sketching the scenario in advance: first Maurras's conversion by the grace of Saint Thérèse of Lisieux, then his election to the Académie française by the grace of M. Bellessort, then grand national assizes and the proclamation of Maurras as *Duce* to the strains of 'La Marseillaise.'"[58] The intellectuals who took part in all these actions culminating in a sort of crystallization around Maurras at the end of the 1930s gave their support to this conservative revolution that was, in part, the National Revolution, and particularly to its return to moral order.

It was those who recognized themselves in this ideological neb-
ula, and not "the French of 1940," who "with morbid fascination"
"turn[ed] over the stones of their national life and contemplated
the crawling things, real or imaginary, that they believed festered
there."[59] Among those crawling, teeming things were bad literary
morals and, according to René Gillouin, "the sexual obsession—bad
boys and vile *garçonnes*" of "hack commoners," whose violent condemnation is not exempt from this fascination that is so characteristic
of the polemical rhetoric of the Action française:[60]

> All French men and French women have their share in the respon-
> sibility for France's disaster. . . . The responsibility of the writer is
> particularly heavy. . . . Wasn't it André Gide who, spoofing an ex-
> pression of Le Play reprised by Paul Bourget according to which
> the family is the social cell, pretended to agree with it completely
> by taking the cell to mean a prison? It is around the same time . . .
> that a president of the Conseil named Léon Blum republished a
> book of his ghastly youth concerning marriage, seasoning it with
> the most impudent publicity, a veritable manual of vileness that
> should have prohibited its author from having any political career.
> Society and literature, each pushing the other, rushed headlong
> together toward the "common cesspool" where there is no more
> literature or society.[61]

Before the war, Gillouin had asked that Jean Cocteau's play *Les
Parents terribles,* which he described as "immoral, antifamily, and antisocial," be banned. He was pleased that, when it was revived by the
Théâtre du Gymnase, it now aroused such "vehement protests" that
it had to be removed from the bill: "Well! the public mind has ceased
to descend the slope and has started to ascend it once again. There is
hope." This hope was predicated on restoring the French family and
keeping mothers at home.

Throughout its publication we find numerous contributions to the
production of the "eternal feminine" in the doctrinal review of the
Action française. The lamentations of Gillouin concerning the Republican chaos—"a people ravaged by alcoholism, rotted by eroticism, eroded by a declining birthrate"—were the basis for his appeal
for a "national, authoritarian, hierarchical, and social" French State.
The "shock" and the "redemptive repentance" that one owes to the

catastrophe of 1940 would make it possible to reconstruct the "traditional family, founded on love and mutual respect and on moral discipline," "any offense against the eternal laws of life [calling down] exemplary punishments not only on peoples but on individuals themselves"; "with Marshal Pétain the truths of private and public salvation [are] installed at the very heart of the state."[62] René Benjamin lists the causes of the general ruin: "The house that no one knows how to build anymore, the woman who reduces her dress to the minimum, the Mass broadcast on the radio, art that believes that the ultimate aim is to reveal what the morality police still hide provisionally, work seen as a sentence, charity detested by the poor who feel humiliated, humility scoffed at as a weakness, here are the proofs that Bolshevism is strangling us after exiling the soul." He preaches "a moral life" that alone can "recognize its rights of inheritance," that alone "knows the family."[63] The family is the family of France and the French family, and when the *Revue* questions "the future of the new France" through the voice of Thierry Maulnier, it affirms that "the origin of French 'nationality' is too ancient to be granted to any comers by a simple legal formality, by a simple decree of naturalization."[64]

The culture of anathema and the catastrophic vision of history specific to the Action française were a perfect match for the National Revolution, as were all the more or less prestigious fellow travelers in whom it always knew how to catalyze commitment in a period of crisis, ceaselessly recreating a noble form of militantism of the right — for use by academics — that casts an indulgent eye on, and experiences vicariously, the street violence perpetrated by the youth of the extreme right, in the same way it has always known how to marry pamphleteer hatred and obscenity with great homilies on the moral order. Eugen Weber recalls the extraordinary influence of the ideas of the Action française on literary and intellectual circles during the interwar years, an influence whose routine and diversified involvement in the fields of journalism and literary criticism was not the least of its mediations.[65] A publication such as *Candide,* launched in 1924 once the success of *La Revue universelle* was ensured, provided a means of access to a wide audience (300,000 readers before the war) by its light tone and its high literary quality, its illustrations, and its increasingly anti-Semitic satirical drawings. *Candide* decried "the foreign invasion," the social disorder, the rise in crime, and public school teachers. Like *L'Action française* (the movement's newspaper), *Candide,* which was also withdrawn to the Free Zone, would not cease to encourage further repression of "those responsible," civil servants, parliamentarians, Freemasons, Jews. From October to December 1940, *L'Action française* ceaselessly called for a toughening of the first Jewish Statute.[66]

It is truly a mixture of political invective and appeal to a golden age, of anti-Semitism and antifeminism, of provincial preachifying and denunciations of the apocalyptic dangers that characterize an article in *Candide* concerning feminine culpability and expiation. Here, the rhetorical violence of the Action française reveals itself completely along with its preestablished affinities with the National Revolution. The text opens once again with Léon Blum's "manual of vileness":

> From what irreparable disaster has the disaster at the bottom of which France so patiently and proudly finds itself saved us? The springs were dried up. . . . And a kind of nonchalance, the pleasures of living well had caused women to lose the habit of looking beyond the self and higher. One of the secrets of our collapse is there, in this blandness, in this indifference. Because intoxicated with herself, in love with direct action, personal ambition — lawyer, doctor, business "man" — woman has little by little turned away from her eternal role. . . . Because she was unable to transmit to her husband, to her sons, the flame that she no longer guarded in the deepest recesses of her being, the French woman of today carries her share, a heavy share, of responsibility for the defeat of France. The new men have understood this. The new laws are as wise as they are severe. They curb the unleashing of feminine avidity, limit young women's access to the liberal professions, and, on the other hand, enable in a way that is equivalent to requiring it that women return home and stay home. What the woman of today, having in her turn said her *mea culpa,* must realize first is all that we were starting to achieve through her. The danger is still there. The beast continues to prowl and is only waiting for peace to better show its teeth. In order to become a better fighter, let her, this guardian of threatened homes, create for herself the soul of a warrior. The task is immense. She is magnificent, we are be-

fore ruins. However, as in these northern cities where the annihilation of houses makes it easier to perceive the shooting spire of the cathedral, we can more clearly distinguish the eternal routes outside of which it is dangerous to venture. We see them rise up from the most distant past. We sense their infinite extension.[67]

2. THE CHURCH AND FEMININE CONTRITION

In the case of men of letters, their support for the reorganization of the social world promised by the National Revolution was consistent with the defense of long-standing, strictly political options (commitment to the Action française, or at least adherence to its conception of order and disorder) and with the defense of specifically literary interests (realism, regionalism) that also expressed the defense of a world of values, particularly Catholic values. In the case of the Church, the question was raised differently, and an analysis of the broad affinities demonstrated between the Church and the social philosophy of the National Revolution leads us to question the limits of what is usually qualified as political. More precisely, the immediate and complete meeting of minds between Vichy and the Catholic Church as institution concerning the defense and promotion of the "eternal feminine" allows us to reflect on the limitations of an approach that would reduce politics to commitments traditionally qualified as political— for example, the ecclesiastical hierarchy's defense of a given Vichy domestic or foreign policy option or the commitment of particular members of this hierarchy or of these groups of clerics in favor of or as active participants in the Resistance. Such an approach overlooks those forms of almost prereflexive adherence to value systems, here the sexual division of the social world based on normative imperatives. We often forget that these forms of adherence have political effects: on the one hand, because these schemes impose exclusions based on the arbitrary naturalization of biological differences (in this, close to the effects of racist logic) and are therefore in keeping with a view of a "natural" social order; on the other hand, because they allow *massive mobilizations* based on shared "apolitical" values, mobilizations that legitimized, strengthened, and gave longevity to the new regime while at the same time endorsing, without always wanting to, all of its political positions.

The national, diocesan or specialized Catholic press unanimously welcomed the establishment of the French State (Cardinal Gerlier, Archbishop of Lyon, who was hostile to Nazism, said of the new national motto Work, Family, Country, "These three words are ours"), enthusiastically supported all the measures for restoring moral order, and was gratified by all the genuine advantages granted to the Church concerning education, religious orders, and diocesan associations. How could the great majority of the faithful have doubted the legitimacy of the new regime and the validity of all its policies?[1] They would have needed a rare clairvoyance to discern the rifts and divisions in this attitude of support when in November 1941 Abbé Lesaunier, superior of the seminary of Carmes, wrote, with the imprimatur of the Archbishop of Paris, in *La Conscience catholique en face du devoir civique actuel:* "I recognize without hesitation the authority of the government of Marshal Pétain; I am neither a Gaullist nor an Anglophile; I submit without recrimination to the occupying authorities." The critical response of Father Fessard, the famous Jesuit theologian, *La Conscience catholique devant la défaite,* drafted as a result of the shock expressed to Cardinal Suhard by certain Catholic circles in response to the allegiance to the German authorities expressed by the preceding text, did not, according to the author, receive any reply: "I was sadly surprised to note that my work had served no purpose, since after November 1942 as before, the 'legitimacy of the established power' continued to be affirmed, without the necessary distinctions, by the entire hierarchy."[2]

The prophetic view of the debacle, the political imposition of a national mea culpa as the only way to conceive of the defeat, and the call for the restoration of family values perhaps contributed as much if not more to the collective recognition of and gratitude for the National Revolution expressed by the majority of Catholic institutions and militant Catholics than the favors the new regime bestowed on the Church. In September 1940, a clergyman who preached during the pilgrimage of Rocamadour chose to exalt the salutary necessity of expiation and "the acceptance of suffering by following Mary's example." In a surprising regional chronicle of adherence, we can gauge the importance of the Church's support for "the enterprise of collective culpabilization that constitutes an insidious but remarkably effective basis for the official ideology."[3]

An analysis of the diocesan *Semaines religieuses,* which appeared from July 1940 to November 1942, also seems to support this hypothesis. The pastoral letters, editorials, and sermon topics borrowed from the vocabulary and the slogans of Vichy ideology, disseminated the Marshal's aphorisms, made him the hero of "edifying scenes," and preached against the city that paves the way for "the masses' lack of discipline."[4] The *Semaines* quotes Barrès, Bourget, Bordeaux, Massis, and de Maistre to condemn the Republican regime and universal suffrage, because "authority is incompatible with election." More profoundly, this study reveals the *linguistic kinship* between the Church and the regime. "The deadly sin," opines the Archbishop of Aire-Dax, "is that the spirit of pleasure has won out over the spirit of sacrifice. We can replace this expression with the one that is directly superimposable: in France, the pagan spirit has won out over the Christian spirit."[5] If clerics sympathized so readily with the new regime, it is because this new regime spoke their language: the little phrase concerning "the spirit of pleasure," the search for collective culpabilities, the call to conversion, the sign of Providence are all signals that have an immediate and spontaneous rallying effect. Henceforth prelates read the regime politically under the sign of "coincidence" and "concordance," for the Gospel and *Les Semaines sociales catholiques* seemed to them to inspire French radio from morning till night: "What gives us all confidence is that the *official voice* of the nation that yesterday warbled light verse, fleeting verse, today trains to grave rhythms with *profound and eternally divine resonances.* The Church recognizes itself in these cadences."[6] Very conscious of their function as transmission belt, the French State did not pass up the opportunity to use such homilies, and the propaganda services used the pastoral letters of 1941 collected in a booklet.[7]

It would, of course, be simplistic to present the situation as though all Catholics were delighted with the Vichy regime. From the start, doubts and oppositions were revealed. Father Dillard, for example, a Jesuit leader of Social Catholicism who expected much from the "French reconstruction" and delivered wildly popular sermons in the church of Saint-Louis de Vichy in which condemnations of Nazism alternated with the defense and illustration of Work, Family, Nation, quickly became disillusioned with the regime and vigorously denounced "clerical-military ceremonies" like the High Mass of the Legion.[8] Elsewhere, the Action française, which delighted in the alliance of army, Church, and state, devoted itself to denouncing Catholics of the opposition deemed "bad Frenchmen" and "bad Catholics" in the columns of its newspaper ("without realizing—at least we want to believe this—that it was denouncing them to the Vichy police and soon to the Germans"),[9] which shows that unanimity was far from achieved. A study of the content of the pastoral letters published in the *Semaines religieuses* also reveals that if, during Lent of 1941, fifteen out of eighteen of these letters focused on topics drawn from Vichy ideology, when the regime hardened its stance in August 1941, they stopped taking their inspiration from the ideas of the regime in power. In 1942, their topics were once again strictly religious.[10] Nevertheless, through the voice of its hierarchy, the Church as an institution by and large supported the National Revolution. In September 1941, the cardinals and archbishops of the Free Zone adopted the text drafted by their colleagues in the Occupied Zone on July 24: "We revere the Chief of State, and we ask that all French men and women unite around him immediately. We encourage our faithful to work alongside him in the recovery that he has undertaken in the three areas of family, work, and nation."[11]

Our angle of approach to the Vichy regime through this reinvention of "feminine" "nature" and the "proper" place of women in the city, which relies on the privileged inclusion of women in the inventory of collective culpabilities, allows us to examine this affinity of languages and rhetorics more closely. This is a truly shadowy area where the rifts and confrontations specific to the Church as a field become blurred or disappear.[12] These rifts are incarnated, for example, at one extreme by the foundation in November 1941 in Lyon of the Jesuit-run *Cahiers du Témoignage chrétien,* which would become one of the active centers of Catholic involvement in the Resistance, and, at the other extreme, by the absolution pronounced by Cardinal Suhard on July 1, 1944, in Notre-Dame de Paris during the funeral of Philippe Henriot, which would result in his being banned from the Mass of Thanksgiving in this same cathedral by de Gaulle on August 26. The crusade to return women to the home and to keep them there was unanimously accepted by clergy and the faithful and in the eyes of the country placed the Church in its entirety within the sphere of influence of the National Revolution. This is a very political consequence of the collective identification with a cause presented as apolitical.

The Revival and Politicization of
Pilgrimages and of the Cult of Mary

The increase in the number of pilgrimages that marked the period, particularly those devoted to the cult of Mary, is both a revelation and a demonstration that exemplifies this confusion of languages. The confusion resulted in an amalgamation of the Christian triptych "sin-ordeal-conversion" and the Vichy triptych "error-defeat-recovery." [13] Yet, the very history of the social construction of pilgrimages during the nineteenth century reveals the specifically political imperatives that marked it from the start.

In his preface to *Histoire du catholicisme en France,* André Latreille writes that a historical work on pilgrimages "would demonstrate to what extent the soil of our old country, of the nation that is the eldest daughter of the Church, is steeped in sacred memories—this soil that has never for one moment ceased to germinate saints and heroes of the faith and that through several naïve legends can finally authentically claim the honor of privileged supernatural revelations." [14] The vision of the historian of Catholicism coincides here with the vision of the Church, which, from the beginning of the Third Republic until the 1950s, published history manuals for private education devoted to demonstrating that shame and misery fall on France whenever she protests her vocation as "eldest daughter of the Church." These manuals enumerate and celebrate the saints and martyrs and strive to restore the past, particularly the Middle Ages, to its due place, thereby celebrating the greatness of prerevolutionary France. [15] The Vichy policy of purifying scholastic manuals that followed the German instructions of July 30, 1940, took the same tack. [16] At the elementary school level, it gave the green light to René Jeanneret, who, in collaboration with the Catholic publishing house Mame, published *Le Miracle de Jeanne* and collections of selected passages in the same vein. [17] His policy of propaganda through images that favored the patron saints—from the most national to the most local—including the patron saint of each trade, followed along the same lines.[18]

This organized revival of so-called popular cults during the Occupation found its most consummate expression in the great pilgrimages to Marian shrines that directly evoked the period immediately after the Commune, such as the pilgrimages of contrition to Paray-le-Monial, whose church was elevated to the rank of basilica and was dedicated to the Sacred Heart in 1875. As a continuation of this movement, the National Assembly voted to build the expiatory basilica of Sacré-Coeur de Montmartre on the very spot where the Commune had gathered momentum. By launching a national subscription drive for the construction of the monument, the ruling class and the Church inspired even more palpably the notion of popular redemption.

The history of Lourdes exemplifies this political use of shrines.[19] In 1872, Emmanuel d'Alzon, son of a legitimist deputy of the Restoration and founder of the Assumptionist Order, through which he intended to fight Protestantism, Voltairianism, and the French Revolution, created Notre-Dame-du-Salut, intending to save France through public prayer and the moral edification of the working class. He organized the first great national pilgrimage to Lourdes, placed, after the Commune, like Paray, under the sign of contrition.[20] In February 1941, under the law that restored the assets of the Church to the diocesan associations, the grotto of Lourdes was given to the diocese of Tarbes.[21] On April 20, 1941, "after having crossed the threshold of many cathedrals," Pétain went to Lourdes, thereby demonstrating in the eyes of the Catholic chronicler that "the regime is saying its prayers": "The Grotto of Lourdes signifies something more. Cathedrals steeped in centuries, laden with history and art are a natural part of the itinerary for an official trip. In Lourdes, which disbelief has so often ridiculed, the spiritual alone attracts. 'What courage has been revived there!' exclaimed the bishop of the diocese. Nothing called the Marshal there, that is, no outside necessity. In Pau during the morning, he had spoken to the peasants;[22] in Lourdes, he heard the murmur of the Gave, the voices of the Virgin and of Bernadette."[23] The prophet was clearly in contact with the divine.

After a period during which Mary appeared simply as the new

Eve, redresser of original sin, the Roman Catholic Church continued throughout its history to develop doctrine, making Mariology a specialized branch of Roman Catholic theology that would find its culmination in the great dogmatic proclamations of the nineteenth and twentieth centuries. The dogma of the Immaculate Conception was proclaimed by Pius IX in 1854 as a solemn affirmation of the doctrinal authority of the Church in the interest of countering the modern world and the revolutionary enthusiasm that manifested itself throughout the period in Italy and Europe. The apparitions at Lourdes and La Salette, which would popularize this spectacular devotion, occurred at the same time as the proclamation of the dogma.[24] If, during these hard times of collective expiation represented by the Commune or the defeat of 1940, the cult of Mary was the occasion for a privileged expression of contrition and return to a Christian France, it was in part because it spoke the language of the eternity of things with clarity and simplicity.

In an article published in May 1942 entitled "La Vierge dans la cité," *Renouveaux,* a journal of Social Catholicism, makes Mary the "concrete and living" form of the Church itself—the Immaculate Virgin is the image of the "ideal city"—and makes the Virgin a symbol of an eternal order: "Immaculate from birth, never having known from the origin of her being anything but order, having remained perfectly in place amid the universal confusion, never straying from the impeccable line, Mary is the image of *the well-ordered city, that is, first of all, returned to the eternal order* where all things here below, intelligence and desires, individuals and societies, poor and rich, citizens and princes, seas and winds, birds and lilies of the field are securely in their place in the order conceived by the creator." The cult of Mary celebrated the woman-eternity link and the return to an order of bodies that "does not lie," as Pétain said of the earth. Just like numerous other religious rituals, it also celebrated a cyclical temporality in a period of historical violence during which it was possible to live only from day to day. In such a context, the clerical-political exploitation of the faithful's believing expectation sometimes took on the explicit character of political manipulation. The mass participation in the great pilgrimages of the 1940s along with the revival of small local pilgrimages, witnessed in photos of the period, like that of Vernet in September 1941, inseparably demonstrate a renewal of religious belief that expressed in Messianic fashion a social demand for explanatory schemes at a time of chaos and despair and the clerical-political channeling of these aspirations in a single direction: "It was the Day of the Virgin who appeared in 1846 on the mountain of La Salette to two young shepherds. The speaker of the day, an army chaplain during both wars, was able to interpret the feelings of this crowd of believers who had come to implore the Virgin on behalf of the mutilated and suffering country. It was also the Marshal's day. His image presided over the religious festival. After the Virgin had revealed to us the meaning of the spiritual values necessary for our recovery, *Marshal Pétain spoke through the mouth of the divine orator* who exalted his devotion to the country. He made the crowd cheer the Marshal's program, Work, Family, Nation, which will save France."[25] In contact with the divine, the prophet speaks through the mouth of the divine orator like the hypnotist through the mouth of the medium.

The most striking manifestation of the organized revival of the cult of Mary during the 1940s was the Great Return. In 1938, a Marian conference in Boulogne-sur-Mer started the movement by launching a tour of France of the statue of Notre-Dame-de-Boulogne. In 1942, when a Marian pilgrimage to Puy was to be organized, the organizers sought out this statue. After the Marian conference of Puy, which brought together sixty thousand pilgrims, it reached Lourdes. But the trip did not stop there, and the successive stations of the statue of Boulogne were the occasion for numerous consecrations to the Blessed Virgin and for distributions of pictures and rosaries. According to its tireless leader, the Jesuit priest Paul Doncoeur, a true spiritual son of Emmanuel d'Alzon, the Great Return was "the symbol, the extension, and the means of the great return of our people to God."[26] The forms of consecration to the Virgin, printed on heart-shaped paper, were filled in by some ten thousand people during the Great Return. At the opening of the official ceremonies marking the arrival of the pilgrimage at Puy on August 15, 1942, Father Forestier, general chaplain to the Scouts of France, addressed the bishop of Puy in the following manner: "After the terrible days of June 1940, we thought that, stimulated by admirable messages, France would pull itself together quickly and completely. And, on certain days, it seemed to us that too many were not concerned with 'taking a lesson from lost battles.' . . .[27] We needed more strength to ascend the difficult path of national resurrection. . . . We walked with the heavy burden of our sins, and we are going to place them at the feet of the Blessed Virgin. . . . France, the Marshal said, occupies too great a place in the Christian civilization of the West for it to subsist without it."[28]

These spectacular and fascinating manifestations were explicitly the opportunity for the ecclesiastical hierarchy to encourage vocations in young people. In 1943, the organizers of this pilgrimage were delighted that, since August 15, 1942, there had been thirty-five priestly or religious vocations among older Scouts in the "province" of Lyon alone. Father Doncoeur, an army chaplain from 1914 to 1918 and an important Scout director, had led campaigns for priestly vocations between the two wars. He committed himself completely to the National Revolution and preached the return to the earth and the mystique of the chief, denouncing the "chimeras of democratic liberalism." Father Forestier, a Dominican—who again in 1943 repeated: "The Marshal's messages expressed what we have dreamed of for a long time"—was the general chaplain of the Chantiers de la Jeunesse and saw the new order prefigured in the Scout movement, as he wrote in *Le Chef* in March 1942: "The structures of the new order, made up of authority, of hierarchy, of the disappearance of class struggle, fit the concept that we had of the world too closely, were too similar to the order that reigned in the small Scout city." In the Nord-Pas-de Calais, Monsignor Dutoit urged the diocese to devote itself to the Sacred Heart in 1941, declared 1942 the Year of Mary, and set the revelation of religious vocations as the objective for 1943. He gave his full support to Pétain, whom, he said, we must "obey blindly," and to the politics of collaboration. Monsignor Dutoit saw in the defeat "the punishment for sins that it is easy for us to acknowledge" and "the guarantee of a Christian rebirth." "Is this not an incomparable blessing, this *tranquility* and this *freedom* in which the novena takes place?" he declared in Saint-Omer in July 1941.[29] As of August 15, 1940, and for the first time in years, a great procession traversed Vichy. A whole clergy numbed by routine rediscovered a missionary zeal and vocations suddenly reappeared.

"Women, get hold of yourselves"

The program of contrition, of mea culpa ("on the breast of others," to borrow Jacques Duquesne's expression) was fully embraced by the dignitaries and thinkers of the regime. Aside from the Church's newly rediscovered advantages and influence, this program was one of the most fundamental bases for the immediate ideological affinities of the Church with the National Revolution. The eschatological tradition permeates the history of Christianity: "Without pain, there is no Church," say the confession manuals.[30] Jean Delumeau traces the *systematic construction of eschatological fears by the clerical culture,* the dominant and educated culture, to the birth of the modern world at the end of the fourteenth century, and situates the first known description of the "terrors of the year 1000" at the end of the fifteenth century, a moment at which the new Humanism, which it was intended to counter, was triumphing. This eschatology, which announced the imminence of the final judgment and proceeded to separate the elect from the damned, was also above all propagated at this time by the men of the Church who were the most driven by a concern for ministry. At the head of the agents of Satan were Jews and women.[31] The organizers of the expiatory pilgrimages of the 1940s were, in the end, very close to those preachers, "nomads of the apostolate," and those religious playwrights who spread the theology of a terrible God—the idea that God punishes guilty men—throughout fifteenth-century Europe. In the Drôme, Father Vallet, a Spanish ex-Jesuit responsible for a retreat house, preached sermons on Hell by adopting a visionary stance: "I see him, I see him burning in Hell . . . I see the former Cardinal Verdier burning in Hell!" In 1940, the most conservative factions of the Church accused Cardinal Verdier of having shown too much sympathy in 1936 for the social policy of the Popular Front.[32]

This defeat was the sign that France had sinned, that the defeat was therefore merited and perhaps salutary. Its sins included the permanent wave, paid vacations, Pernod, political parties, strikes, immoral films, bathing suits, democracy, working women, and the declining birthrate. A man as reserved with respect to Vichy as Cardinal Saliège, Archbishop of Toulouse, wrote in a pastoral letter published in *La Croix* on June 28, 1940: "For chasing God from schools, from the courts of the nation, for tolerating pernicious literature, the White slave trade, for the degrading promiscuity of shops, offices, factories, Lord, we ask you to forgive us. What use did we make of the victory of 1918? What use would we have made of an easy victory in 1940?"[33] However, Monsignor Saliège and Monsignor Bruno de Solages, rector of the Institut catholique of Toulouse, were seen by Vichy in 1940 as dangerous elements; they led an open resistance to the regime and to collaboration throughout the entire Occupation. In September 1942, this resistance took the form of a direct confrontation with the prefect concerning scenes of Jewish children being separated from their parents at the Noé and Récébédou camps during the departure of deportation trains.[34] The fact that a man who would prove to be such a firm opponent of the regime also espoused the Vichy rhetoric of expiation, enriching it with his own personal expression likely to make an impact, clearly shows the extent and the violence of submission to the "hypnotic power of punishment" and, over and above the political rifts, the Church's central role as relay in imposing this program, whose force was all the greater because it presented itself as apolitical. In the same way, the admonitions to youth that Peyrade made his specialty in *La Croix* could appear to be apolitical: "No longer must there be question of being witty, light, libertine, mocking, skeptical, and whimsical—that's enough. . . . *God, nature, work, marriage, love, children*—all that is serious, very serious, and looms ahead of you," he wrote in April 1941.[35] In fact, Peyrade's text plagiarizes Alexandre Dumas fils, who was one of the regime's authors of reference. His moralizing aphorisms quite naturally encouraged the comparison with the Commune. We see clearly in Peyrade's literary appropriation, which does not even need to be announced as such because it is so obvious, the extraordinary kinship of the analyses carried out after 1870 and after 1940. The choice of the patronage of Dumas fils, who had castigated the Commune and the communards with unparalleled verbal violence, suggests just how much the return to marriage, to nature, to children was a sermon that was far from being politically neutral. In an article that appeared on June 6, 1871, "A Letter Concerning the Issues of the Day," which calls for a life full of austerity and sacrifice in order to mend the country, Dumas fils had written: "We say nothing of their females out of respect for the women they resemble when they are dead."[36] These authors of apocalyptic times invent and reinvent a language that privileges the

Vichy and the Eternal Feminine ▸ 50

"magic use" of words, "the emotional atmosphere which surrounds and envelops them," a use specific to political myths.[37]

A study of texts published during this period by various currents of the Church that inventory the social sins punished by Providence clearly shows their political aim. The defense of the family and the return of women to their "true" "nature" is presented as one of the central means of redemption. It allows them to condemn the Republican social order, charged with the sin of individualism, and to encourage the return to an authoritative moral order. The redefinition of the "eternal" feminine "nature" and the marking out of legitimate female territories that resulted were thus very often associated with the condemnation of the Republic and its educational policy, the Popular Front, and, even further, the French Revolution. "The cursed year for us was not the year of our external defeat, but the year of our internal defeat, this year, 1936," the Bishop of Aire-Dax declared in his pastoral letter for Lent 1941. These positions adopted by the Church hierarchy were not new; they were forcefully expressed during the Popular Front and strengthened by the dread of the Spanish Frente popular. In a pastoral letter written in the fall of 1936 that was to be read at all the Masses, the French cardinals had spelled out the Church's position: "Anxiety and anguish grip all souls"; "the crisis is general"; it is manifest in the neglect of "the sacred nature of duty"; "the natural principles of the right of property ownership, of respect for one's given word, and for contracts made are being routinely violated"; the cause of "these events that are so painful and so troubling" is "practical atheism"; we must therefore rid the schools of these "revolutionary viruses" and reestablish "the unity of the conjugal bond." The letter of support sent by Cardinal Verdier to Daladier on March 30, 1939, to assure him of the Church's assistance with his "work of national recovery"[38] was followed only one month later by a long appeal from the cardinals to fight against the declining birthrate: to "restore the moral climate of the country" and to have done with the "social convulsions," divorce and abortion must be condemned.[39] This appeal in favor of natality by the cardinals and archbishops on April 28, 1939, after a long silence was also a way of acknowledging the family as the cell of the Church and a natural organ for propagating the Christian faith. It was also a way of responding to the encyclical *Casti Connubii* of December 30, 1930 (which had not elicited

The Church and Feminine Contrition ▸ 51

much comment up to that point) that condemned contraceptive practices and reaffirmed that the primary purpose of marriage was procreation.[40] The defeat, the establishment of the French State, and the spread of the social philosophy of the National Revolution provided the opportunity to revive these lamentations and the conscious, strategic, and unconscious associations they called up in an offensive without objectivity, a revival in which the perpetual Catholic production of feminine identity would occupy a key position.

In *Réveil de l'âme française*, M. S. Gillet, superior general of the Dominican Order, made the Declaration of Human Rights, individualism, and the Republican school the factors of the progressive dissolution of the national forces given over to "instincts" and "appetites" of "hearts eager for immediate pleasure" and "enemies of sacrifice."[41] The cataclysm of June 1940 therefore saved the country from the harmful influence of the "masters of French sociology" who had established abnormal relationships between scholastic education and family education. For Gillet, the restoration of the family was the primary road to salvation: "Now that an absurd policy and deplorable morals due to unbridled individualism have succeeded in fifty years in putting the French family and, with it, France, in danger of death, in order to restore the family, we must return to French traditions, regardless of the cost, and restore the Christian home"; "divorce, the declining birthrate, and free love have ultimately put the very existence of France in jeopardy and have had an undeniable impact on our lack of preparation for the war and on our defeat." Father Gillet always fought lay public education, and his condemnation of sociologists, agitators of family problems and inspirers of state-controlled education, led him to demand a return to "all the notions that assume an antisocial or extrasocial determinism, such as psychology, heredity, race, and even more so to traditions passed down from generation to generation, strengthened by family education, that can be said, using an expressive image, to be in the blood." A veritable political war machine, this text calls for the return to the voice of blood and returns women to the place their bodies have always and will always assign to them: "Women, as well as men, are endowed with reason and freedom. . . . . Nevertheless, this personal human equality does not prevent their individual inequality that stems not from their soul but from their body, that is, the difference of their sexes. . . . If we consider the events that have occurred in history for centuries, and by which nature betrays its most secret intentions, woman does not possess either the physical strength or the qualities of activity, stability, direction, and authority required of a leader to the same extent as man."

In January 1941, *Voix françaises,* a Catholic weekly, was established in Bordeaux and announced in its first issue that it wanted to "re-christianize souls" under the leadership of Marshal Pétain, "the only legitimate head of France today." A publication could not be established in Bordeaux without offering solid guarantees to the occupying force. The editor, Paul Lesourd, was a man of the right, a professor at the Institut catholique of Paris and a friend of Cardinal Baudrillart, rector of the institute since 1907, who, fearing a new Commune after the defeat of 1940, defended collaborationist arguments until his death in 1942.[42] In particular, the newspaper denounced certain civil servants who had retained their positions whom it considered to be Freemasons. In 1943, it demanded that the "terrorists" be brought to their senses and, in May 1944, made union behind the Marshal the last bastion against "chaos." But it was also a garden-variety Catholic newspaper that recounted pilgrimages and filled its columns with articles devoted to mothers who remained at home and the return to family values.[43] A monthly supplement, *Voix françaises familiales,* lauded the rediscovered family, Mother's Day, and Mary, "Queen of France"; week after week, on the front page, was another picture of Mary borrowed from the archives of the Museum of French Monuments. The newspaper had prestigious contributors, including Father Sertillanges, a Dominican and member of the Institut and a Vichy regular. From 1941 to 1943 he published a series of articles on the "moral renovation of France" through the family in which he claimed to be an expert in feminine nature. In 1944 he collected these articles in a theological-demographic work on the family called *La Maison française,* which Henry Bordeaux greeted in these terms: "The cult of ancestors cannot be distinguished from the cult of fire. Every family has its tomb a few steps from the door. . . . Father Sertillanges emphasizes love in marriage through which he then aims to reestablish the authority of the father of the family."[44]

The Church and Feminine Contrition ▸ 53

Because everything had been "falsified" and what was needed was to "start all over again," for Father Sertillanges the cornerstone was the return to "private virtues," "virtues of the family head, virtues of his diligent partner, a specialist in giving." Let those who "led science astray" beware: "Oh, sociologists, sociologists, or passionate minor politicians, you are so rash in wanting to base society on something other than *nature*." To help "our National Revolution," "Women, get hold of yourselves," "for you, too, have been swayed": "The easy life led you away; your tendency to fritter away your time had taken precedence over the seriousness of family existence and the concerns for a sound education"; "the time has come to reform." But feminine culpability can always be raised by the Fathers of the Church, for they can make "the Samaritan woman with seven husbands an annunciator of the Word," and they can make Mary Magdalene "a holy woman," provided that "our life companions" know how to "correct their failings": "partiality in judgment linked to a restricted view of the whole"; "a tendency toward reverie that is their own brand of alcoholism"; "nervousness, obstinacy, whim." To rectify the error of confusing the "roles of men and women" "that we almost committed of late and that *our* National Revolution will redress," it suffices to remember and recall that "woman is the mother of the human race": "Expand this notion and you will have a complete grasp of feminine psychology, and, at the same time, of what nature expects of her in the just division of human labor." And because, as Dumas fils (again!) wrote, "motherhood is the patriotism of women," the battle is on the natality front: "We must remain ourselves, and we will no longer be ourselves if *the foreign invader* is progressively substituted for our native populations. The remedy for this is for us to occupy our regions ourselves; we must agree to populate our cradles in order to populate our factories, our fields, our administrations, and our public services as well. Nature abhors a vacuum. The suction pump acts in demography just as in hydraulics. Will we resolve this distressing problem?" [45] The link between the declining birthrate and immigration that makes demography a political science would be central to scientists' reflections concerning women and would become one of the platitudes of the regime.

Social Catholicism and "Feminine Humanism"

Much more nuanced in its social philosophy and divided in its forms and degrees of adherence to Vichy, the current of Social Catholicism is particularly interesting to study here, for during the interwar years it established close ties with the Catholic movements interested in women's action. Its adherence to the 1940 version of the ideology of the "eternal feminine" seems obvious, nevertheless. Led primarily by Jesuits, the movement, born at the end of the nineteenth century, found expression in annual meetings called Semaines sociales de France, a sort of itinerant university staffed by prestigious professors, whose official organ, the *Chronique sociale de France,* was based in Lyon. In Paris, the Action populaire, a social information center founded at the beginning of the century by Father Gustave Desbuquois, served as the active core of the movement, which devoted itself primarily to Christian trade unionism and to improving workers' living conditions. It also inspired numerous women's organizations and the study circles of the Catholic youth group the Association catholique de la jeunesse française (ACJF). The principal leaders of this current were in the southern zone after 1940 and published their reviews there under different titles that evoked the hope fostered by the situation and the regime even in a current that might be considered as belonging to the "left" of the Church: from October 1940, *Renouveaux,* which was a revival of the *Cahiers d'action religieuse et sociale,* and from January 1941, *Cité nouvelle,* which replaced both the *Dossiers de l'action populaire* and *Études.*

In the editorial of the first issue of *Cité nouvelle,* "France neuve, vérités retrouvés," Father Desbuquois developed the rhetoric of salvation through suffering and expanded the notion of individual conversion to the national community. Calling for a "renewed patriotism," he wrote: "The contemplation [of France] sets off and gives new momentum to the *millenary forces* that were slumbering in the heart of its sons." [46] To "transform the *exceptional* catastrophe into a *final* solution of existence," the French State must be "strong and authoritarian" and, at the same time, respect "the individual or combined powers that existed before it," that is, the intermediate bodies, especially the family and professional bodies. *Renouveaux* justified its title by the ardent desire it detected "in everyone" for "renovation" now that the

"House of France has collapsed" and "the French work site is open." In his "year-end assessment" dated December 15, 1941, one year after the opening of the "work site," Desbuquois takes stock of the division of tasks: "The more the work site of France is organized, the better the two complementary sectors of its activities can be distinguished: the one we might call 'official institutions' and the other we might call 'private initiatives' or, if you prefer, the sector of the NATIONAL REVOLUTION, and among others, the sector of CATHOLIC ACTION. Catholic action must effectively act in conjunction with the National Revolution. It must act as a *catalyst* or like a radioactive body on a specified tumor." [47]

All the ambiguities in the relationship between the movement of Social Catholicism and the political agenda of the regime are summarized in this extreme expression. It was a question of conveying the ideas of the movement to specific domains — family, work, youth — of making them "take hold" by seizing any opportunities offered by the situation, of somehow *investing* the work sites of the National Revolution. Long-defended values could be made to triumph in these work sites, and through them, Catholicism would have an influence on the new social order as it strove to counter the influence in Vichy of enemy Catholic trends such as the Action française.

So Father Desbuquois settled in Vichy until the fall of 1943 and continually supported the National Revolution. Father Dillard preached in the church of Saint-Louis de Vichy until the day the anti-Nazi tone of his sermons caused him to be expelled. He went to Germany as a clandestine chaplain for French workers and died in Dachau in 1945. At the same time that it supported the family, education, and youth policy of the French State, *Cité nouvelle* published philosophical and literary articles written by Father Fessard and Father de Lubac, founders of the *Cahiers du Témoignage chrétien* and leaders of the Catholic resistance. And while Eugène Dutoit, dean of the Catholic law school of Lille and president of the Semaines sociales de France, published *Rénovation française, l'apport de Semaines sociales,* in which he opened a dialogue with the regime about corporatism and the labor charter, the Lyonnais groups of the Chroniques sociales de France and numerous members of the Commission Générale des Semaines sociales became involved in the Resistance. [48] This demonstrates in highly abbreviated fashion to what extent this movement was internally divided. The contradictory relationship with the Vichy regime was even capable of dividing individuals. And here is where we come back to the theme of apolitical adherence to the National Revolution. By becoming involved, at times massively—as witnessed, for example, by the omnipresence of Social Catholic jurists in the activities of the Commisariat General for the Family, whose policy they largely influenced—in everything pertaining to the family, and therefore to women, education, corporatism, and youth, they enriched the state-influenced rhetoric with their own language and translated it into the *familiar language* used by the many men and women who listened to them. This "honorable" participation in Vichy policies based on *entryism* led to an overproduction of definitions of family order and of feminine "nature" that were ultimately quite close to those disseminated in the most conservative Catholic currents. The logic of competition worked at the very heart of the institutional Church to produce discourse concerning the "eternal feminine" without any limitations. This is one of the mainsprings of the social logic that, in these times of crisis, produced unanimity concerning women's return to the home.

The members of the Action populaire published a series of brochures between 1941 and 1943 that made up the collection "France vivante" from Spes. These brochures were presented as a continuation of the group's work and incorporated the ideology of the National Revolution into the areas of education, family, and work without any apparent difficulty. The Jesuits wrote about the peasant corporation, women's careers, the restoration of the family, and the family policy of the French State, the labor charter, and "our mothers." *Nos mères* opens with Pétain's message to the mothers of France on May 25, 1941, and sees the origin of communism in the "anemia of the worker family." It then called on the inevitable Father Sertillanges, who, to praise mothers, sketched the portrait of the invisible woman as loved by the regime: "O woman, O mother, diamond of intimacy, you whom none see from the outside, whom at times no one thinks of, rejoice! I see her, braving anxiety and worry, accepting thankless tasks, devouring sorrows, enduring the monotony of days that is so heavy," and so on.[49] In the booklet *Découverte de l'âme paysanne* (1942) that reprinted excerpts from a book published in 1935, Father Maurice de Ganay considered the problem of the earth to be a feminine problem:

The Church and Feminine Contrition ▸ 57

"The old mythologies tell us: the Earth goddess is the mother of men. This dual maternity of earth and woman is necessary to give and sustain the life of humanity. And if our current agriculture seems to be suffering from hemophilia, is it not symbolic that it is through women that this disease is transmitted?" [50] Having rediscovered the woman-peasant couple dear to the men of letters, he assigned to country-women (and not to marital structures or economic difficulties) the responsibility for the rural exodus. At the same time, he seized the opportunity to impose the return to myth in opposition to all forms of rational analysis.

Through numerous repetitive articles both *Renouveaux,* a modest review that offered briefs on all the social sectors in which Catholics found a privileged field of action, and *Cité nouvelle,* a more intellectual review, composed a hymn to "feminine humanism" based on the spirit of sacrifice and withdrawal to the private space that approved the Vichy principles governing the sexual division of the social world and that were implemented in the policies concerning the family, youth, and education. The grandiose concept of feminine humanism, whose sociogenesis we must be able to reconstruct, which seems to have no other function than to further radicalize the normative masculine/feminine opposition in the guise of praise for feminine qualities "of the heart," appears in an article published in *Renouveaux* in September 1941 entitled "The Family Household, Civic and Social Training of Women." This article stresses the "present necessity" of domestic education thus defined: "Conscious of its originality, for it is a 'feminine humanism' and will become a general culture; it is already in almost complete possession of its technique; it will soon take its exams."

Thus showing its respect for the poor and the oppressed, to talk about women, *Cité nouvelle* opened its columns to a woman. To "put France's house back in order," it was necessary to confront the "delicate problems" raised by the "woman question" courageously:

> Whereas twenty years ago, only those with an intellectual vocation sought the same education as boys, little by little, this habit became more widespread without any discrimination. Many succumbed to overwork before finishing. Others, worn out before their time, missed out on both a career and marriage. So many

woman doctors without patients and lawyers without cases, who would have been happy just being wives and mothers. The current trend, which seeks to return young women to their domestic mission, seems hard to many of them. . . . This path will make them happy, provided that they understand that circumstances obligate us to live more simply and that life is not made to give oneself every pleasure at an accelerated rhythm.[51]

In the first part of her article, the author praises exceptional women revealed by recent social developments, such as the aviatrix Hélène Boucher. In the texts of these moralizing women who, in these blessed times that offer unexpected strategies of distinction, claim the status of moralists, we often find this dual discourse that is most likely only a means of presenting oneself as being one of the legitimate exceptions that confirm the rule and of enjoying the power of prohibiting pleasure. Among the most active propagandists of Vichy sermonizing concerning women's return to the home, we can count numerous "authorized" women who assumed postures of authority to counsel other women to retreat at the very moment at which they were fully exercising their powers as experts in feminine aptitudes. Catholic "feminism" of the interwar period, often inspired by Social Catholicism, was the breeding ground for these vocations.

Women in the Service of the Church

Vichy is a quasi-experimental setting for studying the Church-woman relationship or, more precisely, the Church-feminine relationship in its most contradictory aspects. There is an obvious antifeminist Catholic tradition based on the identification of the maternal element with nature and of the paternal element with history,[52] an identification that produces "since the beginning" and "forever," in the eyes of theologians, the idea that "the" woman must efface herself to better exist. But there is also a cultivated affinity between the Church and the feminine universe that can be analyzed both as a means of liberation from masculine domination and as a policy of the institutional Church toward women as a religious clientele to be retained and expanded.[53] As Father Sertillanges says in a terse little expression: "Woman is more religious than man."[54] By placing the period of the defeat and the Occupation under the sign of the revival of the cult of Mary, the Church played on these two aspects. On the one hand, it participated in the conservative revolution in the central domain of the sexual division of the social world; on the other hand, it built on Catholic women's works and on their spokespersons by mobilizing all the feminine leaders of "Christian humanism" to glorify the respectability of women who obey the imposed rules of the game. In both cases, women were an opportunity to resolve conflicts of influence.

The Church's interest in defending and promoting the "eternal feminine" during this period of national crisis, which it interpreted and presented as a time of reconquest, can ultimately be understood as a specifically political and strategic interest. By leading the crusade to return women to the home and keep them there, the Church effectively defended two central imperatives of its existence and its vitality. On the one hand, the reminder of women's vocation for family education—at home—was inseparably a reminder of family freedom in educational matters, that is, the defense of education against instruction, of free educational choice, of the supremacy of the family as institution over the school as institution, in short, a *defense of private education* (in France, Catholic by a great majority) against the Republican school. In his analysis of the complementarity of the state and private associations, Father Desbuquois explicitly linked the defense of the family and the defense of "free" education: "We must give up analyzing all the forces of natural right that serve the good of the country and the state itself, all the more so if the state gives itself up to their spontaneous momentum. Among these forces, private education distinguishes itself. The private school is not a school that through a spirit of regrettable independence escapes state control. It is a normal mode, *consistent with the natural order,* of serving the family." [55] It would be fairer to say that the family, as desired by the Church, with the wife performing her job as mother "well," serves the "private" school. The restoration of the family, which the very conservative Father Gillet and Father Sertillanges opposed to sociologists who wanted to base society on something other than "nature," also had the essential function of rearming religious education.

On the other hand, the defense of the woman's return to her sole maternal "vocation" was, inseparably, a reminder of the central role played by mothers of families—and, of course, especially mothers of large rural families that resulted in making countrywomen responsible—in *maintaining religious vocations*. The mother played a preponderant role in family collaboration with the enterprise of inculcating vocation. Maternal training of vocations was encouraged and explicitly recognized by the Church during the years of crises in recruiting priests.[56] In the Nord-Pas-de-Calais, the "Christian renaissance," led by Monsignor Dutoit, praised large families that augured a "good priestly harvest."[57] *Renouveaux* placed the future of the priesthood in the hands of mothers: "The decline in the spirit of faith in women is primarily responsible for the general indifference of young people to the beautiful vocation. . . . If the creator made the heart of women more sensitive to feelings of faith and more accessible to religious intuitions, is this not because he expects her to be a shining influence for training young minds and awakening their aspiration to the most beautiful ideal?"[58] To speak of women, as we can see, is to speak of many other things and not of minor subjects from the perspective of institutional vitality. On these subjects all the currents of the Church were in agreement.

And if Father Doncoeur, who unconditionally supported the National Revolution, in his eyes, the sole opportunity to restore Christianity, wrote one of the most eschatological texts concerning the necessary return of "the race of women" to its single vocation, was this not because he worked during the interwar period for religious vocations and was obsessed by the *crisis in priestly vocations,* the title of one of his books?

> I wonder whether great upheavals are not intended to take us back to our being, to make us accept nature, to follow our vocation. The qualities necessary to a woman of today? None is more particularly necessary for her than *being woman.* I think that she will need great intelligence and audacious initiative to do this. . . . Yesterday I was rereading in Carrel: "Her natural function, which consists not only of bearing but also of rearing her young, should be restored to woman." These decrees are as harsh as they are revolutionary. . . . The more one posits *the natural being of woman,* the more it appears that it is defined by the flesh. We will pronounce this word with the same veneration we would use to speak of a work of God and just as we say "the body of Christ." Eve was taken from Adam's

flesh, and this single trait probably defines her being compared to that of man: he is drawn from the elements of the earth, and as a result he exists in reference to an exterior universe. . . . She exists in reference to man and, born of his flesh, she carries in the heart of her being the memory of her race. Man will cultivate Paradise or the rebel earth; she is dedicated to the supremely eminent work, the work of the flesh. The entire mystery of Mary is there.[59]

3. THE DEMOGRAPHIC SIN

In his speech of June 20, 1940—"The spirit of pleasure has won out over the spirit of sacrifice"—Marshal Pétain assigns a large share of the responsibility for the country's situation to the declining birthrate: "Too few babies, too few weapons, too few allies, those are the causes of our defeat." From a military standpoint, the demographic argument does not seem very pertinent, as both armies were numerically equal when they confronted each other.[1]

France's demographic situation was marked by the hecatomb of the First World War: the drop in the birthrate during the 1930s can be explained in large part by the hollow classes' attainment of the age of fertility and not by any Malthusian desire. The surplus of widows and unmarried women had reached three hundred thousand after the war of 1914,[2] and in 1935, the draft contingent had declined by half because boys born between 1914 and 1918 were so few in number.[3] However, the rise in the birthrate between 1938 and 1939 would continue to be analyzed by demographers as a beneficial result of the increase in criminal measures against abortion and not as an effect of the reestablishment of demographic equilibrium, as the consequences of the war of 1914–1918 had played themselves out. This explanatory discourse would find an unlimited echo in 1940, when Pétain took over and imposed on everyone the simplistic analysis of demographic culpability. If France had been vanquished because of moral disorder and if one of the signs of this disorder was the drop in fertility, recovery would be achieved by imposing pronatalist propaganda and measures. The regime was obsessed with condemning "neo-Malthusianism," and the contrition/woman/expiation scheme would be free to spread throughout the regime as demographic science legitimized a political conception of the moral order.

In a propaganda brochure published by the Commissariat General for the Family entitled *La Vie en fleur,* we find an anonymous text entitled "Dies Irae":

> Suddenly, in a home that is about to close its shutters, the horrible truth is made known. At the foot of the ceremonial bed, where, amid the glow of candles, the inert body of their only child lies, two elderly parents are lost in grief: a grief-stricken mother and a despairing father. . . . The father throws himself into the arms of a cousin: "Why didn't I listen to you when you suggested that we have more children? We only wanted one child so we could make him happier. Any excuse was good for not having any more. And now we are alone." What remorse! The man publicly confesses his selfishness. . . . *Dies irae . . . Dies illa . . .* Two elderly spouses expiate their unpardonable mistake of not wanting to give their child one or more little brothers. In our France, which was called the country of only sons, this story is truer and more common than it should be. Immanent justice![4]

Here, once again, the theology of a terrible God is put to use to re-establish the social order with respect to the fecundity of couples. In this album illustrated with photos of smiling infants and young nursing mothers, this evocation of divine vengeance shows to what excesses of morbid imagination the hypnotic power of punishment had led. We find here the great themes of the regime's pronatalist propaganda (condemnation of contraception, criticism of a "society of only sons," praise for the solidarity between generations) that are perfectly suited to the rhetoric of sin and redemption.

Vichy's use of demography as a political science was in keeping with historical continuity; however, as a result of the exceptional historical period in which it was deployed, it took on apocalyptic tones. It succeeded, with the help of experts ready to collaborate in this particular means of expanding their competencies, in immediately mobilizing an entire learned body of work in which it privileged an eschatological dimension. From this "scientific" perspective, women are the preappointed culprits.

The Sex Police

Michel Foucault traces the origins of the "sex police" and of the "political economy of population" back to the eighteenth century: "At the heart of this economic and political problem of population was sex: it was necessary to analyze the birthrate, the age of marriage, legitimate and illegitimate births, the precocity and frequency of sexual relations, the ways of making them fertile or sterile, the effects of unmarried life, of the prohibitions, the impact of contraceptive practices—of these notorious 'deadly secrets' which demographers, on the eve of the Revolution, knew were already familiar to the inhabitants of the countryside."[5] But the systematic construction of depopulation as both a political issue and a medical issue, that is, as an issue of moral science falling under *hygienism,* began in its modern form as the "socialization of procreative practices" after the defeat of 1870.[6] From 1875, in fact, the annual number of births began to decline regularly, and a violent political debate opened up between neo-Malthusians and pronatalist policy supporters concerning the notion of demographic growth, a debate that would continue during the entire interwar period and in which Vichy family policy would be caught up.[7] The debate was launched in July 1890 by Henri Fèvre in an article in *La Revue d'aujourd'hui* entitled "Et multipliez-vous." In it he develops the thesis that will be taken up by all neo-Malthusians: excessive procreation results in an overabundance of potential workers and soldiers, and therefore in unemployment, poverty, and war. Paul Robin, from the Catholic upper-middle classes of Toulon, was a former student of the Ecole Normale Supérieur and a professor and communard who escaped to London. After the Republican political victory, he founded the orphanage of Cempuis, where he invented a form of pedagogical self-management. He was a tireless propagandist for these theses, and in 1896 founded the Ligue de la régénération humaine. In the opposite camp, the moral "repopulation" leagues—particularly the Ligue française de moralité publique, founded in 1882 by a pastor, and the Alliance nationale pour l'accroissement de la population française, created in 1896 by the statistician Jacques Bertillon and Dr. Charles Richet (Nobel prize in medicine in 1913)—saw the declining birthrate as a loss of the nation's prestige, power, activity, and initiative and as the cause (already!) of foreign immigration that corrupted both the race and morals. It was the harbinger of the collapse of the West. These were the spiritual fathers of the pronatalist demographers and physicians of the Commissariat General for the Family responsible for developing the theoretical bases for and implementing the family policy of the French State.

Scientific discourse after the Commune combined sin and expiation with "degeneration" and once again assigned women a strategic place in the examination it conducted of the causes of and remedies for the "explosion" of 1871, an explosion that was inseparably social and sexual in the eyes of the proponents of the hygienist order. The concept of degeneracy was the cornerstone of this medical construction of social problems that set physicians up as experts of order and disorder, an expertise that went well beyond specifically clinical disorders. The full thrust of this notion was imposed at the end of the nineteenth century by Valentin Magnan, who saw in it a pathological state of being characterized by "lesser psychophysical resistance" and by an inability to produce the "biological conditions of the hereditary fight for life," a state that leads to the "annihilation of the species."[8] Between 1871 and 1877, new theories appeared that shifted the policy regulating prostitution toward increased repression of "deviant" sexual behaviors, henceforth presented as a "crashing wave."[9] A complete reversal of perspectives occurred, which then presented prostitutional behaviors as a symptom of degeneracy. Criminal anthropology supported psychiatry in establishing the heredity of this psychic degeneracy of the "born prostitute." "Prostitution is a pathological organic affliction," Dr. Simonot wrote in 1911 in a work that marked the culmination of this process of naturalizing sin. The medical category of the "insane prostitute" or of the "insane female criminal" haunted the literary portraits of the female communards, who were portrayed as hysterical women drunk with blood, worse than the men whom they incited to even greater crimes. Francisque Sarcey likened the Commune to the incendiary "intoxication" of the Middle Ages and wrote that if "in these fits of madness women experience a more savage exhilaration than men, it is because they have a more developed nervous system; it is because their brain is weaker and their sensitivity more acute. They are also a hundred times more dangerous." Gobineau, who developed the theory of the superiority of the

Nordic race, affirmed: "I am profoundly convinced that there is not one example in the history of any time and any people of the violent madness, of the fanatic frenzy of these women."[10]

On the eve of the First World War, the French eugenics movement lent its assistance to the moralizing activities of the populationist leagues.[11] Just as in other countries of Europe, eugenic concerns arose in France as a result of this same fear of decline and degeneracy. But the neo-Lamarckian scientific tradition gave French eugenics a distinct tincture that distinguished it from the Anglo-Saxon current imprinted with neo-Malthusianism: belief in the theory of the heredity of acquired characteristics would lead French eugenicists to privilege prevention in order to provide biological assistance to the generations to come. The health of the parents, conception, pregnancy, and infant care were identified as privileged sites of intervention for improving the species, and at the same time designated physicians as the predestined theorists of the eugenics movement and women as the primary object and essential focus of their actions. Meetings were held in the great amphitheater of the school of medicine, and prestigious physicians figured among the founders and directors of the French Eugenics Society. These included Adolphe Pinard, the most famous obstetrician in Paris, a patron of the model maternity ward of Baudelocque Hospital, a professor at the school of medicine, and a deputy, and Eugène Apert, a pediatrician. Partisans of scientifically based infant care, in which the mother plays a central role, particularly through nursing, these physicians contributed greatly to reinforcing the image of "total" maternity, which in their eyes was the culmination of feminine "destiny." On this terrain as on others linked to the fight against "biological decline," they encountered pronatalist movements: Charles Richet was vice president of the Eugenics Society, Pinard was a member of the Senatorial Commission on Depopulation, and Lucien March, treasurer of the Eugenics Society, would become director of the Statistique générale of France. *This organic link among women's medicine, eugenics, and natalist policy,* which never existed in the Anglo-Saxon countries where eugenics claimed to be for neo-Malthusianism and *birth control,* conferred an unparalleled burden of symbolic violence on the discourse of French scientists, physicians, and demographers concerning feminine "nature."

After the First World War, whose demographic consequences dramatized the birthrate issue, the door was opened to politicians who, on July 31, 1920, passed a law repressing incitement to abortion and anticonception propaganda. The primary effect of this law was to impede considerably the development of Malthusian propaganda and feminine contraception. Then, with the law of March 27, 1923, abortion was no longer considered a violation falling under the assize court, paradoxically for the purpose of strengthening its repressive power; until then, the jury was "largely open to pity," the recorder stated.[12] The number of acquittals would effectively decline — dropping from 72 percent between 1880 and 1910 to 19 percent between 1925 and 1934[13] — and physicians accused of performing abortions could be prohibited from practicing medicine. The influence of the profamily and pronatalist movement was considerable during the interwar period.[14] In 1920 the Conseil supérieur de la natalité (CSN) was created. In 1922, the term "natality policy" appeared. And the activism of the National Alliance for the Growth of the French Population was strengthened by a critique of the "egalitarian individualism" proclaimed by the Revolution of 1789. This organization would become the National Alliance against Depopulation, whose membership increased from 230 in 1913 to 25,000 in June 1939 under the enthusiastic leadership of the demographer Fernand Boverat, who was also vice president of the CSN and who would work tirelessly during the National Revolution. On the eve of the war, a Haut Comité de la population was created, and, through a variety of measures, the Family Code of 1939 encouraged the birth of at least three children in the "model French family," in which the mother was married and lived at home.[15]

The Betrayal of Women and the Anemia of Civilized Beings

The theory of degeneration, and its ideological offshoots of the 1920s, is marked by a tendency to *amalgamate social determinisms and biological determinisms* so that it is always easy to move from an individual "defect" to a collective deficiency. In the same way, reflection on the defeat — of 1871 as of 1940 — extended the individual notion of sin to the entire society.[16] A declining birthrate, prostitution, and alcoholism are the symptoms of a national decline that must be treated, according to the biological metaphor that invades political discourse during such historical moments of crisis when physicians manage to exert their influence in social prophylaxis. Pressure to improve the birthrate before and after a conflict is a phenomenon common to all nationalisms, as shown by the stages of the Third Reich's natalist policy and its scientific legitimizations. There are many similarities between Nazi biopolitics and French natalist policy with respect to the conception of women's role in the nation and the limitations placed on women's freedom of decision concerning reproduction. As Dr. Schallmayer, winner of the Krupp Foundation prize in 1900 for his work *Hérédité et Sélection dans la vie des peuples,* stated: "Sexual life is not a private affair, it must be a sacred thing devoted to higher ends."[17] This theme of the national interest opposed to individualist "selfishness" would pervade all the Vichy texts concerning the family.

The interwar period saw the publication of a very large number of political-scientific essays on the "decline of the West" that placed the loss of "vitality," the cause and effect of the declining birthrate experienced by the countries of Europe, at the center of their analyses. These works, which all resemble one another, impose commonplaces on the relationship between social order and "natural" order by playing on apocalyptic denunciations.[18] They oppose the "anemia" of "civilized peoples" to the threat of domination through numbers by "barbarian hordes." The only remedy for this imbalance is a "healthy" birthrate in Europe. These works also share a mythic logic and a kinship with divinatory art. The unprecedented success of Oswald Spengler's book *The Decline of the West* (1918) resulted precisely, according to Ernst Cassirer, from this characteristic that made it "an astrology of history, the work of a diviner who unfolded his somber apocalyptic visions."[19] In 1935, Burgdöfer, director of the Office of Statistics in Berlin, published *Volk ohne Jugend* (People without youth), which provided National Socialism with a prestigious scientific justification for its natalist policy.[20] *Le Déclin de l'Europe* by Albert Demangeon (1920) attests to the same fear of depopulation and the sign of a loss of vital force expressed by Spengler, warns of "the sterility of civilized peoples," and calls for a return to nature. In *Mesure de la France* (1922), Drieu La Rochelle accuses France of "semisterility in the order of the flesh" and of having violated the law "that is the very promise made to our species, its pact of alliance with the forces of the world, the patriarchal origin of the human empire": "France committed a crime.

It is paying for it according to this standing rule that, when all is said and done, is the law of retaliation. 'You smothered a son in your bed, you will lose the other in war.'" Drieu La Rochelle's central theme was his regret for France's inability to vanquish alone in 1918, and its use of colonial troops: "Verdun? But there were already so many Englishmen in France and even, O soldiers of the Year II! so many negroes."[21] A Nazi propaganda film on the War of 1914 produced in 1937 with archival footage shows a group of African soldiers in uniform in a Parisian cabaret and comments in the same vein: "How can a country that claims to be civilized mobilize so many savages?"[22] In *Explication de notre temps* (1925), Lucien Romier, a future Vichy minister of state and an intimate advisor of Pétain, decries a "people of only sons" that could succeed only in being a "mediocre people." In *Le Destin des races blanches,* for which André Siegfried wrote the preface (1935), Henri Decugis, basing his ideas on French-style eugenics research, analyzes the phenomenon of differential fertility, according to which the elite reproduce much more slowly than the masses.

However, the seminal book concerning these questions was Alexis Carrel's *Man, the Unknown (L'Homme, cet inconnu),* which had sold 200,000 copies at the end of 1939 (the cover of the 1950 edition boasted 406,000 copies sold).[23] The book allied the social philosophy popular at the time with scientific tools, borrowing particularly from biology and physiology, in the manner of *erudite myths* that satisfy "the unconscious impulse that drives one to give a unified and total response in the manner of myth and religion to a socially important problem."[24] Its dazzling success most likely owed as much to its content as to its author, recognized at this time of crisis as the kind of prophet defined by Max Weber. Carrel was thus a kind of scientific double of Marshal Pétain. Like Pétain, he was a man who grew old in the prestigious past and gave his person to France in this ultimate moment. Carrel expressed his own feeling of the extraordinary nature of his mission in a letter to his publisher, dated September 23, 1942, in which he complained of the poor distribution of his book: "If it were only a question of my material and moral interests as an author I would submit to the common law, but it is a question of the work undertaken for the recovery of the country. The ideas that I put forth have, as a result of events, taken on *a kind of prophetic character.* Well before necessity imposed its laws on us, I had foreseen and indicated the path to follow. It is indispensable that my book be accessible to all those who in France are capable of understanding, reflecting, and acting."[25] Carrel was an internationally recognized researcher who had won the Nobel prize in 1912 for his work on vascular sutures and who established the initial bases for studies on transplanting blood vessels and organs. He emigrated to the United States in 1905 and at the Rockefeller Foundation conducted research on conserving tissue outside the body. Working as a surgeon in France during the First World War, he developed with Dakin a method for treating wounds by antiseptic irrigation. His infatuation with "biotypology," metaphysics, and eugenics came much later. We see here an expression of the resentment of a researcher in conflict with the French medical authorities of his time (he was rejected during the competitive examinations for surgeon of the hospitals of Lyon in 1902, and fought against what he called the criminal routine of military surgery quick to amputate). We also see the expression of a personal concern for the absence of progeny, as he had never been able to have children with his wife: "An entire world is crumbling. . . . There are still here, among the descendents of the Puritans, a few morally strong types. But the number is decreasing rapidly, for women in this environment are willingly and even often unwillingly childless."[26]

Obeying the sociological law that dictates that an author's progressive recognition is accompanied by a move toward great theoretical and philosophical syntheses, Carrel assumed the prophetic role of the intellectual who feels himself called to give his opinion concerning the ultimate questions of ultimate times. In his preface to *Man, the Unknown,* Carrel presents himself as a man of science and refers to himself in the third person:

> He has observed practically every form of human activity. He is acquainted with the poor and the rich, the sound and the diseased, the learned and the ignorant, the weak-minded, the insane, the shrewd, the criminal, etc. . . . The circumstances of his life have led him across the path of philosophers, artists, poets, and scientists. And also of geniuses, heroes, and saints. At the same time, he has studied the hidden mechanisms which, in the depth of the tissues and in the immensity of the brain, are the substratum of organic and mental phenomena. . . . He lives in the New World, and also

in the Old. . . . Before beginning this book, the author realized its difficulty, its almost impossibility. He undertook it merely because somebody had to undertake it. Because men cannot follow modern civilization along its present course, because they are *degenerating*.[27]

Presenting himself as an intermediary between different ages of humanity, as the master of the physiological and chemical mystery of the infinitely small, Dr. Carrel placed the entire weight of his scientific authority behind the diagnosis of "degeneracy" that embodied in this historical moment the "return of myth." In Carrel's book, degeneracy is once again essentially linked to the declining birthrate that threatened "the best elements of the race" with extinction and is a result of our (wrongful) desire to "free [ourselves] from the natural laws." "We have forgotten that nature never forgives," he concludes in the preface that he wrote for a new American edition in June 1939. In its biological dimension, the rhetoric of expiation confers on "nature" the task of punishing the guilty. One cannot but be struck by the similarity among the vengeful text of the Commissariat General for the Family, "Dies Irae," the statements of La Rochelle regarding "the law of the species" and "retaliation," and those of Carrel concerning the natural laws and the revenge of nature: the scientific version of the myth echoes the theology of a terrible God. By a law of November 17, 1941, the French State created the French Foundation for the Study of Human Problems, for which Carrel was appointed "regent." We will return later to this foundation that was the embodiment of this utopia of scientific policy for managing human capital.

The intellectuals and men of the Church who crusaded for woman's return to the home read, reread, and often quoted Dr. Carrel, whose scientific legitimacy provided an exceptional guarantee for the Vichy conception of restoring order. In the Carrelian utopia, women, once again, were charged with the return to nature and with reestablishing submission to the "natural" laws through the return to their feminine "vocation." If man is an unknown, woman, for her part, harbors no surprises: "Women should develop their aptitudes in accordance with their own nature, without trying to imitate the males"; "The same intellectual and physical training, and the same ambitions, should not be given to young girls as to boys"; "Between the two sexes there are irrevocable differences. And it is imperative to take them into account in constructing the civilized world"; "Her natural function, which consists not only of bearing, but also of rearing, her young, should be restored to woman"; "Modern society has committed a serious mistake by entirely substituting the school for the family training. It was obligated to do this by *the betrayal of women.* Mothers abandon their children to 'kindergartens' in order to attend to their careers, their social ambitions, their sexual pleasures, their literary or artistic fancies, or simply to play bridge, go to the cinema, and waste their time in busy idleness."[28] To conclude these observations, Carrel calls for the promulgation of laws aimed at limiting the education of girls, protecting the institution of marriage, and prohibiting divorce, all "in the interest of the next generation."

The Natality Market

Vichy's family policy was for many a natalist policy. The regime would confirm the establishment of the declining birthrate as a political issue and give it an extreme form: "Briefly, it is a question of organizing France for the convenience of large families and not for the convenience of sterile families."[29] In *Le Chef et la Famille,* a propaganda brochure put out by the Commissariat General for the Family intended for the Chantiers de la Jeunesse, the Pétainist eschatology repeated the litany of sins that led to the defeat and pointed to the family and natalist policy as the remedy that would make it possible to right the "moral climate of the France of yesterday" marked by cohabitation, abandonment of the family, divorce, conjugal selfishness, abortion, sexual permissiveness, and debauchery. In the preface to this work, General Lafont, the leader of the French Scouting movement, politicized the issue in the following way: "Led for years by unmarried, divorced, or married but childless leaders, France had neglected, routinely, we might say, to practice a family policy. The cries of alarm raised by several clairvoyant patriots were met with speeches; tendentious information was spread concerning the progress of Malthusianism, of *birth control* in every country."[30] Many lawyers, doctors, and demographers who had led natalist crusades during the interwar years quite naturally found themselves proponents of a social philosophy that wanted to make the family "the basic cell, the very foundation of the social edifice," as Philippe Renaudin, commissaire general for the family, recalled: "This is how the Marshal expresses himself the day after the catastrophe that left Frenchmen bewildered and France without hope. These words of the head of state are a diagnosis, and they resonate like an order."[31]

Renaudin, master in chambers to the Conseil d'État, directed the Commissariat General for the Family from September 1941. This Commissariat, whose structures were established in September 1940, was part of the Ministry of Health until May 1942. It was then attached directly to the head of state through the intermediary of Admiral Platon, state secretary to the head of the government responsible for the family:[32] "This is the first time that in France such a complete official organization has functioned in the service of the family. It is amazing to think that there has always been a Ministry of Commerce and Industry, a Ministry of Public Works, a Ministry of National Education, and that it is only since the Marshal assumed office that there has been a Ministry of Family under the name of the Commissariat General for the Family. Of course, Commerce, Industry, and Public Works are the supports of national prosperity, just as Public Instruction is the condition of national advancement. But the Family is the very foundation of Society, of the Nation."[33] The Commissariat General for the Family was a central institution of the regime, responsible for initiating laws to "protect" the family, laws concerning marriage, divorce, working women, and girls' education. It therefore participated freely in the state definition of feminine identity and the division of male and female roles. It also controlled the enforcement of legislation, the regional action of family associations, whose existence it favored as a political force, and, finally, sponsored official propaganda concerning women and families. The Commissariat General for the Family and the Advisory Committee for the Family, created by the law of June 5, 1941, are privileged examples of "neutral sites" suited to rallying a group around an eclectic structure and uniting agents belonging to different splinter groups of the leading and middle classes, sites whose primary function was to produce consensus.[34]

These institutions that, from the proclamation of the French State, rallied all those who had stood for the defense of the birthrate and of the family since the beginning of the 1930s imposed a *consensual view*

Vichy and the Eternal Feminine ▸ 74

of the family and natalist policy in opposition to the former divergent, sometimes opposing views of family order and demographic order. This process of ideological conciliation played no small part in the extreme simplification of the dominant agendas regarding the family, and therefore regarding women, under the National Revolution. The "neutral sites" where "commonplaces" are developed are always sites where *violence becomes commonplace*. While constructing the family, for example, as a political question, such institutions advance the apolitical nature of their concerns, related "from the very beginning" to "natural" and "eternal" realities of the human order: the family group and the equilibrium of parental roles. In this way, they cause the family issue to be seen as a neutral issue, thereby naturalizing the arbitrary. The widespread thesis of the continuity of family policy between the end of the Third Republic, with its culmination in the Family Code of July 29, 1939, the National Revolution, and the postwar period—a thesis that has a real affinity with the idea that the family is apolitical—always risks making us forget the specific effects of unanimity, which represses controversies and arguments in favor of a single point of view. It also causes us to forget the specific violence of the regime's policy with respect to women, due, in large part, to their collective designation as a key element of the national decline and regeneration in these domains.[35] Like ordinary racism, the identification of feminine responsibility for the defeat works on a subconscious level. "Sexual racism," in its brutal version produced by a period of crisis, can draw on an entire available cultural stock of images of feminine "destiny" always ready for action: the fact that the argument preexists makes it possible to *deny* (in the Freudian sense), at the time and afterward, the specific violence of condemnation in a *historical moment at which the counterpowers and the guardrails have given way.* In this sense, the thesis of the ahistorical continuity of family policy contributed to reinforcing this denial, just as it has most likely made it impossible for quite some time to see any interest in conducting research on women during the period.

To approach this phenomenon of unanimity from another perspective, we can also posit that prompt participation in the debates begun in 1940 concerning the causes of the defeat allowed movements to mark their place—and to increase their share of audience and influence—in this market of symbolic goods. The more the declining birthrate and the weakness of the family institution occupied an important place in the representations of the causes of the defeat, the more pronatalist and family proponents would have an important role to play and the more they could carve out a space of intervention and important action in what could be called the *market of revival*: Conseil National, ministries, commissions, reviews, and collections. And they never stopped condemning the selfishness of couples and the decline in family values, reserving for women, in their turn and in their manner, alongside philosophers, novelists, and spiritual advisors, a leading role among those responsible for the defeat, confining them at the same time to a reserved practical and symbolic space, that of reproduction.

Georges Pernot, a lawyer, a practicing Catholic, and president of the powerful Fédération des associations de familles nombreuses from 1930, a senator from the Doubs (Republican Union), a member of the Haut Comité de la population et de la famille established in 1938, and very briefly minister of the family from June 5 to 16, 1940, in the Reynaud government, voluntarily collaborated with the secretary for the family from the establishment of the French State and was appointed to the Conseil National in November 1941.[36] From the start he chose to place his movement under the slogan Work, Family, Nation, and on July 29, 1940, he submitted a "Note on Family Policy" to Marshal Pétain in which he appropriated Pétain's expressions: "The Nation is not a group of individuals, but a group of Families. As the family is '*the* social cell,' it is according to the Family and not according to the individual that the State must legislate. Laws must receive the sanction of lawmakers only if they are suited to favoring the creation and fertility of homes." This note demanded reform of the school that "must above all train courageous citizens and good mothers of families," a legislative review seeking to curb divorces, a strengthening of the fight against abortion, and a revamping of the organization of labor according to three "postulates": "the mother in the family home"; the father's remuneration determined by the number of children he has; and "the priority of the heads of families" for access to public and private jobs.[37]

In the name of the Alliance nationale contre la dépopulation, Fernand Boverat proposed revising school manuals so that demography and family morals were always part of instruction in history and geography, but also in ethics, reading, modern languages, and arithmetic in the primary, secondary, and higher grades. This revision was accomplished by a decision of March 11, 1942.[38] Vice president of the Conseil supérieur de la natalité, instigator of the law of 1939 by which the Family Code facilitated lawsuits against abortion, and member of the Hauts Comités de la population of 1939 and 1945, Boverat was in the meantime secretary general of the Natality Team of the Carrel Foundation and one of the leading intellectuals of the Commissariat General for the Family, where he led a fight against abortion that was all the more dogged the more abortion was sheltered from any discussion or criticism. Let us not forget that at the time of the debates concerning the repression of abortion that had resulted in the law of July 31, 1920, Professor Pinard himself, an undisputed medical authority in French obstetrics and an ardent defender of the birthrate and the maternal vocation of women, opposed this repressive and, in his eyes, useless law.[39] He also wanted to protect unwed mothers, proposing that they be considered "abandoned mothers," when Boverat argued "in the interest of the country," he said, against giving the unwed mother "a privileged position vis-à-vis the legitimately married mother."[40]

Boverat inundated the head of the Marshal's civil cabinet with mail. He sent him brochures on abortion and "advice to young people so they can be happy," in which he defended the opinion that "marriage is even more necessary for women than for men" from a physical standpoint, as one can see "the rejuvenation that several months of marriage produce in young women who at 25 had already started to fade and to lose some of their charm," and from a moral standpoint, as woman "needs to give free rein to the affectionate feelings that nature endowed her with." He firmly demanded that training in the domestic arts be mandatory for girls: "I take the liberty of pointing out to you another issue that may have escaped the Marshal's attention. According to the present curriculum of our lycées and collèges,* instruction in drawing and music is mandatory. However, domestic education (sewing, knitting, keeping house, cooking)

* The collège and the lycée historically belong to parallel but distinct educational systems. Because translation of these educational institutions into English is both tricky and misleading, these terms are in French throughout this work. — *Trans.*

remains optional. Our young girls are taught two pleasing arts; they are not taught the things that are essential for future mothers of families. This is absolutely contrary to what the Marshal announced and to what he wants. I am therefore convinced that he is unaware of this situation, which is contrary to the interests of the family and the birthrate."[41] Boverat also asked for the Marshal's support in republishing his book *La Résurrection par la natalité,* of which he said, somewhat in the manner of Carrel, that he was "the first to formulate a doctrine of family and pronatalist policy." He was successful in his request, and the book became another prophetic manifesto on the causes of the defeat that this time made demography a total science, just as Carrel did for medicine. In a review of this work in 1942, *L'Actualité sociale* underscored the miraculous resonance between the Marshal's expressions and the demographer's cries of alarm: "One remark by the Head of the State defined the causes of the current defeat of France: 'Too few children, too few arms, too few allies.' M. Boverat gives us an eloquent commentary on this remark." He cites the decline in religious faith and the dissemination of contraceptive practices as one of the leading causes for the declining birthrate, the review, which firmly supported this determination of causality, pointed out. *L'Actualité sociale,* a monthly bulletin specializing in legal commentary concerning family allowances* founded in 1928, devoted numerous articles during the war to French and European demography and viewed the Italian and German models as food for thought: "In our opinion, the German experience demonstrates that the family achieves its potential not because it is an end in itself, but because the idea of nation is exalted: the arrival of children from beyond the Rhine since 1933 is clearly the effect of an essentially political action."[42]

Gustave Bonvoisin, director general of the Comité central des allocations familiales and vice president of the Comité France-Allemagne, where he had contacts with numerous personalities of the Reich, a member of the Conseil national alongside numerous other representatives of movements in defense of the family,[43] senior editor of Éditions sociales françaises, which published collections and jour-

---

* During the interwar period, family allowances were bonuses granted for the birth of a child. These bonuses increased with the number of children. — *Trans.*

nals in support of the family (*L'Actualité sociale, Éducation, Benjamin*), made *La Revue de la famille* a propaganda organ for the regime. The powers of "premonition" on which the family proponents prided themselves made them ready spokesmen for Vichy eschatology: "Like the prodigal sons of the parables, the French are now returning to the family. . . . No large families, no children, and at the time of the offensive, not enough soldiers. . . . Isn't this what we had been saying and repeating here for twelve years before the war? Alas, it is only after the defeat that France is saying its prayers. But it is never too late to do the right thing."[44] In October 1943, the *Revue* gratefully commented on "The Social Policy of the Future," a text-manifesto that appeared on September 15 in *La Revue des deux mondes* in which the Marshal rewrote the Republican slogan Liberty, Equality, Fraternity in the following way: liberty, but "sheltered by a guardian authority"; equality, but "framed within a rational hierarchy"; fraternity, but exclusively within these "natural groups that are the Family, the City, the Nation." By giving an extensive response in its columns to this text of political philosophy that set forth the new principles of citizenship established by the French State, the profamily press also assured it widespread dissemination among its readers, professionals and militants of the movement who henceforth formed a corps of *ideological intermediaries* able to increase considerably the impact of the most political themes of the regime. At the same time, they regularly fanned ordinary Pétainism by the constant reminder of their profound agreement with the Marshal's family policy: "Marshal Pétain has just combined in a brochure the texts of the appeals and messages that he addressed to French citizens from June 1940 to June 1941. Bringing these directives together makes their unity and their rectitude, as well as their wisdom and common sense, clearer. There isn't a Frenchman alive who should not make this little tricolor manual his bedtime reading, who would not gain from internalizing the truths that he [Pétain] recalls with the most paternal tone of authority, from being inspired by the advice he lavishes in the name of the most clairvoyant affection."[45] By easily aligning their rhetoric with that of the Marshal's *Appels et Messages* and with the ideological style of the authorized comments to which they gave rise, the profamily journals participated in their own way in reinforcing the Pétainist myth that made the head of state the father of all French men and women and his "paternal affection" the ultimate motive of authority and submission.[46]

In June 1942, *La Revue de la famille* took part in analyzing the results of the great referendum-competition on the causes of the declining birthrate organized in December 1941 by the Commissariat General for the Family with the very active collaboration of the familialist movements. Five hundred thousand people responded to this survey. The Commissariat had proposed the following causes of the decline in this order: "young couples prefer the cinema or automobiles"; "divorce is possible without children, difficult with children"; "absence or lack of religion"; "one's lifestyle is curtailed when there are children"; "stylish women fear losing their figures"; "women working outside the home: stores, factories"; and so on. "Fear of the pain of maternity" came in fourteenth place. Lack of religion, the difficulties of raising children, and women working outside the home won the "public opinion" vote. In one of the lectures organized by Édition sociale française, Bonvoisin, then president of the Centre de coordination et d'action des mouvements familiaux de la région parisienne, returned to the responses to the referendum, which, he said, easily finding the language of confession and of the "desire to know," "constitute nothing more than *admissions*": "Most of the forms of expression of thought . . . had made the family a subject of derision, a heroine offered for public admiration of the woman who refuses to transmit life." Against this lapse, the return to the obvious is proposed: "For any woman *who is not unnatural* it is obvious; maternity makes her blossom, maternal love is the only human love that deepens in her over time, with *ordeals.*"[47]

An apparently apolitical, consensual, and integrative theme, the defense of the family, which can mobilize both the most learned guarantees and notions of common sense, imposes representations of the social order, naturalizes socially and historically constructed differences (here, of the sexes), organizes symbolic domination (here, masculine domination), reactivates symbolic violence, and imposes legal measures that have concrete effects on the lives and deaths of individuals. The analyses of Rémi Lenoir concerning the social construction of the notion of the "normal family" and the notion of demography as a "natural and political science" through its break with the social sciences and its institutionalization as state science, and the analyses of Hervé Le Bras concerning the archaeology of demographic constructions clearly show that this "apoliticism" has very political effects.[48]

Vichy's legal arsenal regarding the family, inseparably including women (we will return to this later), mobilized certain conservative and Catholic factions of the Bar alongside familialists and natalists. All these "clairvoyant patriots," to borrow the expression of General Lafont, these natalist crusaders, massively contributed their skills, their social capital, and their labor force to the work undertaken by the Commissariat General for the Family, that "superior service of the interests of the family," according to Gustave Bonvoisin. The novelty compared to the interwar period was that by constructing the family politically as the foundation of society and stamping it onto city hall pediments in place of the Republican motto's Equality, the new French State launched a gigantic *call for proposals* with regard to family, demographic, and natalist issues. And technocrats concerned with defending and expanding their intellectual, ethical, and institutional contribution and who had long been devoted to these areas were impelled to respond. It was not a time for controversies. The crisis situation required that one be present at the front, alongside others, with a unanimous momentum fueled by the feeling of finally being fully recognized and irreplaceable. This form of immediate and collective adherence, over and above the internal contradictions of the familiast and natalist movement itself, won out over existing discourses and imposed a *simplification* of the analyses that ultimately reconstructed the family and the natalist order on the basis of the "eternal" opposition, founded in "nature," between feminine and masculine "vocations." The crisis situation and the prophetic discourse that it engendered had the primary effect of negating the very possibility of a debate, of a clash of ideas concerning the mythic foundations of the new social — and sexual — order that would both take over and provide relief. Conflicts between the Alliance nationale contre la dépopulation, with its natalist and demographic aims, and the family associations that recommended a program of moral recovery based on religious inspiration, conflicts into which debates concerning the roles and functions of both sexes could creep, all disappeared in favor of a total vision of demography as a moral and religious science and of the family as the only legitimate female space. Demography itself, at least during international conferences, had nevertheless been a site of adversarial confrontations: at the World Conference on Population held in 1927 in Geneva and chaired by a neo-Malthusian American feminist, participants had in particular discussed the relationships between population growth and growth in resources.[49] The French journalist Renée Duc, who viewed the demographic alignment as consistent with her own desires in 1937, clearly showed, by pointing out the French enemy of the family to German readers, the existence of these spaces of contradictory thought that could no longer express themselves after 1940: "Only women belonging to organizations and to leftist parties in France and to organizations that, on the pretext of helping woman in her fight and with her rights, seek to destroy feminine characteristics and the most precious virtues of the race, reject marriage and children. There are not a lot of children because *people want to enjoy life*. Only a change in regime can improve the demographic situation of France."[50]

The National Revolution thus presented itself as life against death, redemption against sin, renewal against degeneracy: "In France there are presently 25,000 divorces per year, one out of twelve marriages; 400,000 to 600,000 abortions—some have recently said a million— that is as many, almost as many as or more than births. Social scourges are undermining homes. There are some who conclude from this tableau: the family is dead, familial sentiment is dead. Of those we ask: why don't you follow your reasoning to the end, which is: France dead? The body does not survive the cell. But there are forces of renewal. The work will be long and exacting, but it can be undertaken with confidence. An entire education must be repeated."[51]

It is to this type of education that *Françaises que ferons-nous?*, a sort of vade mecum for the new moral order, clings.[52] This is a collective anonymous work of "popularization" that haphazardly mixes poems by Péguy and Supervielle, edifying songs about feminine joy and the courage maker, photos of cherry trees in bloom, and stylized drawings. The result is nothing more than feminine moral lessons, adages, images of infants, framed quotations from the Marshal—for example, "The National Revolution signifies the desire for rebirth, suddenly affirmed in the very heart of our being, a day of terror and remorse"—and suggested reading: Bainville, Thibon, Pourrat, Carrel, Guitton, and Father Daniélou. A kind of almanac for doing better, entirely in keeping with the stylistic taste of the regime, it offers answers to all the questions raised about "nature" and legitimate feminine functions. The opening text, entitled "Our Responsibility," encourages women to examine their conscience: "We have seen France almost die. . . . We protected her as a mother protects her child in danger. . . . You often heard it said after the defeat: do not accuse the leaders. Each of us, the least of us French citizens, is responsible. . . . Weren't you content with the careless distraction afforded by Sunday movies, your fashion magazine, your door closed to protect your happiness? . . . Your indifference allowed your children to grow up with a sensualist mentality. . . . You had lost sight of your role as woman, which is to guard traditions and embody the new values." As the Marshal said, the National Revolution implies the "desire to be reborn" of a "morally degenerate" people "in demographic decline, without children, without a future, without hope." In this sinister tableau, the causes of the declining birthrate, the primary disorder, are selfish couples ("Children interfere with Sundays on tandem bicycles") and women's work. The tandem bicycle is one of the fantasies of the regime, a materialization of both "selfish" pleasure, without children, and especially of the social gains of the Popular Front—"tandems ridden during demagogic paid vacations."[53] In his preface to *France 41,* Raymond Postal, the editor of the Alsatia publishing house and champion of the work, wrote:

> It is only too obvious that the family, the social cell, has in France tragically abused the freedom to commit suicide. . . . The primary quality, in this area, regardless of what is said, is numbers. . . . I have sometimes wondered whether the tandem bicycle of Sunday outings, where the lyricism of popular couplets envisioned the couple moving at the same rhythm through their happy life, was not a symbol that implied much against the family. A couple is not a family. If the tempting machine cost more in the savings books of young households than a birth, a cradle, or a layette, at least it offered nothing but enjoyment. Once the child was born

by chance, some sometimes added a small seat for him or added a trailer to the conjugal bicycle. Most placed the child with a wet nurse. Tandem bicycle for some, social life for others, everything conspired against the fecundity of French homes.[54]

Natality and Naturalizations

This peak time for reconstructing masculine domination, which once again violently demarcated legitimate feminine territories by borrowing from the natural order, was also a peak time for *exclusion*. Discourse concerning homemakers and the declining birthrate was always also a discourse on the dangers of naturalizations and racial contamination. The experts in the "eternal feminine" who were on a crusade in 1940 all related the declining birthrate and immigration, for the family spirit being first a national spirit, and, as Maurras said, "The real country needs to return to its natural organization": "The mad naturalizations granted after 1924 will be reviewed with care. 'The French are at home,' an old song used to say: this was merely a noble cry of our youthful desires. We will live to see them become truths in fulfillment of the great motto, Work, Family, Nation."[55] In a memo regarding the principles of the new social order that he sent to Marshal Pétain on June 28, 1940, General Weygand defined the profound reasons for the return to the family: "By diminishing France's potential, the drop in the birthrate led us, from a military standpoint, to defend our territory with an unacceptable proportion of North African, colonial, and foreign contingents; from a national standpoint, to grant massive and regrettable naturalizations, and to deliver a part of our soil and our riches to foreign operators. *The family must be restored to honor.*"[56]

The biological metaphors that permeate the texts of the French State and its organic intellectuals combine the issues of natality and immigration into a single concern for the national health. The meditation on the "suicide of the family cell" is in keeping with a broader reflection on "the obligation to consolidate French forces whose long heredity has set their characteristics" that, in this period of chaos, easily rediscovered the thesis of the old theoreticians of racist French anthropology and their political-biological view of the national community.[57] The identification of guilty parties, the protection of borders, and the protection of the national health were combined quite naturally in this enterprise: "The review of naturalizations, the law regarding access to certain professions, the dissolution of secret societies, the search for those responsible for our disaster, and the repression of alcoholism attest to a firm desire to apply, in all domains, a similar effort of purification and reconstruction."[58]

As early as July 16, 1940, only six days after Marshal Pétain became head of state, Vichy's anti-Semitic legislation was preceded by a law specifying that a foreigner who had become French could be stripped of this nationality; the law of July 22 followed, instituting a commission responsible for reviewing all naturalizations that had been granted since 1927 to strip French nationality from all naturalized citizens judged to be undesirables.[59] On August 27, 1940, the Marchandeau decree law of April 21, 1939, which punished defamation of or injury to "persons belonging by their origin to a determined race or religion," was repealed. The first Jewish Statute of October 3, 1940, whose primary objective was to eliminate Jews from public service, was followed on October 7 by the repeal of the Crémieux law of 1871 that extended French nationality to the Jews of Algeria.[60] The speed of these initial measures and the extent of the legal arsenal against foreigners and Jews, whether French, foreign, or "denaturalized," can be understood only against the backdrop of the xenophobia and the renewal of anti-Semitism that characterized the 1930s.

The economic crisis, threats to employment, and fear of the Popular Front combined to encourage the extremist expression of a rejection of immigration and of refugees that revived the old anti-Semitic traditions. The victory of the Popular Front reinforced the xenophobia of the 1930s based on the theme that "naturalization has become an electoral industry." In August 1936, *Gringoire* reported that the demonstrators of 1936 "don't talk or look like us."[61] While the number of foreigners in France had declined between 1931 and 1936 (dropping from 2.9 million to 2.4 million) as a result of workers who returned home faced with the employment problem at the end of the 1930s, the problem of immigration merged with the refugee problem. It was this new category of immigrants — "displaced" persons — that became a political and social problem. France received proportionally more refugees than any other country, and it must be pointed out that, faced with the problem of German and Austrian Jews during 1938 and 1939, no nation substantially modified its immigration quota. Michaël Marrus and Robert Paxton point out that if each of the thirty-two nations that participated in the international conference on refugees in July 1938 in Evian had agreed to accept seventeen thousand German Jews, the number of stateless persons would have been absorbed successfully. French xenophobic reactions to refugee immigration during the 1930s must therefore be ascribed to the organized international indifference that responded to the European tragedy. "Opinion does not want to hear about political refugees who are, by definition, future social security burdens or future delinquents, competitors of French workers or intellectuals on the job market, and whose conflicting ideologies can only, by establishing themselves on our soil, create disorder, advise violence, and cause blood to flow," *Le Temps* wrote in November 1938, returning to the theme of the Jewish warmongers who were spreading as the German threat mounted.

During this period marked by an obsession with national deficiencies and the weakness of the "race," the immigration issue and the issue of the declining birthrate had already been combined. In *Gilles,* published in 1939, Drieu La Rochelle sketches the portrait of a young Frenchman in his own image: "He despised and hated with all his man's heart the prodigious, vicious, and asthmatic nationalism of this radical party that left France childless, that let it be invaded and cross-bred by millions of foreigners, Jews, wogs, Negroes, and Indochinese." In the same vein and at the same time, *Candide* protested against the admission of refugees in the name of the protection of young Frenchwomen. "Young girls, love only men of your own country!" wrote a journalist who was troubled by the number of "young Frenchwomen massacred by their *métèque* lovers."[62] In 1938, a tract distributed in Paris urged: "FRENCHWOMEN, make sure you get respect. *If the fat Jew is bothering you* . . . do not hesitate to call for help and *correct him as he deserves!*"[63] Pierre-Étienne Flandin pleaded the case of French renewal through race and family because France had been "bastardized" by foreigners.[64] If there was opposition to anti-Semitism during these years in various social spheres, within the Church, among communists, and even in right-wing movements (in the Croix de Feu, for example), there was no organized, constructed collective expression making it possible to oppose a common front and historical, economic, and cultural arguments to this tendency to focus all grievances on "foreigners." Xenophobic discourse became commonplace, and the press provided "public opinion" racist commonplaces for discussing the demographic peril: "In a country with a low birthrate like ours, it is a priori crucial to seek to palliate the disadvantages of demographic deficiency through the influx of new blood, when this prudently calculated and wisely engineered influx does not threaten national unity or the integrity of the race." However, *Le Temps* concluded in April 1939, the threat is real, and we need to concern ourselves with a policy of "selected assimilation." Georges Mauco, official expert in immigration and demography and secretary general of the International Scientific Union on Population from 1937 to 1953, wrote: "There is a danger that physically inferior or overly ethnically different elements will bastardize the race and bring to it germs of sickness that the race had succeeded in diminishing."[65]

Jean Giraudoux, commissioner of information in the Daladier government in 1939, had conceived of his work *Pleins Pouvoirs,* which met with enormous success, as a health manifesto. The conclusion called for the rapid forging of "a doctrine of population growth, of urban planning, of large projects, and of national honesty." In the second chapter, "La France peuplée," Giraudoux himself analyzes the problem of the "French race" and also links natality and naturalizations, loss of demographic vitality, and "barbarous" immigration. The state must consider that "its principal mission is that of the head of the family" and that "all the fears burdening the French imagination at this time are inspired, without realizing it, by the same sentiment: Frenchmen are becoming rare." But the situation was not without remedy "because Germany, where the birthrate had dropped lower than ours, brought it up to 300,000 in less than four years through simple legislative measures." To "optimists," who pointed to the demographic contribution of naturalized foreigners, Giraudoux retorts: "Our land had become a land of invasion," subjected, like ancient Rome, to a "continual infiltration of Barbarians," this "curious and avid cohort of Central and Eastern Europe." Therefore, "a new senior staff," composed of the "leading figures in administration and science," must determine "the influx and the quality of immigrants," for "what greater mission is there but to shape one's race with love." One would thus avoid "the establishment in France" of this "immigrant who debarked at the Gare de l'Est at eleven o'clock" and was able to "occupy a boutique on the boulevard de Sebastopol at noon and sell his luggage and furs"; such types "adulterate our country by their presence and their actions," "rarely beautify it by their personal appearance," and "we find them swarming over each of our arts or our new and ancient industries in a spontaneous generation that recalls that of fleas on a newborn puppy." Thus, "through an infiltration whose secret I have sought in vain, hundreds of thousands of Ashkenazis, who escaped from Polish or Rumanian ghettos, have entered our country" and "bring, wherever they go, the approximate, clandestine activity, misappropriation, corruption, and are constant threats to the spirit of precision, good faith, and perfection that belonged to French craftsmen. *A horde that manages to forfeit its national rights* and thereby brave all expulsions, and whose physical constitution, precarious and abnormal, brings it by the thousands into our hospitals, which it packs."[66] The images of Giraudoux, the prestigious writer, are consistent with those that were current in the most common and the most racist press. His health-related anger betrays the Vichy ideology of national purification: craftsmen of the old stock and French milk of the Mother country would make it possible to reestablish "a race that owes its value to the selection and the refinement of twenty centuries."[67]

The concern of Vichy's leaders was to restore homogeneity and to fight against the divisions perceived as debilitating for the national organism: cultural pluralism, social classes, party politics, foreigners, and cosmopolitanism. "It was not a happy time to be different in France."[68] Feminist demands were directly in line with threats that spawned divisions:[69] for woman, assimilation meant remaining in her place, blending into the "race" of women, as Father Doncoeur said, to accomplish the mission to which her flesh destines her. It is interesting to note that during the 1930s, a period of crisis and xenophobic growth, feminism was attacked as a foreign invention ("Is it this cosmopolitan influence that makes it so inassimilable to the French organism?" Théodore Joran wonders), antifeminism and anti-Semitism often going hand in hand.[70] Like immigrants, women were accused of taking the place of the unemployed, and feminist leaders were stigmatized as Jewesses. Cécile Brunschvicg, one of three female secretaries of state in the Blum government, combined all the handicaps in the eyes of the extreme right. The journalist Clément Vautel, a champion of antifeminism, wrote in 1936: "Feminism in France is an opinion or an attitude of women lawyers, Jewesses for the most part, of women doctors, bluestockings, female intellectuals who, in the end, are humiliated about being women." He saw in the "immense crowd of wives, of mothers," "of average Frenchwomen," "who humbly and courageously do their traditional duty every day," the rampart against feminist demands, the award going (already!) to the countrywomen who, according to him, gave a healthy response to all this nonsense by "a burst of laughter and a sweep of their brooms."[71] Everything that diverted the feminine vocation from its course was a bearer of chaos, just like the "inassimilable" "nature" of "foreigners," whose extreme incarnation would be the refugee Jew from Central Europe whose image was demonized by Giraudoux, among others. All the fears of the 1930s were at work in the ideology of the National Revolution, and the doctrine of assimilation that the Republican tradition had erected as a rampart against racism could, in times of crisis, take on an exclusionary tone: "In times of crisis, however, when the national lifeboat seems ready to be swamped by a mass of exotic outsiders, the requirement of cultural assimilation can cut the other way. Difference seemed a threat after 1940; pluralism, a form of weakness. At such times, woe to Jews and gypsies or other peoples refractory to assimilation. Deliberate, obstinate, provocative difference then seems not merely a rejection, but a menace!"[72]

Therefore, it was the "average Frenchwoman," as Vautel said, that would support the regeneration primarily through natality and the return to the home. Like those recently naturalized, without hearth or home, women were wrong to leave their homes, their hearths, whose assemblage into little countries established the national order. They had once again to become guardians of the hearth so that the nation could return to a "natural order": "The individual, which is only an abstraction, possesses nothing, neither temporal values nor spiritual values. How could the individual carry in his flesh the national values? How could he understand the values of flesh and blood, he who has no home, no lineage? For us who love the soil that sustains us, for us who love in our children our flesh and our blood, we understand and we love our country, this country whose soil frees us from miserable wandering (like the wandering of the Jewish people), whose chosen lineage assures us of a magnificent heredity and delivers us from racial defects."[73] In this context, demography becomes a political and moral science[74]—a morality that "must not be merely a profamily tendency but a probirth tendency"—because it makes it possible to perpetuate the race of ancestors, to repopulate without diversity, to return to homogeneity in the national body. The French-woman, therefore, first of all had to procreate and become once again what she was: tradition.

> There was a time when there was not only a tradition of the French family, but when one could say that the Frenchwoman *was* tradition. . . . where it was a reality to say that preservation, not only of the race, but also of the essential morals of the Country, was the responsibility of the French woman. . . . The Fatherland was essentially a *Motherland*. . . . If we want to escape the decadence and death that threaten us, one of the primordial conditions of our salvation will be the restoration of woman to her role as mother, as force of conservation, as force of continuation. . . . The young Frenchwoman of today must find the confidence, the faith, and the will to once again become French as well as a woman. The oldest words of our language, those that attach us most deeply to our ancient soil by the roots of the race, are those which, precisely like the word *cradle,* are linked to the family and to the mother. The French race is not as physically decrepit as has been said. It is the duty of young Frenchwomen to prove that it is still as robust and fertile, just like its soil.[75]

Demography was a women's issue, and if France had sinned against the family, it was because "in Paris in 1938, a thousand women did not give birth to even five hundred daughters destined to replace them and to have children in their turn."[76] The demographic science version of the "eternal feminine" slipped naturally into the logic of calculating "net reproduction rates" and "fertilizability" rates that asserted itself at the end of the nineteenth century. From this moment on, in fact, for demographers, it was women who produced children (average number of children per woman); daughters therefore had to be more numerous than mothers.[77]

The "demographic drama," to borrow the expression of the Commissariat General for the Family, that was at the heart of the familialist preoccupations of the French State gave rise to very political analyses that routinely associated the natalist issue and the immigration issue: "You are aware of the fatal curves. This drama has many aspects: insufficiency of life, aging, the transfusion of foreign blood. . . . This population is killing itself. Ultimately, foreigners are replacing Frenchmen; France is the land of European immigration. Due to the anxiety in which her loss of substance places her, she ended up absorbing without selection."[78] The problem of foreign refugees is thus reposited in light of the political project of the National Revolution as a problem that a healthy natalist policy could control, irrespective of the reasons for this particular immigration. Thus, a potential French people rearmed by the natalists was opposed to a composite, heterogeneous people weakened by the contribution of foreign blood. The obsessions of the 1930s were rationalized by the state demography that offered analyses that reduced the historical conditions of border crossings to a theory of communicating vessels. The influx of foreigners was henceforth a mandatory theme of demographic discourse, and it occupied a large place in propaganda brochures. Paul Haury, vice president of the National Alliance against Depopulation, explained the catastrophe of 1940 through "the demographic assessment of the five years preceding it" and believed that the demographic void "encouraged the influx of too many undesirables, which—it was realized too late—gravely altered the national character. France had become the great center of European immigration, and risked becoming its dumping ground. . . . During the census of 1936, while there were a few more Frenchmen and fewer foreigners, it was due to naturalizations, therefore a simple change of label, a paper game, that moves naturalized foreigners into the category of Frenchmen."[79] Once the process of naturalization is compared to a "paper game," the process of reviewing naturalizations follows naturally. The focus on considerations concerning the birthrate, naturalizations, the demographic prophecy, and the denunciation of the stateless peril had become commonplace. In each appeal to maternity we hear the sermon for a homogeneous and "purified" France. Even the most "feminine" and apparently innocuous of the brochures produced by the Commissariat General for the Family, *La Vie en fleur,* abundantly illustrated with photos and drawings of infants and sketches of young, elegant mothers, that disseminated the medical view of beautification through maternity, analyzed "the artificial addition of forty-five thou-

The Demographic Sin ▸ 91

sand children of foreigners" and emphasized how much the France of 1913, with its "thirty-seven million inhabitants (of which only 2 percent were foreigners)," was a "more homogeneous" nation than the France of 1938, with its forty-two million inhabitants and "8 to 9 percent foreigners."

The appeal to French natality and maternity was therefore in keeping with a political view that reconceived recent history in terms of the invasion and pollution of the social body by inassimilable foreign elements. The construction of an official image of femininity centered on maternity sought the same results as the construction of the foreigner, whether naturalized or not, as a threat to the national health. It is probably the darkest basis of the overproduction of the "eternal feminine" in this moment of crisis.

If we choose to go further in analyzing the eschatological dimension of the National Revolution, we see that women occupied a central place in the contrition-redemption scheme. The identification of the declining birthrate as deadly sin was unanimous among the most conservative members of the literary field, the Church, the medical profession, and the legal profession, and made women privileged targets of the collective mea culpa to which the regime invited the country. The designation of an "eternal feminine," which the country, to its misfortune, had forgotten in its periods of misguided democratic ways, allowed one to conceive of the National Revolution as the return to the "natural" order of the world.

In this highly political enterprise of naturalizing differences, experts played a fundamental role by contributing, in their own fields, the legitimacy of their knowledge, skills, and interest (at times, their passionate interest), historically produced against other factions of their profession, to make their view of the sexual division of the social world, which was also a view of the social order, triumph.

If the "eternal feminine" of scientific discourse seems to escape history, it is because there is an entire stock of cultural images of the feminine and of the masculine/feminine opposition—progressively constructed over time, most often in times of crisis and confrontation, during the fifteenth century or after the Commune, for example—whose historical conditions of production have been "forgotten." These schemas, which are part of the social unconscious, can always be remobilized, purified in some way of the contradictions specific to their historical processes of production. They can thus appear as eternal truths, as indisputable values to which it is always good to return. "The eternal paths outside of which it is dangerous to venture," as the journalist of *Candide* wrote, would lead to that golden age to which only the mythic vision of the social world gives access.

4. VIOLENCE AND STATE PROPAGANDA

The Vichy policy of returning mothers to the home, which, as of May 1941, dictated that Mother's Day was to be a national holiday, seemed to disregard the realities of the professional, scholastic, and intellectual situation of French women in 1939 and that had evolved since the nineteenth century. Compared to other European countries, many women in France had worked for a long time and had accompanied the educational market through its successive developments.

From 1906 to 1946, French women represented close to 40 percent of the working population, and married women who worked were common (before the war, 66 percent of working women had a dependent family), whereas they remained an exception in England.[1] Most of the women who worked in industry and agriculture did so out of necessity: in 1921, 46 percent of working women were employed in agriculture, and the rate was still 40 percent in 1936. In 1911, 56.6 percent of women working outside agriculture were employed in industry, 44 percent in 1936. In Great Britain, where unemployment was endemic, the work culture declined before the First World War among women of the working class to the point that in 1913 the expression *working mothers* then designated homemakers. In France, Michelet's lamentations concerning "the female worker, an impious, sordid word" would persist as long as women were insistent.[2] This quotation from Michelet is often found in Vichy anthologies promoting the mother-at-home agenda.

The major consequence of the First World War on the women's job market was the increase in employment in the middle classes linked to the drop in their income and to the demographic imbalance that had increased the number of single women. From 1930, girls outnumbered boys in teacher training colleges, and the nursing school of the Salpêtrière was placing candidates on waiting lists. Banks and insurance companies played a key role in the growth in female employment, and the number of women in public service doubled between 1906 and 1936.[3] In the middle classes and in certain portions of the bourgeoisie, family strategies concerning girls' education and investments in women's education became necessities. The thirst for knowledge, economic survival, and the process of the structural de-skilling of "female" occupations combined to encourage the *consistent rise in the demand for women's instruction.*

Parity between boys and girls in primary education was achieved during the years following the Ferry laws,* and a regular increase in female education could already be observed between 1847 and 1881.[4] According to Ecoles primaires supérieures (EPS) statistics, the presence of girls in the upper primary grades was significant and early; in 1911 42 percent were girls, 49 percent in 1926, and 50 percent in 1936. In professional business and industry schools, the percentage of female students increased during the interwar period, rising from 21 percent in 1911 to 26.5 percent in 1926 and 30 percent in 1936. Lycées and collèges maintained a much more masculine recruitment than the upper primary grades; here, enrollment showed 21 percent girls in 1911 and 30 percent in 1936.[5]

Girls' secondary public education had special status for a long time: five years of study instead of seven; no preparation for the baccalaureate examination, but an end-of-studies diploma awarded by the school itself; no Latin or Greek, but a modern education.[6] Female secondary education was not assimilated to male education until 1924, and the general competitive exam (the *concours général*) was not open to students from girls' lycées until 1930.[7] These belated laws granting full academic existence—and therefore professional existence—to girls' secondary education were necessitated by the changes in the demand for female instruction in the bourgeoisie and the upper middle classes. The legislation once again acknowledged an established fact: in 1912 at the Académie de Paris, young girls had earned 208 end-of-secondary-education diplomas and 66 baccalaureate degrees; in 1921,

* Laws named after Jules Ferry that called for mandatory, free, secular primary education. — *Trans.*

169 diplomas and 606 baccalaureate degrees. As early as 1916, a board of investigation had noted changes in social demand: to provide girls with the means of existence during a period of crisis, of threatened fortunes, of inflation that devalued dowries and annuities and, adding at the end of its work in 1919, difficulties in finding a husband.[8]

The higher women went in the educational system, the more their access was slowed or violently blocked. Thus, in higher education, the number of female diploma recipients was extremely low until the First World War, although they were attending universities, thereby attesting once again to the force of female demand for academic credentials. The legal dissertation written by Edmée Charrier and defended in 1930 is the best source concerning the higher education of women until 1929.[9] In 1914, 480 baccalaureate degrees in philosophy and mathematics were earned by women; in 1926, 2,134, compared to 7,000 and 9,200 male baccalaureate degrees for the same years. In 1929, some 22,000 women held this diploma. At the Académie de Paris, women represented 3 percent of the student population in 1890, 12 percent in 1914, and 25 percent in 1929. In 1928–1929, in all of France there were 12,669 female students compared to 39,319 male students. The medical schools had the highest percentage of women, the law schools the lowest. The number of female diploma recipients remained very low until 1914 and increased slowly during the interwar period: 790 women earned a doctorate in medicine from 1870 to 1928. The statistics available do not allow us to conduct a national survey for schools of humanities, sciences, and law, but for Paris we note strong growth between 1918 and 1928, when the number of female graduates holding law degrees quintupled (98 out of a total of 781 bachelor degrees). The number of bachelor degrees in science rose from 37 in 1914 to 64 in 1928 (over 25 percent of the total number of degrees for the same year). In arts and letters, where the first bachelor degree was earned by a woman in 1871 and the second in 1891, 52 bachelor degrees were conferred in 1914 and 157 in 1928 (33 percent of the total number of degrees).[10] At the École Normale Supérieure, only 12 young women were admitted on the basis of the competitive admission examination until 1930. Finally, although women had been admitted to the École libre des sciences politiques since the war, they were required to have the baccalaureate, which was optional for men, a sign that women's access to the university was still conditional.

Thus, admission to the liberal careers, granted rather early to women, remained quantitatively low: 95 women doctors were practicing in 1903, 300 in 1921, and 519 in 1929. There were 12 women lawyers in 1914 and 96 in 1928. There were only 7 women university professors in 1930. Professional opportunities for female diploma recipients were still mainly in primary and secondary female education.

With a blindness that surprises us today, the discourse that began with the National Revolution disregarded the realities of women's condition and aspirations. The violence of the permanence of an image and an imagery of woman in the kitchen suddenly reappeared intact, untouched by the struggles for women's suffrage, by the presence of three women in the government of the Popular Front, by women's access to higher education and numerous skilled jobs, by the permanence of women's work in industry, agriculture, and offices. In this discourse, the observation, unanimous in the past, of the courage and capabilities of women during the First World War was lost, as though a ground swell had left a blank stretch of sand on which one could begin again to write the history of the "eternal feminine." [11] A reserve army would become involved.

Vichy's Condemnation of Women's Work

Under the French State, the defense and promotion of the "occupation of mother" and the return of mothers to the home—that is, the imposition of the equivalencies women=mother, feminine space= domestic space—was not only carried out on a symbolic level by producing classifications, downgrades, and reclassifications, but became incarnate in a vast legal arsenal with very real potential effects. These laws that sometimes concerned the Family, and at other times concerned Education, Labor, or Health (the capitals refer to the ministries concerned), formed a tight network of incentives, limitations, and prohibitions that sketched a *cartography of legitimate feminine spaces,* designated violations, and, sometimes, set forth sanctions.

During the first batch of exclusionary laws, the Act of October 11, 1940, said to be related to women's work, prohibited hiring married women in civil service and industrial civil service jobs (except for women who had successfully passed a competitive examination for civil service jobs) and urged young single women under the age of twenty-eight to find a husband within two years. This law gave them a nest egg (if they divorced, they could be reinstated, provided they had been the "beneficiaries" of the divorce), gave unpaid leave to mothers with fewer than three children whose husbands were working, automatically retired women over the age of fifty, equated married women and common-law wives for all these restrictions, and, finally, authorized short-term employment, thereby reinforcing the dominant conception of women's work as *additional income,* provided, in addition, that it was carried out close to the family home so that women could "do the household chores." [12] Michèle Bordeaux points out that in the private sector as well, hiring was not favorable to women as a result of the law of October 8, 1940, that gave hiring priority to fathers of families with more than three children, to demobilized soldiers, and to widows with more than two children. Between October and November 1940, the Commissariat General for the Family also initiated a bill regulating *private* wage-earning jobs for married women. [13] The handwritten documents, then the successive typed versions of this bill, which are kept in the Archives nationales, are entitled "Housewife, Working Women," thus demonstrating the *political unity* of a program that ideologically imposed woman's reproductive "vocation" and carried out legal restrictions on women's work. This bill stipulated that a married or cohabiting woman was prohibited from working in the private sector "if the salary, professional earnings, or the industrial, commercial, or artisinal benefits of the husband are sufficient and stable." Any infraction of the prohibition would be punished by imprisonment of one to eight days and a fine of 50 to 500 francs to be paid by the "female offender" to a family allowance fund.

Vichy policy concerning women's work merits an in-depth study that would take into account the regime's contradictions between Realpolitik and social philosophy, the effective methods for enforcing new restrictions in the various administrations and enterprises, and the debates and interpretations to which these measures gave rise. Thus, in Rennes, employers wondered what was the threshold beyond which the husband's salary was "sufficient" and about the immorality of employing common-law wives while honest married women were being dismissed. [14] The regime's policy shifted after May 1942, when feminine labor was once again a necessity, because the STO (forced labor draft) was depleting the reserves of skilled workers:[15] in September 1942, all the articles of the Act of October 11, 1940, were suspended except for the marriage incentive provisions. There are no specific studies for the period concerning the fluctuations in female hiring according to industrial sector, type of office job, and job description, or based on the economic requirements imposed by Germany and the national needs. It nevertheless appears, according to Hélène Eck's analysis, that women's work, which was indispensable to the survival of households in the lower classes and in certain sectors of the middle classes, continued and perhaps even increased during the Occupation.[16]

However, in its terminology, its expectations, and its exceptions, the law of October 11, 1940, remained a particularly consummate expression of the place granted to women in the city by the National Revolution. This sort of bargaining between economic imperatives and the defense of the symbolic order of the mother at home, which in France pitted the Secretariat of State for Industrial Production against the Commissariat General for the Family, also characterized Nazi policy regarding women's work, which shifted toward an intensive exploitation of feminine labor based on the increasing needs of the war economy, though it had begun by recommending that women return to the home under the slogan "German wife and mother."[17] The prohibitions concerning women's work occupied a large place among the first legislative measures enacted after Hitler's accession to power in January 1933. In June 1933, married female civil servants were dismissed. Proposing to perform a comparative analysis of the policies regarding women's work, including under the Nazi regime, Margaret Maruani insists on the central function of the women's work policy in reinforcing masculine domination and in the continuous articulation of the discourses and practices concerning production and reproduction: "Ideological discourse on maternity is often first an argument against women's work. Natalist policy is not only a demographic bias, it is also an ideology of domination. . . . For one does not prohibit women's work without ideological 'justification.' The Nazi leaders spoke constantly of restoring the honor of the 'German wife and mother,' of giving her back her 'dignity' while taking away her right to work."[18] Under the Vichy regime, natalist concerns, defense and glorification of the job of mother, and policies governing the employment of women were not contradictory. Women's work was placed under the sign of "additional income" and, especially when it concerned industrial production, it obeyed the logic of a *reserve army*. These are all ways of stating and restating, in defiance of all the social and economic realities, that it is not in the order of things for women to work. But it is also a discourse that imposes the idea that there are workers who are legitimate in all *economic* circumstances and others who are not. Here, women and immigrants share this precarious status. In an article published in October 1940, Charles Richet, who continued his father's natalist and eugenic crusade, condemned women's work because the "divorce" between work and family life "was in large part the cause of our decadence of the last twenty years." Harmful from the standpoint of the birthrate, women's work was also "deplorable from the perspective of marital honesty. In the common sense of the word, if, in a shop or an office, women and men work together, there is promiscuity. What female laborers and employees call 'a little freedom' is merely the elegant translation of this marital emancipation that more or less contributes to breaking up family life." [19]

Return to the Domestic Sphere and Domestication of Public Opinion

Mothers of the family, family mothers, were called on by the ideologues of the National Revolution so that the French could "anchor themselves on the natural and moral institutions to which [their] destiny is linked." Or so said Marshal Pétain, who, in his message to French mothers on May 25, 1941, set forth the feminine prerogatives ("mistress of the house"), attributed specific qualities to women ("affection, tact, patience, gentleness") that make them the "inspiration of our Christian civilization," and assigned them as their educational duty in preparation for that of the state to "give everyone this taste for work, this sense of discipline, of modesty, of respect that makes men healthy and peoples strong." [20] They were thus also designated as mothers of the social order. Finally, glorified as "mothers of our dead, mothers of our prisoners, mothers of our cities," and "mothers of our countrysides who, alone on the farm, give us fruitful harvests," they became mothers of the Nation. Patron saint of the three pillars of the renovated "house of France," the figure of the family mother is constructed as the only legitimate feminine identity. To a house labeled France and Co. with closed shutters, surmounted by a dark sky where the Star of David is outlined and that is crumbling under the undermining work of moles named democracy, selfishness, Jewry, pastis, Communism, and so on, the illustrator of a propaganda poster opposes the house of France with bright windows built on the pillars of the new order and surmounted by the seven stars that decorate the Marshal's baton. On the second floor of this replumbed house whose trellis is once again adorned with leaves, a mother opens the window to let the fresh air in.[21] As propaganda texts and images abundantly show, a woman without children does not exist, except as a nun or her lay counterpart, the welfare assistant. Little girls play with their dolls to rehearse the only role they will need to play: "Now a game, later a mission," reads the legend of a poster from the Commissariat General for the Family. Maillol's fertility goddesses predominated in artistic representations of the female body, relegating the slender figure of the garçonne to the shadows.[22]

How is state propaganda produced? With respect to women and families, it seems to have been developed exclusively within the Commissariat General for the Family; the documents and archives available do not allow us to reconstruct the discussions, any conflicts, or the social logics of the consensus that presided over its development. So we do not know what negotiations or what proposals resulted in the natalist line that dominated all the action of the Commissariat in this domain, the strictly familialist aspect — the family as the place of moral education, for example — being relatively absent from the iconography and the slogans of this administration. One has the feeling that the demographic crusade succeeded in imposing its shibboleths on state propaganda or, in any case, that its slogans lent themselves particularly well to these forms of *simplification* of the ideas contained in the tracts, posters, and brochures of moral rearmament intended for target audiences. It is likely that Paul Haury was one of the men responsible for the preponderance of pronatalists in the Commissariat's propaganda work. Inspector general of public instruction, he became chief of staff for Dr. Serge Huard, secretary general of health in July 1940, then secretary of state for the family and health when this office was created, from August 1941 to April 1942. He also established the connection between public education and the Commissariat by writing "demographic and family education" manuals for the lycée classes that became mandatory beginning in 1941. During the 1930s, Inspector Haury had been one of the most active leaders of the National Alliance against Depopulation. He became vice president of the movement, and then wrote the premonitory articles for its publication, entitled "Mother's Day, What It Is, What It Should Be" and "Let Us Celebrate the Principles of 1789, but Let Us Know How to Adapt Them," and hymns to the feminine virtues: "If man is thought, you are life. . . . It is to maternity and all it comprises of renunciation, suffering, and concern that the essential traits of the feminine psychology *for all ages* were attached before it was deformed by the excesses of contemporary individualism."[23] The policy of the National Revolution concerning women would allow Haury to develop this theme fully and to impose his style in the brochures that the Commissariat published for the teaching profession (*L'Instituteur et son rôle dans la restauration de la famille française, L'Université devant la famille, L'École et la Famille, Étudiant mon camarade*), which had a print run of two hundred thousand copies and were intended for all members of public and private education.

The brochure concerning the role of the elementary school teacher opens once again with an apology for the defeat intended to put things back in place and each person in his or her place, at the same time pointing out the self-evidence of common Pétainist thought:

> To the erroneous calculations of the average Frenchman of before the war, shriveled into his shrunken self, you will oppose the radiant beauty of a family ideal that other Frenchmen knew how to live, even dangerously. You will find the accents of the heart to evoke these comforting realities that are the joys of the home that woman illuminates with her presence and warms with her activity. . . . It is because this ideal was lived for centuries by millions and millions of French men and women that the words the Marshal spoke the day after the armistice awakened such a profound echo in countless hearts. Finally! the Head of the French State had found the key to the *eternal truths,* by opposing the spirit of sacrifice to the spirit of pleasure, by repositioning the family at the base of the social edifice.[24]

The elementary school teacher must therefore be careful not to produce "déclassés," those nomads of the social order so well depicted by Paul Bourget in *L'Étape*. Instead, they were to leave young country girls to their traditional headdresses, to establish a family atmosphere in class, and to encourage "realistic apprenticeship" for girls who would be taught "how to do housework, to compose and carry out a family menu by handling a broom and saucepans." "Finally, our little girls have precious dolls; let them learn to diaper them, to bathe them . . . or to pretend, to prepare a bottle for them." This brochure, which concerns elementary education, speaks of the working classes and of the natalist propaganda that is appropriate to them according to enlightened elites. It presents this parable wherein the elementary school teacher, a natalist missionary, educates the masses: "In a populated quarter of Paris, a worker's wife, already the mother of three children, comes looking for the school principal. A fourth child is on the way. The 'kind' neighbors gave her certain advice. 'So, what would you do in my place?' The schoolteacher is neither flustered nor indignant. She speaks from her heart, and convinces the lost mother. The baby is born, it is a beautiful little girl. Several years later, seeing her playing and singing on the school playground, the schoolteacher, who had been denied the happiness of having children, could say with a smile 'This one was more mine than if I had given her life; I saved her life.' Who better than the elementary school teacher is able *to enlighten the darkened consciences of these women?*" "Mother" of the students in her class, just as the male teacher is their "father," the female schoolteacher is there to teach them how to become a mother. The Commissariat collected press clippings in response to its brochures that testified to their warm reception. In November 1941, this particular brochure was welcomed by many newspapers, including *L'Action française,* which viewed it as a "masterpiece" and wanted to have a less luxurious version printed in order to distribute "millions of copies."[25]

At the university, the audience changed and so did the rhetoric: the "revelation of June 1940," this "tragic object lesson," was to be the opportunity to correct "the intellectualist error" to train not "minds" but "elites of flesh and blood."[26] Well-known authors were called on to introduce "planned natality." In *Juliette au pays des hommes,* for example, Giraudoux "brings a young intellectual woman who is passionate about independence and avid for experience back to a normal marriage." And the teaching of history was subordinated to the demographic object lesson. But it was left to philosophy professors in particular to "denounce the pseudo-emancipation with which women have been duped under the name of feminism, and that quite simply neglected what is strictly feminine in her": "The equal of man in dignity, but performing different functions in the family and in the nation that conform to her nature and are in no way inferior, the modern woman will once again become the guardian of the home."

This desire to suit the propaganda to the social characteristics of the audiences targeted shows the strictly political aim of the Commissariat, which ran its natalist campaign of family promotion like an electoral campaign. And it is found in other publications that can also be studied comparatively, for example, *Une belle mission des travailleuses sociales*[27] and *La Plus Belle Femme du monde*.[28] The latter was presented as a deluxe women's magazine, punctuated with refined advertisements that extolled feminine beauty illuminated by motherhood. Lucien François, the editor of *Votre Beauté,* who wrote the preface to this special issue, drew up the list of feminine qualities that are revealed only by maternity: a "sense of the concrete and of image" in "direct contact with the real"; "concern for others"; "intuitive power and imagination" — "these are the trump cards that the eternal Eve can only really place in her hand if the care and education of children have given her the pretext to use them." She may thus "*emerge from the dark domain* where, until adolescence, she has been slumbering." Who convinced the team of *Votre Beauté* and the great Parisian experts in feminine beauty to lend their voices to the National Revolution's program with respect to women? And did they really need to be convinced? In this short editorial, which, in the guise of praise, instantly mobilized the most normative stereotypes of feminine "nature," can we not glimpse the hidden face of the magazine that, during ordinary times, simply molded ageless stereotypes to the taste of the day? In *Une belle mission des travailleuses sociales* (the "nurses of social evil,") the recall to order takes on more military accents ("woman's desertion places France in mortal danger") and the designated guilty ones are, as it happens, the fashion designers who transformed woman into a "caricature," "a sad doll that lives only for her body, her clothes, her sex appeal." On the cover of the brochure, the protective shadow of a giant social worker wearing a dark tailored suit and a hat places her hand on the shoulder of a wretched little girl with a sickly looking face: in "our young girls of the working districts," family and domestic education must inculcate "a concern for the domestic." It is therefore suggested that women of the bourgeoisie combat the "selfishness" connected with worldliness by showing them that their beauty can only gain from maternity; to women "of the working districts" and to the little girls in elementary school, one offers domestic education and family allowances. However, in all cases, the professors of natalist morals—the elementary school teacher staged by Inspector Haury as the expert of *Votre Beauté*—placed feminine consciousness on the side of *darkness,* thereby once again giving a new life to the old mythic oppositions.

In November 1941, Dr. Huard sent an *Album of Family Propaganda* to Marshal Pétain, an immense red-bound file suggestive of a guest book, that included posters, tracts, quotations, brochures, and newspaper clippings, and summarized the accomplishments "achieved in less than three months." [29] The Commissariat conducted a systematic policy to mobilize what it called "opinion," "to lead it to understand the necessity of a 'family mystique,'" by working "within the customary framework of each of the magazines according to the audience to which it is addressed." Commissariat items were sent to 825 newspapers. The tracts and posters put out by the Commissariat—"The childless coquette has no place in the city; she is of no use"; "Children without siblings are sad"; "The new France protects mothers"; "The leaders of tomorrow will be the children of large families," and so on—were to be disseminated by large public administrations and lending institutions. Food stores, novelty stores, shoe stores, and the fashion and hairstyling sectors were to distribute them to their female staff and customers. In the cover letter accompanying this propaganda, the secretary general of the Commissariat states that "these posters are one element of the CRUSADE FOR THE FAMILY undertaken at the order of Marshal Pétain as a great opinion campaign."

The Commissariat declared that its ideological activity used "the most modern advertising means"—"massive postings, spectacular competitions, attractive leaflets"—and demonstrated a remarkable capacity for using the feminine press and exploiting the target audiences dear to market studies. It also took to the radio with the program *France-Family,* broadcast three times a week at 7:20 P.M. (*"prime time!"*), that showed families "how much the Marshal's government worries about their fate" and that worked like a "mailbox" to create a daily supplement of "public opinion." The show did not overlook the "persuasive value of the *slogan*" that had proven itself in the field of "commercial advertising": "The greatest pleasure is to spread joy in one's family"; "A young girl must prepare herself early for her mission by helping her mother at home"; "It is your taste for order and neatness that will make your home attractive for your husband and your children"; and so on.[30] The French Family Exhibition presented in 1943 at the Pantheon city hall of the 5th arrondissement, which was then to travel throughout the country, was an apotheosis of this pedagogy through images, slogans, photos, and sculpture: "Oh clear and luminous face of the mother triumphant in her modesty." Reprising the contrition-redemption scheme, this exhibition condemned single life, contraception, abortion, and alcoholism: "Let us escape these evil spheres. . . . This entire exhibition would be vain because it would be negative if we hadn't taken care to show the remedy next to the evil, if we had not realized that the public needs to feel firm ground next to these precipices that make one dizzy."[31]

The feminine press was undoubtedly a privileged medium for updating these themes that are as old as the world itself, endowing mythic figures with the lightness and triteness of the fashion sketches and beauty and household advertisements that inseparably produce a feminine market and a feminine identity, a subculture of gender, according to Erving Goffman.[32]

The importance of state propaganda in the Vichy regime has been underlined by historical research, and certain of its characteristics have been revealed, such as the battles between Paul Marion's Secrétariat général à l'information and the Légion française des combattants and the Amicale de France, the school's central role in conveying propaganda, and the overproduction of parables illustrated within the Vichy system of political symbols.[33] In the field we are studying, the Légion and the Amicale de France—two large movements uniting "active Pétainists," to borrow the expression of Yves Durand—were not silent, but their approach with respect to women and the family differed from that of the Commissariat. The Légion tended more to develop the theme of the family as central element of the new political order; we will return to this later. The Amicale de France, particularly in its *Bulletin des jeunes* that defined what a "young national revolutionary" should be, gave unqualified approval to the fascist models for supervising male and female youth[34] that in its eyes resulted in an exemplary mobilization of girls, the "wives and mothers of tomorrow."[35]

The Imposition of Mother's Day

Although Mother's Day was not, strictly speaking, a Vichy invention, it was nevertheless under the French State that it acquired its full symbolic weight, ultimately becoming a national holiday under the name of Journée des mères when the term "fête" (celebration) was deemed inappropriate given the country's recent defeat.

The idea of a national celebration of French mothers had appeared at the end of the First World War at a time when, as a result of historical circumstances, the experts in feminine identity clashed over priorities concerning feminine social involvement. If the image of the young female pen pal corresponding with soldiers at the front or that of the nurse devoted to the wounded could easily be compared to the "invention of new maternities,"[36] the work of women in munitions plants was the subject of heated discussions between those who supported munitions production and those who supported repopulation. As a feminist journal, *La Française d'aujourd'hui,* so neatly put it in 1917: "We are counting on women workers to give birth to thousands of shells and to turn out dozens of children." For the *Bulletin des usines de guerre,* the "egg" produced by these female workers was equivalent to the egg produced by the average woman of the working class; for Professor Pinard, the director of Baudelocque, who defended a hard-line view of child care, because the mother ministers to the child from the start of conception, the factory was a "child killer." In the Seine region in 1914, women represented 5 percent of the labor force working in steel mills; in 1918 they made up 30 percent of the war workforce. From a national standpoint, the munitions industry employed 430,000 women out of 1.7 million workers at the time of the armistice.[37] For these women, factory work was a vital necessity, and, by and large, it was unskilled work: their ability to sustain monotonous tasks were praised, and they were denied any "inventive attention" or any decision-making capacity. However, the *munitionettes,* as they were called, would represent the majority of strikers in the numerous movements that cropped up beginning in 1916. They preferred the "inopportune" strike that swept away the arbitration and conciliation proceedings established at the beginning of 1917 and demonstrated remarkable capabilities of resistance and negotiation. Their protest actions led the police and the conservative press to accuse them of "bad morals" and to condemn attitudes that were "not very feminine." In this context, and with the war over, repopulationist ideology began issuing extreme opinions: "Woman's price is the child. If she is voluntarily sterile, she falls into the ranks of the prostitute, of the working girl whose organs are nothing more than instruments, obscene toys, instead of remaining the venerable mold of all the future centuries." [38]

With the armistice just recently signed, Louis Loucheur pressed women to return home, without indemnification, to welcome the surviving soldiers and free up jobs. So, immediately following the war, a systematic campaign to return women to the home was organized for the first time,[39] a campaign that simultaneously witnessed the initial outlines of Mother's Day and the ratification of the law of 1920 regarding the intensified repression of abortion and anticontraceptive propaganda. At the instigation of the High Council for Natality and the defense leagues for large families, the public authorities established a day to celebrate mothers through a circular dated April 24, 1920. By a decree dated May 26, 1920, a Medal of the French Family was also created to recognize "mothers of French families who have at least five children living simultaneously, and who, through their enlightened care, their laborious activity, and their devotion, have made a constant effort to inspire their children, under the best conditions of physical and moral health, to have a love for work, integrity, and due regard for their social and patriotic duties." [40] This initial attempt to make the category of mother the national emblem of the celebration of women had relatively little success during the interwar period; it was not until the National Revolution that this holiday was imposed on everyone and became a central ritual of the tactics of maternity. Until that time, the recalls to order issued by the various ministries concerned and by the High Council for Natality bore witness to the lack of response encountered by this initiative. From 1926 to 1935, official circles consistently regretted the failure to celebrate or the restricted celebration of Mother's Day. To breathe fresh life into this celebration, in 1938 on the boulevard Kellermann, they erected a monument "To sublime mothers, the grateful country," at the foot of which the League of Women's Rights placed a derisive spray of flowers bearing the inscription "Homage to French mothers, sublime but not voters,"[41] thereby once again providing an example of the expressions of antiestablishment sentiment condemned to silence by the National Revolution.

Rita Thalmann's research on the Third Reich's policy concerning women reveals the similarities between these national conceptions of celebrating mothers: the grandiose pink granite monument to Maternity measuring 18 by 25 meters was erected in the center of Berlin in 1934. From 1938 on, a medal struck with the motto "The child ennobles the mother" was distributed in grand ceremony to mothers of large families on the birthday of Hitler's mother. In Germany, the cult of the mother goes back to the nineteenth century and is linked to the political and cultural processes of national construction. It finds particularly privileged expression in the veneration of Queen Luisa of Prussia, who was progressively represented as the ideal incarnation of the purest form of maternity: her death mask was treated like a bust of the Madonna by the sculptor Schadow and, after her death in 1910, countless works of plastic art praised her domestic virtues in the bourgeois style while her very real political action was ultimately ignored. The symbolic Nazi woman herself would abandon the figure of Germania as national symbol for the resurrection of Queen Luisa in her dimension as guardian of the family devoted to her maternal duties.[42] In the Mussolinian ideology as well, Italian women existed only to produce children and realize their potential as wives, mothers, and guardians of the family space, even if the division between the sexes was less rigid there than in Germany. And the authoritarian regimes of Spain and Portugal imposed the same masculine/feminine scission and the same sexual division of the social world. For George L. Mosse, these national symbolics contributed to fixing women in their place and reinforcing the distinction between the sexes, at the same time reinforcing the distinction between *the normal* and *the abnormal,* as defined by the bourgeois order during its construction of respectability throughout the nineteenth century that would also, in its turn, be a primary concern of the Nazi regime. The imposition of Mother's

Day as a *state ritual* is a manifestation of the privileged link that fascist and authoritarian regimes maintained with returning mothers to the home and keeping them there.

Returning to the sociogenesis of Mother's Day and to the decisive role played by the French State in its ultimate establishment as a national holiday, I would like to illustrate the arbitrariness of this *state designation of the feminine*—and of the masculine/feminine opposition—whose creation has been forgotten because it has been so successful in asserting itself in fact and mind. We can thus ask the following question: By making Mother's Day a national holiday, did the state act only on the public space?

Beginning in 1941, Mother's Day, the last Sunday in May, became one of the French State's great days of national celebration. May, the month of renewal, had long been the occasion for agrarian rituals with an erotic component well before the Church devoted it to Mary.[43] The state liturgy therefore appropriated an entire collective unconscious with a heavy emotional charge. Against the wayward actions of the lower classes during May that threatened cities, the force of myth was placed in the service of moral order. As described by Bonnard, the last minister of national education of Vichy: "On Sundays in May, when hoards of city dwellers invade the country, it is frightful to see how they slaughter spring."[44] On this national holiday, Pétain himself sent a message to the mothers of France. Municipalities honored mothers of large families, who received the Medal of the French Family. In churches, ministers exalted the sacred role of mothers. Local recreational meetings were organized. The government offered a supplemental ration of dried legumes and a well-stocked bag of groceries to the mothers with the biggest families. And "many war memorials have been adorned with wreathes by pious hands to associate the tribute rendered to Mothers with the memory of the children they mourn."[45] In their tributes to Mother's Day, pro-family reviews evoked its national dimension during these dark years: "Everyone felt the special character it had; Mother's Day of May 25, 1941, will ultimately be the day on which France rediscovered, in the tribute given to those who give us life, the sense of her nobility and the hope of her recovery." Elsewhere it was called a "day of recognition, of contemplation, and of hope." The celebration of the mothers of France was a celebration of France. The heroism of French mothers recalled the national potential for regeneration through the children born and to be born. But foregrounding this patriotic component within the context of the Occupation does not mask the fact that the *political imposition* of Mother's Day, like the establishment of private and public rituals appropriate to its celebration, produced a symbolic *coup de force* whose effects on the symbolics of the sexual division of the social world largely survived the Vichy regime.

Robert Paxton stresses the fever for public ceremonies and collective activities that inspired the new regime, unlike the Third Republic. He writes that state ceremonies had not been designed with such didactic zeal since David worked for the Committee of Public Safety.[46] When he went to the Free Zone for the first time in 1942, Jean Guéhenno described Châteauroux this way: "A strange land, a sort of principality where everyone from children of age six on up, regimented into groups from 'Youths' to 'Veterans,' wearing francisques* or symbols of the Legion, seemed to be in uniform. Where is France?"[47] Mothers of families did not need uniforms, but they are there in the photos, lined up and holding small girls and boys by the hand, holding smaller children in their arms, while Marshal Pétain, the national grandfather, passes them in review and gives them a kiss. Mother's Day was a day of organized mobilization whose preparation, which was not left to chance, was the occasion to remind everyone of the general principles of the regime's social philosophy. On May 12, 1941, Vichy sent the Chantiers de la Jeunesse a circular related to Mother's Day in which each of them was encouraged to continue the work of "restoring the idea of family" undertaken by the Marshal "through his personal example" by evoking "all the sacrifices, devotion, and renunciations and love he has benefited from." Youths were to offer a "gesture of kindness" to their own mothers. Topics for discussion, recitations, skits, and examples of poems for the campfires, study circles, and evenings organized between May 18 and 25 were attached to the circular.[48] In 1941, each student of the 6th and 5th classes had to write a letter to his or her mother celebrating her household work; the best were sent to Vichy and read on the radio. In 1942, all students in the primary, secondary, and vocational schools were to prepare a "Tribute to mothers" during Easter vacation. The best ones

* An emblem created by Pétain to reward loyal service. — *Trans.*

were read on the radio, then distributed by regional delegates for the family; there were plans to publish them in a national publication entitled *The Golden Book of Motherhood*.[49] Seventy thousand copies of the Mother's Day circular intended for the teaching profession and signed by Jérôme Carcopino, minister of national education from February 1941 to April 1942, were distributed in May 1941: "To support his efforts for family renewal, Marshal Pétain has asked that the customary [*sic*] celebration of Mother's Day in the future take on greater splendor than in the past. Therefore, I have decided to involve the University in this effort, and I am sending you the enclosed posters to put up in each of the classes of your educational institution. I am asking you to draw your students' attention to all the devotion, sacrifice, and love in carrying out their daily labors in the service of the family their mothers' lives represent."[50] The poster, displayed in all schools, shows seven children (the seven stars in the Marshal's baton): four girls (one of whom is drying a plate, the three others offering gifts) and three boys (two offering their exceptional academic results and the third offering a framed portrait of the Marshal). In their offerings, the children symbolize the sexual division of social labor. The poster has the following caption: "Your mommy did everything for you . . . THE MARSHAL [in red letters] asks you to thank her for this nicely."[51] For Mother's Day 1941, 3 million postcards were ordered along with hundreds of thousands of posters, including four thousand 80/120cm format posters with the following text punctuated with a francisque: "Have you thought about what your MOTHER'S LIFE represents in terms of daily DEVOTION, discrete SACRIFICES, real and pure LOVE. Haven't you often forgotten to show her: That you understood her advice. . . . By asking all of us to celebrate Mother's Day, the Marshal is giving us the means to REPAIR THIS OVERSIGHT."[52]

In April 1942, the propaganda service of the Commissariat General for the Family sent the regional delegates for the family Mother's Day conference programs that were a veritable organizational chart of feminine identity as defined by the regime: "Mother, foundation of the family. Mother creator, the grandeur and servitude of maternity. Mother educator, enlightening, training, and educating the soul and the body; gives birth to the child twice, physically and morally; quotations from great men. Mother consoler, first sadnesses of the child and the adolescent. Mother counselor and guide in the home;

in her love she finds intuitions that never deceive. The mother has the mystique of sacrifice; maternal love is satisfied more in giving than in receiving, and is enriched in expending itself. The mother is the soul of the house; quotation 'The house is the stone garment of the family' (Father Lemire)." The circular invites the delegates to make this day a "popular holiday" with which "representatives of the various social milieux" must be associated so that it is a "celebration of social union, all classes mixed together."[53] Through the voice of the Commissariat General for the Family, Mother's Day was thus designated by the state as an ideological tool of *social peace* from an organicist perspective that would also be expressed in the corporatist option of the National Revolution. Jérôme Carcopino's comments concerning the new symbolism of May 1 invented by the regime are eloquent in this sense: "One will perhaps recall that the Marshal had wanted to abolish the May 1st holiday, without upsetting the working class, by converting it into a State holiday that would be the Labor Holiday for all classes and that a fortuitous conjunction of dates would make coincide with Saint Philip's Day."[54]

In big cities, Mother's Day was celebrated by representatives of the state, the Church, and the cultural institutions. In Paris in 1941 there was a matinee performance at the Comédie-Française, a celebration at the city hall of the 17th arrondissement organized by the Théâtre de l'Étoile, and a reception given by the chief of staff to the secretary general for the family where there were speeches, particularly by the president of the National Center for Coordinating Family Movements in the Occupied Zone.[55] In Lyon, Cardinal Gerlier gave an address at the basilica of Fourvière; in the evening, at the city hall, the state secretary for the family stressed that this Mother's Day legitimized, "finally and officially, the family policy inaugurated in the past against incredible resistance by an elite of clairvoyant men. Is not the destiny of States forged in the domestic fire?"[56] The show *Le Plus Beau Métier du monde* (The most beautiful occupation in the world) was performed before thirty-two hundred young girls in Bordeaux, and the Paris Mint engraved a Maternal Love medal.[57] At the grand casino of Vichy, *L'Annonce faite à Marie* was performed; during the intermission in 1941, the lead actress recited an ode to Pétain written by Claudel: "France, listen to this old man who cares for you and speaks to you like a father! Daughter of Saint Louis, listen to him and say: Haven't you had enough of politics?" [58]

This reinvention of Mother's Day and its ultimate establishment as a national holiday is a good example of the work of selection carried out, at certain historical junctures, in the available cultural stock of representations of the feminine and of the masculine/feminine opposition. This work of mobilizing symbolic representations and interpreting the meaning of symbols, which limits and contains their metaphorical potential, ends in reinforcing normative statements about feminine "nature" and in producing the illusion of social consensus, since time immemorial, concerning what could have been a subject of conflict or, at the very least, was far from having achieved general agreement. The perceived differences between the sexes were thus channeled through fixed representations that took the form of an eternal binary opposition offering a normative and univocal affirmation of the nature of the masculine and the feminine. [59] Vichy's construction of Mother's Day presented itself as the simple continuation of a "customary" celebration, as Carcopino said, while the process of selecting the masculine/feminine schemes of opposition that accompanied it repressed any alternative possibilities, including the memory of the relative symbolic and practical nonexistence of this commemoration during the interwar period.

The Commissariat General for the Family, which centralized state propaganda in this *cultural selection* of representations of the feminine, received assistance from many institutions. The Church, in particular, supplied its policy with images, myths, and symbols and provided it with the means for rewriting history, thereby contributing to the production of a guided archaeology of the cult of mothers that imposed exemplary filiations and incarnations, foundations and founding ancestors. The family movement would, of course, involve itself fully in the symbolic construction of Mother's Day by helping to invent its rituals and by mobilizing all its militants to ensure its success. The Éditions sociales françaises published a *Petit Guide de la journée des mères,* the first volume of a new collection entitled "Les petits guides des fêtes françaises." [60] Aiming to "reestablish a certain lifestyle in all the homes of France"—as the "great majority of our fellow citizens" have lost the "respect for traditions" and have "a tendency to live from day to day, like animals"—the purpose of this little guide, or so it states, is to "routinize" the experience acquired concerning Mother's Day since 1941. It developed a *social philosophy* of Mother's Day, "a collective awareness" and manifestation of the "unanimous recognition of a nation for which the individual is not all," and offered topics for reflection and inspiration concerning the "occupation of mother": culinary knowledge, furnishings and housework, clothing and laundry, household songs, and more. Finally, it sketched out the plan for a Mother's Day celebration: 8 in the morning at home, then at church, at school, in the hospitals and the maternity wards, in the city for a contest to choose the most beautifully decorated house. In the afternoon, at city hall, the municipal theater, or a large schoolyard for the "official programs" with speeches, diplomas, and medals and the collective audition of the broadcast message of the head of the state, followed by recreational programs. At the end of the day, the unveiling of the Maison de la famille and the results of the display window contest. Then return home for "traditional" songs and games.

The guide devotes a lengthy discussion to the public ritual of the celebration to which, it says, it is desirable to "give a ceremonial character," the aim of which is to "allow the ceremonial acts to follow one another with order and magnitude" and "to illuminate and amplify the sense of an official ceremony." As in any ritual, space is divided up in strict fashion and reveals the separation of groups: the officials, the trumpets, and the choir would be on a raised platform; in the center of the enclosure, in front of the platform, mothers of families would be surrounded by children, young people, and old people, with the audience all around. There would be trumpet flourishes, a master of ceremonies, and crowd control handled by children to make sure that everyone is put in his or her place. Schoolchildren, chosen on merit, would leave their rows to go as a delegation to find mothers in their homes, carrying "symbolic objects (flowers, books, work tools, baskets of fruit)." The mass of children would sing a round; three times the song would stop while the crowd listened in silence for the arrival of the procession of mothers entering the center aisle slowly while pennants wave and songs begin again. The current president's tribute to all the mothers would be followed by a tribute given by the master of ceremonies to those who embody the perfect fulfillment of the occupation of motherhood and to

Vichy and the Eternal Feminine ▸ 118

whom their own children would give official awards. . . . The ceremony would end with a "mothers' thank you" expressed by a giant letter written by an anonymous mother, carried "with a certain theatricality to the platform" to be read by the master of ceremonies. The recreational programs would be the opportunity to mobilize the national cultural resources concerning maternity: legendary mothers and mothers of famous men, with all the poems that men of letters have dedicated to their mothers; tributes by the trade associations to the "first occupation"; a living tableau of little girls "playing mommy"; an enumeration of the mother's tasks ("feeds, cares for, and consoles," etc.); a selection of lullabies and skits that illustrate maternal love among the animals; celebration of the month of May "devoted to the fertile woman." Finally, one chapter inventories the "traditions" conserved in folklore, the "popular civilization," and emphasizes that Mother's Day is the consummate example of "living folklore": earth and maternity; month of fertility and month of Mary; Isis, Ceres, and Proserpine; local family celebrations of the eighteenth century and commonplace books (journals kept by the father of the family); occupation of mother and "mother" of the Compagnons.* The folklorist preoccupations of the regime and its official writers drew from an ideologically inexhaustible notion, that of *living folklore,* for which women are the support and the stakes: if maternity gives and restores life to folklore, it is because women are on the side of the eternal return. Here we find the themes dear to the Action française, which was looking for a way to reconcile the life forces and a conservative role in a reconstructed eternity.

But beyond its systematic exploration of how to give official status to Mother's Day and the teachings that were to be taken from it for the future, the guide recalls, from its first pages, that "this should first and foremost be a *family* day, the day on which each boy and girl, each man and woman thinks of *his or her* mother, serves *his or her* mother, puts *his or her* mother in the *place of honor*." By thus connecting public ritual and the call to order of the private celebration, because everyone, child and adult, was supposed to honor his or her own mother, this ceremonial code conveyed the sociological truth of Mother's Day

* Journeymen. While journeymen completed their apprenticeships throughout France, their landladies, often wives of journeymen, were called "mother." — *Trans.*

as desired by the French State. This national day was in fact a rite of consecration, of legitimization, that is, a *rite of institution* as defined by Pierre Bourdieu with respect to rites of passage:[61] the major effect of the rite is the one that goes almost completely unnoticed, because it is less to transform the person involved in the rite than to establish a limit, a gulf, between those involved and those not involved. The initiation of young people first of all establishes the difference between men and women and *institutes* it by establishing man as man and woman as woman. In the same way, the Mother's Day rite is the magical establishment of a difference that *establishes an identity* and imposes a social essence based on biological differences. By separating mothers in the ceremonial space and in the temporal space of the calendar, the state imposed limits and "a right to be that is inseparably a *duty to be.*" By indicating their identity to women-mothers, it produced an effect of statutory assignment that had real effects, because this establishment imposed a destiny and enclosed those men and women it distinguished within the limits thereby assigned to them and that it made them recognize. This rite of institution embodied in Mother's Day first erected a magic boundary between the masculine and the feminine. Women now needed only to content themselves with being "what they have to be." In January 1942, *La Revue de la famille* and the National Center for the Coordination and Action of Family Movements, the advisory body connected with the activities of the Commissariat General for the Family, organized a great competition of texts, drawings, posters, and photographs to enhance the celebration of Mother's Day. The text that won first prize in the literary section, "The Psalm of Young Mothers," expressed in striking form this celebration of privation that denies privation and imposes on women a univocal representation of themselves and the duty associated with it: "The house is our cloister. Our life has its immutable rule, and each day its office, always the same: the time for washing and dressing, for walks, the time for bottles and classes. Thus chained to the thousand small requirements of life, a slave to all its little complications, cut off, by force, at all times, from our own volition, you see, my God, we live in obedience. . . . There are some who, passing near the closed piano and the slumbering books, listen to their hearts beat the melancholic death knell of their shrouded interests."[62] Each word of this description of feminine destiny, nourished by the feminine culture of sacrifice and withdrawal from the world and that is far from being reducible to a literary pose, calls for comment. The vocabulary of confinement, very close to that of the "little way" of Thérèse of Lisieux,[63] establishes a complete gulf between the outside world and a domestic space where books have ceased to speak. But, for the selection committee for the competition, this woman's work was simply "a magnificent spiritual elevation that rises like a veritable cathedral in witness of our faith in the Mother's mission."

Ritual draws its force from the collective belief of a whole group. Behind every small child who comes home from school with his or her poem, drawing, or embroidery that expresses gratitude for the legitimate feminine virtues placed under the sign of sacrifice and self-lessness, it is the state that reenters the intimacy of the private space to recall the separation of masculine and feminine destinies and the sole feminine identity that it recognizes and for which it officializes the recognition. The rite of institution is always an imposition of cognitive structures. By ordering and controlling the testimonies of private recognition on a national scale, the state, through symbolic force, imposes an *order of bodies* and induces everyone, from the youngest age or with memories from his or her youngest age, to internalize the division of this order: "On Tuesdays, I gathered my 'guys' at home. Quite simply, I spoke to them, even bringing up personal memories in front of them. . . . The young people were moved as I had never seen before. Here and there, concealed tears appeared. . . . Almost all wrote a fitting letter to their mothers. This gesture was so new for most of them that one of my guys confided to me: I didn't know that it was so difficult to express feelings that seemed so natural!"[64] The evocation of Mother's Day will always be an occasion to stress the spontaneity and the "naturalness" of the actions of children, an untouchable guarantee of the legitimacy of such a celebration in the order of things that leaves no need for questions. In his circular for the preparation of the holiday in 1941, Carcopino made childish "invention" the guarantor of this legitimacy: "While we can *suggest* to all the children of France that they show their affection and their recognition to their mothers, it is particularly important that this gesture be sincere, spontaneous, and innocent. Otherwise it would lose any true and profound value. The child must *invent* and *decide* himself what gesture he will offer."[65] It would be naïve to see in the ritual only the

Violence and State Propaganda ▸ 121

organization of spontaneity—even if this aspect exists as attested by our own childhood memories of preparing Mother's Day presents at school. This type of ritual touches the deepest part of us because, by recalling bodies to order, the state mobilizes the first experience of the world. As a ritual of institution, Mother's Day makes us misperceive and recognize an arbitrary limit as legitimate and natural. In his second message to mothers of French families on May 31, 1942, Marshal Pétain turned to the refined discourse of *naturalized arbitrariness:* "By transmitting life, by raising the child you will be proud of tomorrow, you realize women's destiny fully; you find deep joy in this simple obedience of the laws of nature." He was backed up by Admiral Platon, who, the same year, addressed mothers in this way: "You taste the pure, long-lasting joy given by obedience to the natural laws, a joy that selfishness never offers." [66] The Commissariat General for the Family made Mother's Day a privileged feature of the education of young girls and the establishment of feminine identity: "We must show them that the highest glory a woman can achieve is in the perfect accomplishment of her role of mother." [67]

The state would never have succeeded alone in establishing Mother's Day and imposing its celebration within the intimacy of the family. It needed a lot of support. It received state assistance, of course, from the school, the prefectures, the municipalities, and all the propaganda work of the Commissariat General for the Family. But most important, it received private assistance from the mass of Catholic-inspired organizations and publications that have always devoted themselves to promoting the family. The political decision to celebrate Mother's Day officially and nationally beginning in 1941 acted as a call for proposals encouraging the activism of private initiatives that enriched the state ritual by proposing an inexhaustible reserve of expressions of recognition of and toward maternal virtues. The authority of the state allowed this symbolic coup de force that imposed a "duty to be" and succeeded in making one forget its construction. And mothers were not the last to celebrate Mother's Day and to express in their letters to magazines and their responses to contests that they were happy to be what they were supposed to be. Mother's Day honors them by depriving them of the consciousness of deprivation itself.

The triumph of Mother's Day and its continued celebration well after the Vichy regime, without its origin ever again being questioned, as is the case with all successful symbolic coups de force, lead us to wonder about the specific historical circumstances that constituted the *crisis*. In favor of the crisis situation here we have the defeat, the "breakdown," the establishment of an authoritarian state and this specific form of cultural revolution that was the National Revolution, and we can observe a phenomenon of ideological *crystallization*. An entire set of institutions and currents of thought that existed in dispersed order came together in a new way and constructed the new order in which there was no longer a place for the expression of anti-establishment ideas or for ideological confrontation, as these had found expression in the feminist press, the criticisms of recognized doctors with respect to the repressive natalist policy, and the parties and organizations of the left. All the guardrails had been destroyed. The general indifference that had met attempts to establish Mother's Day during the interwar period was replaced by the conjunction of state and individual interests that were each able to express themselves *more fully* and inspire each other, drawing material and symbolic advantage from being able to sell the "eternal feminine." In this unprecedented situation, the logic of bidding led to a massive overproduction of ceremonials, dogmas, and anathemas that constructed a new entity from old elements. Vichy was always already there, but was inconceivable a few years before.

When we examine the archives concerning the family for the period 1940–1941, we note the ceaseless pressure exerted on the services of the Commissariat General for the Family by promoters of the mothers-at-home agenda as if the historical situation of the defeat and the Occupation had not changed anything. Each stated its proposal, renewed its vows for the success of a program to restore family order, contributed its idea, its innovation, asked for loans for a work that had not yet succeeded in seeing the light of day, issued warnings about what it called the slowness or the softness of the measures taken, and proposed going further, always further, on the road to the "natural" order of the family and parental fecundity. A ministry had been created and it needed to make its place, whether or not the regime broke with democratic principles—a "technical" ministry, with which, moreover, one could collaborate without worrying about the political choice involved in collaboration. And what if "the mother at home" is a political slogan? What if the principal political effect of returning women to the sole reproductive function assigned to them and of its legitimization by the imposition of a representation of feminine "nature" organized entirely around the repetition, from one generation to the next, of the maternal function, is a rallying effect? How can we not celebrate Mother's Day, this tribute familiar to little children organized by the schools and churches under the Marshal's patronage?

5. HERITAGE AND INCARNATIONS
OF CATHOLIC FEMININE CULTURE

Female supporters of the Vichy policy to keep women at home were numerous and militant. They provide the opportunity to localize and measure the strong presence in interwar France, where the social logistics of recognition of and gratitude to the National Revolution were constructed, of what the Church calls "Christian feminism," thus clearly showing its desire to be active in the aggiornamento of women's involvement in the social world. The expression appeared around the turn of the century during works conventions at which the necessity of a social commitment by Christian women to combat socialist and lay influences was expressed. Marie Maugeret, who organized meetings concerning the "social duty" of women at the Institut catholique de Paris, founded a review entitled *Féminisme chrétien* in 1896.[1] Based on defending the family as the "basic social cell" and keeping mothers at home, the women's movements, or movements with a large female membership, that are recognized under the name Christian feminism—certain of which paradoxically fought to advance the rights of women who were "obligated" to work—found a particular affinity with the regime. As Yves Durand emphasizes, the Vichy regime "is not superimposed onto French society" but "bound to it by various means"; it strives to "exploit and maintain spontaneous support" as much as to "maintain the tranquility of opinion through persuasion or constraint."[2]

The Commissariat General for the Family exploited and supported the enthusiasm of these movements—private producers of feminine identity, often inspired by the current of Social Catholicism—and the militants and directors of these associations read the National Revolution as a guide book for the defense of the family and of mothers of families, producing for and with the regime a strict marking out of what was "feminine." *Renouveaux* identified and welcomed one of the numerous "surveys" that flourished with the help of the National Revolution and that bolstered the regime through the assent of "public opinion": "Everyone must respond to the census 'What are the problems the family is having at present?' offered in the October bulletin of the ACIF [independent women's catholic action movement of Mme Payen in Lyon] *by and for himself or herself."* [3] The *Chronique sociale de France* provided a forum for Mme du Peloux de Saint-Romain, who, in a talk to the Feminine Civic and Social Union (UFCS), recalled that a married woman who "accepts a broadening of influence" in "the city" must "use it in such a way as to show that a woman outside, as well as at home, must devote the best of her care to her family." [4] The law of October 1940 adversely affecting women's work was judged "highly insufficient" because "the legislative effort will remain futile" as long as "everything that prevents the spirit of sacrifice from bursting forth in the soul" has not been suppressed. [5] The tone had been set.

To understand this commitment to the "eternal feminine" that often provided global support for the regime, we need to take a look at certain historical moments of the Church's involvement with women and women's involvement in the Church. Only such a look backward can take into account the force of the worldviews that were at the source of the unqualified support for what was first of all perceived as the triumph of a cause long defended. To defend Vichy through the "eternal feminine" is here to defend an image of self that touches the very core of these investments in all the senses of the term.

The production by the Church and by the many broad-based institutions it controlled or sponsored of a representation of women and of legitimate feminine territories constructed a subculture of gender that developed without interruption from the beginning of the nineteenth century. I focus my analysis on the most intense periods of this production: the development in the nineteenth century of a predominantly feminine religious culture, including the feminine mystic; the offensives led by the Church beginning at the turn of the century concerning girls' education and women's social and political action in reaction to the Republican laws regarding education that imposed

Vichy and the Eternal Feminine ▸ 126

mandatory public schools for girls and created a state female teaching corps; the encouragement of the establishment of a Christian
feminism and of its development during the 1920s in response to the
rootedness of Republican-inspired lay feminism linked to the radical
movement, Protestantism, and Freemasonry, and to its monopoly in
the fight for women's suffrage; and, finally, in 1925, the creation of
new forms of women's social action that participated in the broad
current of Social Catholicism. However, these moments of "invention" must not be considered solely from a chronological perspective. The force of the Church as institution on the feminine identity
market resides in its extraordinary talent for being able and knowing how to make images from different ages coexist, which lends an
eternal character to its discourse—even its most modern discourse—
concerning the feminine. But it is political struggles that are at the
origin of Catholic advances in constructing femininity, and it is these
battles that outline, from the beginning of the nineteenth century,
what I propose to consider as a field of feminism.

A Separate Female Sphere

For reasons due both to the concern for the apostolic reconquest of
French society and to the demands made of the Church by women—
demands whose social and cultural conditions of production require
an in-depth study—the second half of the nineteenth century appears
as a golden age in the relationship between the Church and women.
The signs are evident in the sharp increase in female religious vocations, in the revival of the cult of Mary, in the reinvention of the
miracle as apostolic policy, and in the official recognition of new
forms of feminine piety that found its culmination in the beatification
of Thérèse Martin. From the first visions of the Virgin and the heart
of St. Vincent by Catherine Labouré (beatified in 1912) in 1830, several
days before the "Trois Glorieuses,"* and the apparitions of La Salette
and Lourdes in 1846 and 1856, through the apparition of the Virgin
in Pontmain in the Mayenne in January 1871 and up until the miracles
that followed these visions (the miraculous medal of Mary, the grotto
of Lourdes) or that were worked through the intermediary of a saint

* July 27, 28, 29, 1830.—*Trans.*

such as Thérèse of Lisieux, the figure of the Virgin and of women and children intercessors dominated the forms of religiosity of this period, reinforcing or inducing a privileged link between the Church and women in a period in which historians of Catholicism note a decline in religious practice and faith. The statistics for the miracles due to the miraculous medal established in 1842 and 1878 show that two-thirds of those miraculously saved or healed were women. This is also true for the miracles of Lisieux.[6]

However, the most dazzling manifestation of this feminine investment of and in the Church was the uninterrupted growth in the number of women in religious communities and the incessant creation of new religious orders from the beginning of the nineteenth century to 1880, growth that is even more impressive when compared to the limited increase in the number of priests and monks.[7] The consequence of this disparity in numbers would be an increase in the independence and autonomy of the women's congregation movement and institutional segregation that encouraged the development of a *feminine religious culture*. Between 1808 and 1880, the number of nuns and female congregants increased from 13,000 to more than 130,000. A total of 200,000 women passed through the novitiates of the orders during this period, and we note the progressive feminization of the cadres of French Catholicism. The anticlerical Charles Sauvestre, a former follower of Fourier, wrote in 1867: "This type of training that draws 100,000 women away from the world and makes them renounce the pleasures of youth and the joys of family amidst a skeptic and materialistic society is a phenomenon worthy of serious attention."[8] It is significant that maximum recruitment was achieved between 1855 and 1859, during the "very favorable political climate" of the authoritarian empire, as Claude Langlois observed, and also, it must be added, in the climate of the renewal of the cult of Mary, of apparitions, and of the Vatican's proclamation of the dogma of the Immaculate Conception in 1854, all elements that invited women to "dedicate themselves" to the Church. In a century during which the Church tirelessly attacked modern civilization, industrialization, and urbanization and idealized the Middle Ages,[9] its fallback to a feminine clientele, its valorization of feminine belief and mystics (the *fiat* of Mary) and its reduction of the cult of Mary to an ideal femininity (modesty, devotion, and resigned acceptance)[10] resulted in an overproduction of the women-eternity connection and a symbolic and practical space of refuge for women.

"The impact of religion is anchored in the interface between the reinforcement it offers for the ideologies of the most diverse groups and the language of desire that it addresses to individual subjects: this device wins over individuals to social strategies whose specific nature is thus *obscured* for the actors themselves."[11] The work of Jacques Maître on the articulation between psychoanalytical and sociological approaches to religious phenomena, particularly to the feminine mystic studied through the case of Thérèse of Lisieux, are invaluable for an in-depth analysis of these controlled affinities historically propagated between the Church and women. They show, for example, the violence and intensity of the relationship with the mother and of the trauma produced by her loss in the stories of Thérèse and other mystics, and the way in which the religious world was invested as a maternal world. The maternalized vision of Jesus in mystic experience allows us to posit a correspondence between the mother's religion and the archaic relationship of the subject to her mother. The religious space thus appears to be marked by matrilineal filiation and maternal omnipotence. The investment of cultural objects imposed and controlled by the religious organization allows one to avoid psychological engulfment in symbiosis, and the official Catholic code makes it possible to organize a socializing discourse in the field of the original symbiotic bond. The institutional Church incorporated these profoundly psychosomatic experiences (we need only think, for example, of the miraculous cures well before the canonizations that institutionalized these miracles). It offered the narratives of the lives of the saints as a recall to the order of "naturally" "feminine" "virtues" — selflessness and self-sacrifice — by developing overtones that associated maternity, withdrawal to the private sphere, recognition of hierarchies, and the *celebration of a separate feminine sphere,* thus playing on feminist social demands enclosed within the enchanted circle of "one's own kind." The processes of beatification and canonization of the great modern saints should be studied (as Carlo Ginzburg did with respect to witch trials in sixteenth-century Italy)[12] as the translation into the high culture of the Church of these feminine mystical experiences now managed in the logic of edifying history. The controversies and the prunings they occasioned should be analyzed, and we should learn to decipher the skillful rewritings of "popular" beliefs: Thérèse died in 1897 and, after the first miraculous cures of 1903–1904, particular care was taken to show the compatibility of her message with the anti-modernist doctrine of Pius X. The process of beatification, which began in 1910, developed the theme of weakness transformed into strength along with the values of family and nation. Women's religious orders were thus recalled to the social order.

A primarily rural recruiting effort slowly replaced the more urban recruiting effort of the first half of the century in female religious communities, and the rare data available reveal a tendency toward democratization and a shift toward the most modest professions of each social group.[13] The strong hierarchization internal to the orders and of the orders among themselves made it easy to manage this social stratification. In a period when the ruling classes had little interest in ecclesiastical careers and when this career was relatively inaccessible for men from the peasantry, which was still not very literate, the female orders allowed Catholicism "to maintain close contact with the dominant classes and to broaden its influence over the working classes."[14]

Women, who, for their part, were subject at the time to strict legal subjugation and who had little hope of being emancipated through access to professional life and had no other social protection than family dependencies, which were often intolerable, found real forms of security, professional practice, and *access to knowledge* in these religious spaces. As Claude Langlois points out, "women of action" as well as "middle managers" found a means of self-expression in the orders, a large number of which, we must remember, were oriented toward teaching, from large boarding schools to rural schools. And if the unequal but continuous dissemination of primary education throughout the century appeared to be a factor in democratizing the recruiting efforts of these institutions, it is also reasonable that the popular demand for instruction that was expressed with such force in the nineteenth century played a primary role in their remarkable growth. The theme of the worker and the peasant corrupted by culture haunted the discourse of the conservative factions of the ruling class. In 1869, there were 33,600 adult courses that enrolled almost 800,000 people.[15] Women's demand for education played a central role in the success of the religious communities, and the inauguration of Republican, free, secular, and mandatory education for girls upset a cultural landscape where, in 1863, 70 percent of elementary public school teachers were members of female religious communities and 69 percent were uncredentialed, while 85 percent of male elementary school teachers were laymen and 88 percent were credentialed.

Works, the teaching provided by religious orders, and the nursing activities of nuns, who held a monopoly over women's nursing work until the end of the century, thus constituted an important *market for women's work* in which a culture of women's relationship with the city was forged and nurtured by the old Christian oppositions of masculine and feminine relationships in the social world that was constantly capable of enriching them. Aiding, nursing, and educating were merely ways of exercising a *symbolic maternity*. The specific constraints applied to female contemplative orders further reinforced these limitations and the imposition of reserved spaces: whereas for men the cloister existed to keep women out, for nuns, the cloister was total, forbidding them to leave, the parlor divided by a double grill bristling with pointed barbs.[16] This confinement came to symbolize the almost total exclusion of the nun from the *public* functions of the Church. Thus, whether in the active communities or in the cloistered orders, a nun's life in the nineteenth century was entirely conceived of as "an isolation from the outside." This isolation and "regulation of life," the insistence on household concerns and cleanliness, the rule of modesty that imposed corporal reserve placed under the sign of prohibition, humility, and restraint, the superior's authority based on "sweetness and love," the maternal position attributed to the nuns affiliated with boarding schools[17] — here is a catalogue of legitimate feminine qualities inspired by "feminine nature" as defined for all eternity by the Church Fathers (Saint Paul, Saint Augustine, and Saint Thomas, in particular), suited to guiding the education of girls well beyond the cloister. The symbolic weight of this model results at the same time from its omnipresent and diffuse reference to the sole legitimate female role, that of mother of a family, from the fact that it inspired the great majority of skilled female professional identities throughout the entire nineteenth century, and from the fact that it had no real competition, from a symbolic standpoint, from the new lay feminine identities proposed by the Republican school. The upper elementary teaching schools for girls of Fontenay and the elementary teaching colleges largely incorporated the religious rules. Their implicit definition of the proper feminine occupation of the position slipped, at least until the First World War, into the religious model for exercising "feminine aptitudes." There were never any women among the "black hussars of the Republic." An analysis of the subjective relationship to the elementary teaching profession during the years 1880–1914 reveals feelings of social and emotional solitude based on the internalization of a "just" social and cultural place — "worthy and modest" — that imposed restraint and separation with, for company, "our friends, books," according to those who gave evidence.[18]

The Church's symbolic management of women did not stop with the establishment of the Republican educational system. Quite to the contrary, the anticlerical educational measures (enrollment in religious primary and upper primary girls' schools fell from 750,000 in 1880 to 520,000 in 1890 and dropped to fewer than 50,000 in 1905)[19] and the establishment of secondary public education for girls provided a new momentum and an aggiornamento in female confessional instruction. A vast institutional complex of private primary education and, to a lesser extent, secondary education, was created, along with Catholic teacher training colleges and access for girls to the bachelor's degree in humanities at the Institut catholique in 1909.[20] From 1878 to 1901, the student ranks of free denominational schools swelled from 623,000 to 1,257,000. With the restrictive Combes* measures, the number of students dropped to 188,000 in 1906, but, at the same time, the private "lay" schools attracted 700,000 students, the Combes law having deprived primary confessional schools of a little less than one-third of their students. The percentages of girls and boys in private schools, 33 percent and 14 percent respectively, remained very unequal from 1906 until the eve of the First World War.[21] Public secondary education for girls experienced weak growth between 1880 and 1900 and did not issue any useful diplomas. The students that had to work at the time most often took the advanced certificate.

Secondary education was the real site of the private/public confrontation on the highly symbolically charged battlefield of female education, which, during the 1920s, became the terrain for the profes-

* Emile Combes, president of the Conseil from 1902–1905, proposed the law establishing the separation of Church and state, a separation which entailed the closing of numerous Church-sponsored institutions. — *Trans.*

sionalization of women: "The education of girls is one of the sensitive points between 'clericals' and 'men of progress,' the liberals: this explains the dimensions assumed by the episcopal campaign against the secondary courses of Duruy in 1867, or the hostility toward the lycées for young girls founded by the Camille Sée law."[22] For some twenty years, secondary confessional education slumbered as the state assumed many of the ideological traits of clerical education. Paradoxically, it was the very archaism of public education (essentially, the lack of female preparation for the baccalaureate until 1924) that once again placed private education in a position of initiative: at the Collège Sainte-Marie of Neuilly, students were explicitly prepared for the baccalaureate during the years preceding the First World War.[23] Thus, the Church remained influential in the central field of girls' education through its strong presence in primary education, through the continued existence of the private provincial institutions, which continued to prepare students for the certificate of competency, and through the innovative advances, born from its awareness of the feminine demand for education, that would compete with the public secondary school. The importance of feminine engagement in Catholic action during the 1930s is most likely related to the Church's continual invention in the field of education. Nevertheless, accommodation remained limited and essentially involved the Paris region. During the interwar period, private Catholic secondary education would not be able to challenge the supremacy of public secondary education for girls, which would assure the mass education-professionalization of women. The Church continued to maintain a conditional discourse regarding girls' education that also drew from its most archaic cultural stocks.

The Church, the Republic, and
the Political Mobilization of Women

An analysis of feminist movements and women's action, more or less committed to demanding the vote for women since the turn of the century, also reveals the active presence of the Church in this new field of production of feminine identity that can be perceived in part as a battlefield of influence and symbolic struggles between Catholicism and the Republican state. By considering together the specifically feminist movements and the Catholic women's action movements — which also waged partial battles in defense of women and recognized themselves under the title Christian feminism — or rather by considering *all of these movements as a "field,"* a *champ* in the theoretical sense of Pierre Bourdieu, we can better account for the social logic of the positions taken (that would carry the subsequent biases with respect to the Vichy policy toward women) as structural constraints that weighed on symbolic feminist battles in France. I suggest that it was with the advent of the Third Republic, which revived the Church/state opposition, that feminism established itself as a field subject to the oppositions and scissions that also polarized the university field and the political field.

From 1880 to the First World War, "Republican" feminism was expressed in groups with different objectives and ideologies, certain of which would unite into the two large movements that dominated the public scene until 1940.[24] The National Council of French Women (CNFF), which resulted from two conferences held in 1900, one overtly feminist, the other marked by philanthropy, united over thirty societies; its influence was particularly felt in Paris. Although the movement was dominated by Protestant and Republican women from the upper class (Mme Jules Siegried, the daughter of Pastor Puaux, from Ardèche, and Sarah Monod), we also find women of the Jewish upper class and renowned figures in education (Pauline Kergomard) and from the health field (Mme Alphen-Salvador, founder of the first nursing school of Paris). The CNFF incorporated the French League of Women's Right (LFDF) with a prestigious feminist past (founded in 1882 by Léon Richer, a Republican journalist and Freemason, and Maria Deraismes, comrade in arms of Louise Michel, with the support of Victor Hugo). This union met opposition both from Catholic women's groups and from radical feminists who preferred direct action. The second movement, the French Union for Women's Suffrage (UFSF), which united the suffragist action during the 1920s, was weaker before 1914; it owed much of its drive to the support of the Feminist University Federation, whose network of teachers would make the UFSF the best-represented association in the provinces. Chaired by the Protestant Mme de Witt-Schlumberger and directed by Cécile Brunschvicg, wife of the philosopher and daughter of a Jewish Alsatian industrialist, it used the weekly *La Française,* founded in 1906 by the journalist Jeanne Misme, to disseminate its propaganda. In the radical wing of feminism, we find groups that allied radical and reformist tendencies (such as the Fraternal Union of Women, a pro-Dreyfus, anticlerical group that became heir to *La Fronde* upon Marguerite Durand's departure), groups oriented more toward the left that objected to the UFSF's too moderate methods (such as the National League for Women's Suffrage), the Socialist Women's Group, founded in 1913, subordinated to the party, whose positions were divided concerning alliances with "bourgeois feminism," and militants who found themselves deprived of associative foundations on the eve of 1914 (such as the neo-Malthusian Madeleine Pelletier).

During this period rife with clashes between Church and state, particularly with regard to education, and faced with this important development of the Republican-inspired feminist current, with its mobilization in university contexts and its relatively successful association with more radical feminist groups, a broad movement of Catholic women's action became established. Marie Maugeret, who in 1896 launched *Le Féminisme chrétien*, seconded by *La Femme contemporaine* (1903–1913), an anti-Dreyfus, anti-Semitic newspaper, founded the Nationalist Union of French Women. In 1901, the year during which the law regarding freedom of association, which required authorization only for religious communities (and therefore targeted the teaching orders) was ratified, the League of French Women was created in Lyon and devoted itself to propagating religious faith among the working classes. In 1902, the Paris committee of the League founded the French Women's Patriotic League, an association for freedom of education and against socialism, the "Masonic plot," and "Jewry," that protested the transfer of Zola's ashes to the Pantheon. The number of members remained around 500,000 until 1914 and reached one and a half million in 1932. In the middle of the Dreyfus affair, the League of French Women put out a poster using Épinal imagery in which, under the patronage of Clothilde, Geneviève, and Jehanne, it launched this appeal: "Give your mite to support the nation, property, and freedom. Make your husband, your sons, and your brothers vote for an honest candidate, and 35 million French will escape the yoke of 25,000 Freemasons and France will belong to the French." [25] Wishing from the start to modernize French political conservatism according to the English model, the League soon lined up under the banner of the newspaper *La Croix,* for which it expanded distribution and worked to strengthen Catholic education, even founding schools in the provinces. As far as the police were concerned, the movement's allegiance was to the Liberal Alliance and to the Assumptionists, but it appears in fact that the League members acted autonomously. Their success, attested by the spectacular growth in membership, also testified to a feminine demand to participate in public life in the name of typically "feminine" interests arising from the private space of the family (defense of the freedom of education and development of family social action, for example).[26] In 1900, the wife of Chenu, president of the Bar, had created Women's Social Action, which received the sponsorship of Brunetière, Jules Lemaître, and Goyau, famous figures of the anti-Dreyfus movement. At the same time, more modestly are established the premises of Catholic social work with the foundation in 1911 of the École normale sociale that sought to "develop and train female social elites in all social milieux for broad, competent, enlightened action to establish the Christian social order."[27] Among the leaders of these new forms of assistance, we find members of the League of the French Nation, the union of anti-Dreyfus intellectuals.[28]

Thus, from the beginning of the Third Republic until the Great War, the scissions between the Republican feminist movements and the Catholic feminine action movements, like the scissions internal to the feminist movement itself, were largely subject to the logic of the oppositions of the political field. The different movements wore the colors of the masculine parties and the ideologies that confronted each other there. The CNFF and the UFSF were led by women who belonged to the Republican world and, often, to the sphere (very influential at the beginning of the Third Republic) of the Protestant and Jewish industrial upper class, mostly from Alsace, and therefore tied to the developments of the Republican school and to the invention of modern forms of social protection.[29] Both movements received much male support from radicals, socialists, and the League of Human Rights, and also had important relationships with Freemasonry through the intermediary of the LFDF, whose successive directors belonged to the Obedience of Human Rights. In the Catholic women's action movements, the nobility and an anti-

Dreyfus sentiment prevailed. Here, too, the Dreyfus affair was the apparent polarizing principle for all these movements, which were massively involved in the ideological debates concerning "the method for legitimizing ruling classes and concerning the social function of intellectuals."[30]

But the confrontations in the political field must not mask the strong consensus that reconciled all the dominant classes concerning the symbolic limits within which modes of expression of feminine engagement in the political scene were to remain confined. Among the men who were sympathetic to Christian feminism or to Republican-inspired women's suffragism were politicians and intellectuals such as the anti-Dreyfusard François Coppée, one of the founders of the League of the French Nation, who gave his support to the Patriotic League of French Women, and Francis de Pressensé, a member of the League of Human Rights, who gave his support to the UFSF.[31] They agreed to pay tribute to a moderate, worthy, and well-bred feminism that could be called "conditional." Joseph Barthélemy, a Catholic defender of women's suffrage, thus opposed a "contorted feminism coiffed with the Phrygian bonnet" that emphasized "the fear of family responsibilities and maternity" to those women "in whom Joseph de Maistre recognized a special aptitude to yield to superiors" and who would therefore know how to put their clairvoyance into their voting ballots.[32] For his part, paying tribute to his mother, Mme Jules Siegfried, on the occasion of the fiftieth anniversary of the CNFF, André Siegfried adopted a similar tone: "I believe that her expression was 'The more feminist one is, the more feminine one must be.' . . . She used to say that a woman must be a woman, that she must be elegant, that she must be a woman of the world, that she must be different from men. . . . This is how she managed to transform a certain number of ideas into an acceptable form."[33] To strengthen "acceptable" expressions of feminist demands, all of these movements turned to masculine sponsorship, in all likelihood bearers of various forms of self-censorship. During the 1920s, the UFSF worked to set up a parliamentary group of women's rights uniting communists, socialists, and radicals who soon rallied men of the right and the center, including statesmen. The same male support came from the conservative constituencies of the advocacy committee of the National Union for Women's Vote (UNVF), a Catholic suffragist association founded in 1920 that included Jean Ybarnégaray, a militant of fascist-leaning leagues and later deputy to the French Social Party after 1936, who was state secretary for youth in 1940 and who, in correspondence with the prefect of the Basses-Pyrénées department, asked for the dismissal of two female elementary school teachers who were opposed to Vichy, calling them "female muzhiks." [34]

The power structure in the Republican and conservative women's movements was ultimately dominated (both with respect to the proportion of unmarried women in all the movements and in the country) by married women in the governing bodies; the UFSF recommended that the local sections select as directors "creditably known women, family mothers if possible, but especially levelheaded women with a tolerant attitude. One wastes no time in identifying the group with its president." [35] The often dramatic destiny of radical feminists, who advocated single life at a time when unmarried women had no socially legitimate outlet other than the modesty of female elementary school teachers or the apostolic action of religious and lay Catholic action, and who sometimes dressed like men, reminds us that the social and cultural conditions for a symbolic revolution in this field were far from being met at the time. A comparison of the lives of Blanche Edwards-Pilliet and Madeleine Pelletier, an acceptable feminist and a violently criticized feminist, is richly informative in this regard. They were both medical doctors. The former was the first female intern of the Paris hospitals in 1885; the latter was the first female intern of the asylums of the Seine in 1903. The former was a member of the CNFF, the National Association of Freethinkers, and the League of Education and vice president of the LFDF between the two wars, and was made a knight of the Legion of Honor in 1924; the latter, who published *Droit à l'avortement* in 1913, was progressively deprived of any associative foundation and, in 1939, was denounced as an abortionist and committed to the asylum of Perray-Vaucluse, where she died. The former, the daughter of a doctor, married with three children, founded the League of Family Mothers; the latter, born into a poor family, single and without children, wrote that it was necessary "to be men socially." [36] The social verdict set the limits of what was historically tolerable in the symbolic order. Pelletier was clearly "the blemish" and could be included among the "angry individuals whose position is interstitial," endowed with an "antisocial psychic power,"

Poster by Prud'hon; Alain Fournier team. Commissariat General for the Family. Courtesy of Musée d'Histoire contemporaine–Bibliothèque de documentation internationale contemporaine (BDIC), Hôtel national des Invalides, Paris.

Tract of the Commissariat General for the Family, May 1943. Courtesy of Bibliothèque de documentation internationale contemporaine (BDIC), Nanterre / Photo P. Pitrou.

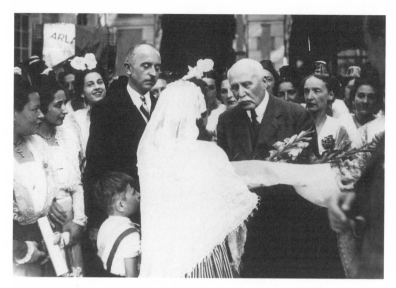

"Living folklore" women. The Marshal's trip to Arles, December 1940. Courtesy of Musée d'Histoire contemporaine–Bibliothèque de documentation internationale contemporaine (BDIC), Hôtel national des Invalides, Paris.

The Marshal's trip to the Limousin region, June 1941. Courtesy of Musée d'Histoire contemporaine–Bibliothèque de documentation internationale contemporaine (BDIC), Hôtel national des Invalides, Paris.

The pilgrimage of Le Vernet, September 1941 (see pp. 46–47). Courtesy of Musée d'Histoire contemporaine–Bibliothèque de documentation internationale contemporaine (BDIC), Hôtel national des Invalides, Paris.

"The procession of Grand Supplication takes place at Notre-Dame de Paris for the first time in thirty years." Courtesy of Musée d'Histoire contemporaine–Bibliothèque de documentation internationale contemporaine (BDIC), Hôtel national des Invalides, Paris.

"Mr. Henri Pourrat, recipient of the Prix Goncourt, whose work is entirely situated in his native Auverge region, photographed at the home of a bonnet presser from the countryside of Ambert, discussing the local customs, customs that Marshal Pétain wants to see return," 1941. Courtesy of Musée d'Histoire contemporaine–Bibliothèque de documentation internationale contemporaine (BDIC), Hôtel national des Invalides, Paris.

Praise for women of the earth. Courtesy of Musée d'Histoire contemporaine–Bibliothèque de documentation internationale contemporaine (BDIC), Hôtel national des Invalides, Paris.

The return to nature. Rural service of young unemployed women of Marseilles. Pernes-les-Fontaines (Vaucluse). Courtesy of Musée d'Histoire contemporaine–Bibliothèque de documentation internationale contemporaine (BDIC), Hôtel national des Invalides, Paris.

"Running around like that, from expensive amusements to tiring outings, have they gotten to know each other, learned to understand each other?

"Deep qualities are less likely to please than charming defects . . . seen from the outside. And, with a disconcerting lightness, they decide 'to try marriage!' For, after all, divorce is always an option."

Excerpt from *Une belle mission des travailleuses sociales,* Commissariat General for the Family. Courtesy of Bibliothèque de documentation internationale contemporaine (BDIC), Nanterre / Photo P. Pitrou.

Tracts from the Commissariat General for the Family. Courtesy of Bibliothèque de documentation internationale contemporaine (BDIC), Nanterre / Photo P. Pitrou.

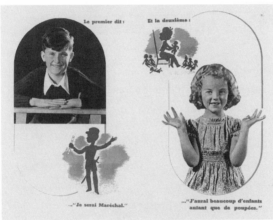

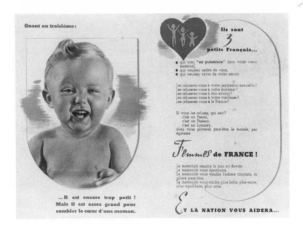

Saint-Désiré Center in Lons-le Saunier. "Young girls making dresses and baby dolls for distribution during the Quinzaine for youth to the children of the city of Lyon." Courtesy of Musée d'Histoire contemporaine–Bibliothèque de documentation internationale contemporaine (BDIC), Hôtel national des Invalides, Paris.

Group portrait with Marshal Pétain. Courtesy of Musée d'Histoire contemporaine–Bibliothèque de documentation internationale contemporaine (BDIC), Hôtel national des Invalides, Paris.

Center for young girls of Bussière-sur-Ouche. "Young girls spinning like our grandmothers did in the marvelous setting of an old abbey." Courtesy of Musée d'Histoire contemporaine–Bibliothèque de documentation internationale contemporaine (BDIC), Hôtel national des Invalides, Paris.

Delegation from the domestic science school of the Jeunesse agricole chrétienne féminine (JACF) of Cussac. Courtesy of Musée d'Histoire contemporaine–Bibliothèque de documentation internationale contemporaine (BDIC), Hôtel national des Invalides, Paris.

Oath of the athlete ceremony at the velodrome of Vincennes, May 17, 1942. Courtesy of Musée d'Histoire contemporaine–Bibliothèque de documentation internationale contemporaine (BDIC), Hôtel national des Invalides, Paris.

Chantier de la Jeunesse. Courtesy of Musée d'Histoire contemporaine–Bibliothèque de documentation internationale contemporaine (BDIC), Hôtel national des Invalides, Paris.

"pollutants" who are "always wrong," whose place Mary Douglas analyzes as follows: "In one way or another, they are not in their place, or they have crossed a line that they should not have crossed, and this displacement results in a danger for someone."[37] Having neither economic nor social capital nor male support, her transgressions condemned her to social death. This sentence recalls the limits imposed for all practical purposes on feminist battles, the most acceptable feminism being the most "feminine," as André Siegfried put it so well.[38] Recalls to the symbolic order of the masculine/feminine opposition thus traverse the entire field of feminist movements and feminine action, manifesting the force of the resistance, in the military and psychoanalytical senses, that such movements awakened. These veiled forms of rejection operated largely with proclaimed or tacit acquiescence in Vichy's antifeminist policy.

This relative submission to the political field and its struggles allowed the feminist and women's action movements to construct and strengthen their social existence; it also allowed the women of these movements ultimately to escape the representation as militant "viragos" largely developed in the male political class since the Revolution and, with unparalleled violence, after the Commune. But it must not cause us to underestimate the extraordinary means of access to public life for these women constituted by strictly feminist forums, and also by this vast sector of Catholic women's action. Thus, the feminist struggle for women's suffrage and recognition of their abilities in the university and professional spheres led by the feminist movements linked to the political and ideological Republican universe was pitted against a feminine struggle for women's right to defend publicly the values of their private sphere threatened by Jacobinism. The Catholic women's action movements had not yet given full meaning to the notion of Christian feminism, but they contributed to developing a Catholic women's culture that incorporated participation in the public space, provided that only what affected the "traditional" spaces of feminine responsibility was defended in this space.

Catholic Women's Action in the 1920s

After the war of 1914, this Catholic feminine culture also expanded to suffragettism and to professionalizing women in separate spaces.

The struggles in the political field continued to polarize the symbolic oppositions, and the policy of re-Christianization, which worked through Catholic social action, gave a new impetus to women's participation in public affairs while subjugating feminine action in its own way.

Despite single attempts such as the States-General of Women organized by the CNFF in 1929, 1930, and 1931, which provoked a call to order from the Holy See authorizing the participation of Catholic women as individuals only, the religious split persisted with force during the 1920s and 1930s. The Republican movements focused their battles on women's suffrage. Suffrage also quickly became an issue among Catholics after a pontifical declaration was pronounced in its favor in 1919: in 1931, the encyclical *Quadragesimo Anno* ultimately recognized women's right to vote and to education while ordering their return to the home. In a context marked by the decline in religious vocations in which the Church devoted itself to the "crisis in the priesthood," creating the Work of Vocations in 1934,[39] the consolidation of the Republican school, the rise in women's demand for education and professionalization, and the increase in female celibacy after the slaughter of the war, the Catholic Women's Action movement found a new energy. The UNVF, founded in 1920 by the Duchess of La Rochefoucauld, did not hide its sympathies for the right. For its founders, among whom one finds the Catholic women leaders of the anti-Dreyfus movements of the 1900s (Mme Chenu, the founder of Women's Social Action, the Marquise de Moustier, president of the Patriotic League of Frenchwomen), defending the vote for women was first a defense of Catholicism, because the Russian Revolution converted conservatives and Catholics alike to suffragettism during the 1920s (Maurras declared himself to be a supporter of women's suffrage).[40]

It was also early in the 1920s that the current of Catholic social action expanded greatly, fostering new expressions of Christian feminism, and occupied different sectors of public life. This aroused strong opposition from defenders of traditional Catholicism such as General de Castelnau. Each of the many Catholic youth movements created after 1922—Fédération française des étudiants catholiques (1922), Jeunesse ouvrière chrétienne (1926), Jeunesse étudiante chrétienne (1929), Jeunesse agricole chrétienne (1929)—soon saw the advent of its female counterpart. Specialized Catholic action thus offered young girls new ways and means of acting in the Church and of intervening in society that constituted an innovative model for mobilizing the feminine elite in the Church.[41] In a historical context marked by a crisis in vocations, the idea of a lay apostleship as a natural extension of Christian life underwent broad development, and the exaltation of consecrated celibacy was progressively disparaged through the promotion of Christian marriage and the celebration of conjugal spirituality.[42] This religious renewal—concomitant with the conversion of many intellectuals who saw Catholicism as the antidote for the modern world and who developed Thomistic studies—was reinforced by the Church's condemnation of the Action française, which many of its sympathizers abandoned. These various and sometimes antinomic currents of Christian renewal also encountered the yearning for "spiritual renewal" that was alone capable of putting an end to the "established disorder," or so thought the "nonconformists of the 1930s." "We want and must find our deep soul. . . . We must join the most authentic tradition, rediscover the spiritual values that the modern world constantly attacks and debases," Jean-Pierre Maxence responded to Brasillach's inquiry concerning the postwar period. "Subversion of values" for Thierry Maulnier, "spiritual blossoming of man" for *Esprit,* "recognition that we are first and foremost soul" for Jean de Fabrègues—such are the levers of the "necessary revolution."[43] The audience for this Christian renewal was embodied in the great religious events that bracketed the Popular Front: the commemoration in the Parc des Princes in 1936 of the fiftieth anniversary of the ACJF, the Catholic Association of French Youth that united young and not so young youth movements, and gatherings in 1935 in Lourdes and, in 1937, in Lisieux for the consecration of the basilica dedicated to Saint Thérèse.[44]

In this context, a vast sector of Catholic social work developed that definitively marked its distance from the feminist movement inspired by Republicanism. The Conference of Welfare and Social Hygiene Institutes of 1921 was the site of a break between Catholic social action and the action led by the UFSF, which, to the indignation of the Catholic movements present, ended the conference with a motion concerning women's suffrage that was deemed too radical: "Thus the feminist movement ended—at least among female social workers—during this conference in July 1921. Never again would they venture such risky statements."[45] In France, unlike in the English-speaking countries, this new labor market also imposed the postulate that social service could be entrusted only to women and only to women defined as "lay sisters." In 1925, *La Rose des activités féminines pour l'orientation professionnelle des jeunes filles* stated that social careers were appropriate only for souls "of apostles" and for single women. Abbé Grimaud, a reputed specialist on the Catholic family, wrote in 1933 that the social worker is always an "unmarried" and "universal mother."[46] At a time when the family was recognized by the Catholic hierarchy as the cell of the Church and the natural organ of apostleship, the Union catholique des services de santé et des services sociaux was founded and maintained close ties with the numerous Catholic associations for the defense of the family.[47] Thus, during a period of Catholicism in France when condemnation of modernity and the invention of modern forms of proselytism coexisted, the important Catholic sector for the professionalization of women, which did not escape the effects of the increase in the female demand for education, incorporated the symbolic heritage of the nineteenth-century communities that promoted the obligation of celibacy, even for laypersons, in certain professions such as teaching, and thereby propagated the idea that there were specifically female occupations in education, health, and social welfare.

At the point at which all these issues converge, we find the movement created in 1925 by Andrée Butillard, founder, in 1911, of the École normale sociale: the Women's Civic and Social Union (UFCS). This movement sought to expand women's social action to defending "the ideal of Social Catholicism" and "all the freedoms challenged for several months now by the governmental policy of the 'Cartel des gauches.'" It also wanted to fight against the "erroneous doctrines" that subtended actions in favor of women's suffrage. The UFCS wanted to reflect on "the causes of social injustices" and "to study their solutions in the light of Catholic social doctrine." The superior of the Seminary of Carmes, Cardinal Verdier, was the movement's spiritual advisor. He defined well-tempered feminism thus: "In a certain number of its demands, particularly concerning the vote for women, the feminine movement is not unfair and may be timely, provided, however, that the family hierarchy and the mission of wife and mother, which is woman's honor, are safeguarded."[48] The UFCS developed its action along three main lines. First, following the encyclical *Quadragesimo Anno* of 1931 ("The work of mothers of families is at home, above all, or in the appurtenances of the home, among the domestic occupations"), it set up a national Mothers at Home Committee that within several months attracted thirty thousand members. The League of Mothers at Home, a branch of the Maternal Home Committee, worked for the establishment of special allowances for mothers who were not working. Second, in pursuit of the work of its commission on public morality, it launched the idea of educating parents and took part in creating the École des parents (the Parents' School) in 1930. Third, the UFCS trained "proponents" and "propagandists" of Christian feminine organized labor (whose bent in favor of workers must not be exaggerated) and organized women's union weeks.[49]

"Christian Feminism" and the
Politicization of the Field of Feminism

Combining the heritage of philanthropic action of the end of the nineteenth century and of the Catholic women's movements against the policy of secularizing education in existence before 1914 with the new Church-women relationship that began to take hold in the 1920s, "Christian feminism" marked out the social spaces that were legitimately feminine. This work of symbolic cartography allowed it both to recall woman's "true" mission—mother at home—and to identify substitute missions that placed women's work in a direct line of succession with congregant tasks. In 1927, the Semaines sociales de France, an itinerant university that united clerical and lay intellectuals to posit the Church in the modern world, devoted itself to "Woman in Society"[50] and set up the general assemblies of "Christian feminism," an ideological alternative in response to the growing pressure for higher education and the professionalization of women. During these meetings, where conservative and innovative positions were expressed, the majority agreed to recognize a feminine "nature"—scientifically certified by Dr. Biot: "What biology teaches us about woman's nature"—and the definition of a specifically feminine territory. Eugène Duthoit, president of the Semaines sociales, opened the proceedings with "The family, Essential Given of the Woman Issue"; Catholic legal experts focused on "The Wife and Mother in French Law"; and economists presented "Queen of the Home, the Woman as Director of Family Management." Father Gillet, a professor at the Institut catholique de Paris, remarked that although there is "moral equality" between the two sexes, "material inequality" is "a fact against which one cannot rebel without damage," because "the individual consequences of woman's sexual inequality" have to do with "her physiological life and her intellectual development."[51] With all its evidence sublimated by the praise of Christian virgins, mothers, and widows—"Christianity having made woman into a more human type of humanity"[52]—feminism had to be reengineered as a "claim by woman to her essential status as a person" that excluded this "feminism that has become individually useful," the feminism of "freethinking, anarchistic, and Masonic feminists," from which it was necessary to save "Christian feminism."[53] If the UFCS was greeted as an exemplary institution of "Christian feminism" by Church authorities, it was because it fought on the very terrain of feminism, respecting feminine specificity, and against the ideas of the left without dabbling in politics: "Before the painful consequences that unhealthy ideas have produced in the feminine masses and in anticipation of our participation in universal suffrage that will apparently be an actuality in the not so distance future, the apostolate of the École normale sociale finds a field of action in the civic terrain that can render great service to Catholic works in general. . . . It is not a question, and you have clearly understood this, of throwing women into the fray of political parties, but of training them for social action that is clearly spelled out and further specified by the apostolate that the UFCS created for this purpose."[54]

Beyond the political and religious ideological oppositions, the division that has structured all women's movements as a field since the end of the nineteenth century is the issue of women's education and therefore of their professionalization. The issue of women's work was at the center of the Republican feminist movements. The numerical importance of working women among their militants and, among them, the preponderance of teachers, lawyers, journalists, and social service workers, women of letters, and doctors,[55] was reinforced by the personal and institutional relationships that existed between the professional women's associations, such as the Association française des femmes diplômées des Universités, founded in 1920, the Union nationale des avocates, the Fédération internationale des femmes médecins, and the Société des agrégées, also founded in 1920, and the feminist movements founded at the beginning of the century with the blessing of Ferdinand Buisson, one of the fathers of the Republican school. We can thus wonder whether the efflorescence of all these groups of women intellectuals at the start of the 1920s was not the real reason for the creation, in 1920, of the UNVF, that foray by the Church into the terrain of women's suffrage. For the Catholic movements, the issue of investing in female education was, on the one hand, caught up in the condemnation of the Republican school that would at times be the explicit reason for founding a Catholic women's association (the Patriotic League of French Women waged a long battle against the secular school) and, on the other hand, was subject to the recurrent Catholic conception of female education suited in the majority of cases to supporting the primacy of the woman-at-home agenda. There were no teachers in the UNVF and few lawyers, but there were many women of nobility or from Catholic industrial circles devoted to charity, and the right to work remained subordinate to motherhood and the family. In the women's movement as well, *the education issue was a political issue,* and women's access to secondary and higher education, a condition of their professionalization, was the central feminist issue of this period and the real field of its symbolic battle. Symbolic and political battles were inseparably linked here. Women of action defended their conception of the elite and of its reproduction through their images of female elites and women from the working class. When the secular school was muzzled and "purified" by the French State, the spokespersons for the Catholic action movements and those for private education proceeded with the unrestricted development of their program for a minimum female education and a minimum education for the children of workers and peasants.

The irreducibility of these two positions in the field of the feminist movements and Catholic action increased and hardened with the increase in social and political battles during the 1930s. Thus, while it attacked women's employment in industry and deservedly denounced their work and salary conditions, at the same time, the UFCS developed a defense of women's domestic and family work that was keenly criticized by the UFSF which, during a meeting at the Mutualité in 1935, affirmed women's right to earn a living, "a right that must not be withdrawn either for questions of sex or for reasons of marriage," and the equal harmfulness of unemployment for women and for men. The UFSF also attacked the proposal made in the Chamber by Philippe Henriot, a militant of the Fédération nationale catholique, a deputy from the Gironde of the National and Social Republican Party, editor of *Je suis partout,* and a future star of collaborationist radio in 1944.[56] He wanted married women who gave up their job to an unemployed man to be given the indemnity previously collected by him. Why not to an unemployed woman, the feminist associations retorted. For the UFSF, this proposal by the right-wing deputy was in keeping with the viewpoint of the Catholic women's associations that accused feminism of defending and propagating cohabitation by defending woman's economic independence.[57] Confronted by the civic and social indignation of the feminist movements and their call to unite for the defense of women's work that was so violently under attack, the UFCS did an about-face, stating: "The immense work of restoring spiritual and social values demands that we return motherhood to a place of honor with its responsibilities and duties, its joys and its rights. Nevertheless, in the current state of economic life, we believe that the salaried work of a mother cannot be subject to legal prohibition." However, in 1937, the UFCS organized a large international conference on the topic "The Mother at Home, Worker for Human Progress." This perseverance earned Andrée Butillard, the founder and director of the movement, a private audience with the Pope, a sign of the importance the Church accorded these issues.[58]

The second open confrontation exploded on the occasion of the reform bill concerning the civil capacity of married women. At the beginning of the 1930s, a legislative commission that included feminist suffragists (particularly the legal section of the UFSF) and Catholic feminists (particularly the UFCS) looked into reforming the legal status of married women. The first group wanted to get the most from a reform they considered a diversionary tactic with respect to women's suffrage. The second group, allied with the pressure groups that made up the profamily faction, represented by Senator Georges Pernot, defended provisions to this bill that would leave intact the notion of the husband as head of the family and would retain his right of veto concerning his wife's work. In February 1937, the two groups confronted each other when some ten Catholic women's action movements, including the UFCS, the League of Homemakers, and the UNVF, asked the Senate legal commission that marital authority be recognized by law and that the husband be able to oppose his wife's practicing a profession. It was on this latter point that the battle was the fiercest, and the conservative current won the day. The husband, "in the interest of the household and the family," was to be able to oppose his wife's practicing a profession; the wife, in this case, was to have recourse to arbitration by the courts.[59] The associations that mobilized to restrict the scope of this law that was ultimately ratified on February 18, 1938, with the Pernot amendments that retained the notion of head of the family and the authority of the head of the family in numerous areas (Articles 213 and 216), found themselves alongside the Commissariat General for the Family and supported it in its practical and ideological tasks. The violence of these confrontations also stemmed from the tense social climate marked by the fallout in France from the crisis of 1929, the demonstrations of February 1934, and the Popular Front.

One cannot but be struck by the permanence and vitality of the broad Catholic Women's Action Movement from the beginning of the nineteenth century. This movement was caught up in the conflicts between the secular state and the institutional Church that accommodated the growing force of women's demand to participate in public affairs. Through this attempt to sketch the social history of the "field" of the women's movements and women's action movements since the 1880s, we see that the "eternal feminine" is produced through symbolic and practical battles, covert or explicit, concerning the definition of feminine identity. The study of the sociogenesis of these confrontations and the representations of the masculine/feminine opposition that it constructed there seems to me to constitute a sort of *psychoanalysis of the social conscience* against the amnesia of genesis that tends to eternalize and reify classifications and identities. The definitions of the feminine, those concerning women's place in the city through their access to academic degrees, professional positions, and civil rights, are expressed all the more clearly and all the more violently when they are produced during intense periods of political and ideological debates that one would not at first have expected to be concerned with the "woman issue." Ultimately, the struggle to impose a representation of femininity participated fully in political battles. For example, it accompanied the stages of confrontation between Church and state concerning the education question: the foundations of the women's Catholic action movements had always joined in defending confessional education, then private education. Even more striking, it slipped into the social oppositions for which the Dreyfus affair is the telltale sign to the extent that it is tempting to draw a parallel between the processes of integration through education among Jews and among women. Here the Patriotic League of French Women aligned itself with the League of the French Nation to defend the "natural" elites "naturally" produced by the presence of mothers at home, those "true" elites so dear, we will see, to the social philosophy of the National Revolution. Representations of the sexual division of the social world are always representations of the social order.

Appropriations, Internalizations, and Incarnations of the Catholic Culture of the "Eternal Feminine"

The harshness and persistence of these battles, their inscription in the political field, the force of the *beliefs* that they mobilized and mobilize and of the *investments* they produced and produce, are the hidden heritage—the social unconscious—of the production of feminine identity that the National Revolution occasioned.

The existence and the resurgent capacity of "Christian feminism" since the 1880s cannot be reduced to the mere political and apostolic will of the Church deploying successive, unprecedented strategies for winning over an expanded number of female supporters. The various historic currents of this movement were borne, embodied, and invested by women who belonged to diversified social and ideological spaces, and who recognized themselves in these currents and gave and restored life to them on the basis of defending interests that often went beyond the strictly religious. The first of these was, paradoxically, the interest in education, to which the communities and private education responded in their own way. Just as paradoxical was the interest in professionalization that was defended by developing a space for "women of action" and a broad sector of "women's" work.

By registering these social demands, on the one hand, the Church maintained and strengthened its influence over women or, rather, developed the Church-women bond, established during the nineteenth century; on the other hand, it continued to impose its vision of femininity and of the masculine/feminine relationship through all sorts of aggiornamentos. Thus, in movements that were structurally young and old, conservative and progressive, whose coexistence constituted the force of the Church as an institution because this coexistence allowed the Church to respond to aspiration schemes of different ages, a *Catholic feminine culture* developed that was capable of integrating the old and the new. Perhaps we can see here one of the springs of the *recurrent production of the eternal feminine:* by reinventing social forms of the Catholic feminine presence in the world, the Church let go of what was subsidiary while conserving the essential. And it was once again Father Sertillanges, a virtuoso of the symbolic policy in this area, who, by separating "good" feminism from "bad" feminism, traces the limits of what cannot be transgressed: "If by feminism one means: first a battle of the sexes, second an individualism, a selfishness for women, and finally a tendency to suppress the difference in human work by distancing women from the family roles to place her on an equal footing with men in public life, then we are not feminists. But if, by feminism, one means the progressively effective emancipation of the moral female person, its growth in value, its enhanced application to all occupations with relation to her skills and her duties . . . , in this case, we are [feminists]." [60] There is only one vocation for women, that of the mother-homemaker. The others are additional; the consecrated celibate, the lay apostolate, all these occupations are "symbolic maternities," along with participation in the public space on the basis of the defense of the family, which obviously included the defense of "freedom"* of education. As I have attempted to show, this symbolic universe was invested and reinvested in part, paradoxically, on the basis of a feminine demand for knowledge, work, and participation in public life. It was because the Church produced and reproduced a feminine culture over time that it produced generations of women capable of embodying this culture and of appropriating it for

* In France private education, i.e. Catholic education, designates itself as independent, suggesting that public education is non-independent. — *Trans.*

themselves on a prereflexive level. By taking only what they had already been given, they reconstructed *separate feminine spaces* in each era, denying the social and cultural determinisms that are at work in the principles of separation and thereby continually restoring a dynamic force to this culture of enclosure.

Take, for example, this woman from Brittany, won over during the 1930s by the local feminist propaganda for women's right to vote, who wanted to encourage the creation of a women's group in Vannes and brought in a lecturer from Paris. Her success was complete and a section was quickly created. However, she realized very soon that certain statements concerning divorce and the role of women were not consistent with her "line of thought," and she ceased her activities. Learning of the existence of the UFCS, she wrote to its founder, who agreed to give an initial talk before the five hundred women she brought together: "I was unaware of the Church's social doctrine. I had all the seeds in my heart, and Mlle Butillard would make this potential blossom. The courses on social doctrine, so luminous, were a revelation for me. All that I had sensed in rather confused fashion concerning the state of the social order, I finally understood!" This woman became a propagandist for the UFCS, founded local sections, and split her time among the cadres of Vannes, Lorient, and Rennes.[61] Words like "feeling" and "revelation" belong to the vocabulary of deep-seated agreement, that agreement that is given immediately, the discovered truth known for all time, borne by this feminine teaching of the ageless Church. It was this internalized culture that manifested itself in complete freedom in a National Revolution that was based on the "eternal feminine" to bring women back to the home.

Its most official ideological expression was a program-text written by Vérine, "The Family," the only feminine contribution to this thematic manifesto on the restoration of order undertaken by the National Revolution called *France 41*. Vérine, the pseudonym of Marguerite Lebrun, the mother of a large family, took part in this work produced by experts on moral and social order as founder and president of the École des parents. The publisher, Raymond Postal, said in his introduction that, whereas in other times this movement could "only display a concern for more reliable science and greater perfection, it is today an imperious and virtually general necessity." We do not have any details concerning the steps taken to obtain the author's consent to appear in this ideological anthology of the regime, or the circumstances behind her consent, but a brief history of the École des parents reveals the political interest for the French State to be legitimized through the support of the president and founder of such an institution rich in social and cultural capital and in respectability.

Born into the medical milieu—the daughter of a doctor from Ivry who was an enthusiast of social issues, married in 1904 to Émile Lebrun, a pathologist—at the end of the 1920s, Vérine, a member of the Commission on Public Morality of the UFCS, published several works on sex education in the family and on married life under the auspices of the Association of Christian Marriage (founded by Father Viollet, leader of the family social works of Moulin-Vert).[62] During the first board meeting of the École des parents, on January 25, 1930, Vérine recalled the context in which this institution, which claimed to come from the English "schools mothers," had been founded. It was in fact founded to block the plan to include sex education in the lycées that was about to be approved. Vérine, at the request of the members of the UFCS, wrote six articles in 1927 and 1928 for *La Femme dans la vie sociale,* the movement's newspaper, that demonstrated that "this individual and progressive education must be given by the mother." The idea of a parents' school stemmed from this defense of an "education of the senses and emotions by the family" in the context, once again, of a battle against public education. In January 1929, the first official activity of the École des parents was a lecture at the lycée Louis-le-Grand to announce its opposition to sex education in the lycées. Among the first members of the École were representatives from the family movements and from private education and numerous physicians. The UFCS withdrew its too markedly confessional sponsorship so that during its first conference at the Musée social the École could unite "families of all creeds." At the end of 1929, the École des parents asked the National Alliance against Depopulation to "adopt" it to take advantage of the Alliance's infrastructure and in exchange committed itself to developing pronatalist teaching consistent with its own program of moral education. Born in a Catholic movement and in opposition to a secular project, this institution succeeded in integrating the representatives of other creeds: Father Dassonville of the Action libérale populaire, Pastor Marc Boegner, president of the Fédération protestante de France, and Rabbi Louis-

Germain Lévy of the Union libérale israélite, discussed the role of religious feeling in adolescent education at the second conference in 1931. At the same time, the École joined modern pedagogical currents and new advances in child psychology to the defense of a traditionalist view of family education that would enhance the mother's role through a wealth of medical-psychological baggage. Vérine's repugnance for Freudian doctrines continued to prevail nevertheless.

During the 1930s, the École des parents defended the family ("the most precious conquest of Western civilization") and its supremacy over the school ("the school belongs de facto and de jure to fathers of families, they are the ones who should govern and control it"), non-coeducational schooling, including in lycée classes, and the absolute difference in the training of young boys and girls: "We would like our young men to know that they are not called on solely to be Heads of professional bodies, but also Heads of the Race. . . . It is specifically because we are for equality in difference that the École des parents intends to prepare young men and young women for marriage differently. . . . Whether certain feminists like it or not, we women are not the life powers. We hold them. We are their depositories. This is as noble and as laden with responsibility." We must therefore "rehabilitate the domestic arts, culinary science, child care, too often disdained today by our young female intellectuals hungry for diplomas."[63] Elsewhere, Vérine states that she is "entirely in agreement with the feminist cause," defending women's right to vote that will give "mothers in particular a new and powerful means of action."[64] The colloquia, lectures, and publications of the École des parents hammered home the "eternal" principles of feminine culture and values in a traditional or psychologized form: "The mother must prepare her daughter for marriage from her earliest childhood, inculcating in her the spirit of sacrifice. Conjugal happiness requires self-denial and giving of self with smiles and cheerfulness";[65] "Sometimes mothers, in the weakness of their tenderness, repress the personality of their children with the unconscious fear that they will lose them. Those mothers must be reminded that *the crux of education is in self-sacrifice: knowing how to suffer and make oneself suffer to prevent causing suffering, knowing how to die to one's self to make others live.*"[66]

"Christian feminism" found its scientific version, new legitimizations, new forums, and a new audience. Vérine drew from all this authorized and, in her eyes, predictive knowledge to make her contribution to the ideology of the National Revolution. But the historical context hardened speeches, and many young listeners of the École des parents—and, we might imagine, certain of its lecturers—were unable to acknowledge their interest in the new sciences of education in this threatening defense of the homemaker, "the true French mother":

> We will therefore never tire of repeating this: *woman, wife, and mother is made for man, for the home, for the child. As long as all the young wives of France do not understand this, will not live this truth of nature, nothing will be built in the city.* Woman was given to man to be his companion . . . and not to be his competitor or his rival, and to take such a place in all the domains and in all facilities that the poor man would no longer have found for himself tomorrow if the scourge of the War . . . had not restored level heads. . . . For many years, the League of Homemakers, feeling the gravity of the danger of "hominization," had undertaken a magnificent campaign of recovery. This campaign is more necessary than ever, for it is human, civilizing, and it will reestablish the eternal order: each in the place that nature assigned to it.[67]

The UFCS and its affiliate, the League of Homemakers (founded in 1933, disbanded in 1946), also mobilized themselves to participate in the work of "recovery" and "French renovation." Reading *La Femme dans la vie sociale* of the war years, one notes the extraordinary vitality of these associations that began to multiply campaigns and membership, created new sections, supplied new town councilors appointed as competent family mothers (115 members of the UFCS were town councilors in 1942), served as relays for the government concerning feminine issues,[68] and actively participated in the work of the Advisory Committee on the Family, where all their national directors and also "true mothers at home," as they used to say, were appointed. Their timeless and ahistorical representation of the family group,[69] the manner in which they found the motto Work, Family, Nation forever at work in the social doctrine of their movement,[70] and the key words of the new ideology found throughout the issues of their newspaper[71] give their adherence to the new regime the appearance of a self-referendum as much as of a referendum. These elements probably allowed them too to invest with a naive enthusiasm the new social order that they reduced to a forum of mothers for families: "To remake the country through the family, to remake the family through the mother at home"; "Woman serves the country by serving the family." The old slogans of the two associations were not invented for the National Revolution, but the National Revolution was the occasion of a veritable explosion of these movements that, according to their theoreticians, had only been awaiting this historical moment to find their true dimension: "When a fire has been well laid, it suffices to bring the match near and everything blazes in an instant. It is currently much the same for the LEAGUE of HOMEMAKERS. Everywhere it is created, the LMF meets only with sympathy. The movement is growing rapidly. Many mothers are joining, some are showing themselves to be great propagandists, others are better suited to organizing. In this way the section comes to life; far from being a 'flash in the pan,' it becomes a living, acting organism, a light for all households."[72] One might think that the Marshal's little phrase about the "spirit of pleasure" and the "spirit of sacrifice" was the spark that set the whole thing ablaze.[73] In the Camargue, the city hall of Sainte-Maries made the city council room available to the LMF for lectures on "everything a family mother must know." In Avignon, the newly created League already had four sections and one hundred members. In Marseille, a competition was won by a militant who brought in thirty members, and Andrée Butillard "showed how the LMF has always fulfilled the motto that the head of the State is now proposing to us: Family, Work, Nation." In Ardèche and in Le Puy where the UFCS created numerous cells led by women of the upper middle class, the propaganda and recruiting activities seemed tireless.[74] There were many material reasons, but the isolation of many women confronted with very difficult family situations probably also contributed to the success of this expansionist campaign: the meetings provided information on governmental and municipal assistance, the rights of widows and war prisoners' wives, offered cutting and sewing classes, and dealt with food issues.[75]

But the inauguration of the French State first and foremost offered such women's movements the opportunity to impose their hierarchical view of the masculine-feminine relationship and their subordinated representation of feminine identity. To women who found it hard to accept the loss of their job following the October 1940 law prohibiting women from working in the civil service, the LMF offered moral reeducation and rearming: the discovery of "the superiority of their family and social mission over their former professional tasks."[76] The objective limits historically and socially assigned to work, education, and the professionalization of women and to their involvement in public affairs became "senses of limits," a *"sense of one's place which leads one to exclude oneself from the goods, persons, places, and so forth from which one is excluded."* And the continual reinvention of a feminine Catholic culture played a central role in mediating this correspondence between social structures and mental structures that predicates a perception of the social world by which "dominated agents . . . tend to attribute to themselves what the distribution attributes to them, refusing what they are refused ('That's not for the likes of us'), adjusting their expectations to their chances . . . consenting to be what they have to be, 'modest,' 'humble,' and 'obscure.'"[77] A photo of a little girl, a doll in her arms, younger brother and sister seated in the grass near her: "She keeps in her arms the doll-baby that already in her young heart awakens the maternal feelings. . . . Mothers, let us use this charming game of the doll to teach our little girls how to sew, do laundry, and iron; . . . thus while having fun, the gestures will become nimble, an apprenticeship will be accomplished preparing the would-be mother for her future task."[78] The Commissariat General for the Family could not have done better. And if the UFCS claimed to be "nonpartisan," indifferent to the government in power,[79] it took explicit positions when it had to, maintaining the union around the Marshal that appeared to the UFCS to be the condition of its growth of influence and the survival of its social action: "Marshal Pétain said in his moving New Year's speech: 'The unity of spirits is in peril.' Why so many divisions in the spirit: We note them around us and if they were to enter 'us,' they would threaten to paralyze our social apostolate." It is thus a question of "unifying" France, "not in imposed words and gestures, but in a *tension of spirits, of hearts and muscles* toward the accomplishment of the motto 'Family, Work, Nation' [*sic*] that was formulated for us when the Armistice was signed. . . . French women, we will continue our activity with courage renewed by the vision of increased necessity and by the observation that the leader who, in this tragic moment, is responsible for France,

Catholic Feminine Culture ▸ 169

made us hear the call to the civic virtues to which we have devoted all our efforts against winds and tides since our foundation."[80]

The National Revolution constitutes an almost experimental framework for studying the dynamic force of this Catholic culture of femininity, for it allows us to become aware of its unconscious internalization that is the true spring of these immediate investments lived in the register of "feeling," of "revelation," of the "tension of spirits, of hearts and muscles," the whole vocabulary of this unprecedented encounter between prophecy and the aspirations of those who receive it as a long-awaited message. There were numerous political stakes involved in defending the new regime on the basis of the defense of the "eternal feminine." It was also the occasion for winning or broadening markets—both markets of symbolic goods and professional markets such as social work, which would experience extraordinary growth under Vichy. At the same time, adherence to the sexual reorganization of the social world undertaken by the new order capitalized on the total identification of these women of influence with the Catholic feminine culture that would find itself reactivated by its accession to the state forum. The culture of enclosure born in female religious communities, the culture of sacrifice, of renunciation and selflessness would nourish—and be nourished by—the subculture of gender produced by the French State. The feminine section of the Spanish Phalange[81] had made it possible to sublimate the contradictions between the defense of feminine abnegation and recognition of a feminine heroism capable of pushing this abnegation to its end by valorizing the notion of sacrifice that imbued most of women's education to make it accede to the rank of *political value*.[82] So too, the French State's recognition of "eternal" feminine values, largely produced by the Catholic culture, resulted in an immediate mobilization.

6. FAMILY IMPERIALISM
AND FEMININE SUBJECTION

In 1940, the situation was no longer at the stage of debate; it had become a monopoly. The representation of the "eternal feminine" with all it implied concerning the naturalization of the arbitrary—founding social destiny on biological destiny, for example—thus seemed to have been an essential precept for all time. The amnesia concerning its genesis repressed the competing historical processes of the construction of femininity and, by authenticating the viewpoint that had become dominant as the historical product of social consensus, at the same time made the myth seem to be an obvious fact.

The unprecedented situation created by the National Revolution and its program to revamp the social order—one of "those rare moments when things are malleable"[1]—offered supporters of the "eternal feminine" a *government forum.* Here all facets of Catholic feminine culture, the calls to order of the pronatalist factions, the condemnations of the Republican school, the slogans of women's works and professions placed within the Church's sphere of influence, those of the movements for the defense of the family and the head of the family, and finally, of "free" education, would find expression *together.* State propaganda was thus able to draw from this inexhaustible reservoir of what was then perceived as "common sense." The Vichy construction of feminine identity was therefore a *collective construction.* The ranks of the Commissariat General for the Family were completely filled with representatives of the private associations that had been fighting to return mothers to the home since the beginning of the century. The former opposition between familialists (concerned with privileging the moral value of the family institution) and natalists (defenders of demographic realism) lost much of its relevance in the "atmosphere of spontaneous fermentation" that characterized the early history of the French State.[2]

If this vision managed to impose itself so easily, is it not because the values that inspired it had a much older history than the competing values that were being defended, particularly by the feminist and university women's movements involved in the slow and recent process of secondary and higher education for women? The cultural revolution led by the new regime mobilized "the person we were yesterday" that Durkheim writes about: "For in each of us, in differing degrees, is contained the person we were yesterday, and indeed in the nature of things it is even true that our past personae predominate, since the present is necessarily insignificant when compared with the long period of the past because of which we emerged in the form we have today. It is just that we don't directly feel the influence of these past selves precisely because they are so deeply rooted in us."[3] This unconscious part "deeply rooted in us" can easily find the path of return to representations constructed in other times and for which we have forgotten the successive social processes of production, once again giving them the blind force of "mythic demons."

Adherence to the National Revolution on the basis of the defense and promotion of the "eternal feminine" appears to be an adherence without limits that probably equaled the violence of the symbolic battles that had marked the processes of construction of feminine identity for a century. The elimination of competition and the unhoped-for accession to *the monopoly of the legitimate definition* played in this area, as in others, the role of accelerator that led to overproduction, raised bids, and rigidification. And though no one invented anything, strictly speaking, something new was invented during this collective creation: a new mode of exercising symbolic violence in an unprecedented situation of established monopoly. The experts and militants for women's maternal "vocation" and keeping mothers at home would effectively produce feminine identity in the service of a political cause, that of establishing the family as the "initial cell" of society and the privileged agent of political life. It is because the French State opposed family hierarchy to the individualism inherited from the French Revolution and made family values the basis of and model for civic virtues that women's recall to the maternal order goes well beyond the cause traditionally defined as familialist to become a central element of the new political order.

The establishment of the family as one of the key elements of the new French State was, inseparably, a process of female subjection that inflicted on women a subordinated identity restricted to the domestic sphere. These redefinitions of a new subculture of gender were consistent with the construction of a family political order that in many respects largely exceeded the simple implementation of the Family Code of 1938 and its pronatalist measures. It was now a question of returning to the "natural" hierarchical structures undermined by the French Revolution and the sin of individualism.

The Family, the "Initial Cell" against Individualism

The fact that the familialist rhetoric developed within the ideological sphere of influence of the Church since the 1880s and, with a particular vigor during the interwar period, used and abused notions of "eternal values" and "natural right" and drew its inspiration largely from the political philosophy of the regime with respect to family matters helped foster the thesis of the extraordinary continuity in family policy before, during, and after Vichy.[4] This thesis, which tended to *banalize* the family measures of the National Revolution and, by the same token, prevented them from being viewed as political measures, integral parts of a system that in six months swept away democratic principles, privileged the technical aspect of a policy whose ideological weight seems to me rather considerable in the processes of legitimizing what was explicitly given as a new order.

In "Politique sociale de l'avenir," a program of social philosophy of the "new French State" and a defense for a "strong state," Pétain gave the place of honor to the family: "The right of families is, in fact, older and higher than the right of the State just like the right of individuals. The family is the basic cell; it is the very foundation of the social edifice; it is on the family that we must build; if it gives way, all is lost; as long as it holds, all can be saved." This commandment, which would be elaborated on ceaselessly by all those who defended a place in the family market, introduced a new civics lesson concerning the limits of the Republican slogan revoked in July 1940:

Family Imperialism, Feminine Subjection ▸ 173

When our young men, when our young women enter life, we will not deceive them with fine words and illusory hopes; we will teach them to open their eyes wide to reality. We will tell them that it is wonderful to be free, but that real "Freedom" can exist only in the shelter of a guardian authority. . . . Then we will tell them that "Equality" is a good thing, from certain standpoints and within certain limits; but that . . . various kinds of equality must be framed within a rational hierarchy, founded on the diversity of functions and merits. Finally, we will tell them that "Fraternity" is a magnificent ideal, but that in this difficult period we are passing through, there can be real fraternity only within these natural groups that are the family, the city, the nation.[5]

The family is also the prime example given by Marshal Pétain to condemn "the false principles of individualism": "The necessary preliminaries to any reconstruction are to eliminate destructive individualism, destroyer of the 'family,' whose ties it breaks or loosens, destroyer of 'work,' against which it proclaims the right to idleness, destroyer of the 'nation' whose cohesion it disrupts when it does not dissolve its unity."[6] Finally, in his first message to the "mothers of French families," the head of state first saluted the family: "For ten months, I have been urging French men and women to tear themselves away from the mirages of a materialistic society. . . . I have invited them to depend on the natural and moral institutions to which our destiny as humans and French men and women is bound. The family, initial cell of society, offers us the best guarantee of recovery."[7]

"Initial" and "essential" cell, "natural" institution par excellence and exemplary embodiment of these "organic" unities that would be the new intermediaries between individuals and the strong state in the fight against Republican individualism and universal suffrage, the family occupied a strategic position in the political apparatus of the new regime. The family metaphor even made it possible to bring the Republican slogan back to its rightful proportions, freedom, equality, and fraternity being overseen by "guardian" authorities, "rational" hierarchies, and "natural" groups. From the most political commentaries to the most technical texts of ordinary familialists, the strictly political content of the regime's family philosophy was integrally repeated and therefore widely disseminated, as if the condemnation of universal suffrage that constituted its backdrop was self-evident.

René Gillouin, an influential ideologue of the regime, defined the new state as "national, authoritarian, hierarchical, and social." National, "it banishes from within itself or it strips of all leading influence the individuals and groups that, for reasons of race or conviction, cannot or will not subscribe to the primacy of the French fatherland: foreigners, Jews, Freemasons, Communists, Internationalists of all origins and of all convictions." Authoritarian, it "denies the validity of the freedom principle" but admits "concrete freedoms," for example, the rights inherent in "natural groups." Hierarchical, it "denies the validity of the equality principle." Social, it "excludes individualism," "universalism," "political liberalism." And, to these various "equally ruinous systems," it opposes the four principles of the professional, local, regional, and national "family community."[8]

William Garcin, head of social services of the Légion française des combattants, secretary general of the Federation of French Families, and head of the legislation office of the Commissariat General for the Family, participated fully in the ideological construction of the National Revolution by drafting two volumes, *L'Individualisme* and *La Famille*, of the very official collection "Cahiers de formation politique." In the first volume of the collection, *L'Individualisme*, the authors state that they are addressing students to disseminate the essence and substance of "the Marshal's luminous messages" in a "logical plan of governing ideas," each reader being able "to push further in the determined direction," to "take the new principles from texts to deeds and mores." The "Cahiers de formation politique" are combined into three sets: "The Real," "Realist Politics," and "Liberal Politics." In each of the thematic parts of this collection of social philosophy in which Thibon's influence is obvious, the family figures prominently and explicitly in its support for the new "political doctrine": alongside the "Cahiers" devoted to *The Race, The Commune,** and *Intermediate Communities,* it appears in the constructive part entitled "The Real"; alongside *Corporatism, Regionalism, Marriage,* in its "traditional conception," it provides a basis for "Realist politics." In the critical part entitled

* Here, the smallest French territorial division, not to be confused with the Commune. — *Trans.*

"Liberal Politics," *Divorce* is associated with the *Trade Union,* the *Department,* and *Parties* as one of the elements that shatter "communities." In his contribution concerning the family, Garcin explicitly links the critique of individualism, the condemnation of the rights of man, and the necessity of feminine subjugation: "How could our society lose interest in the family, the source of its life? Let us spell it out, this suicide is one of the effects of the individualism . . . legalized by the Revolution of 1789 and codified by the Declaration of Human Rights. There are still Frenchmen who proclaim themselves to be 'sons of the Declaration of Human Rights.' Strange father! The Declaration of Human Rights uproots man and his family, and proclaims that men are born free and equal in rights, in some sense adults and without any family."[9] Now, *La Cité antique* by Fustel de Coulanges clearly shows that "families developed with this paternal authority that was all powerful. Right of life and death over women, over children, over slaves, over servants, over customers, and over beasts." "The Roman matrons who had lost their sense of dignity" were responsible for the fall of Rome. We must therefore return to the family, "an entirely natural and spontaneous society" that "comprises a head indicated by nature and accepted by its members" and "a natural counsel, and this is the role of the mother."[10]

The draft constitution proposed by the Conseil national in July 1941 stated in its Article 3: "The nation is not only composed of individuals but of natural or spontaneous groups. The State respects them, controls them, organizes them, and harmonizes them." The third title of the draft was devoted to "social groups" that were "the organic elements of the Nation" (Article 52) and first of all to the family, which is the subject of chapter one. It is "the basic social group" (Article 53); it has a head: "The husband is the head of the household, the father is the head of the family" (Article 54). "The law, through a set of real benefits and effective measures, encourages marriage, facilitates the founding of households, supports maternity, assists large families, *keeps* mothers at home, and protects childhood" (Article 56).[11]

Under the French State, the family issue thus became an explicitly political issue. The condemnation of universal suffrage, of individualism, and of human rights goes hand in hand with the condemnation of abandonment of the family. The state definition of feminine identity was subject to this political logic. Women had no other legitimate destiny than that of guardians of this "initial cell," of this "natural group" whose survival and validity must be defended. Redefining women's place in the city by virtue of their "natural vocation" thus now had stakes that were important in other ways than those of the old familialist battle. It was to tear the word "family" from its antiquated connotations, to give it the youthfulness of a political slogan that the Commissaire General for the Family saw as the task at hand: "The word Family is inadequate. . . . Too often, Family only evokes a virtuous household, dusty associations with perfectly honorable Presidents, assistance from well-meaning and charitable souls frequently housed in the bodies of unmarried individuals. The family movement thus merely appears to be an embittered activity of protest. . . . If the family program allowed itself to be reduced to these petty concerns, would it really have become the basis of a national policy?"[12] This *national policy* first passed through a legal reform of the rights and duties of the family, a legal entity, which would provide as many opportunities as there were legislative enactments to recall the eternal principles of the sexual division of the social world.

Family Rights and Duties

A very broad set of laws sought to strengthen the family institution (*L'Actualité sociale* congratulated itself for having called attention to "ninety-nine laws, decrees, or orders concerning the Family" between October 1940 and December 1941),[13] define the rights and duties of each spouse and of parents toward their children, and protect family assets and the "essentially" hierarchical family structure, acting like so many recalls to a family order in which the place of each was defined by law. This legal partitioning of the family institution, one of the three pillars of the renovated house of France, appeared inseparably as an attempt to fix women in their function as homemaker and men in their paternal duties: "Free, [a man] refuses to bind himself for life to a woman. He knows no sexual discipline. What can this robot teach his son begot during a chance encounter?"[14] Lawmakers and their familialist and natalist exegetes could thus defend the idea that the spirit of the law was the desire to protect women and minors rather than to treat women as minors who would not be able to leave the family space, where lawyers protected them, without risk. Symbolic violence was at its height here, for the repetitive hammering concerning women's family vocation posits itself and presents itself as protection against male "selfishness." We could almost call it symbolic blackmail, for the slightest priority, benefit, or allowance fed the imaginary of the "eternal feminine."

Of course, *L'Espoir français,* "a French propaganda organ," included the family question in its special issues concerning "topical" subjects. In March 1941, in an issue entitled *Pour le relèvement de la France,* the editorial "France Kept in Order" expressed pleasure that Marshal Pétain "saved the French order" by hunting down communists, destroying Freemasonry and "red" unionism, and ousting mayors and "partisan" municipalities, and placed the guarantees and privileges granted to the family, "the basic cell," at the center of what it called the "new French grandeur." An accompanying illustration shows the soup tureen being served at the family table around which the father, the grandfather, and two children are already seated; the mother carries a baby in her arms and the grandmother remains standing. The editorialist comments: "The family's place in the national order was no longer what it should be. Safeguarding the family estate, the traditional property of the family, the concern for the education of children by their parents were sacrificed to the mystique of equality. Drawn by illusions of independence and ease, too many young women abandoned their homes and the too few children for whom they had the pleasant responsibility of overseeing and guiding the first steps in life." Today, "MOTHERS OF FAMILIES *have been compensated for their devotion to home* by a monthly benefit equal to 10 percent of the average departmental wage," at the same time as "THE DESTRUCTION OF THE HOME *has been proscribed* by reforming the divorce laws." Here the illustration, drawn in the style of an object lesson, and the imposition of slogans through the typography, as is often the case in the propaganda texts we have examined, reinforce the carrot-and-stick rhetoric that characterized the family ideology of the regime.

The law of April 2, 1941, regarding divorce radically changed the law of July 27, 1884, which had been untouchable under the Third Republic.[15] The earlier law, which restored divorce to the Civil Code, had cited three valid grounds: adultery, sentencing to an "afflictive penalty involving the loss of civil rights," and "*serious* excesses, brutality, or abuse." Deeming this wording suitable for all overzealous interpretations and therefore for all liberal interpretations, the new law strove to "specify in a restrictive sense the notion of serious excess, brutality, and abuse to which case law had given an indefinite extension."[16] Alfred Naquet, the instigator of the law of 1884, figured prominently on the list of enemies of France drawn up by anti-Semite tradition, because divorce, for Drumont, for example, was "an absolutely Jewish idea." Similarly, the book by Léon Blum, *Du mariage,* published in 1907, and later the school sex education program proposed by Jean Zay would be analyzed as the same Jewish attempt to systematically demolish the family.[17] In March 1942, *La Révolution nationale,* a collaborationist weekly founded in 1941 by the Mouvement social révolutionnaire, spoke of Blum's book as a "pornographic book (filth and collectivization of women)."[18] Among the ideologists and supporters of the National Revolution, this work was routinely condemned in the most innocuous and in the most technical writings on the family. In his preface to Jean Guibal's *La Famille dans la révolution nationale,* René Gillouin wrote: "My dear Master, you have cited a truly atrocious text by Léon Blum, the sorry author of this book on marriage that could be characterized as a conscious and orchestrated manual of filth."[19] In *Le Divorce,* Dauvillier speaks of a "vile work." The political reconstruction of the family institution had much in common with state anti-Semitism, for which it would provide specific weapons.

The new law subjected divorce proceedings to numerous difficulties and calculated delays at the same time that it gave special weight to conciliation procedures and imposed financial sanctions on the "guilty" spouse. To the three-year period from the date of marriage during which no petition for divorce could be filed, a one- to two-year postponement was left to the discretion of the judge. Then, if neither of the spouses was sentenced to a "punishment involving life or fixed-term imprisonment coupled with banishment or civil disqualification" in the grounds for separation, another two-year period could be allowed to run before the court decreed the divorce. The reflection period could thus reach seven years. The only exception to this concern with protecting the legitimate family was the case of mixed couples. Because there were to be no delays in the "aryanization" of Jewish property implemented by the law of July 22, 1941, in September

1942, Barthélemy sent state prosecutors a circular intended to accelerate divorce proceedings for mixed couples for this purpose.[20] This law was also supposed to be retroactive, contrary to the principles of French law. This was justified in a radio speech by Minister of Justice Joseph Barthélemy broadcast on April 12, 1941: "All the old laws concerning divorce were inspired by political prejudices, by philosophical conceptions, by religious beliefs; the current law overlooks all these considerations. It is solely concerned with the good of the State."[21] Divorce was no longer a subject of debate, but it was subject to reasons of state, because "the stable family must be the rule" and divorce must remain "the exceptional remedy for desperate situations." Thus was Barthélemy quoted by Franck Alengry, who added to the minister's remarks: "These are the very words of M. Joseph Barthélemy, author of the new law, the eminent and faithful interpreter of Marshal Pétain's thoughts on this subject, a profoundly human interpreter of the human heart and of the leader's heart."[22] Barthélemy, so "profoundly human," actively took part in developing the second Jewish Statute of June 2, 1941, on which he remarked: "[The Jews] have refused for centuries to melt into the French community. . . . The French government is merely forbidding them from the functions of directing the French soul or French interests."[23] It would appear that in the mind of this eminent legal expert, the "stable family" is at the heart of the "French soul."

By recognizing as grounds for divorce only the "serious or repeated violation of the obligations of marriage," by increasing the time for converting legal separation into divorce from one to three years, by rejecting "mutual consent," by punishing "instigating offices" specializing in divorce proceedings with imprisonment and fines, by shielding the public from the arguments that would henceforth take place in the room to which the court usually withdrew for deliberations, the lawmaker dramatized the procedure and gave it an exceptional character. He urged young couples to submit to the paternal wisdom of the law and the magistrates who laid down the "eternal" principles that make up the couple and the moral philosophy of marriage. Extending the legal period between marriage and divorce was, effectively, to remind us that "the concessions necessary to adapt to communal life and to create the harmony of tastes and characters" must be made. The new form of the arguments, secret and sheltered, would perhaps be the opportunity for the "appeasement propitious to pardoning offenses and reconciliation." [24] "Harmony in us and around us" was the new motto for the women of the new France proposed by a social catechism of the regime: "She must live just in this point of harmony of her power and her submission. She is only fully mother if she is fully wife." [25] This conception of the woman who makes concessions and creates harmony, omnipresent in the family philosophy of Vichy, fed (and was fed by) collective unconscious representations of sacrifice; the component of feminine honor as such was defined by the regime.

Although the French State had not purely and simply forbidden divorce, as Mussolini's regime had, its authorized commentators deplored it and viewed the law of April 2, 1941, as a "timid attempt," an "insufficient stop-gap measure" pending the ultimate elimination of divorce.[26] To conciliate general and individual interest, one legal expert even proposed asking future spouses to waive the right of divorce during the civil marriage ceremony. This commitment would prohibit them from seeking a divorce at a later date, which in this case was tantamount to assimilating civil marriage and religious marriage.[27] The UFCS regretted that the new law was "not as strict as we would have hoped," for it was necessary to "take into consideration a mentality created by habits and an education with no solid moral basis." [28] The logic of bidding worked together with the appeal to vigilance and to the increased severity of the magistrates to solidify family policy and give it a fundamentalist slant. The competitive battles within the legal field certainly played their part in this process. By multiplying its legislative reforms, the new regime effectively expanded the legal market of the family, giving rise to logics of conquest likely to multiply commentaries and accommodations, whose analysis would require a history of the legal field and of its ideological and professional rifts during the interwar period.

The same desire to strengthen the family institution legally was expressed in the law of July 23, 1942, concerning abandonment of the family, which extended this notion well beyond financial abandonment and made abandonment of the conjugal home for more than two months a criminal offense subject to imprisonment of from three months to one year: "The evil, already acute before the war, has worsened amid the tragic disturbances of the torment. . . . Into too many families, separated by events, a wind of independence has blown, which causes the spouses to disregard their most basic duties." This is why the new law sanctioned physical abandonment "as equal to desertion for, by destroying the home, this abandonment dangerously undermines the cornerstone of French society on which everything must be rebuilt."[29]

Only an in-depth study of legal precedents and the legal commentaries concerning these laws during the period would allow us to evaluate the specific contribution of legal professionals and legal practice to the Vichy program to return women to the home and keep them there. Danièle Lochak has done this with respect to the banalization of anti-Semitic law in legal practice, revealing the conformity tainted with corporatism that largely characterized the legal profession during the period and led it to contribute to legitimizing state anti-Semitism.[30] In January 1943, *La Revue de la famille* explicitly called on magistrates to be strict: "It was time after the defeat for France to react and extend the protection of the law to the family. . . . This resulted in a new tendency of the courts to crack down severely on crimes committed against children and the home. During the single week that has passed, we saw the regional criminal court sentence a mother of a large family to imprisonment because she had abandoned the family home, and the State Court gave twenty years of hard labor to an abortionist. In a France that wants to revive itself on the basis of Work and Family, there is no longer any place for assassins and deserters. As the family has become the basis of society, any crime against the family is a crime against the nation." As we can see, the tone is not light: to speak of "deserters" is to appeal to the severity of this exceptional justice that is the military court, and to designate agitators of family problems as "assassins" is to call on local vigilance in maintaining family order. In the department of Lot, "bad Frenchmen" were denounced by anonymous letters sent to the new local authorities; "mothers of families," for example, were indignant about the "gay life" led by wives of prisoners.[31] To parody Marshal Pétain, we might say that the *family mystique,* according to the sanctioned expression of those who served the National Revolution, "is not nonpartisan."

The Government of Family

This abundant legal work in defense of the family that was very much in line with the new order finally focused on the respective rights and duties of spouses, the privileged territory of a symbolic imposition of masculine and feminine roles and skills through the law of September 22, 1942. This law, which is often presented as a simple extension of the law of February 18, 1938, recognizing married women's civil rights, further associated the married woman with family management. It thus appeared to be a supplementary step on the way to the equality of spousal rights and duties. But this overlooks the fact that, as we saw earlier, the law of 1938 had arisen from violent clashes in the Senate from February to April 1937 concerning an amendment, proposed by the profamily leader, Georges Pernot, that ended up in adding "the husband is the head of the family" to Article 213 and the husband's right to prohibit his wife from practicing a profession to Article 216. Overlooking these close debates and the forces they mobilized in the women's movements and in the political and legal fields clearly illustrates Joan Scott's comment concerning the amnesia of ideological conflicts and battles that characterizes the normative, here legal, viewpoint that became dominant concerning the nature of masculine and feminine. From 1938 to 1942, profamily legal experts advanced the expansion of feminine prerogatives in the legitimate household and finessed the central and eminently political question of the masculine function as head of the family. The law of September 1942, which marked the triumph of the Catholic and conservative factions of profamily jurists, once again upheld marital power and ultimately created the expression of the husband as "head of the family." The commentaries on this law and the ideological climate to which it belongs infer that the *hierarchical structure of the family* is and always will be invincible; at the same time, the law subtly allows exegeses of the division of powers that succeed both in promoting the regime's concern for expanding the rights of married women and in reaffirming specific feminine "vocations" in the private sphere. As an editorialist for *La Française* who signed her name Marianne (the name that had become suspect under Vichy) wrote concerning the Pernot amendments on April 10, 1937: "The senators of the Right, while ardently suffragist when they hope to win women's votes for their party, are the most solid pillars of conservatism as soon as this concerns their civil or economic rights. . . . Who wouldn't be fascinated by the 'feminist' sentiments of these gentlemen after their efforts in and out of session to make the husband remain 'the head.'"

The law of September 22, 1942, was presented by commentators as a true family "constitution," because "*having two people live together*" is to raise "*a problem of government.*" Now, "French law has always entrusted this prerogative to the husband. Was it wrong or was it right? Some people are arguing about this, but the majority of minds accept that it must be so in *the order of nature.*" So that the father can satisfactorily carry out the "outside activities" incumbent on him, his wife must be his "vice chairman of council" and "minister of the interior," his "second," must give him "objective and devoted assistance" and re-place him if necessary, "provided, of course, that she is worthy, and the courts will be the judge of this."[32] Henceforth, the wife enjoyed a "housewife's power"; that is, she represented the husband "in all day-to-day acts concerning the needs of the household."[33] Catholic lawyers such as André Rouast, a professor of civil law at the Faculty of Paris, a member of the Commission Générale des Semaines so-ciales de France, and advisor to the UFCS, played a central role in con-structing and imposing these agendas. In a work published in 1941 that defended the legal reforms concerning the family, he welcomed the timely prudence of the law of 1938 that had sought to "proclaim that the husband is Head of the family, which the Civil Code had not stated expressly," refused to be moved by the plight of the un-wed mother, whose "emotional reasons" must not excuse the situa-tion, and endeavored to specify the role that fell to the woman of the house: "We would do well on this point to take inspiration from Ger-man law and Swiss law that acknowledge a specific function for her under the name of 'power of the keys,' by coordinating this power with the duties of general management that fall to the husband. 'The husband is head, the wife is collaborator': this should be the expres-sion."[34] It is clear from these texts that family law, like labor law, is a production site for classifications concerning the feminine and the masculine capable of mobilizing and feeding the social unconscious concerning the sexual division of the social world through a specific form of wordplay that imposes, with the force of law, binary oppositions that are as old as the world: chief/minor ("collaborator"); exterior/interior ("power of the keys," "housewife's power"). In August 1943, a family conference organized around the theme of the conditions for recovery took place in Lourdes, attracting forty thousand participants. The focus of discussion was the "overriding problem of the authority of the head of the family," viewed, said the commentators, "not as academics, but as architects who have a house to build, like men of action who want to lay out the social habitat for their grandsons." For the Church during this time of crisis, the authority of the head of the family was the symbol of the "union that involves the abandonment of personal preferences to unite with discipline around responsible leaders," "by ceasing to be partisans to once again becoming Frenchmen."[35] Union around the head of the family is most decidedly a problem of government.

The Culture of Home: Devotion and Renunciation

At the same time it designated the family as a rampart against individualism, that sin of democracies, and assigned it a central function in the return to a "natural order," the political philosophy of the regime defined the feminine responsibilities in constructing the new order through the family. It thus established a classification of positive and negative feminine virtues.

A subculture of gender developed at the intersection of the *political* stakes of family imperialism and the *ethical* stakes of the familialism inspired by Catholicism. The definition of Christian feminism tirelessly produced for a century would be conjugated with the assignment of legitimate feminine territories subtended by the political aim of a return to "natural" communities. It becomes almost impossible to untangle what, in this production, comes more specifically from the ideologues of the National Revolution considered as a political regime and from the old combatants for family and family virtues, who always referred to the long-wearing doctrine of Le Play. In this set of unique circumstances that would have been unimaginable several months before ("divine surprise"?), the profamily tidal wave imposed a repetitive, univocal discourse. The same expressions concerning feminine "destiny" are found from one text or declaration

Family Imperialism, Feminine Subjection ▸ 185

to another, a discourse whose content of symbolic violence is very much the result of this meeting of the old and the new, of the "eternal" cultural, and the unprecedented historical and political situation.

La Femme dans la France nouvelle is exemplary in this regard. Armed with quotes from Marshal Pétain, Father Sertillanges, Gina Lombroso, Monsignor Dupanloup, and prestigious representatives of Catholic social action, the book appeared in 1940 to defend the trilogy Work, Family, Nation, "the sacred triptych that awakens deep emotions in us."[36] The "exaggerated emancipation of woman," her "competition with man," the fact that she wanted to "live her life, follow her whims, win her freedom to lead an existence without control that is happy in appearance," according to the author and the author's references, destroyed familial traditions. It is therefore woman's responsibility to rebuild what she has destroyed: "The *new* tendency is to revive the *old* expression of homemaker," "recent provisions henceforth [raising] before her thousands of barriers that will distance her from situations from now on reserved for men." The woman of the new France must once again become capable of "silent self-sacrifice," of "the most complete renunciation," and once again find her timeless qualities: "This marvelous power to love, to admire, to devote herself, this prudent wisdom, this strength in weakness." In short, she must once again find the forms of action and the feelings that are "characteristic of the feminine soul": "Selflessness, the total gift of self to others . . . , all the characteristics of maternal love to which more or less all the forms of love in woman are ultimately related."

The Vichy ideology of the homemaker mobilized a *feminine culture of renunciation* in that it gave expression to a network of mythic oppositions and equivalencies that stem from the fundamental opposition between "spirit of pleasure" and "spirit of sacrifice." On the one hand, there was the coquette: "a coquette without children has no place in the city, she is useless," according to the tract of the Commissariat General for the Family. On the other hand, there was the mother of a large family, devoted to "alterocentrism" (a concept developed by Gina Lombroso, an Italian antifeminist, in *L'Ame de la femme,* published in France in 1924): "This tendency to place the center of pleasure and ambition *not in oneself,* but in another person, to keenly feel the pains, joys, and disappointments of other beings, not to be able to dispense with the approval and the recognition of her neighbor is the cornerstone of the female soul."[37] There was now only one path of feminine honor. The repeated appeals for respect of woman were as many reminders of her "primary vocation" as wife and mother. A respected woman was a woman who respected herself by respecting the limits and the functions her "nature" assigned her. And the Légion française des combattants easily rediscovered the Church's old tactic of idealizing woman correlative with her separation from the world: " 'Fall at the feet of this sex to which you owe your mother,' the poet sang. . . . Let us no longer give our favor, our applause to music-hall starlets, sterile women, divorced movie stars, or to all the painted and plucked figures that go about with short hair and in men's attire. . . . We must no longer allow feminine purity, chastity, and modesty to be insulted and ridiculed with impunity. Far from ignoring it, we must honor the dignity of women who are mothers and educators devoted to domestic life and the care of small children, which are their true nobility."[38]

For the National Revolution, feminine honor and dishonor were basically connected with the body. The body learns early. The only apprenticeship young girls have to undergo is to mimic motherhood, and the condemnation of the child star supports the profamily, pronatalist denunciation of "selfishness," that female expression of "individualism." "Under the influence of fashion and the movies in particular, parents see their little daughter only as a budding star. The havoc caused by Shirley Temple's polished smile is incalculable. Accustomed to overly elegant clothing—it takes so little cloth to clothe a child before the age of reason!—the little girl becomes a demanding and frivolous doll. Ten years later, she is a coquette and an egotist."[39] The mother worthy of the name can only train a future mother, teaching the body of her female child to listen with all the secret fibers of its being to the call of maternity. Ultimately, this is the essential task of women once again enclosed in the enchanted circle of similar souls specific to the feminine mystic culture: "The deepest aspirations of our young girls tend unconsciously, first, then more and more consciously toward marriage. Rocking their dolls, *rocking themselves* to the recitation of nursery rhymes, seeking to penetrate further, as new feelings awaken in them, into the mysteries they sense and that are hidden from them, is to create a home they are preparing for themselves." To assist in forming this feminine unconscious, the mother must "glimpse" in her young daughter "the future mistress of the house": "By acting in this way, *both* obey the most ineradicable instinct of their nature." [40]

The "selfish" coquettes, that repulsive pole of femininity constructed during the National Revolution, were in the image of the woman-weasel, the woman-mare, the woman-monkey or the siren, representations of evil women that Nicole Loraux studies in the Greek myths and who all transgress because they do not bear children. On the positive side, the mother of a large family, honored by Mother's Day, was the image of the woman-bee, *melissa,* "the good and loving wife who grows old alongside her lord and master," who ensures "the flourishing growth of the household assets" and its "long longevity by bearing beautiful offspring." [41] The response to Inspector Haury's fantasies concerning the polished teeth and too short skirts of little girls already lost for the reproductive function was a work of reshaping the feminine aesthetic conducted by experts, journalists of the feminine press, beauticians, hairdressers, and couturiers who distinguished themselves from the "artificiality" of the prewar period imposed, they said, by American films, to reconstruct the face and body of the "true" Frenchwoman, the one who no longer cheated with appearances. In April 1941, *Votre Beauté* launched an ethical and aesthetic manifesto: "This woman used too much makeup; we returned her to her true nature." "A new style of fresh women, wearing hardly any makeup and with a natural charm, is born. Real women," Marcel Rochas exclaimed. The magazine wanted makeup so transparent "that the many expressions of the life of the soul are written on the face." [42] Woman must be transparent, legible, without makeup, like the earth that "does not lie," to borrow Marshal Pétain's expression. On her aging face she bears the stigmata of her feminine accomplishment—renunciation, sacrifice, and selflessness—in the only legitimate feminine territory, the family, that is the sign of true beauty: "The woman who surpasses in altruism the basic precept of charity, 'Love your neighbor as yourself,' by loving her fellow man, her husband, her children, her entire family *more* than herself, this woman will prove to the institutes of beauty that their arguable effectiveness gives way to the radiance of generous hearts." [43] This line of argument borrows widely from the Catholic rhetoric concerning feminine aging: "And then the years fly by, the wrinkles become more apparent. . . . And, then, one has suffered! Honest suffering is the great secret of life. Even though it leaves its mark on a woman's face, it leaves the charm of her smile intact."[44]

This feminine culture of sacrifice therefore had to be internalized from childhood through an apprenticeship that was inseparably corporal and moral: "Do not make your little girls idols by adorning them like shrines; do not keep telling them how pretty they are. . . . If our little girls began their exercises of *moral gymnastics* early in order to forget themselves and think of others, they would succeed in experiencing a feeling of well-being by practicing these virtues, the true release for the soul just as sports (not excessive) are for the body. . . . To build a home, the husband and the wife, *but especially the wife,* must put into the foundation lots of renunciation, devotion, and selflessness!"[45] Thus, the *culture of home* could be constructed, which, as the legal experts reminded us, would make it possible to resolve a "problem of government."

On the strength of his experience as father of a large family and from his responsibilities as vice president of the Advisory Committee for the Family created in 1941, where he chaired the commission responsible for studying the statute of family associations, Vice Admiral de Kervéreguin de Penfentenyo drafted a guide to marital duties that provides a good example of the family reeducation undertaken by the regime. Addressing his young daughter-in-law Marie (a name predestined for a family civics course), wife of his son François, he reminds her of the duties of the wife:

> If François is the head of the family, you are undisputedly the queen of the home. . . . As François is the head, it is his responsibility to make the important decisions concerning the family; but far from being uninvolved, you must give him your counsel after thoughtful reflection. . . . When François has made his decision, even and especially if it goes against your advice, do not be cross and act as if you had made this decision yourself. . . . The errors committed by women have much more serious consequences than the weaknesses of men. It is your responsibility therefore to give all the good examples: moral conduct, piety, dignity of life, candor, loyalty, good humor in all circumstances. . . . The wife therefore deserves the deep respect of all, *provided that she remains on her path.*[46]

Reduced to only the "power of the keys" ("Our grandmothers always carried a large set of keys. Nothing was beyond their control. They were truly 'Queens and Mistresses' in their domain"), Marie, like extern sisters, has only to manage the separate space that is hers, ordering her actions and her moods according to the rules of the *Traités de l'humilité, de la modestie et du silence* that subjected the life of the nuns of the nineteenth century to constant restraint.[47]

The family community was the primary model for all organic communities henceforth responsible for weaving the social bond sheltered from conflicts and in the eternal complementarity of roles and skills. The definition of this culture of the family community was thus the opportunity to bring about a division between masculine and feminine qualities, a division on which the hierarchical structure of the family founded itself: "In this community of which man is the head, in which he represents effort, contributes power, suggests initiatives . . . , woman represents love and all that this great word evokes and implies concerning patience, vigilance, constancy, hope, devotion, charity, courage, and holiness." Woman "suggests and encourages." . . . 'To obey in order to rule better,' this is the ideal expression."[48] This work, written by two clinical pathologists, places its successive chapters under the authority of a quote from Marshal Pétain. It attacks the "individualism" that found "in each of us, in our fundamental selfishness, so many relatively secret complicities, to the point that it received, in our country, official recognition in the form of the Declaration of Human Rights, a veritable 'catechism of individualism' (Barrès)."[49] There could be no clearer statement that the imposition of a feminine destiny in the family community, a destiny founded on woman's natural qualities—selflessness and silent subordination—was a political arm against the egalitarian principles of the rights of man. Men and women are not equal, and in the family community, which endures only in the complementarity of their skills and functions, they are even less equal than elsewhere. The family is thus a society in which each contributes his or her know-how; it is the model of all societies. Through the error of individualism and the "mania for egalitarianism," through the error of "deviant and leveling intellectualism," "we have lost sight of the sense of the ultimate purpose of nature, as if man and woman were interchangeable in their individual functions! The young girl must one day be a wife and mother.

Whatever prepares her nobly for this role, keeps her in it and helps her derive her full value from it *is in the order of things*. Whatever makes her deviate from this noble end *is evil*."[50]

Feminine Civic Sense

The French State would mobilize the feminine culture of sacrifice and thereby enlist women who became its spokespersons or recognized themselves in it, in these times of crisis, in the construction of a *family political order*. In this order, they would have to defend publicly the structural limitations of their private functions, thereby offering an image of citizenship that subjected the "principles" of liberty, equality, and fraternity, to borrow Gillouin's phrase, to the principles of authority for which the family structure, hierarchical by "nature," is the primary field of application. Alongside them, the state called on professional women working in social services, those "unmarried women,"[51] dedicated to "symbolic maternities," who would broaden their sphere of action and influence because they would ultimately leave the limits of the role of "visiting nurse" to become technicians of the "country's moral health." Counted "among the most important agents of the family policy of the new State," they must henceforth "maintain or reestablish the cohesion of the family community."[52]

It was on the local level, that of the commune and the "small fatherland" dear to Maurras, that women were called to make their contribution to the work of national regeneration that aimed to restore "the fundamental values, those that draw from nature and life."[53] By a law of November 16, 1940, mayors of cities with a population over two thousand were no longer elected but were appointed by the government. Municipal councilors were chosen from a list submitted by the new mayor. County councils were also replaced on October 12 by an administrative board whose members were appointed. The justifications given after the fact for a Toquevillian return to local notables who managed the commonweal "en pères de famille [as prudent men]"[54] should not mask the opportunity for a political purge and increased control of the state over the most urbanized municipalities that these enactments constituted.[55] The new municipal council was to include among its members a representative from the family associations, a father of a large family, and a woman qualified to handle private assistance and national charity works. This law was thus welcomed by women's action associations dedicated to Catholic familialism as a liberating and "feminist" law, and the municipal councils were heavily padded. The new authoritarian principle of their constitution and the settling of political accounts were ignored. Tacit adherence to this legislative reform by the local representation seems, however, to have been a given. Thus, the UFCS advised its female members, new municipal councilors, to arm themselves with a spirit "of universal charity" "where the communal environment is deeply infested with material concepts that convey social and civic trends contrary to the social order."[56] The law was also welcomed enthusiastically by the Associations of Parents of Students of Independent Education (APEL), which were pleased with their "consistent, constructive, and confident contacts with the public authorities," to which they contributed "the perspective of family men": "The law of November 16, 1940, provides that in all communes with populations over two thousand, a family man will be appointed. We sent the list of our members capable of filling these positions."[57]

The philosophy of female participation in local political life was the occasion to recall the areas falling under "legitimate" feminine competence that could be fully deployed only in a situation of family imperialism suited to the expression of a specifically feminine civic sense: "The complementary roles of man and woman, which make their collaboration in family life so necessary, also make it necessary in municipal life. While woman does not usually have the same mental scope as man, she has a very realistic view of things, a practical sense that is closer to reality"; "Through her innate family sense, woman effectively has an *intuition of social sense* that allows her to contribute enriching social views in her collaboration with public services."[58] The new municipal councilors of the UFCS contributed "slices of life" involving childhood, hygiene, prostitution, provisioning, all the concrete spaces of domestic reflection, to their first meeting in the Unoccupied Zone. Thus, responding to an old wish of Joseph Barthélemy, women entered participation in political life "by steps," the commune being "the primary school of freedom" and the occasion for exercising "*municipal house-keeping,*" as noted by the English-speaking commentators on women's access to the process of government.[59] At the end of the 1930s, the issue of female municipal councilors was raised. This concerned deputy municipal councilors whose method of election and functions varied depending on the commune; whereas Pierre Mendès France imposed election by universal suffrage and the participation of female councilors in all aspects of communal life in Louviers, this was not the case elsewhere, where any real power was taken away from them in advance. Vichy chose the apolitical model of "women of works."[60] Thus, a symbolic cartography of women's political competence was developed during this paradoxical time of female participation in public affairs, which we have not stopped witnessing and from which we continue to experience the fallout. In the fall of 1942, the Légion française des combattants itself, a masculine institution if ever there was one, created a service called Dames SMS (women of the medical social services), a sort of female social action section whose goal we might think was to increase the movement's local influence. In any event, this unexpected creation testified to the expansion of the model for the application of feminine virtues in the city and its weight of political respectability. Organized by department, SMS women were to devote themselves to issues concerning childhood, to the families of prisoners of war and families of war widows, and more broadly to all the usual tasks of social action. Subject to "Légion discipline," they wore a uniform and an armband. The Légion recruited them only after inquiries; candidates had to prove that their family situation was exemplary (no divorce decrees against them), that they had "experience with social works," and that they had a "clarity of spirit preferable to culture that is too often theoretical." Of course, they must not have been members of the Communist Party or the Freemasons.[61]

The access of women and the family to appointed municipal councils was presented as a way of fighting against the vices of the city that encouraged "the relatively artificial needs of a population that was too sensitive to the contagion of individualism and selfishness." The new urban municipalities would have the delicate task of "raising the rampart in whose shelter the family condition will improve."[62] In an antiquated vision that shared this nostalgia of the eternal return of the same, whose idealization of the Middle Ages became a recurring theme, the commune, that is, the National Revolution's version of it, became the family's rampart against the urban disorder of the street and the slums: working classes, dangerous classes . . . "Is not the

Family Imperialism, Feminine Subjection ▸ 193

commune like the Family of our Families? Its very name, 'commune,' evokes the idea of solidarity, which, during the Middle Ages, further united the inhabitants, the hearths of the same parcel of earth, for, during this era, the elements of the commune were not counted by individuals, but by *fires*." [63] As the writers of the defeat wrote and repeated, woman, the mother of the home, is the guardian of the fires. The commune of the Middle Ages, the "family of families," is clearly the antidote for the Commune of 1871 as it was reconstructed as a demonized vision of the Popular Front.

The Family State

The law of December 29, 1942, known as the Gounot law,[64] which created a Federation of French Families that was semipublic in nature and was recognized as a Family Charter homologous to the Labor Charter, crowned the state-sponsored promotion of the family: "The law related to family associations is also a *preconstitutional law*. It aimed to set up the organization of the new State. On December 2, 1940, the National Peasant Corporation was organized. On October 4, 1941, the Labor Charter was promulgated. Today, a Family Charter is born. 'This law,' as M. Philippe Renaudin so rightly said, 'does not bring the family into the constitution, but it prepares the way for tomorrow, when constitutional enactments will be reviewed, for the family's admission to the vital bodies of the country.' Families, as legal communities, are coming out of the shadows where they have been relegated since the declaration of human rights." [65] According to Serge Huard, then secretary general for the family and health and coordinator of the preliminary work for this law, "If the family is to be one of the bases for the new State, it must be organized in the State, or the State must be given a familial structure, just as it will have a professional structure." [66] Each commune established a single family association grouping all the families "constituted by marriage and legitimate filiation or adoption, whose head and children are French. . . . In its detailed provisions, the Gounot law had a clearly family character. Effectively, each legitimate French family was considered to be a community. It was represented in the association by its Head, the father, if he was worthy, present, and able to express his will, and by the mother in all other cases." [67] The steering committee for the association of families was elected by family suffrage; in addition to his individual vote, each family head had one vote per living minor child, and one additional vote per group of three children who lived to the age of twenty-one. Family suffrage, the old demand of the most traditionalist factions of the family movement, became a political project that was frequently cited under the French State. William Garcin recommended family suffrage from the municipal to the national level "if we adopt the electoral system," for "the head of the family must be the political representative of his children." [68] Jean Guibal saw the family vote as a rampart against the "fiction of individualism": "We can no longer conceive of the French State with the limits of a man's life or the selfishness of a bachelor. A man who has a family behind him is already a reasonable national intellect; by thinking of the family, he is naturally thinking safety, stability, he is already thinking according to the standard of the French State." [69] The Gounot law reserved a choice position not for the representatives of the associations of large families, but for the heads of large families; the steering committees were effectively to comprise a majority of fathers and mothers with at least three children.

In fact, the central power's share in these new institutions was considerable, for control of the administration was continuous, elections of presidents and members of the executive committees of associations or unions required the approval of the regional delegate of the Commissariat General for the Family or of the Commissariat itself, and the executive officer or the commissaire general were ex-officio members of the steering committees of the departmental unions and the national federation: "Thus, with regard to first-level family associations, the central power, in other words, the active administration, permeated the entire family organization." [70] In a confidential memo to the regional delegates of the Commissariat, Philippe Renaudin, after directing that "you must let the associations establish themselves freely, and give the impression that you are making suggestions," clarified the extent of their powers and the necessity to do something new: "If the currently existing movements want to create a Gounot law association, they may not do so without your approval." He recommended that they make sure that "new men come to work in the movement" and not only "members of traditional family associations," for "it is possible that these new men are ready from the standpoint of the *family State* to devote themselves to protecting the family" and "they must not be turned away." It was therefore a question, "without denigrating the movements presently existing," of "not remaining in the old molds." The Catholic associations of heads of families must not "transform themselves into Gounot law associations, and it is necessary to make sure that their members join individually."[71] This aspect of the issue had not escaped the representatives of the old private associations for the defense of the family, who took note of this unexpected competition between a "private law movement" and "a new semipublic law movement" and wondered about the simultaneous recruitment of these heads of families, new militants, and potential competitors. They responded, a little bitterly but with the masculine sense of sacrifice, by affirming their solidarity with the government: "The sacrifice of certain preferences [not being] to discourage experienced heads of families from placing duty before all else."[72] The Commissariat General for the Family finally succeeded in ridding the family movement of its "dusty" aspect and in giving the word family a dimension that was no longer "inferior to its size," according to the expressions coined by Renaudin. It was a state apparatus that was henceforth preparing itself to control the advances in "climate" and in the "family mystique," and the family association became "one of the bodies, one of the administrative organs of the new State."[73]

The Gounot law was repealed after the liberation and replaced by an order of March 3, 1945, related to the creation of the National Union of Family Associations. Although the new government was inspired by natalist concerns and the defense of family values was very present within the MRP (Mouvement républicain populaire), a centrist party of Catholic faith, the family political order established by the National Revolution was rejected.[74] Family policy became more technical, and the defense of the family no longer appeared as a powerful factor of opposition within the political field.[75] The Gounot associations lost their privilege of semipublic law. The new order based itself on the multiplicity of private associations consolidated into departmental and national unions, a pluralism that opposed the "unity" of the Gounot law, whose "spirit appears incompatible with the restoration of a regime of freedom," according to the preamble of the order of March 1945. The new family representation was henceforth compared to trade union representation. The political left was heavily involved in managing family allowances, and the MRP, fearing that action in favor of families would be lost in an all-powerful social security system, succeeded in seeing that family allowance funds remained separate.[76]

Family policy was surely marked by a certain continuity between 1938 and 1945, a continuity linked to the presence of the same personalities from the pronatalist and familialist movements in the various proceedings during which this policy was constructed during the decade and to the very great influence within the MRP of Social Catholic currents of family action. Yet, the situation I have designated "family imperialism" comprised specific characteristics that prevent this policy from being considered a single moment in a progressive and cumulative movement in favor of the defense of the family or as simply an opportune time for producing technical measures. The historical situation of crisis and monopoly placed all the profamily currents within the ideological sphere of influence of the most traditional among them, who seized on the National Revolution as a prophecy come true to cause a familial political order to come to pass. During a debate between members of the Popular Family Movement during the war, Marcel Viot stated: "If it is true that Vichy duped all the family movements when it established family representation, this was done with the complicity of certain traditional family movements. For the men who were behind it and who prepared the Gounot law were not only politicians. Among them were people from certain family movements who took advantage of the coincidence between their interests as representatives of traditional families and the political power in place. This weighed heavily at the Liberation."[77] It was these groups that directed the preliminary steps for the constitutional construction of the family as a legal person (Gounot law, family vote, outline of a family wage, etc.), providing Vichy's family policy with the eminent function of legitimizing a new order that wanted to sweep away the principles of 1789 and the Republican regime. The total victory of familialism thus produced a context of raised stakes and rigidification that consolidated the competitors of yesterday (pronatalists and familialists, for example, or defenders of popular family interests and old paternal leagues in defense of large families) into a single front of blind conquest and expansion of markets of material and symbolic goods. The silencing of trade unions, of the political forces of the left, of public education, the civic exclusion of communists, Freemasons, and Jews, and the sly progression on the corporatist basis of state anti-Semitism, the public proclamation of an "eternal" feminine vocation against all the rather recent historical realities related to the education and professionalism of women—all worked together to produce an *exceptional familialism linked to an exceptional state,* as witnessed by certain projects conserved in the National Archives.

They include the documents sent to Dr. Sautriau, the chief medical officer and the head of state's representative to the Advisory Committee for the French Family, that proposed a constitutional family charter: "Family institutions must replace everywhere elective institutions founded on the myth of universal suffrage." The Declaration of Human Rights must be "replaced by a new preamble to the new constitution of the French State": "Whereas the family is a natural group that existed prior to civil society; Whereas the family, founded on marriage, constitutes the essential cell of the social edifice; Whereas the commune is a federation of families; Whereas the French nation itself is merely the community of French families; Whereas the State is constituted only by the hierarchy of families and professions federated in the communes . . . , the Marshal of France, head of the French State, decrees that the family based on marriage forms one of the essential bases of the new constitution." The following articles of the draft constitution come from this preamble:

> Article 1: "The family body must be part of all bodies constituted by the State." Article 2: [The size of the commune] "is no longer calculated according to the number of its inhabitants, but according to the number of its 'fires' or 'households making up the communal body of families,' that is, all the French families domiciled in the commune." Article 3: "At least half of the municipal Council will represent the communal body of families." Article 5: "Communal elections will be decided by family suffrage."

The author of this draft concludes, "The Family Revolution will complete the National Revolution and will ensure the establishment of a new French and human order."[78]

This draft seemed to receive wide approval among profamily groups, for it was reproduced in many of the reports in the files kept in the Archives. The same is true for the unanimously received project for a single family association that proposed an organizational chart starting with a "communal council of family heads" and ending with the "head of the State" by way of a "national council of family men,"[79] an institution presented as a "Legion of families"[80] in which one can see an unprecedented form of the single party. The role of women, or rather of "the" woman, to be consistent with the regime's rhetoric, was central to this political project: "The State guarantees the family in its constitution and its authority, as being the necessary basis of the social order and as being indispensable to the well-being of the nation and of the State. In particular, the State recognizes that, *through her life within the home, woman gives the State support,* without which the common good cannot be achieved."[81]

The family order thus conceived did not stop at the family cell. It was constructed as the model of the political order; family virtues and divisions of the family roles functioned as so many metaphors for civic virtues and "true" citizenship, citizenship that is consistent with the "real" and not with the dangerous abstractions of the individualism of the rights of man and "leveling intellectualism." Fathers of large families were the ideal embodiment of the "good" citizen and of "healthy" elements. Thus, in the judiciary, single men or men without children could advance only if they declared themselves ready to accept a position anywhere the government chose to assign them.[82] And the tracts of the Commissariat General for the Family reminded heads of families that they were an elite on which the Marshal was counting to rebuild France.

But it was the representation of a "naturally" hierarchical family order subject to the "natural" authority of the father of the family, where the child would encounter the initial model for all hierarchies and would learn how to integrate himself into a society of orders,[83] that was at the center of the family metaphor for the political and social order, recalling once again that the familialist definitions of feminine subordination had political effects. When he laments the decadence linked with the change from the "family-state" to the "family-school," then to the "family-inn," Inspector Haury sees the source of recovery in the return to the large family, alone capable of constituting a "community": "If this is true, by *force of circumstance,* it will retain something of the State—with a head, the father who works outside, and a soul, the mother who watches over the home, with a collective conscience and morality, an accepted discipline."[84] In March 1943, Abel Bonnard presided over the induction ceremony for the first students of the new leadership training school at Uriage; since the ordered closure on December 27, 1942, of the school of Uriage managed by Dunoyer de Segonzac, the Militia had used its facilities. The inspector for propaganda of the Militia gave a speech in which he equated family community and national community: "The family community, the basis of the national community, has three elements: autocracy, represented by the father; aristocracy, represented by the mother; and democracy, which corresponds to the children. We find this trilogy perfectly transformed into the national trilogy under the monarchy: here, autocracy is the king, aristocracy is the nobility, and democracy is the people. In 1789, we witnessed the revolt of the children against paternal authority and maternal aristocracy."[85] Although the rhetoric is a bit confused, the message is clear, and it invites the eternal minors who essentially need love and authority to deliver themselves over to it. Thus, in the eyes of many ideologues of the regime, the ideal political system placed the relationship between the managing elite and the people under the sign of "tough love." Gustave Thibon put it explicitly: "I believe in the necessity of restoring patriarchal social forms (where more than in the soul of a father are these two things that the people essentially need combined: love and authority?). There is no salvation save in the return to this 'paternalistic' ideology considered by many to be extinct."[86] The countless litanies concerning the paternal figure of the Marshal are consistent with the direct continuity of these political representations.

This paternalistic and, it could be said, maternalistic representation of political and social relations borrows largely from the culture of notables concerned with maintaining professional heredity and from the small-town mentality that Marc Bloch analyzed in *Strange Defeat*. The family model of the regime, and the model of the social relationship between elite and mass that it sketches, harks back to these social and family structures that were untouched or barely touched by the rural exodus, factory work, and the economic necessity of women's work. If anything is extinct, to repeat the expression of Thibon, it is the big city and the Popular Front. In the new social order, women of the elite would have to play an intermediary role between the classes, preaching by example but also acting as teachers of "good" femininity, working to keep the daughters of peasants in the country and encouraging the daughters of workers to recognize their "vocation" as homemaker. They would thus rediscover a role that had been traditionally granted to them since the start of the industrialization that had introduced a threatening confusion into the division of sexual roles.[87] They could revive old institutions for overseeing the popular classes, such as the rural housewife works founded at the turn of the century to fight against the primary school.[88] They could rediscover the function of domesticating peasants previously exercised by the chatelaine: "It is curious to observe the difference in mentality between villages where chatelaines *conscious of their duties* have continued to live and those in which no influence has arrived to counterbalance the ideas of the Popular Front. Between the two there is a world of difference!"[89] Thus, these women of the elite who embodied "good" femininity would, in their own way, contribute to the social peace by educating "the respectable poor,"[90] respectful of the "natural" hierarchies.

The participation of many influential women in this symbolic and practical redivision of masculine and feminine spaces of action, which presented itself as "the order of things" against chaos, gave the National Revolution irreplaceable legitimacy with regard to family politics. By placing the capital stock and the mobilizing potential of the institutions they directed in the service of these politics, they gave the regime the endorsement of Christian feminism and of all the forces with and on which it acted to both recognize and channel feminine aspirations of different ages. The culture of sacrifice, which embraced the state definition of the feminine, was thus easily able to appropriate all these new forms of identification for the role of homemaker. In this sense, the National Revolution fixed a situation that, as a result of the competition and contradictions among the systems of feminine aspirations, including within "Christian feminism" itself, still carried within it unexpected spaces through which more or less living forms of awareness of domination could slip in. Feminine involvement in the National Revolution, like that of the feminine section of the Spanish Phalange cited earlier, is an example of *sociological tragedy.* When the victims of domination become the agents of domination—with a zeal that is probably equaled only by their unconscious resentment of the limitations imposed on them and that they overcame in their own way by becoming "women of action," dedicated to the qualified revival of the definitions imposed concerning the limited place of women in the city—discourses and options congeal and tighten. This tightening, expressed in the language of limitation, of good and evil, becomes the condition of their participation in the power, the condition of their speech in the public space. In a tract of the Équipes et cadres de la France nouvelle, "Civic Role of Women and Girls," we find this striking formulation: "Woman's civic action 'outside.' First, she will have to speak. Under penalty of being silent, she will exchange remarks with others. She will have to say out loud what she thinks sanely to herself." Therefore, "outside," for the common good and in this political-social situation in which she need only say what she has the right to say for all eternity and need only claim her submission, woman may override the Paulist precept: "Let women be silent in meetings, for they are not permitted to speak; let them remain submissive as the law itself commands."[91] To leave the (familial) ghetto without leaving the role (as family mother), to require selflessness (on the private scene), to exist (on the public scene), is a way of sublimating the limitations by becoming the legitimate spokesperson for the necessary limitation. Symbolic violence is at the heart of blind activism. Public life is not open to women but to the "maternal influences" of women, and "outsiders" are co-opted only if they contribute new strength to the dominant norms.[92]

The model was internalized in bodies and in minds, as witnessed by several letters from women sent to Marshal Pétain and conserved —by what chance?—in the National Archives. Young girls wrote to him in a very personal style, just as one would write to a respected parent, to request the rapid creation of the "National Matrimonial Office" they had heard about, to express the anguish of "young middle-class women who are not particularly well-off but who are too well-off to work, particularly since the recent decrees," and for whom marriage "is the only ideal." Or, more simply, to ask him for a husband:

My dear Marshal Pétain,
For some time now I've been telling myself daily that I want to write to my, to our dear Marshal Pétain; today I will put this off

no longer. I am eager, dear Marshal, to show you my gratitude for all the devotion that you give to France, our dear Fatherland. . . . May God keep you with us for a long time and protect you from all dangers and against the malice of men so that France can live again and be reborn stronger than ever. The young Frenchwoman who speaks to you is twenty-eight years old. I will take the liberty of briefly recounting my short life. I lost mother and father at the age of eighteen and nineteen and a half. I remained with two young sisters. . . . Dear Marshal Pétain, since my sisters are mostly grown, I want to establish a home and one day be a Christian and French Mother. . . . I consider you to be my family, and I would be very grateful if you could put me in touch, in contact with one of your dear sons, a soldier or The One you believe suits me the most. I would like an orphan who is not rich, not being so myself. I am anxious to be in my home so that I am no longer lonely and to find support in the one I love, to unite our joys and our sorrows and to move together toward a future that, with the help of God, will be happy and prosperous in the company of our dear children whom we will give to God, to You, dear Marshal, and to France.[93]

7. "NATURAL" HIERARCHIES: SEXUAL PREDESTINATION AND SOCIAL PREDESTINATION

Examining the field of women's education makes it clear that the state definition of a feminine identity subjugated to the family and the reproductive function, the imposition of a legitimate feminine territory plotted using the prohibitions of the culture of sacrifice, and the construction of the family as a political unit were central to the construction of the new political order. Intellectual and practical feminine "aptitudes" were scrutinized by the regime and its ideological allies, resulting in the development of a program of female education distinct from male instruction suited to preserving and fostering the feminine "vocation" for maternity and for taking charge of the interior space; the space of the home and of feelings. Men are related to the sun, the outside, command, the brain and reason; women are related to the moon, the interior, submission, the heart, intuition. There is no competition: hierarchies and inequalities are "natural." Woman's relationship to education, work, and social life is subject to the logic of mythic reason, a dualistic logic that admits only a few exceptions to better confirm the rule.

Viewed from the perspective of the sexual division of the social world, the issue of education belongs to the eschatological register of the National Revolution: women's recent access to secondary and higher education, the lack of sexual differentiation in the primary programs, and the progressive professionalization of women in the social spaces traditionally occupied by men of the middle class ranked high in the inventory of causes of the social "degeneration" that led to chaos and defeat. The recovery, the "disciplined renewal of French thought," to borrow the sinister expression of the Havas agency,[1] therefore depended on restoring a distinction between the masculine and the feminine relationship to the school. How better to establish this distinction than by basing a classification of "tastes," of "gifts," of all those positive and negative qualities linked to anatomical destiny that make Latin and mathematics clearly the business of men on the nature of the two sexes.

For reasons both ideologically similar and strategically diversified, the state's plan for an academic redivision based on the sexual division of the social world mobilized defenders of private Catholic education, influential women under the influence of Christian feminism, and long-standing opponents of the Republican school and its meritocratic ideology, who were relatively close to the doctrines of the Action française. In the name of all old and more recent battles involving the education question with which they identified, the supporters of the National Revolution would rewrite the relationship of women to the school and make old systems of thought concerning the necessary and sufficient education of girls a timely issue. Once again, the crisis situation and its prophetic elaboration produced an ideological crystallization, rigidifying and freezing in place both the classification systems (by once again giving them an eternal nature) and the explanatory schemes (by constructing a system that was ultimately closed on itself).

Analyzing the processes of production of a restrictive discourse concerning women's education leads to the hypothesis that the defense of a "just" education of women and the defense of a "just" education of the masses go hand in hand. The school's sole purpose is to teach women what they need to know to continue to be what they are, from generation to generation, forever and always: charm, domestic arts, management of the middle-class interior where the male elite restores itself, management of the working-class interior where husbands retreat from urban and political promiscuity. To speak of the relationship of women to the school is inseparably to speak of the maintenance and renewal of elites, of the access of the middle and working classes to secondary and higher education, of social mobility through the school, of birth and merit, and of social "deracination." To speak of women's place in the school, and therefore of their place in the social world, is to speak of the place of everyone, man or woman, in the social world and of the school's role in the conquest by each of his or her social place. To define a hierarchical *sexual order* that classifies minds is to reconstruct an eternal model (because it is natural and biologically founded) of a hierarchical *social order* legitimized by the ideology of the *natural gift*. To go against these two orders thus established on the nature of things would be to open the door to all the perversions and perverse effects resulting from the social production of "deracinated individuals," regardless of which sex they belong to.

The ideology of *"true" elites* dear to the regime, which wanted each to best occupy the place to which he or she was socially predestined, made the masculine/feminine opposition concerning education one of the cornerstones of its hierarchical representation of the social order and of the correlative disqualification of social advancement through the school. The biologically "verified" predestination that thus opposed the nature and functions of masculine and feminine learning was conceived of as the inescapable model of all social predestinations that cannot be contravened without risking collapse. Individual action was henceforth limited to preserving traditions in the spirit of Taine's social philosophy illustrated by Barrès's lessons in social morality, *Le Jardin de Bérénice* and *Les Déracinés*. The protagonists of these two books belong to those who accept these "fatalities" that must not be seen, writes Taine, "as abstract formulas, but as living forces mixed with things, present everywhere, acting everywhere, true divinities of the human world, who extend their hand downward to other powers that are masters of matter just as they are masters of spirit, to form together the invisible choir of which the old poets speak, which circulates through things and through which the eternal universe palpitates."[2]

The production of the "eternal feminine" thus crossed paths with the battles between the antagonistic conceptions of the relationships between scholastic order and social order that had made the education issue a political question even before the inauguration of the Republican school. While it presented the opportunity to strengthen the legitimacy of masculine domination at a historical moment when women had won access to secondary and higher education and to the professional spaces this education opened to them, the violence that was deployed must also be related to the recent violence of the political and social debates concerning the school.

The Education War of the 1930s

As we saw earlier, women's real breakthrough into secondary education occurred after the First World War; it was not until 1924, when the increase in female demand for secondary and higher education had become an irreversible social fact, that women's secondary education obtained the same status as men's. In this context, Victor Margueritte's novel, *La Garçonne*, published in 1922, met with extraordinary success in bookstores (three hundred thousand copies were sold the first year and 1 million by 1929) and was the subject of widespread debate in the press.[3] The female protagonist of this novel takes courses at the Sorbonne and, disappointed by her family and her fiancé, acquires social and sexual independence through her job. The extent of the scandal provoked by this book (its author was officially expelled from the Legion of Honor, a singular measure in the history of this institution, and repudiated by the Société des gens de lettres of which he was vice president and from which he resigned) can only be explained by the fact that it went to the very heart of the questions that society was asking about itself and that divided it deeply. Behind the quasi-unanimity of the rather virulent accusations of moral indecency leveled by the press, we can also hear the abruptly liberated condemnation of women's right to education and work at the very moment this right had been earned.[4] As Paul Bourget wrote in 1922 in a reflection on feminism that prefigured the Vichy condemnation of the "individualism" encouraged by the Republican educational system:

> It is as an *individual* that the little patrician takes her seat in the lecture halls of the Sorbonne to gain knowledge and earn degrees. It is as an *individual* that the shorthand typist sits in front of her typewriter to assure an independence that, as a woman of the lower middle class, she would never have dreamed possible before, any more than this other woman would have dreamed of developing a clientele as a doctor or lawyer. We are therefore confronted with one of the consequences of this universal movement that from one end of society to the other results in personal demands. Some ad-

Vichy and the Eternal Feminine ▸ 210

mire this individualism as emancipation and as progress. These are quite naturally feminists and democrats, socialists, even Bolsheviks. Others deplore in this rapid multiplication of individual wills a decrease in this collective sense for which family and nation remain superior expressions. That in individualism there is a threat of anarchy is too obvious.[5]

However, women were not alone in upsetting the relationship between educational order and social order during this period. The interwar period was also haunted by the issue of the democratization of education and by the theme of *déclassement*. In 1917, those who called themselves the Compagnons de l'Université nouvelle, teachers who had become young officers, began at Verdun to question the rigid and hierarchical educational structures. In 1919, they produced a manifesto that proposed to call on everyone to rebuild the country, to demolish the primary/secondary barriers, to offer everyone an educational opportunity regardless of his or her original social milieu by establishing free secondary education and combining primary education and small lycée classes.[6] This program, known as the *école unique* (the single school), gave rise to confrontations concerning the education question during the twenty years following and constituted Vichy's legacy in a key sector of its thought regarding the social order.

The name école unique referred primarily to the establishment of a unified elementary education giving all children the same educational opportunities for entering the secondary system. But for conservatives, the formula quickly came to symbolize a multiform threat to the humanities, to quantitative and qualitative thresholds in a secondary system reserved by definition for a small number, and to private confessional education. In the mind of its detractors, free secondary public education necessarily strengthened the state monopoly over education by diverting the least well-to-do Catholic clientele. As of 1919, in response to these "threats," a Catholic Association of Heads of Families was created along with its magazine, *École et Famille,* which led the fight against this reform project. Spearheaded by Jean Guiraud, editor in chief of *La Croix* and a specialist in education issues, this forum contributed to politicizing the educational options defended by the Compagnons de l'Université nouvelle by interpreting them as an attack against the rights of families concerning educational matters. But Catholics did not have a monopoly over dogmatic rhetoric, and very quickly, radicals and anticlerical professionals such as Alphonse Aulard would in their turn make the école unique a political warhorse, subordinating strictly pedagogical discussions to tactical aims. Under the Cartel des gauches, the politicization of the educational question swept away all chances of any real social and technical debate. In October 1924, the Catholic Association of Heads of Families united eighteen thousand people against the école unique, daughter of the "Atheist State," and, very quickly, General de Castelnau called for the creation of a National Catholic Federation that widely disseminated this propaganda, while Minister for Public Education François Albert spouted grandiloquent tirades against the Jesuits.

In October 1926, Édouard Herriot, minister of public education of the National Union government formed by Poincaré, initiated specific reforms ultimately intended to establish free secondary education and to eliminate the *collèges* (fee-charging municipal secondary schools that competed with the upper primary schools). These measures were ratified in March 1930; in 1933, the seven lycée classes became free. The issues of selection, orientation, and the status of small lycée classes that, in the mind of the Compagnons, were intrinsically linked with free secondary education, were ignored. Under the Popular Front, Jean Zay, the youngest minister in the history of the Third Republic,[7] extended mandatory education to the age of fourteen and prepared a "general statute" for the three orders of education. This statute sought to transform the elementary lycée classes into public schools aligned with the programs of the primary system, to make the certificate of primary studies both the final diploma for the primary system and the entrance examination for the secondary system, and to require all students entering the lycée to take one year of orientation studies to determine the choice of secondary section. "Does not justice demand that, regardless of the point of departure, everyone be able to go as far and as high as his abilities allow him, in the direction he has chosen?" one reads in the preamble of the plan. By a decree of May 1937, the minister began to break down the administrative barriers between primary and secondary school and created orientation classes in some forty institutions. But the war put an immediate stop to this set of reforms. During this period, some professors worried about the number of students who would descend on the lycées and thereby compromise the quality of education. After remaining stable from 1880 to 1930, the number of secondary students skyrocketed, marking the start of what would later be called the "education explosion."[8]

Beginning in 1926, when the plans for the école unique were starting to be implemented, opposition to the measures undertaken and to the social and educational options that subtended them took three main directions. First, the Catholic defense of confessional education encouraged very traditional institutional stances and the creation of new institutions: free secondary education was seen as an "antidemocratic, immoral and antisocial" measure by the feminine contingent of General de Castelnau's National Catholic Federation.[9] In 1930, old-fashioned associations such as the Catholic Association of Heads of Families lost their influence to the new competitor, the Associations of Parents of Students of Independent Education (APEL) that claimed fifty-two thousand subscribers to its publication, *École et Liberté,* in 1933. In 1938, APEL, like the National Catholic Federation, violently opposed the establishment of orientation classes in which it saw a plan "for the mobilization by a totalitarian State, in a Soviet future, of human equipment manufactured by mothers and fathers."[10] It was also in this context that the École des parents, mentioned earlier, was created in 1929. This movement sought to fight against sex education in the lycées based, once again, on the defense of family prerogatives against the educator-state.

A second current of more political reactions attacked these plans and their implementation by defending a closed secondary system, primarily reserved for children of the dominant classes and a few rare, individual exceptions. Maurras found all the measures for bringing the primary and secondary systems closer together "insane." *Le Temps,* which in 1922 wrote that nothing good could come of "mixing manual laborers and intellectuals," for the "elites of the people" would benefit more from a "special and separate" type of education, called on Parliament in 1926 to stop "the demagogic devaluation of secondary education." The direction of the Federation of Associations of Parents of Lycée and Collège Students spoke out in 1930 against the école unique, because the measures it proposed could apply to prestigious lycées like Louis-le-Grand.[11]

A third set of later reactions testified to a change in attitudes, or, more precisely, to the existence of internal discussions that shaded positions and seemed to presage real debates on these problems that were both pedagogical and social. *Le Temps* took an uncharacteristic position in 1937 concerning orientation classes, which, it acknowledged, took parents' rights into consideration; Jean Zay had stated that parents would always have the right to reject an orientation. Certain Catholic currents such as the Dominicans, who spoke through *La Vie intellectuelle* and *Sept,* believed that the école unique was a step toward social justice, and, like *Esprit* and Daniel-Rops, were in favor of orientation classes. Even APEL was divided, as its president, Philippe de Las Cases, and his rather progressive Lille section adopted a somewhat more conciliatory position than the entire movement concerning orientation classes.[12] During these same years, the relations between Church and state had been relaxed, and the issue of state assistance for private confessional education had also begun to be considered in more serene fashion.[13]

Despite this softening from 1938 to 1939, Vichy's legacy concerning education was first and foremost that of a battlefield deeply scarred during the interwar period by confrontations specific to the political field and by the Church/state opposition. It is not without interest that the *conflict between family rights and state rights* had been one of the hottest issues of the debate concerning the école unique. To view the school as a threat to the family was at the same time and inseparably to defend confessional education, which presented itself as the "school of families,"[14] and to defend the primacy of the family heritage of positions and dispositions that the school has no other function than to uphold, excluding from its prestigious sections those who are not socially predestined to enter them. The symbolic place of women was central to this debate. Metaphorically, the relationship of women to the school made it possible to posit and impose all the "natural" inequalities between individuals and the school. Concretely, the defense of woman and the family as educator made it possible to privilege social selection over educational selection. And it was probably not an accident that antifeminism returned in force during the 1930s, the most lively period of clashes concerning educational reform. Girls were not inconsequential in the "educational explosion" and in the threats that it leveled against the elitism of the secondary school, both because they contributed to the increase in students and because they risked departing from the role of mother as educator.

The Inspiration behind the Vichy Conception of the School

The establishment of the National Revolution led to a new hardening and alignment of all the positions against everything involving the école unique program. This was marked by unanimistic violence focused on searching for a scapegoat, and the nuances that began to mark the debate, including among opponents during the period immediately before the war, were lost. This designation of the guilty led in particular to a dogged attack on primary education,[15] its union members, its pacifists, its communists, its Freemasons, its Jews, its feminists, its "female muzhiks," as Jean Ybarnégaray called them—in short, all the bad teachers. It even succeeded in repressing the price paid by the primary teaching profession during the war of 1914. Pétain himself told Ambassador Bullitt in July 1940 that France lost the war because the reserve officers had had socialist teachers.[16] In fact, the great majority of the thinkers and those responsible for education under the National Revolution belonged to the most conservative and the most aggressive current of thought concerning the school during the 1930s, the Cercle Fustel-de-Coulanges.[17] This organization, created by the Action française, was a laboratory of antidemocratic ideas concerning education, ideas that would be embodied in the educational policy of the French State and, more particularly, in its conception of the relationship between educational order and social order, between social reproduction and educational meritocracy.

The first meetings of the founders of the Cercle took place in 1926 to fight against the école unique project, the "decadence" of classical studies, free secondary education, and the "establishment of State control over all of French education."[18] Its originator, Henri Boegner, was a professor of literature in Mulhouse, then in Paris, born into a Protestant family with a Republican tradition who converted to Catholicism and was won over by Maurrasism. He strove to unite "members of education *of French origin*" (as the notice of creation of the Cercle says on the inside cover page of the first *Cahier*), writers, academics, students, future teachers of the École Normale d'Auteuil, male teacher training students of Ulm, and female teacher training students of Sèvres who attended Maurras's lectures. Further, he sought to disseminate the ideas of the Action française in the academic world and to establish "the collaboration of school, family, and the major institutions of national, regional, and corporative life for the good of the child and the greatness of France."[19] The Cercle, officially founded in 1928, published a review and organized banquets presided over by intellectual, political, and military personalities whose lectures were reprinted in the *Cahiers*. Among them were Marshal Lyautey, General Weygand (the Cercle wanted to work to bring the university and the army closer together), the academics Abel Bonnard, André Bellessort, and Louis Bertrand, the writer Daniel Halévy, and Henri Massis. The Cercle claimed 1,400 members in 1934 and drew 250 people to its annual banquets, which were Parisian events. The president and the secretary of the Cercle were members of the Study Commission for Youth of the Conseil national, where they were responsible for establishing the "principles of a civic education," and a number of active members had educational responsibilities under Vichy: Albert Rivaud and Abel Bonnard were the first and last ministers of national education of the French State; René Gillouin and Henri Massis were advisors to Pétain; Serge Jeanneret[20] was future assistant chief of staff in Abel Bonnard's office; and Bernard Faÿ replaced Julien Cain as deputy head of the National Library.[21]

In June 1935, the Cercle's banquet was presided over by Henri Massis, who, in 1913 using the pseudonym Agathon, had published a survey with Alfred de Tarde concerning "elite youth," the awakening of the "national instinct," and the "Catholic renaissance"; they attacked the parliamentary regime, Republican education policy, the Sorbonne, "which includes so many cosmopolitan elements," and "primary anarchy."[22] In opposition to internationalism and pacifism, against the secular morality of the professors of the Sorbonne, and particularly of Durkheim, Massis-Agathon praised the "taste for action," the "French rebirth," the "cult of bellicose virtues," and the "Latin idealism" of the young people of the time whose testimony he solicited. In doing so he prefigured all the confrontations that would mark the interwar period and contributed to nurturing the rejection of all processes for democratizing the secondary system, which the Fustel circle would later make its credo. Thus in Agathon's survey we read this criticism of the students of the modern sections of lycées whose recruitment was known to be less middle-class: "We could never make friends (says a *bachelier*) with the students of the modern section. What distanced them was the impossibility of having an elevated conversation in their presence, one of those conversations among young people that is nourished by enthusiastic ideas and feelings. They were only ever moved by an immediate, practical result. Almost all of them affected an *arrivisme* without nobility."[23] It was this same "arrivisme without nobility," this taste for "immediate results" that conservative educational thinkers condemned in girls who ventured into the secondary system and who had been kept so belatedly in a cut-rate modern section that did not even prepare them for the baccalaureate. Armed with classical culture that "imparts to the conscience some form of disinterestedness," the young elite of the day, dear to Massis, also had a taste for action itself and wanted to build an "order of moral standards" marked, he stressed, by the "precocious concern for a career" and "the acceptance, from early youth, of the responsibilities of marriage and family." The "tendency toward the equality of the sexes" thus had the effect of inciting vocations among young family men freed from an "attitude of analysis and licentiousness" to discover the force of "natural feelings."[24] This love life of the "true" elites would become standard under the National Revolution, just as the critique of intellectualism and the critique of immorality would be intimately linked in the process of *national reeducation* that subtended its education project.

The Cercle Fustel-de-Coulanges was the direct heir, through the Action française and theoreticians like Massis, to the old anti-Republican tradition of criticizing the new Sorbonne—personified in its eyes by Lavisse, Durkheim, and Seignobos, Kantian philosophy, intellectual internationalism, and sociology, the moral sciences taught in the teacher training colleges, and the "primary" "pretension" of the primary school proponents[25]—that expressed itself with such force at the turn of the century. During the 1930s, the Cercle completely questioned the Republican concept of education since Condorcet, in which one finds all the guidelines for the reforms undertaken by Vichy. Thus, its legacy came from afar. At the annual banquet of 1932, presided over by Marshal Lyautey, Louis Dunoyer, the president of the circle and a professor of science at the Sorbonne, was applauded when he cried: "In the Cercle Fustel-de-Coulanges, we say: Democracy, there's the enemy."[26] And Henri Boegner wrote that intelligence and democracy were incompatible, the first being fatally sacrificed to the second.[27] The école unique was quite obviously at the heart of these attacks, as it was "born of a cloud — Equality—ultimately inspired by a rather base sentiment—Envy." To fight against the "primary philosophy," "revived by the teaching of sociology," which defends the equality of opportunities, one author proposed that elementary school teachers henceforth receive their "general education" in lycées, in a type of "teacher training section" close to Latin-sciences, to experience the beneficial influence of the humanities on social judgment.[28] Ultimately, the spirit of enjoyment (in the very political sense of skipping social steps) was already stigmatized and its filiation well traced: "It took the individualist philosophy of the Rights of Man separated from his Duties for people who wanted to enjoy from the first generation what in the past it prepared and ripened for two or three generations to tend toward a negative leveling of all discipline."[29]

From 1932 to 1939, the Cercle increased its contacts with officials, and Pétain became one of its heroes: "His speech at the Banquet of the *Revue des deux mondes* in 1934 had been devoted to the problem of education. In it he cited ideas that were very close to ours." Having met General Weygand, the secretary of the Cercle was introduced to Pétain, with whom he had two lengthy meetings in 1936. Pétain's article was commented on during a banquet and its themes were widely disseminated by the Cercle.[30] In this article, Pétain defended a "true system of national education" based on the "tightening of bonds between the school and the army" to "establish the charter of patriotic education in school" and to "spell out and establish the duties of all." If this attack against the school, taken over a bit later by Weygand, got such a response, it was because it occurred at the very time Pétain was the hero of the press campaign promoting his candidacy for the position of savior-dictator. But the Marshal's interest in national education was quite real, and he would have preferred to take over the Ministry of Public Education rather than the Ministry of War in the Doumergue government in 1934: "I'll deal with Communist schoolmasters," he said.[31] After the defeat, the officers of the "armistice army" tolerated by the Occupier subscribed to this tradition, defending, after Lyautey,[32] the idea that the school and the army had the same function — to train young people — and must work together. The generals monitored and commented on Vichy's successive educational reforms, and their insistence on the need for moral regeneration conducted jointly with activities concerning the school allowed them to give special weight to the thesis of the moral causes of the defeat, leaving its military causes in obscurity. The Chantiers de la Jeunesse were one expression of this investment through which the army claimed to be the extension of the school and the veritable "school of character" accompanied by a critique of intellectualism, of the university, of the école unique, of female education, and of elementary school teachers. They welcomed the return of a school that must not only instruct with an eye toward individualism but "adapt young people to the family, to work, to the community."[33]

In *Comment élever nos fils?* published in 1937, General Weygand had already sketched out the program for this scholastic reeducation under the patronage of officer-educators. Girls are absent both from the content and the title of the work, which suggests the educational place the new order would assign to them: "France does not have a real national education system. A great voice was raised to say this, the voice of a leader of men, humane and firm, Marshal Pétain, who, by restoring the morale of our army in 1917, showed himself to be without a doubt the greatest educator of our time." For Weygand, *education and instruction are inseparable,* because, as Le Play said, it is not so much a question of training men "to be tradesmen as having them practice a man's trade": "Instruction without education would be worth nothing, whereas education even without instruction would remain profitable for the common good." This primacy of education must inspire the "collaboration of the schoolteacher and the officer" to restore to honor "the respect for authority," ridiculed by the civil service unions haunted by the class struggle, to develop "the moral value of manual labor," and to train true elites, for "little by little France is watching its elites sink into mediocrity through equalization from below." The primacy of education over instruction ("the dissemination of knowledge does not improve man") makes it possible to reposit the disastrous notion of the equality of opportunities in favor of that ultimate equality shared by family men: "Equality is being pursued in the material order where it is a chimera, and one forgets to seek it in the moral order which alone can procure it: in the most modest setting, the head of the family, who a few moments ago was merely a *minuscule cog* in a factory or in an administration, can, once he returns home, become *the equal of a prince* in accomplishing his duties vis-à-vis his children and in the satisfaction he will derive from this."[34] In this conception, stemming from a long right-wing tradition, of the relationship between educational order and social order that sees instruction separated from education as a factor of demoralization, it is ultimately the "natural" and "eternal" family hierarchy and the preeminence of the family over the school that, by putting the school back in its place, would make it possible to put everyone back in his social place and to put women back in the place they never should have left.

The Fustel Circle's involvement in the National Revolution was immediate and unhesitating, which is not surprising if one takes seriously the idea that, for this group, real educational reform could be accomplished only in the context of complete political upheaval.[35] For its directors, although passionately interested in military honor, the reform of the school was equal to resisting the Occupier: "When, therefore, the day after the crushing defeat, Marshal Pétain invited the French to 'draw all of its fruit from the calamity,' we answered his call, which seemed to arm us for two essential tasks. 1. To show young people, consumed by the desire to wash away the shame of the defeat, other ways of serving France than exciting through vain gestures the ferocity of a vanquisher who was absolute master of a disarmed population. 2. To initiate the major reforms that French education had been awaiting for a century."[36]

An Elitist Educational Policy

Reforming national education was one of the regime's priority objectives. It was on the agenda at Vichy as early as July 4, 1940, during the height of the Mers el-Kébir drama,[37] and in his "Social Policy of Education," which appeared in the *Revue des deux mondes* on August 15, 1940, Marshal Pétain disclosed its principles: "There was a profound illusion at the basis of our educational system: it was to believe that it suffices to instruct minds in order to form hearts and to temper characters. Nothing is more false and more dangerous than this idea. . . . You know this well, you parents who are reading this: a well-raised child is not produced without vigilant use, both intransigent and tender, of family authority. School discipline should support family discipline. . . . We are committed to destroying the disastrous prestige of a purely bookish pseudoculture, councilor of laziness and generator of uselessness." Therefore, the primary school had to be reorganized "according to simplified programs, stripped of the encyclopedic and theoretical character that turned them away from their true objective," and a larger place had to be made there for the manual arts, "whose educational value is too often misunderstood." For Pétain, the école unique "was a lie among many others; behind the appearance of unity it was a school of division, of social struggle, of national destruction. We who are horrified at lies, we shall undertake to establish for you, for France, the true École Unique; *the one that will put all Frenchmen and Frenchwomen in their place,* in the service of France; the one that, granting them all freedoms *compatible with the necessary authority* and granting them all equalities *compatible with an indispensable hierarchy,* will make all French men and women servants of a single faith." [38]

Between 1940 and 1944, the educational policy was torn between contradictory priorities defended by different public figures—or opposed by them, as demonstrated, for example, by the rivalry and divergent opinions concerning the Church-state relationship of Ministers Jacques Chevalier and Jérôme Carcopino. It was subject to pressures from the Occupier, which imposed Abel Bonnard in April 1942; it was also deeply marked by the issue of private confessional education, and greatly affected by the anti-Semitic purge. As J. A. D. Long demonstrates, Vichy's educational history also shows that the regime was not monolithic, but made up of conflicting groups and interests, rivalries, resentments, and cliques that gave themselves free rein in a situation that opened the way to power struggles governed by new rules. Nevertheless, the major educational options of the National Revolution reprised the conservative positions that were expressed before the war. Their targets too were the école unique and the "devaluation" of the secondary system; primary "anarchy"; the separation of education and instruction that provided dangerous weapons to newcomers to knowledge and competed with the educational power of the family on the public and the private scene; and the scholastic certification of social qualifications that tended to impose an educational method for reproducing the dominators and encouraging the dominated to skip steps and to blind themselves to the limits of an assimilation that would bear the mark of "envy," of "egotism," of "individualism," all the stigmas of deracination. All these themes appear in Pétain's text. His anti-intellectualism and his questioning of instruction in favor of moral education, as these were articulated in his defense of the Croix de Feu's platform between the two rounds of elections in 1936, are also evident: "The Croix de Feu represent one of the healthiest elements in this country. They want to defend the family. I approve of that. Everything stems from it. . . . I also see that the Croix de Feu occupy themselves with the moral and spiritual improvement of youth. You know that this is an idea I have held for a long time. One can make nothing of a nation that has no soul. It is up to our schoolmasters and our university teachers to forge a soul for the nation. We do not ask them to make our children into learned men. We ask them to make them into men, into Frenchmen."[39]

Among the important reforms—in addition to political, union, and racial purification and the dissolution of all civil servant associations[40]—that were consistent with these ideological options, the following are primary: the elimination of elementary teacher training colleges, those "evil seminaries of democracy,"[41] and the reform of the departmental boards of primary education and of the second cycle of the upper primary system taken over by secondary education, all measures intended to fight against the dangerous "primary school spirit," a bastion of the Republican educational ideal; the reestablishment of fee-paying secondary education starting with the third-level class; the return to the primacy of Latin and literature over mathematics; the reestablishment of elementary classes in the lycées that aimed to restore the elitism of the secondary system;[42] and the establishment of separate manual arts programs for the city and the country, for boys and girls, "the 'enlightened citizens' (of the Third Republic) giving way to members of unlike communities," according to Robert Paxton.

Le Temps justified the reforms by tracing this history of the threat represented by the école unique, a threat that was finally eliminated: "The true plan of its initiators was to create alongside classic and traditionalist 'bourgeois' secondary education an extended primary education that was intended to blend into the modern secondary education, or rather to absorb it; it was a question of building a 'bridge' between primary education strictly speaking and higher education. This class instruction was naturally supposed to eliminate traditional secondary education in the end. The École unique, when all is said and done, was first of all a *revolutionary war machine*."[43] The political stakes of educational reform are clearly evident in this commentary. There must be no "bridge" between primary and higher education, and the lycée must remain " 'bourgeois,' classical, and traditionalist." The elimination of teacher training colleges and the obligation for future primary school teachers to take the baccalaureate exam were supposed to put an end to the political culture specific to primary education: "From his direct or indirect familiarity with the humanities, the primary school teacher will draw this spirit of wisdom and tolerance bequeathed to us by the masters of antiquity. A disastrous moral divorce, which was threatening to spread, will thus be avoided. A moral divorce that was at the same time a social divorce."[44]

To the complex debates of 1935 concerning the école unique, in which the positions of the initial opponents were characterized by a recognition of the rise in the demand for education, and for the progressive Catholic currents by a concern for increased social justice, Vichy once again provided simple answers. *Among these simple answers was the necessary and sufficient relationship of girls to the school.* The social order must follow the order of the body: man's body, woman's body, middle-class, worker, or peasant's body, depository body of the "true" apprenticeship, that which is not learned in school but through accepting one's place in the lineage, the heir letting himself inherit— the "true" elite—and the others not letting themselves be taken in by the mirages of social deracination. As Gustave Thibon said, after Barrès, social equality is a fatal illusion: "From the equality of *souls* before God, one also draws the equality of the *members of society* among themselves. Christian egalitarianism, founded on love that elevates, implies the *surpassing* of natural inequalities; democratic egalitarianism, founded on envy that debases, consists in their *negation*."[45] The feminine version of deracination, of "envy," this master word of Vichy's social philosophy, is the education-professionalization of women that led them to "deny" their biological "destiny" instead of "surpassing" it by slipping into the symbolic and practical molds of the "culture of sacrifice."

Fellow travelers of the Action française such as René Benjamin, Albert Rivaud, and Abel Bonnard, who were concerned about the issue of education and who participated in developing the educational project of the Cercle Fustel-de-Coulanges that the Vichy government worked to implement, did not disassociate their condemnation of female education from their attacks on the "primary system," from their condemnation of sociology personified by Durkheim, and from their defense of the elitism of the secondary system. The *feminine education issue was thus clearly a political issue,* as women were quite "naturally" able to become examples of the bad social use of education, the one that questions all predestinations.

In 1941, René Benjamin published *Vérités et Rêveries sur l'éducation. La Revue universelle* printed large excerpts from this work the same year, thereby conferring on this text the status of a manifesto for reorganizing education. Opposed to the "primary school mentality," Freemasons, sociology, Jews, and science, and in favor of the humanities, home schooling of children until the age of twelve, a fee-paying secondary system, and "mystery," this work traces the alarming panorama of the ravages wrought by the "invasion" of the secondary system by those who had no "vocation" to enter it and, more particularly, by female secondary education. It is therefore an exemplary expression of the form of condemnation of the school of the Republic that jumbled together the defense of Latin and of an elitist secondary system with the condemnation of "outsiders," primary school students, women, and Jews: "We must seriously discourage these hoards of schoolchildren from rushing toward the secondary system. Let us dare to say that this education must be *privileged.*" To avoid producing "failures, embittered youths and rioters," we must restore "disinterestedness" to secondary studies. We must cultivate only students who have "no concern for the future," "no fear of living":

> This fear has corrupted the meaning of studies over these last few years, and it is this fear that casts unfortunate young girls into this hell alongside unfortunate boys. . . . I want to express what pity I have had for these fathers who solemnly confided in me: "I can die tomorrow. I wanted my daughter to have her baccalaure-

ate degree, a bachelor's degree, her teacher qualification, her doctorate. At least she won't die of hunger." With serious airs, what scatterbrains! An old doctor who had been there to see (he is attached to police headquarters) told me recently: "In Paris there are three hundred qualified female lawyers who are selling themselves on the streets!" . . . Well done! Here is an unexpected result that is laughable! Oh, no one is laughing at prostitution. They are laughing about how the law has gone astray, and while recalling these family men so sure of themselves. They are content to poison and weaken their daughters. They poison her with useless notions. They weaken her, which is culpable, before approaching marriage, which is a joy to her the first day but a trial thereafter. We have to think twice before educating girls. To give them all the sciences without the rule for keeping them under control is to load them with explosives. I will not offend anyone by saying that these are fragile creatures: it would be better to protect their nerves. It is thanks to these nerves that [girls] assimilate so well and get ahead of boys; but it is these same nerves, prematurely worn down, that will cause them to lead crazy lives and make these same boys crazy. And it is studying that will have accelerated this madness. . . . The perfect sense of life (and that is the very summit of culture) must come to young girls through other processes than to young men. A girl must first and foremost *be the double of her mother,* in the home and in the family, that is essential.[46]

Every word of this text deserves commentary, for the quasi-totality of the agendas concerning feminine nature and the legitimate feminine spaces under the French State are united here in a minimum of space. Benjamin first clearly condemns in its turn the "convulsed feminism" on which, twenty years earlier, Joseph Barthélemy had heaped opprobrium: "It is not my intention to dwell on the instruction of girls. This is a subject where tempers flare too easily. It is impossible to say anything true on this subject. One is immediately surrounded by vehement women who are ready to scratch your eyes out." The psychiatric metaphor that allows medical expertise to be convoked to the court of history and the assimilation of the certified female lawyers to prostitutes working the streets immediately evoke the opinions of conservative thinkers about the leaders of the feminist movement. Because a large percentage of them were academics and particularly law school graduates (one of the most famous among them, Maria Vérone, was a lawyer), these leaders were often branded as prostitutes, unbalanced individuals, and half-wits. Benjamin never does more than give a harsh version, in a moment of revenge, of the opposition between the two models of feminine identity that opposed each other even over the central issue of the education-professionalization of women: lawyers, doctors, academics, always suspected of immorality and psychic imbalance, or mothers of families who entered the public space only in the name of the defense of mothers and family. This text subjects women to the expertise of those who are presented as their natural mentors—elderly doctors tied to the morals police—and warns of the explosion, always to be feared, of the overflow specific to this sex and the fatal link that it has with madness. Prematurely worn down by intellectual work, like prostitutes used up by sexual work, educated women must disappear in favor of the "eternal feminine." Girls should be the eternal "doubles" of their mothers. Education that "poisons" girls and "makes them anemic" ultimately compromises their sole legitimate activity, that of reproduction. To conclude his remarks, Benjamin offers the example of India, where he sees the model of sexual division after his own heart: "I would be quite willing to think as the Hindus that woman is more noble than man, and that it is this nobility that must be cultivated instead of inculcating in her notions of chemistry. If you have a daughter, instead of having her write a thesis, prepare her for her task, which is to help a man and to refine him."[47] Évelyne Sulle-rot points out the echo and the revolt caused by this condemnation of the prostitution of law school graduates under the Occupation when she herself was still a young lycée student: "Our neighbor called me into her kitchen to show me this article, 'you whose head is always in your Latin and Greek dictionaries.' I returned to the house bewildered and asked my mother what it meant to 'walk the streets.' . . . That evening, she gave me a brief complement to my sex education, but I learned above all that it was necessary to defend intelligence at any cost against this tide of debasing lies, and that at the age of fifteen a schoolgirl could, in her own way, be in the front line of resistance."[48]

But the medical metaphor does not only speak of the order of bodies; it also speaks of social order. "To give knowledge without the rule for keeping it under control" and, at the same time, to load "fragile" beings with "explosives," to use Benjamin's expressions, is quite exactly what conservatives accused mandatory Republican education of doing at the end of the nineteenth century: "Our fathers would not have understood how anyone could claim to raise a child without educating him, but they would not have been any more receptive to the suggestion that the child be educated without being raised, that is, that he *be handed a weapon* without any warning as to when, in which cases, and especially *with what precautions* he might use it."[49] Close to the Action française, a friend of Léon Daudet, and an admirer of Maurras, to whom he would dedicate a glorified portrait (*Charles Maurras, ce fils de la mer*), René Benjamin was in a direct line with those who vehemently attacked the Republican school at the turn of the century with polemical essays of great violence, such as *La Farce de la Sorbonne* (1921) and *Aliborons et Démagogues* (1927). During the interwar period, he aroused the indignation and anger of the primary teaching profession and of defenders of the Republican educational project by increasing his lectures on the "primary peril," during which he sometimes took advantage of the strong-arm support of local royalist groups to prevent protesters from expressing themselves.[50] Defining primary students as the "nouveaux riches of intelligence," "intoxicated" like "grape harvesters who get drunk without having drunk anything," he naturally assumed the tone of the psychiatric expert when, attacking female elementary school teachers, he drew the portrait of a female convention participant who came from the Basses-Pyrénées. The "nervousness," the "stammering," the "nervous laugh" of the speaker led him to conclude that "women are weak, they are not made for meetings, and that female militants are disturbing."[51] To speak about school women and women at school allowed conservative ideologues to introduce this dimension of insanity into their criticism of the school that is the basis for prophetic rhetoric.

In 1926, Abel Bonnard, an activist of the Fustel Circle, had written *Éloge de l'ignorance,* in which he associated the "danger of learning" for men of the people and for women. Bonnard rehabilitated the ignorance of simple minds "firmly established in their place, patriarchs and magistrates in their families, old women devoted to caring for the home like obscure priestesses." Against this happy ignorance stood the "barbarism of knowledge," the "public fountains of instruction," and those "militias of schoolteachers" who want "to prove to inferiors that inferiority does not exist, that there is no difference between men but the circumstances in which they have been placed and that their aptitudes are equal." Women exemplified what he called the confusion of the era:

> The way in which some are attracted to the vocabulary of the sciences reminds us of the greed with which the girls of savage tribes throw themselves on the shoddy goods a foreign merchant spreads out before their eyes. . . . Most women study provided only that they can profit *right away*. School jargon exerts such an attraction on them that it prevents them from going to the heart of what it covers. Even in studying, they do not escape *their nerves*. They need dramatic events, fits of giddiness, swoons. Precision bores them: they are Baccantes of knowledge. . . . Sad, weary, uncertain, and still chatty, they can *serve as a sign* of the immense confusion of their time and, despite the extreme difference in conditions and appearances, they cannot help but recall the *poor disorganized worker reader* I spoke about earlier.[52]

Appointed minister of national education in the Laval ministry in April 1942, Bonnard, associated with the team of the Fascist weekly *Je suis partout* since 1936, defended the idea of an elite with "character" and condemned "the abject eroticism spread among us in these last few years," a mix of eighteenth-century smuttiness and "heavy Jewish sensuality."[53] With the same vigor, Agathon-Massis had denounced the "arrivisme without nobility" of the students of the modern sections, newcomers to the secondary system, and praised the vocation of young family men witnessed by those who, in his eyes, constituted the "elite youth," freed both from "the spirit of analysis and licentiousness." Just so, Bonnard in his turn in May 1942 defended the ideal couple of the National Revolution, the unified criticism of intellectualism and immorality, once again allowing the establishment of a "healthy" social order: "Henceforth let there reign among the Young Men and the Young Women of our France this frank and gay camaraderie, without prudishness and without equivocation, that excludes all unauthorized familiarities and does not allow any other love than that which will loyally unite spouses."[54]

True elites marry young, and the feminine form of altruism is disinterestedness with respect to all forms of "immediate profit," those that pervert the "proper" use of secondary education. As "woman is more noble than man," according to Benjamin, who slips easily into the old Catholic rhetoric of the ennoblement of feminine nature that founds feminine subjugation, she can exemplify, for all newcomers to secondary education hungry for immediate pleasures, social patience, the primary condition for the "proper" use of knowledge, that "explosive" that must be handled carefully. Let them be content with what they have for all eternity: an "instinct" that puts them in communication with nature (similar in this to genuine "naïfs," the philosopher peasants and artisans dear to Bonnard, Pourrat, and Thibon, whose thoughts reflect the mirror of the seasons) and shelters them from "envy," the capital sin that democracy bears within itself: "We remain a bit disappointed to see the woman withering away in them, the more they study. The essence of their nature is not to know but to feel. What distinguishes them is that they have retained their instinct. They are the mirrors of the sky, the sisters of the clouds. One sees in their eyes what the weather will be like and, when they stretch out their arm to pick up their coat, it seems as if their gesture will draw in the entire landscape."[55]

A Subculture of Female Education

In the field of national education, the accession to power of a National Revolution government mobilized supporters *in a totally new way* because the Republican school, and more particularly primary education, were severely condemned, muzzled, and brought into line. These were supporters of an educational order that privileged education over instruction ("character" over "mind," as Marshal Pétain put it), family over school, an elitist secondary system in which the humanities prevailed over plans for democratizing education united under the term école unique, and all those who fought for the state-recognized and -guaranteed parity of private religious education and public education. Many different interests converged to support the education project of the National Revolution. The age and intensity of the battles that marked the university field since the 1880s, the political charge of the national educational options during the

1930s, the competition, constantly resumed and renewed, between the Church and the state, the crisis situation and the arrival of a strong right-wing power that silenced the adversaries of yesterday—these would contribute to hardening positions and to encouraging raised stakes. Confronted with the antisecular campaign developed by *La Croix* beginning in July 1940 that called for the purification of primary education, Paul Baudouin lamented to Cardinal Gerlier the action of certain clergy: "I told the Cardinal that I thought this attitude was dangerous, that at any cost, it was necessary that this situation not appear to be payback either by the Church or by people of the Church."[56] The assessment of the advantages of the situation drawn up by Paul Claudel in his journal on July 6, 1940, is exemplary of these avenging excesses: "France has been delivered after sixty years from the yoke of the anti-Catholic Radical party (teachers, lawyers, Jews, and Freemasons). The new Government invokes God and gives La Grande Chartreuse back to the monks. There is hope of being delivered from universal suffrage and parliamentarianism and also from the evil and stupid domination of teachers who, during the last war, covered themselves with shame. Restoration of authority."[57] We are clearly in the realm of "national reeducation," as suggested by an editorial in *Le Temps* that betrayed the unconscious of the regime's educational reform, an unconscious weighted with history in which female reeducation occupied a choice place: "For education, the first thing to do most likely is to give it back its integrity. It was being poured out in streams like money weakened by inflation. Each year we saw an alarming increase in the number of ignorant baccalaureate and bachelor degree recipients thrown into an impasse by a futile diploma. A strict raising of the level of studies should make true culture valuable again. At the same time, an educational organization in which almost everything needs to be set up must open paths to all occupations and all horizons for young people who deserve better, through their character and their aptitudes, rather than producing failed 'intellectuals.'" Thus, in the primary school, little girls should not all be raised "as if they were to be postmistresses and all boys as if they were to be future railroad employees. We need housewives, laborers, and artisans." Education must take precedence over instruction, for "we need to train men for whom the most natural attitude is no longer hands in their pockets, shuffling feet, and a cigarette butt stuck to their lip. We need to find the French woman again—she is not so far away, and the model has not been lost—who, up early in her little house, makes man's life more pleasant through the order and thrift she brings to it."[58]

A *culture of feminine education,* a cartography of legitimately feminine aptitudes and intellectual territories, and a demarcation of authorized feminine professional spaces was thus "invented" under the Vichy regime at the intersection of all these inherited struggles. Even though the question of the masculine-feminine relationship was central to its vision of restoring the order of the social world, the French State would never have succeeded in developing the rhetoric of this particular exclusion and in fleshing it out solely through the action of its official services. The work of imposing an "exact" definition of women's relationship to the school and to knowledge and the symbolic violence that it produced were largely the result of the identification with this new order of values of a vast set of institutions that had long been involved in defending family education and the "second family," that is, private education, against the state monopoly over lay education. Ultimately, it is difficult to trace the paternity of this or that educational project aiming to distinguish girls' from boys' education, because the offers of service, the reform proposals, the suggestions for implementation, the adaptation of old classifications and old institutions to contemporary tastes, suddenly presented as the prefiguring of this new golden age, preceded, accompanied, and followed the slightest proposals of the ministries involved. For women of the elite as for women of the people, and for women of the elite who educated women of the people, the culture of sacrifice had at the ready an inexhaustible stock of images of necessary and sufficient feminine knowledge and of the proper feminine use of knowledge.

Léontine Zanta was an influential Catholic intellectual, the first French woman to receive a doctorate in philosophy for a thesis defended in 1914 on *La Renaissance du stoïcisme au XVIe siècle,* a theoretician of "Christian feminism" who published *Psychologie du féminisme* in 1922. In 1941 she called the female students of the prewar years back to the Pétainist family order: "Let our young female intellectuals understand this and loyally examine their conscience. . . . I believe that many of them, if they are sincere and loyal, . . . will admit that they wanted to assure their future situation if they didn't marry, since they had not found a husband to their taste or because they were horrified by household work . . . , which means that the poor things, in their blindness or their obliviousness, did not see that this was merely self-ishness, culpable individualism, and that it was this sickness that was killing France." Today we need to "accept the challenge" and look life "squarely in the face with the pure eyes and direct gaze of our Maid of Lorraine. It is up to you, as it was up to her more than five centuries ago, to save France." To once again become the heroines of the national recovery, women in 1940 had only to make their education bear fruit at home: "We are not telling you to give it up, but to give it to your husband, for whom you can be the intelligent coworker, and to your children. Have the courage to endure and be patient; our Leader also advises you to do this and, before criticizing it, act; action will show your true worth more than all your diplomas."[59]

In secondary education, which more or less concerned only young middle-class girls, the decree of August 15, 1941, of the Carcopino re-form produced little upheaval except to specify in its Article 4 that "the education of girls comprises special disciplines that *conform to their aptitudes and to their role:* in correlation, the programs of other disci-plines have been lightened." However, in the baccalaureate exams there were only two special exams for girls for the oral portion and among the elective exams, music and home economics, whereas as an elective exam boys had a second mathematics exam. The manda-tory written and oral sections were the same for both sexes in all the sections for the two baccalaureate diplomas. Until the final year of secondary education, girls had one hour less of exercise replaced by one hour of home economics. In philosophy and mathematics classes, the schedules for the different disciplines were strictly identical, the only difference being the mandatory hour of home economics for girls.[60] In the letter to the Marshal in which he presented this law, Carcopino states: "Girls will receive a special education suited to their dispositions and to their role that gives special attention to sewing, cooking, hygiene, and child care."[61] In its commentary on the reform of girls' secondary education, *Le Temps* designated music and home economics "education of feminine discipline" and stated: "The intel-lectual disciplines will be adjusted by *tempering equality* [the expression makes you dream] with boys by doing away with scientific equality in the next-to-last and final years."[62]

In primary education, the manual arts and applied sciences had different contents for boys and girls. The content also differed in schools for city boys and schools for country boys preparing for life as workers or peasants (in the former, home building, tinkering, tools, machines; in the latter, subjects related to farming and agriculture). Working-class girls learned cooking, housework, clothing care, and hygiene; they also studied child care, kitchen and pleasure gardening, and small stock farming. It is striking to see to what extent this new feminine specialty of elementary education was spelled out this time in the legislation. The hygiene portion, for example, comprised eleven items, which made it equivalent to the training of a health assistant, because in the mind of the legislator home economics appeared essential for the working classes. For the education certificate, the girls-boys distinction was maintained through the written exams: the science question for girls had to do with "home economics, hygiene, child care, horticulture," and the question for boys concerned "applied sciences for rural life or city life." The practical exercises followed the same divisions in the second series of exams.[63] Programs for working-class children were simplified through a firm refocusing of masculine and feminine educational disciplines. Preparation for "real life" was supposed to prevent the bitterness, envy, and upward mobility that, in the eyes of the regime, the fatal primary school spirit—and its "evil little knowledge," according to the still active expression of Guizot—was dispensing liberally. The topic for pedagogical lectures for fall 1941 is one sign of the interest that Vichy attached to these practical aspects of working-class education: rural primary school teachers were invited to reflect on "the importance of agricultural education and domestic education for the national renewal and on the organization of this education in the primary school."[64]

The sexual division of the scholastic world was thus much clearer in the primary system than in the secondary, where it probably struck the legislator as difficult to reconsider the recently acquired equality of girls' and boys' lycées that testified to the rise in demand for women's education-professionalization in the middle and upper classes of which the state had finally taken official note.[65] In the primary system, this sexual division developed further and created a veritable social blueprint. Commenting on his reform, Carcopino pleaded for aca-

demic respect for the difference in "natures": "In secondary education, I imperatively encouraged manual work for everyone: the study
of drawing for boys and the study of music for girls. Likewise, in the
primary school, I oriented boys toward technical education in agriculture and girls toward home economics and child care. . . . Everywhere I preferred *unison* to unity, in the hope that this *harmony* would
be a prelude to the harmony of the City; and with the certainty that
public education would achieve its goals of national education all
the better if it were *modeled after the nature* of the young people whose
human worth it is our responsibility to enhance."[66]

However, although the reforms that defined a feminine culture of
education were primarily concerned with primary education and only
made a few changes to secondary education, the state redefinition of
a masculine/feminine distinction in the educational order was immediately interpreted as *an invitation to reconsider all education of girls* in
the primary, secondary, and higher systems. By commenting on and
expanding this program of national reeducation directed toward constructing a specifically feminine educational culture, supporters of
the distinction between a masculine and a feminine order of access to
knowledge thus subjected all girls, regardless of their social origin,
to the logic of restricting intellectual learning. In so doing, they also
proposed that female secondary education be channeled into separate circuits, thereby abolishing the threat of competition with men
and delimiting a space of qualified feminine professions that had as
their central function teaching other women, particularly women of
the popular, rural, and urban classes, the only occupation for which
they were truly fit: the occupation of mother.

From July to September 1941, to some extent laying the ground-
work for "public opinion's" acceptance of the Carcopino reform,
Le Temps published fifteen articles on job opportunities for baccalaureate recipients that identified as masculine the careers open to
young people of the middle class. It thus restored the social selec-
tivity to this diploma that the école unique project had wanted, or
so *Le Temps* claimed, to devalue by opening it to everyone. The final
article of the series took a feminine slant on social Malthusianism
and listed the careers "especially open" to young female diploma recipients. Leading the list were feminine education, nursing, and social work; then came those jobs "specially reserved for young women

who have received a bachelor degree or a technical diploma with a sound knowledge of foreign languages": shorthand typist and secretarial positions. As for careers "similar to male careers," the newspaper was pessimistic: rather than becoming an engineer, the paper recommended "technology" to become an engineer's assistant and even, with a little shorthand typing, a technical secretary; in administrative careers, the trend was now to "limit the hiring of women," the journalist delighted. In medicine and pharmacy, where overcrowding was commonplace, young female graduates should set themselves up in the country and specialize in caring for women and children or become herbalists. Finally, in the "saturated" legal careers, they had only to become "assistants and secretaries to colleagues who are already established."[67] In October 1940, at the enthusiastic beginnings of the National Revolution that authorized one to say out loud what one used to keep to oneself, the tone was ironic, and the female baccalaureate was presented as a sin of youth—of a society and of women who had returned to reason—that no one needed to worry about any more:

> Some papers this morning are filled with lists of the baccalaureate recipients of October. Throughout these lists there are many girls' names. Perhaps a day will come when women's names will be published in the papers because they have given birth to their fourth child. What were the aspirations and ambitions of the young girls who had just earned a diploma whose singular fortune is to be all the more envied the more widespread it is? My God, they had neither aspirations nor ambitions. Docile, they followed the crowd. . . . Graduated with distinction. She is superior in not being more exuberant; she puts away the manual and takes up crocheting again. In a few years, surrounded by her children, she will still be crocheting and will tell them what she had written in her brilliant composition on the contributions of Romanticism. In telling this, she will experience a sweet, but slightly vain satisfaction. However, she will be happy in her heart because knitting will have taken precedence over the baccalaureate degree.[68]

The question of private education was central to the relationship between the Church and the Vichy government.[69] It granted religious schools considerable subsidies, because the ambient political condemnation of lay public schools contributed to encouraging the militantism of the associations representing "free" education, their policy of conquest and their desire to impose educational values that defended the preeminence of the family over the school. It is therefore not surprising that the meeting between the Marshal and APEL, which had fought against the école unique projects and Jean Zay's orientation classes beginning in the 1930s,[70] was placed under the sign of election: "Bordeaux, July 1, 1940. Marshal Pétain, On behalf of one hundred twenty thousand French families registered in the regional associations that form the National Union of APELS, I come to fulfill before you a duty, that of telling you how much these families are with you in heart and in deed. . . . The words you spoke, the warnings you gave, had a profound repercussion throughout the nation. But no one in France welcomed them with more emotion than we did, because in them we found *the amplified yet faithful echo* of all that we have thought, written, and said in the ten years since our Association was founded among families whose sons and daughters were entrusted to free education."[71] In the next issue, the triumphant tone of the APELS was expressed without reserve: "For ten years, we have been preparing to live this hour that has finally come, the hour when the French family, once more in possession of the fullness of its rights, will be able to exercise them."[72] The association would not cease to call "family men" to cooperate closely with the public authorities to whom it tirelessly proposed its own reform projects, taking up in its turn the Marshal's educational recommendations, particularly the necessity of training hearts and characters rather than instructing minds. Women, of course, were on the side of the heart and, since September 1940, spokesmen for the association had been drawing the attention of the public authorities to girls' diplomas, programs, and education that "are not in any way distinguished from those of boys, which is nonsense." Their desire to establish a specifically feminine education on a national level ("dominated by the idea that a girl's normal vocation is to be a wife and mother") was once again accompanied by the demand for an elitist secondary system ("fee-paying and reserved for a portion of youth" and "based on literary education"), for a lightened primary system ("rudiments," "introduction to manual work," "exaltation of family values"), for practical professional instruction ("systematic repetition of precise gestures," "general culture administered with prudence"), and a clearly understood professional orientation ("each man was created with gifts that assign him a certain place").[73]

A vast survey concerning *L'Éducation des filles* occupied those in charge of the APELs in the Occupied Zone and in the Free Zone for several months, from October 1940 to June 1941, particularly Henri David, who presented it and commented on it in the movement's publication, then in the brochure specially devoted to it.[74] The questions asked of parents of students, of educators, and of "young people" were the following: "Are you satisfied with the education that girls are currently receiving? Do you want to see fundamental reforms of the methods, the plans and programs, and the schedules? Do you want your daughters to be educated differently than your sons? What would you propose?" The survey was explicitly presented as a means of pressuring the public authorities "at the time when plans for the future reform of education are being developed."[75] In the brochure in which the national results of the survey were presented, published after the Carcopino law of August 15, 1941, APEL noted with satisfaction that several of their demands had been taken into consideration, such as the requirement of special subjects reserved for girls. But they wanted to go much further and establish a "feminine culture," from primary education (where one must "already be concerned with awakening and maintaining in the child what is feminine"), to technical education (responsible for training in the "feminine occupations that must be rediscovered and returned to honor"), to the secondary system, which must comprise "special parts for each sex." For "woman's place is at the center and at the heart of the home. If she does not occupy this place, everything will be finished for this national renovation to which we are invited, but which we will not achieve if we do not take the means to do so. In times of crisis, citizens are conscripted. The crisis is real, it is serious. It will only be exorcised by conscripting wives and mothers. A girl's education must be a distant but effective preparation for the indispensable conjugal and maternal function. *Under pain of death for the country.* This is, clearly, a very vast issue. *It concerns the entire organization of social life.*"[76] Therefore, there were to be no more women in "masculine careers." However, if an occupation was necessary, there would be "higher education for women giving access to the highest levels of social and family careers," where they would have "the possibility of *serving,* whether or not they marry."[77]

For those responsible for this survey, pedagogy itself had to bend according to the sex of the students. Once again, praise of feminine "precociousness" and "intuition" ended up placing girls apart: "The manner of teaching girls must be as different from that of teaching boys as the two sexes are different from each other. This is a question of practical psychology that cannot be ignored. The young girl opens herself earlier than the young man. She is intuitive. It is impossible, without harming her, to place her in the same rigorous training cycle." It is therefore necessary in "girls' schools" to have "uncluttered programs," a climate made "for calm and contemplation" and propitious for "religious training." "And culture will be dispensed at all stages in a family ambience. Let us not forget that it is a question of placing strong feminine personalities in the service of the country. We will succeed in this by training character very early, by developing the sense of discipline, by inspiring a taste for disinterested effort, by honoring the spirit of sacrifice, by cultivating femininity instead of suffocating it. Thus, little by little, these chosen creatures who, for their husband, will be the friend who understands and who supports and for her children, the competent, indisputable and irreplaceable educator, will become a reality."[78]

From the standpoint of the education issue, feminine Catholic culture was able to place in the service of the French State the classifications, limitations, and all the positive and negative prescriptions that it had elaborated since the beginning of the nineteenth century without its being easy to determine whether it was imposing its views on legislators or legislators were using it for their own purposes. The complex tactical compromises that marked the relationship between Church and state concerning the place of private confessional education during these years certainly weighed on the state's recognition of a feminine educational identity that responded to the desires of an important portion of the Church. Old and new, modernist and traditionalist institutions invested the site of feminine educational culture with equal energy. In this space we find at the same time the ideological rallying force of the feminine culture constructed by the Church and the political rallying power of oppositions, adamantly bent during the 1930s on "democratizing" the Republican school.

The review *Éducation* was a forum for modernist discussions of private education focused on the family-school relationship. It was founded in 1935, a time of battles over the educational question, by the merger of the *Revue familiale d'éducation* (founded in 1916 by Abbé Viollet and an organ of the Confédération générale des familles) of *L'Éducation,* a magazine of family and school education (founded in 1909 by Georges Bertier, the director of the Les Roches School)[79] and of the more recent collection of the École des parents (founded by Vérine in 1929). The review called itself a witness to the evolution of ideas in education and the advancements in psychopedagogy: "*Éducation* proposes to study the qualities that parents must acquire to be good educators worthy of this name. Both very modern and very traditional, without being denominational, it will strive to conciliate the principles that must remain at the basis of education with the newest ideas and methods that an educator can no longer ignore."[80] In its October 1940 issue, *Éducation* welcomed in its turn the new times in which one could verify the accuracy of its projections and offer one's experience and services: "The speed of their crumbling and the immensity of their disaster abruptly revealed, last June, to many French men and women that they had not succumbed only to the superiority of troops but also to their own intellectual and moral breakdown. Returning to the past they attributed the initial causes of the defeat to the deficiencies in French national education; they did not lack reason in doing so. But in matters of education, less than in any other, one does not improvise. Times have changed. The French State accomplished its national revolution. The total reform of education is the order of the day." Very quickly the magazine participated in restricting the education of girls, starting with disposing of the biases it gave rise to:

> Thus one whispers to women, to detach them from the great movement of national renovation, phrases that tend to make them believe that one wants to humiliate them. "You are done with high culture, intelligent activities, freedoms and initiatives. You will be asked to bear children and to grow vegetables. Your beautiful time is over. You can't see that you are being enchained!" Well, no. That is all false. . . . If little women, pleasure seekers, egotists, and lazy women for whom the words "devotion" and "family" do not exist, will soon have something to complain about, all the better. The others, those who think of the national interest—and who see it

as clearly inseparable from their own dignity—will only be able to congratulate themselves more to see the principles of a plan focused on the general good applied.[81]

During the entire war, the review called for a "true education of girls," for a "more specially feminine education," for the "organization of all feminine teaching" around procreation, going beyond the options of the National Revolution and placing the scientific gains in educational matters that it made its specialty in the service of a tougher and more complete expression of the sexual division of the educational world in times of crisis: "The readers of *Éducation* undoubtedly still remember the controversies raised in its columns by the education of girls. Today the circumstances imperiously call for a radical solution. We must give girls a feminine training related to their family and social function; there must be a female education parallel to male education, but not identical to it. This will be a return to the logic from which it would perhaps have been better not to have deviated in the first place."[82]

Family and Domestic Education

The law of March 18, 1942, that made "home economics" mandatory for young girls fulfilled the wishes of the family factions. This education was mandatory in all lycées and collèges for seven years for at least one hour per week; in vocational collèges, national vocational schools, and women's vocational business, industry, and artisinal courses, the requirement was three years on the basis of one hundred hours per year. Sanctioned by a certificate of attendance, it provided "an apprenticeship in home upkeep and in making simple clothes and linens. Laundering and ironing. Cooking with several concepts pertaining to diet. An introduction to family psychology and morals. An introduction to ordinary women's law. Elements of household accounting. Theoretical and practical instruction in child care. Theoretical and practical instruction in bodily and domestic hygiene."[83]

This law was welcomed by supporters of the "eternal feminine" as decisive progress in the state's recognition of a feminine educational identity, as a means of combating working-class "slums," and as the opportunity for a "magnificent efflorescence of initiatives that are indispensable for young women and families," initiatives that purveyed the most legitimate feminine occupation, that of instructor of domestic arts. As of May 1941, *La Femme dans la vie sociale* was delighted with the promising vitality of this career, which, it said, lacked only the sanction of a diploma; the magazine then announced the creation of a planning committee to establish a "certificate of aptitude for the duties of home economics instructor."[84] It is easy to imagine what an active role this committee played in establishing the law. Commenting on this reform in June 1943, Henri David suggested increasing the number of hours of home economics instruction to the detriment of other subjects in order ultimately to "demasculinize" girls' academic programs. He cited the need for "several thousand instructors in the near future" trained in leadership schools (*écoles de cadres*), whose skills would be certified by a "board for the development of home economics instruction." An assessment of the candidate's "morality," a French composition "on a subject related to the role of woman and the family in society," examinations in hygiene, child care, family management, and ordinary women's law would make it possible to evaluate the feminine excellence necessary and sufficient for supervising working-class girls.[85] The Secretariat General for Youth oversaw the women's leadership schools responsible for training managers of young female worker centers, schools that "tend to become permanent institutions of moral and vocational training with an original feminine education format." Its texts awkwardly recite the litany of customized classes and point out that the leadership training meetings aimed to "seek an authentically feminine scholastic life."[86]

The commentaries prefiguring or accompanying the law did not fail to compare this new form of girls' education to the slant given to female education during the prewar period: "Yes, the House of France needs to be 'set up'; in the joint work of the National Revolution this is the prerogative of our women. It is the ideal for which French women have prime responsibility. But, alas, are there still women who even know how to set up a house? Is the young girl who has finished her schooling and earned her diplomas, whether these are higher, secondary, or primary education diplomas, prepared for this noble task?" The author thinks not, and finds that "the philosophy of the house has been lost." The remedy? A return to educating the body, the gesture, an education that will never be forgotten and that imparts a second nature: "What was responsible for these condoned desertions of the homemaker's life? The almost total lack of basic actions. The thimble, the scissors, the iron, and the kitchen knife were no longer present at this age when fingers are nimble and reflexes are learned; for the love of certain tasks requires natural ease in performing them, and ease supposes a prior plasticity that little girls really only have between the ages of eleven and fifteen."[87] The Commissariat General for the Family also speaks about the body when it asks young girls of the middle classes to give up their "selfish evasion" in studies and masculine careers: "If all young Frenchwomen between the ages of twelve and eighteen from now on truly study home economics, we might have a lot of hope for the future. . . . since it has been agreed that boys will have more sports and physical education than before, girls, who would do well to be moderate in this area, will use the corresponding hours constructively for work that is more suited to their nature and their mission."[88]

All those who welcomed this new law as a key means of putting the "house of France" back in order agreed to recognize the educational primacy for girls of *corporal training*. Only such training was capable of internalizing from infancy the idea of a feminine "nature" and a feminine "destiny" through the acquisition of a gestural familiarity with feminine tools and through the continual inculcation of this apprenticeship in bodily care, the feminine domain from time immemorial. Laundry, food, care of small children and the sick, the entire feminine "vocation" is focused on care of the body in the same way that the feminine use of one's own body in childhood and adolescence must be marked by the prudence, reserve, and moderation likely to preserve the fullness of the reproductive capacities. In his praise of the occupation of mother, a specialist in the dangers of industrial work praised the "work of food, courageously and patiently assumed by the mother," that a "literature created for our misfortune" scorned, as it scorned the "value of any activity pursued *outside of words*."[89] Through this apparently anodyne law, whose banality wards off all astonishment, the masculine/feminine opposition once again found the force of symbolic constructions that make the body the ultimate point of all differences. It is these *techniques of the body,* as defined by Marcel Mauss, these "habits that vary according to society and education," these "acts that impose themselves from outside, from above,"[90] that the National Revolution used when it wanted to reeducate little girls:

> When, then, can the maternal instinct be awakened in a tiny woman of tomorrow, still wobbling on her tiny feet, who clutches against her heart a bear, a puppet, or a "doggy"? So fragile and small, already her gestures are no longer like a boy who hits things, knocks them over and rages, and we must take this into consideration by placing the "baby," whose name she says so quickly and lovingly, into her arms as fast as possible. Let's not misuse strange and comical animals with our little girls and let us direct these first impulses of moving tenderness that are the first indications of femininity. Let's not accuse them of "whining like all girls" and of playing outmoded games. Do not point to their brothers as examples.[91]

For brothers, there was sports education and the Chantiers de la Jeunesse, new sites for learning virility supervised by the officers of the armistice army: "A very hard life that requires constant contempt for fatigue, a community life that always requires saving face are well suited to forcing an adolescent to surpass himself and to free the man within him. The law of daily effort, desire, and tenacity honored above all other qualities, confirm and ripen a virility that is still fragile and fallible."[92]

But while Uriage and all the men's leadership schools and the Chantiers de la Jeunesse, reserved for boys to "mold character," as Marshal Pétain, the first of the officer-educators, liked to say, were the subject of a considerable number of publications during the National Revolution and of an important number of studies after the war, home economics and the women's leadership schools remained more or less unknown.[93] There are few documents concerning these schools that, according to a report of the Conseil supérieur de la famille dating from 1944, resulted from a "difficult reform to enforce, as there were no trained cadres [leaders] to teach home economics."[94] A memorandum dated November 1943 lamented that the French State's family policy was "in jeopardy" because the budget had recently denied the necessary allocations for enforcing the law of March 1942 making home economics mandatory: "If this denial is maintained, the law will remain a dead letter, and French women will continue not to know how to keep their houses or educate their children."[95] This gap between principles and actual achievements with regard to girls, this striking disproportion in the interest manifested with respect to Uriage and with respect to Écully (its female counterpart, whose trace just barely reaches us) testify, it seems to me, to an additional form of disqualification of the space of female education. The École nationale de cadres *féminins* d'Écully, established near Lyon in the villa of a silk merchant, was organized by a leader of the JOCF (Young Christian Women Workers) with support from the Secretariat General for Youth. The "eminently practical" courses aimed to train cadres for the young women workers' centers that were to admit "any young girl of French nationality between the ages of fourteen and twenty-one who was without work and in need," and who were given a "family life education" and taught "the meaning of a Christian home."[96] We are a long way from the "chiefs" of the château of Uriage and the chat sessions of Beuve-Méry. The women's institutions are doubly silent. They speak little of themselves and are not spoken about. And their silence is comparable to the silence one demands from women, as indicated by the only text devoted to women by the review published by Uriage: "Does woman have a mission to fulfill? Yes. She is to carry out her 'occupation' as woman, as man carries out his. She must be woman with the same faith, the same constancy, the same perfection as a man may be an engineer, architect, philosopher, carpenter, or plumber. . . . Whatever happens, man would like to find her at his side always true to herself, mistress of her nerves and her spirit, smiling, relaxed, composed, silent, but a rich silence."[97]

Ultimately, female apprenticeship is not on the side of history, utopias, excitement, or condemnation with respect to the new order. It is on the side of repetition, of the ahistorical, of the banal, of that of which there is ultimately nothing to say, either at the time or afterward. The best domestic instruction is still that instruction learned in the family, passed on from mother to daughter in the private space through the example of the eternally renewed gesture, the gesture related to food or care. When it theorizes about girl's education, the review *Éducation,* so taken with the advances in psychopedagogy and the Anglo-Saxon methods for boys, finds nothing to offer as an example other than the "instructive experience" of a mother of ten children based on the principle of *imitation,* a key concept in feminine pedagogy: "It was inspired by this principle, on which we have never ceased to insist, namely that what adults wrongly call children's games are exercises that the child takes very seriously and that, in and of themselves, have a training value. Among these exercises, there are a large number that lead the child to imitate the occupations of adults and to repeat the gestures he sees them make. . . . A whole series of other apprenticeships involving domestic life succeed the apprenticeship of sweeping. That of washing laundry, when the little girl positions herself near her mother to imitate her in these delicate operations, by dipping her doll into the laundry tub herself."[98] Finally, for girls, it is simply a question of telling them "the truths that have existed for all time" to make them "this ideal woman who harmoniously unites in herself the qualities of Mary, the intellectual woman of the Gospel, and those of Martha, who is also indispensable."[99]

The specialists in symbolic production who joined in the defense and promotion of the "eternal feminine" and who fought for the monopoly of legitimate symbolic violence in the domain of the sexual division of the social and scholastic world produced, for and with the French State, a system of feminine aptitudes that allowed the construction of "reserves," in the colonial sense of the term. Symbolic reserved spaces are always also spaces of social exclusion, as demonstrated by home economics. Nevertheless, it is so easy to return to them and to feel at home in them. By mobilizing all the schemes of the feminine culture of sacrifice, of disinterestedness and closure, these producers of feminine identity had only to reactivate a highly internalized tradition of apprenticeship to arouse the total adherence and the willing acceptance marveled at by the review of "free" education. "The law of March 18, 1942, makes home economics mandatory and, consequently, it is necessary to lighten the girls' program, 'to eliminate certain subjects that are useless to girls,' writes a very young girl from Ardèche whose sincerity and good sense we applaud." Once again, to go further they proposed in no uncertain terms stripping the science program of its theoretical part in secondary education for girls.[100]

The "Mystique of the Family" versus the "Mystique of Equality"

The construction of a necessary and sufficient academic culture for girls was thus marked by a logic of raised bids. One of the essential springs of this logic was the desire to impose a *new definition of the relationship between scholastic order and family order.* If everything united to entrench women in the family space, it was because they occupied a strategic position in the regime's conception of the relationship between education and instruction, and because this conception had always been at the heart of private confessional education's struggle to maintain and expand its place in the scholastic market. The recurring accusation leveled against the public instruction of the Third Republic during the 1940s was that it separated education from instruction; it thereby reduced, if not annihilated, the role of the family in education and its control over the school. The new order had to reestablish the preeminence of the family in the domain of education and to invent a "pedagogy of national revolution" in opposition to the "dominant educational power" blinded by "a kind of intellectualistic intoxication" for which the sociological training of schoolmasters, raised to the level of morality in primary education, was purported to be largely responsible.[101]

If the sociology of Durkheim was one of the bêtes noires of the ideologues of the regime in educational matters, this was primarily because, in their eyes, it questioned family power both vis-à-vis the school and vis-à-vis the child. In his derisive attack on primary school supporters, René Benjamin expressed this view with the pamphleteer violence of the intellectuals of the Action française: "We must free the child from Religion. That's not all: we must free him from the Family, a deadly group that smothers him. Durkheim, a real scientist, that one (a lecturer at the Sorbonne), wrote in his plodding prose: 'The family is not set up to be able to train the child for social life. By definition, as it were, it is an inappropriate body for this function.' Pardon me for giving you this savage text as is; but you get what he wants to say. Are we to deduce that Public Welfare is preferable to the family? Durkheim didn't say that, and since he is dead, we will have to wait until we meet him in another life to find out."[102] In the Cercle Fustel-de-Coulanges as well, sociology was on the *index expurgatorius,* because it was seen as culpable bad philosophy of individualism. For Henri Boegner, the nation "is an association of families and not individuals"; he accused Durkheim of having claimed that the trade union would fulfill "the functions exercised by the family in the future." In the Circle's arguments against the école unique, sociology is presented as the unhealthy philosophy of teacher training colleges: "What point is there in telling young people, most of whom arrive at school after kissing their daddy and mommy, that the family is disintegrating and that little by little 'it has lost certain of its primitive functions'? For this is the beautiful domestic sociology program M. Lapie has prepared for the teacher training colleges." [103]

Albert Rivaud also accused intellectualism of being one of the causes of the defeat and recommended the return to the Greco-Latin-Christian tradition and to the authoritarian university. He condemned Durkheim as an "imperious and evasive master" for having "imposed his authority on our educators" and "reconciled for them the taste for disorder and the desire to dominate." This "facile and popular" philosophy that, according to Rivaud, "charms many Jews, abruptly admitted into the teaching profession," and allows them to "shine without penalty" in the "reorganized" competitive examinations that were "their business," was also, according to him, a delight to those whom Bonnard called the "bacchantes of knowledge": "Philosophy, school of the critical spirit . . . has spared neither religion nor the family, nor the nation, nor authority. . . . The young women who have passed the teacher qualifying examination of our women's colleges bring an almost sadistic ardor to this work of destruction. They comment on the works of Gide, Marcel Proust, the most audacious novels, they give troubling advice concerning Freudianism, sexuality, cohabitation. They increase shamelessness through pedantry." [104] Sociologists, Jews, women, and primary school proponents, all those who defend the "democratic mystique," the "mystique of equality," to use the expressions in force, had to be brought into line and challenged by the "family mystique," as Inspector Haury called it, alone capable of "forming character" and reducing the ambitions of the school.

When it defended the family against the school in order to defend the Church against the state, private confessional education preferred to reiterate women's assignment solely to the family space and prescribed for them an education limited to their role as mother. Girls' education was therefore a central political issue. We can better understand why the École des parents, which defended the supremacy of the family over the school and the distinction of sexual roles in the family based on a different education for boys and girls, responded so favorably to the educational reforms of the National Revolution that gave such a large role to parents' education. "Don't let people come and tell us, the family-educators, that we are poor utopists, ideologues. . . . We are builders who work only for the family; as a consequence, we are sociologists, producers," writes the founder and president of the École des parents in her defense of the new regime.[105] Abbé Viollet, the indefatigable leader of the old works of the Moulin-Vert, who teamed with Vérine and the director of the Les Roches School to found the modern review *Éducation* earned, in April 1941, the recognition of the state for a new association intended to promote "the study and advancement of family sciences," a new discipline capable of competing with sociology: "We can speak of *family sciences* as we speak of *political sciences* or moral sciences. If this has not been done up to the present, it is because family problems have not had the place that their importance merits. Thus sociology has made a better study of the various forms of marriage than of family life itself, and psychology has given more attention to general psychology than to the psychology of sexes and functions." The association wanted to create a *Revue des sciences familiales* and higher schools for family education in which one would teach family assistants general psychology and ethics, "with application extended to each member of the family according to his age and sex."[106] The specificity and the hierarchy of gender and function within the family would from now on be scientifically founded thanks to the new "family science" based on the biological nature of things and would thus ultimately be purified of sociological questioning.

The state's recognition of a fundamental inequality between male and female intellectual aptitudes founded on the irreducible difference of male and female destinies brought women back into line in the scholastic order. Putting women in their place is at the heart of this "eternal sociodicy" that relies on "apocalyptic denunciations of all forms of 'leveling,' 'standardization,' or 'massification,'" to identify "the decline of societies with the decadence of bourgeois houses, i.e., a fall into the homogeneous, the undifferentiated."[107] This is the most political level of signification of the feminine education issue, and it is omnipresent in the outline of the educational limitations for girls drawn up under the National Revolution. The marking out of the intellectual ambitions of each sex, and therefore of their legitimate use of the educational system, is inseparably a marking out of the legitimate educational and social ambitions of each level of society. Just as the female lycéennes always run the risk of what might be called ontological deracination, the access of the masses to knowledge is always a bearer of social deracination and therefore of illicit ambitions, envy, and revolts. Marc Bloch expresses his indignation on reading Albert Rivaud's article on the teaching of philosophy, which he denounces as a call for a necessary purgation of undesirable professors who persist in "reasoning about social iniquity." He accuses Rivaud of seeking authoritarian promotion (finally possible) to positions of professor of philosophy of "morally gauged citizens" likely to transmit "respect for what is in place and exhort one to obedience." In this very political text, Bloch condemns both Rivaud's anti-Semitism and the social philosophy that he defends with "the tone of a Statesman": "In this eminent brain, there reside, in fact, great plans, final causes, constructive ideas, the definition of beneficial hierarchies. The populace has more short-sighted views. What it is demanding is freedom immediately, equality immediately, justice without delay, and the end of oppression."[108] To reposit the education of girls and the school-occupation relationship that falls to them is also to posit "final causes" and to define "beneficial hierarchies."

The society of the National Revolution was an inegalitarian society, or rather, a society that defended inequality against "the undifferentiated" and "massification." "The new regime will be a social hierarchy," Marshal Pétain announced. "It will no longer rest on the false idea of the natural equality of men, but on the necessary idea of the equality of the chances given to all Frenchmen to prove their ability to serve."[109] And, we might add, to serve each in his place: women at home, peasants in the field, artisans at their workbenches, and the true elite in positions of command and supervision. Harmony in difference and not the amorphous mass and its demands: "Let us pause for a moment on the democratic myth of the 'sovereign people.' . . . There should not be any 'masses' according to the meaning given to this word today. I imagine a healthy people as a highly differentiated multitude of professional and local organisms attuned to one another, but each functioning at its own particular level. This amorphous *mass,* brandishing the *sledgehammer* of its *massive* demands like a bear brandishes its stone, is the product of an extreme social decadence."[110] Thus, to the people, just as to women, the new state must not give any "fictive and sterile" power, as Thibon put it, but rather this "limited, but authentic and fecund power, that falls to it by nature." It is this demarcation that the Republican school jeopardized, for scholarly individualism counted for something in the decline of the spirit of sacrifice in favor of the spirit of pleasure that wanted everything, right away, without adhering to social steps. The poor, like women, would be accused of having a utilitarian relationship with education, the only proper relationship to the scholastic system being the "disinterested" relationship of those who are socially predestined to follow its royal path. This was how the free, secular, and mandatory schools and all the plans for an école unique sinned in the eyes of the regime, of the supporters of academic elitism, and of the defenders of "free" education and the priority of the family over the school. "We can never emphasize enough the harm that such an education had on the young generations, or the moral ruin that such anarchical individualism accumulated in individuals, in families, in society, especially among workers and peasants in whom it is easier to incite passion by flattering their desire for well-being and pleasure than to train their conscience and affirm their desire by teaching their duties rather than their rights," wrote Father Gillet, who defended the woman-at-home agenda with the same zeal.[111] Carcopino ultimately saw an unhealthy conception of equality in the feeless secondary system: "The ranks of certain collèges tripled or quadrupled in several years; . . . classes were overcrowded with parasitical elements that are unsuited to classical studies, often thrown into the so-called scientific sections. . . . very few of these newcomers made it to the baccalaureate; most stopped along the way. Annoyed with their failure, unprepared for an occupation, victims of an awkward ambition, they swelled the ranks of an intellectual proletariat, ripe for all renunciations and all excesses."[112]

The "newcomers" must return to wiser ambitions, give up this "egalitarian fever," and learn again how to wait, learn again the "spirit of economy" that, "in the highest sense of the word, coalesces with

the spirit of fidelity and sacrifice." This social philosophy of renunciation promoted by Gustave Thibon was constructed to oppose egalitarianism defined in this way: "The deadly sin against harmony—
which is nothing more than a set of inequalities founded on functions
and duties—egalitarianism breeds chaos." [113] Woman, "maker of harmony," easier to make submit, must be an example of social patience
and symbolize in the eyes of all the impossibility of transgression.
The idealization of countrywomen and the exaltation of the return to
rural virtues against urban chaos borrow from the same logic, and the
list of texts that celebrated woman's return to the earth and that idealized women of the earth—"true" women par excellence, who cumu-
late feminine patience and peasant patience as desired by the regime,
the "ancient docility that it supposes to be innate to modest peasant
people," according to the ironic expression of Marc Bloch,—is end-
less. The culture of notables has annexed the culture of sacrifice. [114]

Virilizing the Elites

Against anything that, in their eyes, constituted the Republican
school ideology, the social philosophers of the National Revolution
imposed the idea of a natural inequality inseparable from a refocusing of the definition of the elite concerning corporal virtues. Against
the "primacy of intelligence" that must now, "after this tragic object
lesson," be understood to be only "an arm in service of the will," the
university was assigned the duty of training "not brains" but *"elites
of flesh and blood."* [115] We can read the pedagogical philosophy of the
Chantiers de la Jeunesse, [116] of the Jeunesse de France et d'Outre-mer,
that of the male leadership schools, particularly Uriage, and of that
other educational innovation of Vichy, the Commissariat for General
Education and Sports, like so many manifestos for an educational refocusing on the body capable of remasculinizing the masculine body
and making the elites virile. This educational project borrowed from
the Scouting movement, from the Les Roches School, and from its
reference to the cult of sports and to the anti-intellectualism of the
public schools responsible for arming the ethos of the imperial elites
who expressed themselves unrelentingly from 1940 to 1944 in the review *Éducation*. It borrowed also from the hymn to action sung by
the Agathon-Massis survey of French youth of quality cited earlier,

and from the call for an "internal revolution" of elites launched by "nonconformists" searching for a "third way," particularly the personalists of the 1930s.[117] It incorporated the ideas of officer-educators who wanted to make the army an institution that competed with the school, and the ideas of those engineers, fed by the ideas of Lyautey—whose model was Georges Lamirand, secretary general responsible for youth at Vichy—that the regime would ultimately establish a social group conferring legal status on the category of "cadres."[118] This type of project sought to redefine masculine excellence, leadership training, and "true" elites qualities. It completed a process of integrating the values of the dominant class, reconciling the old provincial notabilities and new incarnations of state technocracy around the idea of the "corporal virtue" of leaders. Uriage became one of the showcases of this integration by proposing a definition of the total man that the leader of the future must be, a definition that borrowed heavily from the old officer-educator model. Virility as a virtue of the elite took its unifying value in a crisis period from the fact that, like the "eternal feminine," it relied on the force of an ageless mythic logic.

"The decadence of the race began, with respect to our education, on the day Descartes proclaimed the independence of thought with respect to the body. . . . The Canadians who, far from our effeminate civilization, have maintained the health of our race in its original force, have muscles, stomachs, and lungs of a quality different from ours," the director of the Les Roches School wrote. It was therefore a question of "turning our back on the ideal weakling of the single-child family," to relearn "the immediate and unconditional acceptance of authority," and to "dream of great athletic meets where, in the sun-drenched stadium, handsome young men will arrive in great numbers, torso bare, singing."[119] This desire for education and for the reeducation of the body was entirely consistent with a prophetic interpretation of the debacle. To return to the comparison with the days following the defeat of 1870, we once again find in the ideology of the National Revolution the same accusations of softness and sloppiness that led to a cult of sports and exercise during the 1880s.[120] Educational and familialist reviews that lent their experience to Vichy as tools for active Pétain propaganda castigated youth, "little wimps," and "relaxed indifference" that called for recovery of self-presentation, because the school had failed in this task that makes all the difference between education and instruction:

> For want of discipline and high virtues, of which few teachers would dare give them the example, a nonchalant, physically and morally slovenly youth loafed around the streets and in the cafés. Young women themselves had adopted mannish manners. No more faith, no more respect, no more pride, no more bearing. . . . Bearing is part of the overall reform. It is both the spirit and the condition. It is the rule of soul and body. It requires that casualness and carelessness make way for order and discipline, that each being and each thing have style and charm. . . . Bearing is therefore the agreement of the moral and the physical. Each condition has its own, and the peasant cannot have that of a military man. But regardless of his rhythm, the man who walks well is the man who knows where he is going.[121]

Vichy was a moment of overproduction of a *state idea concerning the body* in which new legitimizations of domination, new definitions of masculine excellence and of a masculine order of leadership combining bodily and spiritual mastery were developed. "If you want to lead others, know how to govern yourself" was the advice given by the radio program *France-Famille*. This ideology of *self-control* imbued the vision of elites after the debacle. In the recurring condemnation of slovenly youth, we can easily read the criticism of the "permissiveness" of the prewar period and of all the "facilities" accorded to the masses by the Popular Front. The permissiveness of these young workers for whom the social laws of 1936 marked "the rush toward pleasure," "the loss of energy," and "hostility toward the constraints of duty," of all these "youth dressed in short-clothes" who "at the end of the week pedaled toward the countryside and in the summer brought the slovenly exodus back to the beaches." But the Popular Front was not the only institution criticized, for "can one affirm that the ruling classes opposed the seduction of easy pleasures with the resistance they should have and that a virile conception of existence and the sense of their responsibility dictated to them?"[122]

Uriage, the special leadership school born of the initiative of a cavalry captain from the provincial nobility and fed by the ideas of

Lyautey concerning the social role of the officer and the educational role of the army, sought to "rebuild" a virile order.[123] Like Lamirand, Dunoyer de Segonzac reflected both on the respect for obedience and on ways of commanding, on the social divisions that divide the recruits and on the "job of leader." He promoted the truth of the body's language and wanted a new style of intellectual, firmly anchored in the "real," so dear to Marshal Pétain: "We would be grateful for an intellectual to present a healthy, vigorous appearance, to hide the finest soul in a very carnal envelope; we would find pleasure in noting a perfect balance between the soul and body of these thinkers who, after all, are men first. It is entirely reassuring to note that this philosopher specializing in the study of love and its refinements himself has a loving wife to whom he has been able to give several beautiful and good children."[124] Although the history of Uriage has been widely commented on, we know less about the text of two lectures given there in December 1940 by Jean-Jacques Chevallier, *L'Ordre viril* and *L'Efficacité dans l'action*. Combined in a brochure from the Uriage collection, these two lectures were repeated at each school session, before the departure of the students, like a kind of "order to action."[125] To reconstruct the community based on a virile order was to once again find "a certain strength of soul, a moral vigor, courage," a "climate of force, the force of a man's body, the force of a man's soul." "In this sense, the *viril* is, of course, opposed to the *feminine,* and also to the *childish* and also to the *senile,* in other words, to all forms of weakness, regardless of how graceful or touching they may be. To the *feminine.* It is not a question here of speaking ill of the eternal feminine, eternally necessary to man. . . . No. Woman has her own order that is complementary to the virile order. If she is not spoiled by false ideas, conventions, and snobbism, what she asks of man is first to be a man. And the more and the better she is a woman, the more she despises a man who is a woman." The virile order has its way of "classifying beings" that "involves a sense of hierarchy, of choice," and "excludes a certain egalitarian baseness." There was "a kind of *sickness of the decision-making spirit* among some, a sort of *sickness of the spirit of execution* among others"; "words had a tendency to replace acts." "Speech is feminine, but action is masculine, says an Arab proverb. Leaders, tomorrow you will need to restore a male order, a virile order."[126]

Vichy and the Eternal Feminine ▸ 254

8. CONTROL OF BODIES

Hygienism occupied a central place in the program of the National Revolution.[1] Making France "healthy" again was the slogan. And the archives have kept surprising texts that show the strength of support for the medical representation of the social world in this period of crisis. In an anonymous letter addressed to the Advisory Committee for the Family, the usual condemnation of the declining birthrate blends easily with the organic metaphor: "France was sick. Too many laws for abandoned children who die unmarried have created an individualism that marks many organs." It was therefore necessary to purge "the body" (the nation), "the basic cell" (the family), and the "nutritional environment" (work).[2] The French corporative sanitary group that brought itself to the attention of the French State and offered its services sent Dr. Ménétrel, Pétain's personal physician and secretary, this "PRESCRIPTION": "Criticism is a DISEASE. Confidence is a REMEDY. The HEALTH of France must be ensured, LOOK AFTER THE MARSHAL."[3]

The biological metaphor invaded political discourse, and the social philosophers of the regime constructed a kind of political medicine. The social body was constantly threatened by disease, the cure required a surgical procedure, and if Pétain was the grandfather of the nation, the father of all fathers, he was also a miracle worker, the premier physician. This dimension is omnipresent in what was called the "cult of the Marshal": during triumphant trips to the provinces, everyone wanted to touch him, to touch his coat, and women knelt along his route. In Toulon, a woman kissed the hand of a journalist who had touched the hand of the chief of state.[4] "Leader and father, with devotion, intelligence, love, and faith, he brought the only balm that could return France to its great destiny: the affectionate remedy of truth."[5] Under the pen of Gustave Thibon, this medical solicitude is combined with severity: to care for a patient, you have to cause pain and restrain the patient. "The Marshal is the physician who watches at the bedside of France. But the best doctor in the world is not enough: the patient must want and be able to get well. Even plunged into the healthiest and most natural environment, an organism that is too altered continues to die. . . . a period of strict authority will be necessary for the national restoration. This authority will be applied to a France that is worn out and torn, as the supporting stake is applied to the tree or a bandage to a wound. . . . A deep wound calls for a tight, durable—and uncomfortable—bandage. A person who is saving a drowning man does not hesitate to dig his fingernails into his skin a little."[6] Submission to the "natural" laws encouraged and guided by the chief-physician is what would make it possible, according to Thibon, to escape from the "democratic exhibitionism" that had led "the mass of men to conceive opinions and experience feelings vis-à-vis reality that infinitely surpassed their *normal* intellectual and emotional sphere."[7] We must not seek too much to understand the social order. Political biology leads to the return to the "real," the real of corporal differences, of sowing and reaping, of parturition, which constitutes the true order of the world.

Alongside Marshal Pétain, many national health experts—biologists, doctors, and demographers—pointed out the social ills and suggested remedies for them. Abortion, immigration, alcoholism and workers' slums, juvenile delinquency and childhood maladjustment, poor physical education (lack of muscles for boys, deficient preparation for motherhood for girls) were the great health concerns of the French State. Many experts invested old and more recent interest in them, constructing a particular form of medical imperialism in this new historical situation that created new markets or expanded old ones. The *hygienism of the National Revolution* was born of the conjunction of disparate interests—the demand for a doctors association expressed since the 1930s by certain factions of the medical profession, and the interwar crusade against abortion waged by familialists and pronatalists, for example—and the political philosophy of a regime that used and abused the health metaphor that carried within it exclusivities and exclusions. "No neutrality is possible," explained

Vichy and the Eternal Feminine ▸ 256

Pétain, "between true and false, between good and evil, between health and sickness, between order and disorder, between France and the anti-France."[8] Biology would speak of order and of anti-France; politicians and social philosophers would speak of the relationship between the cells and the social body. In this hygienism, women once again played a central role: the health-related discourse of politicians and health experts would contribute to reinforcing the image of an "eternal feminine," this time in the service of a biological view of the social order. Primarily responsible for the declining birthrate and therefore, in the eyes of the regime, for its corollary, anarchic immigration, responsible for the poor upkeep of bodies in the domestic space, women had to undergo a hygienic reeducation under the direction of family doctors, obstetricians, and biologists. In this area, the construction of femininity easily combined old medical myths and new sciences.

But women's role in political-biological thought concerning the social world was not limited to their reproductive function. The "natural" inequality between men and women allowed one to posit other inequalities for which medical-psychological science would provide numerous examples. Vichy was haunted by the classification of natural aptitudes, tests, professional guidance and graphology, as well as by biotypology or morphopsychology that made it possible to reposit the problem of the social order by minimizing the role of the school. From this perspective, the Doctors Association and the Carrel Foundation appear during the National Revolution as the tribunals that were competent to rule on the *biological foundations of domination*. Inequality was everywhere: between sexes, nationalities, races, "leaders" (the "true ones"), and the "masses." It was a question of recognizing and measuring it. The eternal masculine/feminine opposition legitimized by the medical sciences is at the heart of an inegalitarian view of the social world that condemned individualism in favor of organicism.

Political Science as Medicine

The eschatological dimension of the National Revolution fueled this process of biologizing the political fault already at work immediately following the Commune. Biological and medical discourse concerning social pathologies reached a vast audience at the end of the century that greatly exceeded professional circles to become a common element of the political language and the culture of crisis.[9] The theme of national decadence became omnipresent, and alcoholism, tuberculosis, and syphilis were presented as "social dangers" that attacked the "social organism." Comparisons with Germany haunted this biological view of the national decline, reinforced by the demographic cries of alarm of pronatalists of all persuasions. The theory of degeneration became a social theory, and the telescoping of social and biological determinisms founded a political rhetoric in which the biological metaphor was central. "Medicalizing" the social question[10] and the national question led to imposing the same framework of analysis on domestic health problems and exterior security. This medicalization most likely resulted in large part from the appearance of a new relationship between medicine and public space (administrations, journalism, literature), between doctors and the political field, and from the consecration of a new medical figure—the national hygiene expert—that were accompanied by new forms of expanding medical competence and the political use of medical legitimacy.

The humiliation of the defeat of 1870 and fear of the Commune played their part in raising the notion of degeneration to the ranks of a political concept, and the images of the lost provinces acquired a corporal and biological form with Barrès. In 1914, organic metaphors and typologies exerted a kind of rhetorical and linguistic imperialism over all forms of comparison between France and Germany. The contributions of Social Darwinism and of the conceptions of the human community as inseparably historical, biological, and social specific to Le Bon, Soury, and Vacher de Lapouge would, at the end of the century, give its consummate dimension to this political-biological view of the national community. The determinism of the new nationalism, which condemned democracy, was a physiological and naturalistic determinism that affirmed the principles of subordination of the individual to the community and of the integrity of the national body, according to the analysis of Zeev Sternhell. This anthropological construction that resonated in harmony with the image of the national community forged by Barrès ("beings can only bear the fruits produced for all eternity by their stock") was anti-individualist and anti-intellectual (rationalism, specific to "the deracinated," that judges everything by the abstract kills the driving forces of the national activity).[11] It likened the nation to a living organism, to a tree, an image dear to Taine and to thinkers who posited a national instinct, an image that evoked the genealogical tree of French families of "old stock" and the oak dedicated to the Marshal in the Tronçais forest.

This ideological heritage permeated the social philosophy of the National Revolution. *Biologizing the rhetoric of the culture of crisis* merged quite naturally with political thought that made organicism, and particularly the family cell, the rampart against individualism and democracy:

> Biologists may know whether cells commit suicide. It is only too obvious that the family, the social cell, has, in France, tragically abused the freedom to commit suicide. . . . It is a commonplace to say that the physical and the moral are closely linked and act on one another. Let's go further: moral life is conditioned by the organic state; conversely, virtue has a biological value; morality is therefore *ipso facto* conjoined with medicine, whose domain this is. . . . a country is as healthy as its politics (just as it can, in return, have the politics of its health), and this is why the heads of the totalitarian States of Germany and Italy have done so much over the last few years to remind doctors of and, as needed, impose on them the sense of preventive medicine. . . . We must purchase our health or our cure through effort. But what a field of action for medicine! So many areas to be monitored, activities to be guided, in the family (and even before marriage), in education, instruction, sports, work, urban planning, architecture. . . .[12]

The National Revolution would thus enlist medical knowledge to reflect on the relationships between what is biological and what is social, what is preventive hygiene, and what is corporal education.

The individual repercussions of the exodus, food shortages, cold, and family separations mobilized the knowledge and actions of physicians, who were divided concerning support of the regime.[13] Resistance was important in the medical profession, and it quickly proposed a counterdiscourse to the dominant ideology: "In our time when truth is falsified in an astounding manner by the men in power, when *Paris-Soir* and the State radio wage a campaign against 'graduates,' when the Marshal speaks of Revolution while the country is plunged into the blackest reaction, a veritable return to the Middle Ages, . . . we want physicians to reorganize medicine themselves. The medicine of tomorrow, the medicine of France that edifies socialism, will be what French physicians will practice as they fight alongside the people."[14] Through his duties as president of the Laennec Conference, Paul Milliez led many young Catholic physicians into the Resistance who, like him, he noted, were expected to side with Marshal Pétain.[15] We need to be able to relate the political positions that divided the medical profession to the professional positions taken within the medical field by the supporters of this or that political agenda during this historical period of crisis and during the interwar period. Indeed, intense debates related to the appearance of new conditions for practicing and entering the profession began to break out in 1925. These concerned medical studies, the relationships between specialized and general medicine, medical and surgical procedure, the question of the "overproduction" of doctors, and the question of the relationship between private practice and state-controlled practice that began to crystallize with the establishment of social insurance. A study of these debates and the conflicts that marked them is the only way to give a complete accounting of the expectations and contradictions that marked the relationship between medicine and the public authorities between 1940 and 1944, and its evolution at the Liberation.

I have chosen to place special emphasis on the founding of the Doctors Association in 1940 and its sociogenesis during the previous decades. This study, which has never been done, proved indispensable to my approach to the collective construction of the "eternal feminine." Here, I present only the elements necessary for understanding the medical contribution to this representation of femininity but reserve a complete analysis of the birth of the Association for a subsequent work. I have particularly sought to establish what certain forms of adherence to the ideology of the National Revolution owed to past battles specific to the medical profession. I must add that the ideological appeal sent by the regime to the medical profession, the expansion of the medical function to the role of advisor to the prince, the insistence of the biological metaphor in political discourse, and the renewal of the state demand for national hygiene were all akin to a call for proposals from the public authorities to the medical profession. Its less irreducible differences were thus attenuated in favor of collaborating with a state power that gave such importance to the contribution of medical competence and experience to its undertaking for national regeneration. From this perspective, one might think that the medical overproduction of the "eternal feminine" also had something in common with this process of establishing consensus that at the same time defended family medicine and the family physician. That representation of the profession so dear to a large majority of the medical profession had viewed as a threat the transformations in training, in practice, and in the medical hierarchies that marked the interwar period. By calling for a total medicine for the total man, the French State allowed a large portion of the medical profession who felt rejected in the past to reconcile with itself and with the entire profession. Now encouraged to revive its most "noble traditions" and its former definition of the family physician, the medical profession rejected Parisian anonymity, the medical "plethora," the "coldness" of specialized medicine, the "dangers" of socialized medicine controlled by the public authorities, and the threat of becoming mere civil servants.

"We are not unaware to what extent biological comparisons applied to social life are deficient; nonetheless they are the best, and it is certain that the medical profession, if those who practice it assume it with all their being, is still the best school of political wisdom."[16] To reposit the relationship between medicine and society as the increased participation of medical wisdom in the national reconstruction is to make each doctor an educator of social understanding, a political hygienist, a privileged collaborator of the powers that be. The regional health education centers were to spread "the new trends of individual hygiene that are to develop the individual's social understanding and his mission in the collective effort of general improvement." So wrote Dr. Serge Huard, secretary of state for the family and health until April 1942,[17] in his preface to a medical work focused on the idea that physicians are less caregivers than "health educators." "Materialism has neglected moral health, the health of the spirit. The new order will take care of spiritual health as much as of physical health. Moral health will be protected from the countless viruses that threaten it through the hygiene of public opinion, through the sanitization of the streets, recreation, and publications. . . . France and the French need a hygienic cure; and all the more so in a country with a low birthrate, it is necessary to offset the numerical insufficiency of citizens by their good quality."[18] In 1936, judging medicine to be "at a crossroads," Dr. Delore, who praised Dr. Carrel and deemed himself to be "in line with the medicine of the future," was already calling for a "complete medicine," a true "human science," situated "at the intersection of biosocial problems." Delore confidently announced: "Medicine will be the center of the society of tomorrow. It will be responsible for making a major contribution to restoring elites."[19] Professor René Leriche, the first president of the Higher Council of the Doctors Association from 1940 to 1942,[20] saw the National Revolution as the opportunity to develop a public health policy that joined the state and the medical profession on new bases. This policy would finally free the profession from the threat of "civil servantism" that, according to Leriche and all those who were invested in constructing the new social and medical order, marked the social policy of the 1930s: "The past is past. We now face the future. So that this future is what the Marshal's National Revolution wants it to be, it is necessary that all measures be taken according to the interests of the nation's health, the physical interests that condition its moral behavior. And so that this comes to pass, physicians must become advisors the government listens to for everything concerning health, and they must establish a tireless collaboration between the administrative bodies and medical thought."[21] *Le Concours médical,* an influential professional newspaper, also supported the National Revolution on the basis of support for a "renewed conception of the state" that, by defending corporatism as the political principle of an organic society, defended all corporatisms: "Let us therefore leave to the prop room of the defunct regime the counterweight gearwork inspired by Montesquieu and let's say that there is *one Body that is the nation.* All its parts are only organs that live on its soil and from its blood. . . . But this community will only live within an elite, an active core, whose members will also be professionals. At the same time as they lay the foundations of the State, they will make up the cadres of the corporations. And this common birth will perpetuate the community of doctrine and action between the guardians of the country and those of the professions."[22]

Professor Sergent, former president of the Academy of Medicine, won support for the new regime from the old generation: "I have the satisfaction, amidst the hard and cruel trials we are enduring, of clearly and indisputably perceiving the reestablishment of the fundamental principles that constitute the necessary bases of professional, social, and national organisms." He defended a conception of the elite that had placed him, he said, in the category of "outmoded" thinkers: "The strict idea of absolute equality is the worst and the most toxic of viruses. I am not afraid to repeat it: the brain directs; the feet must obey its orders; a human organism, deprived of its cerebral rudder, errs into imbecility, insanity, madness, bestiality; a social organism deprived of its intellectual and moral direction falls into disorder, anarchy, turpitude, barbarism." Ultimately, the great physician, he who trains the new elites, must, like Marshal Pétain, "behave with respect toward them like a father, remembering that in 'patron' [boss] there is 'pater.'"[23] Dr. Laffite, who in 1936 drafted a survey on the crisis in the medical profession in which we find all the themes that would be debated in 1940 in the Doctors Association, concluded his work with praise for the political lucidity of the medical profession that resonated with foresight: "We must attack false dogmas. Idols must be overthrown. To the Revolution, a source of evil, a new revolution must be opposed that will be a renovation. . . . The return to traditionalist and, let's use the word, antidemocratic ideas in considerable environments took place, Dr. Pierre Mauriac writes, at the same time as the ceaseless confirmations of experimental medicine, particularly by the laws of biology. A scientist as detached from political contingencies as Dr. Carrel has, in his recent book, condemned the democratic principle."[24]

A member of the most prestigious of elites, the embodiment of the "brains" who must think and direct the social world to save it from disorder and imbecility, but also a paternal elite who knew the weakness of the weak, Alexis Carrel exemplified the ultimate dimension of the physician as scientific advisor to power, and medicine became the science of sciences. All physicians—and, among them, all those who prided themselves on their knowledge of social philosophy—referred to Carrel, who made them the ultimate experts concerning the moral and biological decline of the nation. As early as 1935 his book had pointed out this decline, which the "hard lesson of things," as one said of the times, confirmed, giving this book prophetic value.

"What particular science should be caused to grow and absorb the others? . . . Medicine has received from anatomy, physiology, and pathology the more essential elements of the knowledge of ourselves. It could easily enlarge its field, embrace in addition to body and consciousness, their relations with the material and mental world, take in sociology and economics, and become the very science of the human being. Its aim, then, would be not only to cure or prevent disease, but also to guide the development of all our organic, mental, and sociological activities. It would become capable of building the individual according to natural laws."[25] By establishing the French Foundation for the Study of Human Problems in 1941, the French State provided Carrel, who was appointed "regent," with the resources to form teams to develop "the systematic construction of civilized man in the totality of his corporal, spiritual, social, and racial activities," by creating a "new technology, *Anthropotechnics*": "Thus, less than two years after the most complete defeat in its history, France affirms not only its desire to revive, but also its desire to develop to the greatest extent the hereditary qualities which are still untouched, though dormant, in its population."[26]

The Vichy regime offered both the opportunity to expand medical competence to the summits of what could be called "biocracy," particularly with the Carrelian utopia that borrowed from the most recent technocratic and scientific advances as well as from science fiction, and the possibility of once again reactivating the old images of the profession, still active in such a diversified space where representations of the profession from different ages, like the old and threatened image of the family physician as health educator, co-existed. This moment was also the opportunity to reconstruct concretely the profession's relationship with the state, for, on October 7, 1940, the Doctors Association, whose creation had not been possible during the interwar period, was established. The medical defense of the preeminence of the feminine "vocation" for maternity and the imposition of the feminine identity that it implies are caught up in all these professional images ranging from medicine as total science of the social world to the new promotion of the family physician and the defense against the state of "liberal ethics" concerned with the prerogatives of its clientele (and therefore the prerogatives of mothers of families).

The Inauguration of the Doctors Association
(L'Ordre des médecins)

To understand the issues that governed the foundation of the Doctors Association under the French State, we need to return briefly to the reasons a large majority of the medical profession sought to create collective organizations. In the beginning of the century, they established medical trade unions, which they later confederated.[27] During the 1930s, they fought to create a doctors association (comparable to the bar association in the legal field) to which membership would be mandatory and that would have professional jurisdiction, allowing it to mount opposition to state initiatives.[28] Motivating these affiliations were two concerns. One was the threat to private practice by the advancement of social laws that would push doctors toward becoming civil servants and would place the practice of medicine under "state control." The second was the "plethora"—an overproduction of physicians. These two concerns betrayed numerous fears about the devaluation of the entire profession or of certain of its subsectors and about the questioning of traditional methods for entering the profession. Thus, like all those who had condemned the école unique and the democratization of education, Professor Sergent lamented the decrease in the number of physicians' sons and the increase in new recruits: "children of the 'nouveaux riches,'" who had not, perhaps, always received "ancestral training"; young women; and particularly foreigners, most of whom "arrive here from Danubian countries and represent the elements deemed 'undesirable' in their own country."[29] These arguments were even more influential during the 1930s, because medical hereditary transmission and attainment of middle-class respectability were clearly affirmed in the medical teaching profession between 1901 and 1932. The social closure of the medical elite and the conservatism of its positions went hand in hand: defense of the social values of the conservative Catholic middle class, ethical rigor, concern for the future of the race, and the Malthusian and xenophobic defense of the profession.[30]

The first action of the Confederation of French Medical Trade Unions had been to demand the revamping of the law of 1928 concerning social insurance and to require that this law fully condone the principles of the confederation charter (free choice of physician by patients, respect for doctor-patient privilege, freedom to prescribe, direct understanding between physician and patient, and excluding the "tertiary payer," that "factor of subjection and demoralization"). In 1929, the general assembly of the confederation voted to create a doctors association.[31] The struggle to revamp the law regarding social insurance and the fight to obtain the ratification of a law creating a doctors association went hand in hand. The law of April 30, 1930, which amended the law of 1928, satisfied doctors with respect to direct understanding and gave the medical unions a representational role. Many doctors between 1930 and 1940 thus agreed to denounce "threatening state control" and to present the medical corporation as "a natural phenomenon of self-defense." Furthermore, the state was constructing new medical figures (state medical functionaries for Public Welfare and asylums) and a new market (factories, free clinics, hospices, insurance companies). All these elements were suspected of introducing immorality into the practice of the profession, as functionary doctors were alleged to have laxer individual responsibilities because they were shared with the state, and of threatening its nature as a liberal profession.[32] The Action française expanded its audience in the medical profession during the interwar period to the extent that it founded a monthly journal, *Le Médecin,* in 1926. This response was based on a defense against state control and a call for corporative organization that did not really contrast with the positions of other medical groups:

> It suffices to observe the lack of harmony and the disagreement that oppose state control that is increasingly monopolizing the proud and necessary independence of a profession that wishes to and must remain *liberal,* that is free (let us avoid confusion). Yet another proof that Liberty with a *capital* L kills liberties, ours in particular. . . . The State boss, State socialism, this is the great external cause of our anxiety. . . . Armed with this light, do you want to explore the social insurance project? We cry no, not only because our legitimate interests would be endangered, but also because the interests of patients would suffer from this process of making doctors functionaries.[33]

These initial traits of the "medical malaise" that had given rise to the demand for a doctors association in 1926 became the source of the support of a majority of the medical profession for the establishment of an association in 1940. In apparently paradoxical fashion, it was also the source of problems in the relationship among the association, physicians, and the Vichy government carried away by statist passion, problems that would end in 1942 when a second version of the association, more respectful of the major corporatist options defended up to then by the medical unions, was established.

The second concern at the origin of the demand for an association was designated by the profession as the "plethora" issue. Physicians who wrote about the crisis in medicine during the 1930s felt that the plethora was caused by "lowering the barriers at the threshold of secondary education," "the influx of a feminine contingent that the conditions of the postwar period no longer allowed to devote itself to its primordial task, the home," and "the intrusion of a crowd of foreigners, too often undesirable, attracted by the mirage of the ease of life in France and the hidden complicities of power, or expulsed from their country by political convulsions. If there are more physicians, there are fewer customers and no loyalty at all. The family physician of fifty years ago is a dying breed."[34] This refuge in corporatism since the 1930s that led doctors associations to support, then apply, exclusionary measures against foreigners and Jews also characterized a large majority of the German medical profession. Beginning in 1929, a National-Socialist League of Physicians was founded and counted almost three thousand members at the beginning of 1933, that is, before Hitler's ascension to power; in October 1933, the League had eleven thousand members and demanded that Jews be excluded from the medical profession. During the interwar period, the theme of a plethora was omnipresent in the profession, and women and Jews shared responsibility for this state of affairs. The resentment against socialized medicine and the growing influence of medical insurance companies were also at the heart of the declaration of a crisis in German medicine.[35] The return to a strict corporatism also led German engineers, teachers, and lawyers, who had been in a mode of relative decline and threat during the 1920s, to throw the weight of the crisis on the weakest: youth, women, the least educated, Jews.[36]

In 1931, a tract published by the medical students of the Action française warned about the proportion of "foreign and Jewish doctors,"[37] and in September 1934, the *Action française* devoted a series of articles to "French medicine and métèques." In his assessment of the medical malaise of the 1930s, Dr. Lafitte devoted two hundred pages to the plethora and, although he was less alarmed by the presence of women in the profession, he gave a central place to foreign doctors: "To cap it all off, the borders of the country are largely open to political refugees of all sorts, to the unemployed, in particular, to all those that the foreign races are pushing out and sending to us."[38] In 1930, a report was presented on behalf of the confederation by Professor Balthazard, dean of the medical school of Paris, and Dr. Cibrié. It warned of the increase in the proportion of foreign medical students and foreign doctors between 1920 and 1930[39] and linked the weakening of medical traditions in France to the newcomers, "who do not have the same morality as French doctors because they have not received an education in medical probity in our French schools."[40] Finally, the Armbruster law (named for the doctor of the confederation who brought the bill to the Senate) of April 21, 1933, required that the French State doctorate in medicine be earned in order to practice medicine in France and required naturalization if a foreign doctor wished to practice before the age of thirty or practice socialized medicine or perform public service. At the beginning of 1935, the medical students in Montpellier launched a strike movement that spread, fanned by the Action française, and that was punctuated by violent demonstrations during which foreign students were attacked.[41] In July 1935, a new law nullified all equivalencies in medical studies and required possession of the French State diploma and French citizenship or status as a French subject or citizen of countries placed under French protection as conditions for practicing medicine; only naturalized citizens who had completed their military service could practice medicine.[42] The establishment of the French State would very quickly make it possible to go much further, for "as much as we hesitated to adopt drastic measures in the past, this time we are being categorical."[43] The law of August 16, 1940, specified that "no one may practice medicine in France if he does not have French nationality as a native as a result of being born of a French father." The problem of foreign and naturalized doctors—which included a majority of Jews—was ultimately settled, for the implementing circular of November 1, 1940, specified that the law was effective retroactively. In March 1941, during a lecture at the Rive Gauche bookstore, Dr. Desmarest described the plethora and the tasks of the Doctors Association. Denouncing "the intrusion of foreigners into French medicine," foreigners who "cross the border on the simple pretext that their country of origin no longer offered a favorable climate for their political ideas," he wanted the Association to undertake "a vast work of purification" of these "new, freshly painted French elements," and to fight against "the increasing penetration of the French medical profession by the Jewish element."[44]

As of October 7, 1940, the Doctors Association was responsible for enforcing all the laws specifying the conditions for practicing medicine. The doctors unions were dissolved (Article 17 of the law creating the Doctors Association), and membership in the Association became mandatory. The first article of the law required that all doctors had to be authorized to practice their art by a departmental association board that registered them on a public roll. Doctors who did not satisfy the conditions of the law of August 16, 1940, and its implementation circulars could not be included in this roll. Then, with the second Jewish Statute, a number of Jewish doctors affected by the *numerus clausus* imposed in the liberal professions, where their number was limited to 2 percent of the effective total of practitioners, were also excluded from enrollment. A law of May 26, 1941, extended the notion of illegal practice to any doctor who practiced without satisfying the nationality and enrollment conditions.[45] The Association was divided over the issue of Jewish doctors: certain departmental boards collaborated voluntarily with the aryanization of the profession;[46] others protected the doctors threatened and took advantage of all derogations possible; the Higher Council of the Association, chaired by Professor Leriche, frequently opposed the Commissariat General for Jewish Affairs.[47]

By decreeing the dissolution of the medical unions, by imposing appointment by decree of the members of the Higher Council of the Association and the appointment — by the minister of the interior and at the proposal of the Higher Council — of members of the departmental boards, by giving positions of responsibility in health policy to men who had not taken part in the recent professional battles during the interwar period, the Vichy government, even if it was carrying out certain wishes of an important part of the medical profession, ended up driving a wedge between doctors and the Association on the basis, once again, of the rejection "of centralizing, statist, and dictatorial tendencies" and the desire to promote autonomy for the corporation. The expression comes from Professor Mauriac, dean of the medical school of Bordeaux and president of the Doctors Association of the Gironde. During the same lecture in 1942, he called for the restoration of the power of the medical corporation against the "diktats" of the central power and for the pursuit "without weakness" of "the elimination of métèques from the medical profession."[48] The leaders of the Confederation of French Medical Unions were opposed from the start to an association that they qualified as "a statist agency" because, unlike the Bar, it was not entitled to elect its boards and had called unsuccessfully for the draft project to be amended in a corporative sense.[49] They thus forgot that in the heat of the battle with the state concerning laws regarding social medicine they were ready to sacrifice the union to the Association, for, because the union was not mandatory, it had no legal efficacy.[50]

Tax measures aimed at increasing control over medical income by imposing a stub book—which the doctors' unions had already succeeded in 1934—ignited the situation in January 1942. The new health minister of the Laval government, Dr. Raymond Grasset, greeted by his colleagues as a practitioner and former president of the Puy-de-Dôme union, in other words, as a true defender of the interests of a profession whose demands he knew well, returned to these measures at the same time that he promulgated, on September 10, 1942, a law regulating the powers, duties, and functions of the Association in a new way.[51] He was thus responding to the wishes of President Laval, a senator from Puy-de-Dôme: "Marshal Pétain agrees with me concerning the reconciliation of the medical profession and the government. Your past experience as a union member allows you to try and succeed with this issue."[52] During the convention for the Association advisors of the Unoccupied Zone held in Aurillac on August 23, 1942, Grasset presented the project to reform the status of the Association and the main points of the new public health policy. Among them was the issue of foreign doctors. After clarifying that 1,388 doctors had been definitively prohibited from practicing as of August 11, 1942, and that 400 were authorized but "will never practice because they are Jewish and affected by the departmental *numerus clausus*," he indicated that he was in favor of pursuing the "full enforcement of the law in all its severity" ("prolonged and lively applause").[53]

In the "new" Doctors Association of 1942, the principle of election was a fact, and legal and management powers were henceforth separated: at the departmental level, the medical councils were responsible for professional organization; at the regional and national levels, the boards had a disciplinary function. However, whereas the members of boards of departmental councils were elected by their colleagues, regional board members were appointed by the state secretary for health. The national board had elected members, but in accordance with the conditions set by the public authorities, and a chairman appointed by the minister, who ultimately appeared once again to be the "supreme wheel of the Association, the head of the corporation," worried Le Concours médical in October 1942, aligning itself with the expression of other fears concerning continued subordination to the ministry.

In July 1943, Grasset appointed Professor Portes, "head" of obstetricians in France, since he had been a professor of clinical obstetrics at the Paris school since March 1942 and a hospital gynecologist, as president of this reformed Association: "Your specialization designates you quite naturally to watch over the life of the nascent Association. . . . The qualities of the heart, tenderness, social spirit, generosity of spirit, all that, your daily contact with the ardent joys of motherhood have only sharpened all this, and we thank you in advance for glorifying your new presidency with it."[54] Louis Portes was the incarnation of the modern version of medicine for all times, that of women and of birth. He was an old partisan of the medical charter voted in by the Congress of Medical Unions in 1927, a manifesto of private medicine that defended patients' free right to choose their doctor, the right of prescription, and understanding and direct payment of professional fees.[55] It was his charge to reconcile the medical profession with itself and with the public authorities. The appointment of Professor Portes presented itself as apolitical, an appointment that created consensus and appeasement. Trained at the school of Baudelocque Hospital, where modern hospital obstetrics were established, he was also a staunch defender of the principles of medical "liberalism," in the name of which the medical unions had fought against the social advances in the health policy and in the name of which, ultimately, many had given their trust to the new regime. It was a trust that Vichy's statism would ultimately seriously breach even if its policy concerning the prohibition against allowing foreign doctors to practice seemed to have been widely approved and welcomed by many as a "cleansing" of medicine itself.

The experience of the secretary general of the doctors union of Seine-et-Oise is an example of a relationship with the Association that went from hope to disenchantment. On July 8, 1940, the secretary general sent the head of the French State an enthusiastic report on the necessary reorganization of medicine: "The French doctor, by virtue of his distribution throughout the Country, his penetration into all the social milieux, often also through his general knowledge and the example of his work, can play a major role in the Country's recovery." The fight against "FOREIGNERS" topped the list of proposed reforms: "The invasion of medicine by 'Stateless persons' with a crassly mercantile mentality is the major reason for the decline in medical morality." It was therefore necessary to review naturalizations, to exclude foreigners from public service, and to prohibit them from practicing medicine. In the second place, it was necessary to eliminate "state-bureaucratic" social insurance, free medical clinics that were merely "centers of agitation," and reduce to powerlessness their "communist-sympathizer promoters and directors," who had succeeded in interfering with the country's entire health structure." In short, it was necessary to give medicine back its "spirituality that 150 years of liberal individualism has caused it to forget." On January 28, 1942, this doctor, who was a member of the first Higher Council of the Association, noted that "the immense hopes that, along with the National Revolution, had given rise to the creation of the Doctors Association" had been replaced by "profound disappointment": this was once again "the state-socialist imprint" on medicine, "opposed to the wish of all doctors." [56] The Association's alliance with the state was thus marked by disillusion.

The desire for the consolidation of conservative elites demonstrated by medicine and the familialist movement in both cases ran up against Vichy state control, perfectly illustrating what Stanley Hoffmann called "the self-destruction of the National Revolution." [57]

Medicine and Family

The avatars of the relationship between the medical corporation and the French State should not lead us to underestimate the profound adherence to the National Revolution of a large portion of the medical profession. Among the reasons for this adhesion, the wide concurrence given to a biological representation of feminine destiny, oriented toward and devoted to motherhood and to the reproduction of the family, seems to me to occupy a central place. *This medical defense of the family and of the feminine "vocation" is in fact first of all a defense of a certain image of the profession* that rejects modern forms of professional competition. An image of the family doctor,[58] still widely shared at the time, that tacitly combined the nostalgia for families of doctors, those provincial medical lineages, and for the large medical family[59] of an idealized period when the savage economic competition of large cities had not yet supplanted genuine emulation, was linked to the denial of the economic aspects of the profession. The responsibility for "commercializing" the profession, so often denounced during the 1930s, was attributed both to foreigners, "come from far away to sell medicine in France as one sells rugs on café terraces,"[60] and to the sons of the nouveaux riches, those newcomers to the "caste" of the liberal professions.[61] The image of the family doctor was the very image of rootedness: "Alas! we are far from the time when the family doctor gave level-headed and objective advice with full knowledge of the facts because he was as much friend as doctor, because he knew the family whose older members he watched disappear and whose children he saw born."[62]

Article 11 of the Ethics Code published in the first issue of the *Bulletin de l'Ordre des médecins* of April 1941 discussed the "relationship between doctor and families": "It is entirely desirable that the family physician continue to exist and that he remain a heeded advisor as he was in the past. . . . He is better qualified than anyone to guide parents in educating their children and sometimes in marriage plans." The hygienist project of the National Revolution, placed under the aegis of the defense of the family, reaffirmed the central role of the family doctor in the country's moral and health education, and therefore contributed to this form of reassurance provided to itself by a method of practicing medicine that had been relatively devalued during recent years and that felt threatened by the state and by socialized medicine, specialized medicine, and all figures of the plethora. In 1942, Professor Sergent called on all doctors of France to listen to "the moving appeals of Marshal Pétain: 'Doctors!—the Marshal tells us—your mission is great and noble, to appease suffering and heal, but also to advise and guide. What a grand title in particular is deserved by the family doctor! He is a friend and confidant. He knew the grandparents and best understands the grandson. He cares for bodies, and souls are open to him. He remains the sure and laborious craftsman of this restoration on which the France of tomorrow depends!' "[63] Addressing the doctors on the day after his appointment, Grasset suggested that they unite in a "corporate body established according to the intentions of the Marshal" and forget their "excessive individualism." The unifying model in the eyes of the new health minister was "the doctor-confidant of families, charitable by nature, social by destination."[64]

The representation of medicine as family medicine is inseparably a representation of the familial reproduction of the medical profession. In this sense, too, it is consistent with rootedness and suspicion of those who are deracinated. The Maurrasian conception made family heritage the best guarantee of national heritage and rejected individualism that allowed the social ascent of "foreign" families to the national heritage (Maurras cited the example of the social rise of the Monod family, a Protestant family).[65] This notion of heritage was embodied in exemplary fashion in this familial transmission of medical notability greeted by *Le Temps* in 1940: "In the past, the medical profession was often transmitted from father to son, and we had families of doctors just as we had families of magistrates and soldiers. However, for several years now, cosmopolitanism in the liberal professions has tended to destroy this admirable and precious continuity of the elites who were the deep-seated strength of our country. Science itself could only gain from this hereditary transmission, guarantee of the highest virtues. The family became the support of the corporate body. Thus the new law tends toward a true restoration of the national, family, and corporate spirit, at the same time as a restoration of the elites."[66]

In these families of doctors, just as in the home of the family doctor, women, wives, and mothers played a major role whose defini-

Vichy and the Eternal Feminine ▸ 274

tion can be traced to antiquity: "If you want to deserve the beautiful title of a true doctor's wife, you must, oh woman, in giving yourself to the man who holds in his hands the health of citizens, fathers, mothers, children, family confidences and who saves the healthy life of the city, you must know: That you must be even more virtuous than other women, be good, cheerful, and discrete."[67] It was first of all within their own families that doctors who defended this form of medical tradition defined the sexual division of the social world based on the opposition between interior and exterior, visible and invisible, reason and emotion specific to the culture of sacrifice. And if Mme Pasteur is one of the emblematic feminine figures of the National Revolution, she owed this to her philosophy of devotion, constructed like the legend of a saint: "With her good grace that always gave an air of ease to everything she did, Mme Pasteur reconciled the most diverse duties. She was her husband's secretary and copied his scientific notes with the intelligence of a true collaborator. Any entertainment, sometimes even Mme Pasteur's outings, were subordinated to the laboratory work. She found that entirely natural. 'It's quite simple,' she would say to the stupefaction of so many young women for whom couturier appointments filled the week to come, 'I never make plans.' "[68]

Professor Castaigne and Professor Sergent sketched a portrait of a doctor's mother that was similar to the portrait of a priest's mother drawn by the Church: "To be a member of the elite, a man, according to Sergent, must first receive basic moral training. Sergent had the good fortune to receive it from a very early age in his family. During a lecture to my students, I said one day that often it is at his mother's knees that a child learns this infinite kindness without which one cannot become a doctor worthy of the name. Sergent insisted, in the course of his book, on all he owed to his mother's influence."[69] In accomplishing their role fully, doctors' wives, often themselves daughters and mothers of doctors, allowed the medical elites to forge themselves and the medical lineages to perpetuate themselves. In October 1941, the periodical *Médecine et Famille,* the publication of the Association of Large Medical Families and of Doctor Friends of the Family, praised the government and Dr. Huard. It called on doctors' wives to send them a report of their family situation so that the review could draw up a list of "fine medical families"—it began with those that had had at least eight children—those large families that must be "a model for the profession and for the country." In this professional milieu, the defense of the housewife thus took on the overtones of a manifesto for the defense of the body and the return to a protected medical order.

It is therefore not surprising that the medical definition of the "eternal feminine" made a forceful comeback during the National Revolution. Besides the fact that medicine has always practiced expertise concerning women and that it could therefore immediately mobilize a whole background of learned knowledge concerning the biological foundations of feminine "nature," its commitment to the firm redefinition of the masculine/feminine oppositions of the 1940s also resulted from a form of redefining professional identity that totally combined medicine and family and in this way harkened back to a mode of practicing the profession that was threatened and in competition. By establishing the family as the basic social cell, the social philosophy of the regime gave new life to these representations of the family doctor, of families of doctors, and of the large medical family. The omnipresence of the family metaphor in the medical field and the omnipresence of the biological metaphor in the political field worked together to bring into the National Revolution those who recognized themselves in this image of the family doctor who had designs[70] and perspectives on the family and therefore, of course, on mothers of families.

The privileged contact of the family doctor, a health educator, was, in fact, the mother of a family, the guarantor of the longevity of his clientele, from one generation to another. One of the ardent defenders of the image of the family doctor during the interwar period wrote: "As soon as he is established in a family, the doctor remains there. Called by the parents, he will continue to care for the children and the little girl he brought into the world; he will deliver her child much later, just as he did for her mother."[71] The ideology of medical liberalism had to find in her a faithful ally, just as had "free" education in its fight against the state as educator. In this sense, feminine subjection to this medical view of the relationship between biological and social order was also the condition for the "proper" functioning of a market hurt by the professional crisis of the 1930s. The work of Dr. Delore, *L'Éducation et la Santé,* published in 1941, clearly demonstrated the medical profession's ambition to exercise moral authority and therefore, indirectly, the reasons for the commitment of a large number of doctors to the National Revolution on this basis: "The National Revolution demands profound reforms in all areas. . . . You lived in complicated fashion and against nature, you will return to the simple life. . . . You considered the doctor to be a healer, you will see him first as a health advisor. . . . Young people, do not abandon your sexual education to often unfortunate chance. See your family doctor. . . . Learn the basic notions of eugenics, that is, the laws of healthy procreation. . . . Future mothers, learn the basic notions of child care, how to keep house and educate children." And if instruction in child care had to become mandatory in medical schools, it was because, "through this, doctors would be prepared to carry out their task as *educators of mothers*."[72] It is in once again becoming "the home hygienist," who "gives a taste for clear, sunlit houses," that the family doctor would recover the full extent of his function between "social doctor" and "specialist."[73] In this way he once again found the role assigned to him in 1933 by the medical lectures of the Écoles des parents, that of a "spiritual advisor" and of an "educator of souls" capable of training the young girl to be "the nurse for her own," according to the expressions of Mme Vérine, herself the daughter and wife of doctors.[74] In the image of the ideal doctor's wife, each wife may invest her "innate" taste for caring—the medical version of the culture of devotion—in the domestic space. She would thus contribute in her turn to defending the biological heritage.

In the professional sphere, the issue was more complex. The same qualities of endurance and selflessness that led doctors to encourage the caregiving domestic activities of mothers of families led them to fear the practice by these women of a profession that "hardens the heart." Women threatened to increase the plethora, and they should limit their practice of the profession to "working with children, the aged, women giving birth, and with free clinics," subordinated professional sectors, and an institutional version of the space of private care.[75] On the other hand, nursing training was encouraged because it was "useful to all women in preparing for family life" in a France that, "under the aegis of Marshal Pétain, is regenerating and renewing itself."[76] And if it was certain that the material situation of France during the years of Occupation necessitated the unusual capabilities of nurse, hygienist, child care giver, and dietician from mothers of families,[77] the recall to order of caregiving feminine virtues was first a recall of feminine culpability and an appeal to feminine sacrifice. By becoming the hygienist of her own body and nurse to her family, the French woman could redeem herself and work for regeneration: "Because you are woman, you will be responsible for the *health of France*. . . . It is up to women to watch over the health of all. It is up to her to make homes in which each can blossom fully, morally, but also *physically*. We are no longer a race of strong people. . . . We are no longer a race of young people. . . . We are a country of sick people. . . . We are a house without a cradle. . . . I am calling you to a crusade."[78]

The interests of this "friend of the family" medicine, often marked by the Catholic tradition, tallied with those of the natalists who belonged to the Commissariat General for the Family and the Carrel Foundation to make maternity the only legitimate feminine "destiny." Between natalist crusade and medical expertise there would therefore develop without impediment a *policy of control of the female body* founded on a representation of femininity enclosed in the circle of biological and demographic expertise. Aside from its omnipresence in the eschatology of the National Revolution and in its conception of the new order, the defense of the birthrate imposed itself so easily as central agenda of the national regeneration only because it was a "commonplace" apt to reduce the oppositions and conflicts within the dominant class. Acknowledging with sympathy the request for a critique of the brochure *La Vie en fleur* sent to him by the Commissariat General for the Family, Professor Sergent underscored this shared concern for unanimity and quoted at length from the official letter accompanying this request: "We would be very grateful if you would ask a particularly qualified editor to present in an original fashion all the merits of this album in favor of the family and natality. We insist that union be based on these merits. If government leaders and directors of family movements wish to have suggestions and take observations into account, it is indispensable to avoid any polemics, any public criticism on this issue. Your feelings as a Frenchman will remove you from these criticisms, at a time when we want doctors to understand the urgent necessity of the union of all French men and women concerning the problems that condition the survival of our race and our country."[79] Although the political desires to impose a collective medical celebration of the natalist activities of the government were clear here, this letter of recommendation also let it be understood that there could be differences of opinion concerning this subject, and that it was neither the opportunity nor the time to note them. But if, in spite of everything, the medical profession mounted this battle horse with collective enthusiasm, it was also, it seems to me, because it allowed them to deny internal dissensions within the profession—in which different professional positions were expressed—and to associate portions of the medical profession that would be opposed on many other subjects with this work of public health. Thus, Professor Sergent was constantly concerned with separating biology from the clinic, going so far as to want different studies for two types of doctors, practitioners and scientists, and criticizing the overloaded aspect of the scientific portion of curricula.[80] His stances were probably echoes of arguments and conflicts of the interwar period concerning medical training, the relationship between general medicine and medical specialties, and even the definition of professional competence. The appeal to natality and maternity made it possible to move beyond these arguments and to unite biologists, specialists, and family practitioners in the defense of a national cause for the greater benefit of broadening the medical audience. Unanimity was in keeping with the defense of the body, and the medical discourse concerning the feminine body could only become more restrictive in practicing it.

Abortion: A Crime against the State

The old classifications specific to medical thought concerning positive and negative feminine virtues—classifications that are ageless by dint of being repeated—were easily mobilized. So too were the theses of the French form of eugenics defended by Professor Pinard and the entire tradition of medicalizing pregnancy developed particularly at Baudelocque, which linked the health of the country to the conditions of procreation, gestation, and infant care and as such gave women a central responsibility in this area, requiring them to sacrifice everything to the maternal function. This encouragement of total maternity also suggests the mobilization of women in the service of the community of the people recommended, under the Weimar Republic, by the men of the Conservative Revolution who were already evoking a regenerated Reich. According to them, love, conception, and birth constituted the "heroic summits of feminine life," and the rejection of maternity was tantamount to "desertion."[81] In 1935, Hitler declared that "woman also has her battlefield: with each child that she brings into the world, she fights for the German nation."[82] The same notions imbued the texts of the National Revolution concerning women's mission: "An eminently national role, since, owing to her, the Country endures, it is through her that the Country becomes more prosperous and stronger if she gives it lots of vigorous children who are well brought up and with a high social spirit. Woman's National Service lasts for her entire existence at home, and it is through her pregnancies that she pays the blood tax."[83] The metaphor of a national feminine service — a blood tax — immediately calls to mind desertion, which is punished by death in wartime.

Although not strongly repressed until the beginning of the twentieth century, abortion was subjected to increasingly severe penalties and to more rigorous enforcement of these penalties during the interwar period. But this repression appeared insufficient at the end of the 1930s. The National Alliance against Depopulation was worried about the dissemination of the Ogino-Knauss method* and the renewal of Malthusian discourse. And it was fascinated by the demographic efficacy of the fascist regimes, particularly Hitler's Germany, whose policy of repression (sending abortionists to concentration camps) and propaganda it saluted even if it rejected the German conception of race and forced sterilization. Convincing the Daladier government to establish a High Committee on Population, the Alliance's campaign resulted in the decree law of July 29, 1939, called the Family Code. This law strengthened the penalties against abortionists and women who had received abortions, abolished the notion of "impossible offense" (the offense was considered impossible if one could not prove the woman's prior pregnancy after the fact), gave each brigade of the mobile police a special section, authorized doctors to alert the police to any abortion matter, regulated therapeutic abortion, and established a veritable oversight framework for pregnancy from diagnosis to delivery services.[84] The content of this law shocked the medical profession. Although doctors had achieved the recogni-

* The rhythm method of birth control. — *Trans.*

tion for therapeutic abortion that they had been demanding for a long time, they were at the same time forcibly enlisted in the fight against "criminal" abortion. They were urged to report their patients who had had abortions; pregnancy tests were subject to strict regulation; and, finally, the doctors and midwives unions, like the family associations, were encouraged to take part in civil suits against abortionists. In general, the medical organizations refused to play the role of informer.[85] So it is difficult to know what the real effects of the law of 1939 would have been if it had been enforced during a normal period of history.

In 1939, the review of the National Alliance against Depopulation published a drawing showing three executed prisoners tied to posts to which are affixed the plaques "male abortionist," "female abortionist," and "traitor," and the legend: "Abortionists kill one small French man or woman in three. Those who protect them betray France for the foreigner. What punishment do they deserve?"[86] With the defeat and the establishment of the Vichy regime, this tone would dominate. The growing intransigence and the conquering imperialism of the demographic interpretation of the defeat, the self-promotion of demographers to the rank of accusers and public saviors, would lead the defenders of the family and the birthrate into an escalation of figures, cataclysmic predictions, horrifying descriptions, and calls for repression. "Out of two children conceived, only one is born, the other is killed before his birth by abortion," claims the banal propaganda brochure *La Commune rempart de la famille*, which called on municipalities to support the state's vigilance and to rely on the lists of practitioners established by the Doctors Association to monitor potential abortionists. William Garcin referred to the 1938 projections of 28 million inhabitants by 1985, and on the impact of the war (death, prisoners, undernourishment): "We are marching toward disaster. France will soon die with the last of the French."[87] In a pamphlet "that is not for children," Fernand Boverat likened a woman who has an abortion to a child murderer assassinating a baby in its crib with a revolver, and established a sadistic and complacent equivalence between abortion practices and Chinese torture, with sketches in support, going so far as to compare the probe to the stake and to evoke the "abortionist's" oven in which "live children" were burned.[88] *Voix françaises familiales,* a profamily supplement of a conservative and pro-Pétain Catholic review, took up the theme of the masked female criminal and associated it with sinful beauty: "You see this young woman who walks down the street? Isn't she elegant! Admire her blouse, her stylish hat, her painted nails, her plucked brows, her bearing, her perfume. You say Oh, what a beautiful woman! What a mistake! This woman is quite simply an assassin. Under her rice powder, she is a monster. She has done what animals will not do. Animals fight to defend their young. This woman killed her own child . . . the flesh of her flesh."[89] The French Legion of Combattants spoke of "prenatal murder" and was pleased that the new Code of Ethics of the recently created Doctors Association "mitigated the old rigor of secrecy" and allowed doctors to "inform the legal authorities about women who have had abortions."[90] Professor Portes, a staunch partisan of repressing abortion, lent the Commissariat General the support of medical competence to fight against abortion: emphasize all the subsequent risks to the health of women who then become "singularly fearful"; use "emotional arguments" to make then understand that "in spite of appearances, this is truly murder"; gain time; show those who cite "aesthetic reasons" that the birth "will only increase their physical blossoming"; examine closely the legitimacy of therapeutic abortion, "a breach through which criminal abortion enters," "particularly in the upper classes"; for "unyielding" women, "repeat offenders with respect to abortion," remind them that it is becoming "infinitely more difficult to escape scandal and the inexorable severity of the law."[91]

In this type of ideological context in which abortionists were designated as assassins of the country and abortees as child murderers — abortion being presented as the ultimate and unpardonable form of feminine "selfishness" — repression of abortion developed rapidly. In 1940, it was initially simply a question of enforcing the Family Code, whose repressive measures were quickly extended by court decrees. In Toulouse, the mere "intention" to abort resulted in a woman's punishment; in Riom, the intention was punished, although the woman was not even pregnant; in Poitiers, a second offense was considered a "habit" and severely punished as such, even though the first act took place before the decree law of 1939. Then, on September 1, 1941, a new law deprived abortionists of the right to a suspended sentence (*bénéfice de sursis*), and even a woman who performed an abortion on herself for the first time could no longer plead extenuating circumstances.[92]

On February 15, 1942, the so-called 300 law (the 300th act passed by the French State) made abortion not only a crime against the individual but a *crime against society, the state, and the race*. This law, which targeted only abortionists for whom "criminal repression was difficult to accomplish," gave the state judicial system two new arms. One was administrative internment, "created at the start of the war for individuals who were a danger to the national defense or public safety": at the proposal of the secretary of state for family health, the secretary of state for the interior or the prefect ordered the administrative internment of any individual against whom there existed "precise, serious, and concurrent presumptions." The other was judgment by the state tribunal, instituted by the law of September 7, 1941, that "judges any individual guilty of acts or dealings likely to harm the French people." This designation, concluded Dr. Huard, who introduced the new law in this manner, "applied perfectly to those who chose to depopulate our country as their profession."[93] The judgment of the State Court was final and immediately enforceable; among the penalties set forth were death, a life sentence of hard labor with deportation, hard labor with deportation for a given period of time, or imprisonment with or without a fine. The sentence of the court was to be posted on the doors of the professional offices and private residences of the accused. Special proceedings and special courts designated abortion as an act against the national defense and public safety. The German law of February 28, 1933, "regarding the protection of the people and the state" had prohibited abortion and family planning institutions. In 1939, through an addition to Article 218 of the German Code, the death penalty was introduced in the case of the abortion of an Aryan fetus "for attack against the life force of the German people."[94] Just like the abandonment of family cited earlier, during a time of crisis, abortion is akin to sabotage and treason. It is the feminine form of desertion. The champions of repression contended that the law had the approval of "public opinion"; they relied on the results of a survey conducted by the Carrel Foundation in 1942 in which 70.5 percent of the people questioned purportedly answered yes to the question: "Do you think that abortion is a crime that should be punished like murder?"[95]

During the Occupation and liberation, there was a sharp increase in abortion cases before the courts. In 1941, there were double the number of the preceding years; between 1940 and 1944, there was a 30 percent increase (22.6 percent between 1944 and 1947). Overall, the courts continued to be relatively lenient: in 1943, in the department of Seine, out of 750 people accused of abortion, 237 were acquitted, 380 were sentenced to less than one year in prison, 112 received a sentence of between one and five years, and only 15 were sentenced to more than five years. But exemplary judgments were also handed down. A laundress was guillotined on July 29, 1943. In August, another woman was sentenced to death but was not executed. A seamstress was sentenced to life imprisonment and three other women, including a midwife, to hard labor for life; two others, a nurse and a midwife, were sentenced to twenty and ten years of hard labor. A single man in this list received a life sentence at hard labor in Lyon.[96] And appeals for severity were numerous. The *Bulletin de liaison* of the Commissariat General for the Family found the professional sanctions too weak and suggested that the Doctors Association impose additional sanctions, for example, "the prohibition to practice medicine during a period of time longer than that set by the order of the court." Further, the *Bulletin* invited the regional delegates, "thanks to the relationship they had succeeded in establishing within medical circles," to "bring about additional sanctions in serious cases through this corporative path."[97] Boverat took a stand against doctor-patient privilege concerning abortion and ended his brochure, *Le Massacre des innocents,* with an appeal for denouncement, giving the list of public prosecutors ("send the letter to the Head of the Prosecution Department at the Court of Appeal") and regional police brigades ("send the letter to the Division Superintendent"). Some doctors also wholeheartedly cooperated with the repression. Dr. Roy, a professor at the medical school of Tours and president of the Center for Coordination and Action of Family Movements of Indre-et-Loire, demanded the acquittal of a woman who received an abortion and who denounced her abortionist, publication of sentences, loss of parental authority of convicted individuals, and "the creation of a special Court composed of a professional magistrate, assisted by a representative of the family movements and one Mother decorated with the Medal of the French Family."[98] Sentences are easy to conceive. The Carrel Foundation was not idle: it helped publish Dr. Roy's book, *L'Avortement, fléau national,* and undertook investigations in Tarn-et-Garonne, Tarn, and Lot to "study the repressive methods used and their effects on the regression of evil," "the initiative against abortion" having been taken for several years in these departments by a state police commander with whom it collaborated.[99] For Carrel, the evil stemmed from the fact that "abortion has ceased to be considered a crime": "Men and women have stopped obeying the law of propagation of the race. Nature remained silent at first, the transgressors themselves were not punished or were only mildly punished. Then terrible catastrophes arrived. France declined, England is following the same path, and a great qualitative transformation is occurring in the United States. The severity of the punishment shows how serious the offence was."[100]

Although the medical profession was certainly divided concerning the means for fighting abortion and particularly concerning the threats this struggle presented to the principle of doctor-patient privilege, no protest seems to have been raised concerning the execution of a woman who had performed abortions or concerning penalties of imprisonment and hard labor for life. The death penalty and the serious penalties introduced by the law of February 15, 1942, thus affected only women, including some who belonged to the health care professions, and a single man about which nothing is known; no doctors were involved. Women from the lower classes living in provincial cities suffered the worst because they were the easiest to accuse and sentence during a stage of the fight against abortion that made it a crime against public safety. In any event, no one came to their defense, and their designation for national opprobrium evoked the opprobrium that stigmatized the *tondues** during the liberation.[101] After the war, while the repeal of the law of September 1941 and that of the State Court made enforcing the law of February 1942 impossible, the repression of abortion continued. In 1947, 2,022 cases were brought before the courts, compared to 205 in 1936.[102] The natalist policy was again at the heart of the policy of "national reconstruction," and demography was more than ever a "neutral" science.

* Women whose hair was shorn as punishment for "horizontal" collaboration. — *Trans.*

"Tota mulier in utero"

Through the prestige of its founder, the priority that was accorded
to medicine over the other human sciences, and its interdisciplinary
dynamism that created new markets, the Carrel Foundation played a
central role during this period when medical legitimacy was being re-
defined. Contrary to what the modernism of such a project might lead
one to expect, apparently far removed from the traditional objectives
of family medicine, Dr. Carrel constructed motherhood as the only
legitimate feminine identity based on a pessimistic vision: the end
of a world. His desire to elaborate a total human science in the service of a future city, for which the National Revolution would make
it possible to lay the foundations, mixed futurism and archaism, as
is often the case in prophetic undertakings. The archaism concerned
women's bodies. It was through control of the female body that one
could return to a golden age where the physiological laws founded
the social laws. Denying the recent lessons of history concerning the
sexual division of the social world, refusing to take note of the necessity of women's work, and condemning the scholastic and professional advances of women, Carrel, cited by everyone and everywhere,
placed all his scientific authority into imposing the idea of an "eternal
feminine" founded, this time, on biological and physiological determinisms. Women were thus, once again, guarantors of continuity in a
universe perceived to be chaotic because it had lost its "natural" reference points. From this perspective, Carrel reprised the nostalgic ideology of the Action française, whose medical spokesmen saw in feminine "deviance" the very image of "the Formless": "It is the Formless
that in religion seeks to make cosmopolitan formlessness conspire
against organic Catholicity. It is the Formless that in the masculine
subject desires the predominance of the feminine principle. It is the
Formless that desires a femininity that mimes man, that cuts short
her charity like she cuts short her hair, that exhibits its forms in her so
well that she loses all form; that interferes in everything, stirs everything up, overcomes everything, conquers everything, but through
which the race is no longer."[103]

As obsessed as it was with the scientific knowledge of degeneration and with the scientific construction of a regenerated race, the
Carrelian utopia also drew up a pessimistic report on the scientific

and technical advances concerning the evolution of societies and the quality of individuals. In this way, it was close to the *völkisch* nostalgias such as the lamentations of Thibon concerning the destruction of millenary equilibrium, and it resonated in harmony with the theme of the return to the "real" so central to the National Revolution. Carrel wanted to construct a science of sciences capable of "remaking" man, who "transgressed natural laws," and of restoring him "to the harmony of his physical and mental activities," in opposition to the harmful uses of science that did not take into account the "nature of human beings."[104] The declining birthrate, the voluntary sterility of women—and the involuntary sterility of the "best" among them—were the cost of progress against nature, of the "modifications brought about in the ancestral habits by industrial civilization."[105] In the Foundation's vast program of the study of human problems "to raise the biological level of France," feminine reeducation was given a place of honor. Teams devoted to the biology of lineage, the declining birthrate, childhood development, habitat, and nutrition, and departments devoted to the biology of population, the biology of childhood and of youth stated that "it is the mother who animates the family home and therein accomplishes the essential part of her work as housewife and educator." But the current education of girls left something to be desired in this area: "The preparation for the role of mother of a family will be completed by carrying out a family service at home," by studies on "the rationalization of woman's work in her interior" (which began with a study of how to lay out the kitchen), and through the Foundation's cooperation with primary education to develop agricultural and domestic education.[106] Under the guidance of experts, this feminine work that revived the "natural laws" was informed and framed by one of the five large specialized establishments of the Foundation, the Mother and Child Center, which determined the conditions for the "optimum development of the child from conception to age six."

Like the ecclesiastic institution, the medical institution had at the ready an entire cultural stock constructed over a long period that mixed old myths and successive historical expressions of high culture concerning feminine "nature." The central theme of this medical culture of femininity was that motherhood was the *civilizing process of women* in a dual sense: it pulled them out of the "savagery" into which their unsatisfied instincts always risked making them fall back, and it enlisted them in the historical process of civilization. It replaced chaos (uterine furies, nymphomania, hysteria) with harmony, "formlessness" with form, and gave women their full social utility. "Motherhood beautifies woman," according to the doctors drawn by the propaganda of the Commissariat General for the Family. "An attractive woman without children has no place in the city," added the social philosophers who intoned Vichy's profamily social philosophy. In short, the only way for women to leave their condition as minors, as incomplete beings stalked by every imbalance, was motherhood. Demographic balance and feminine psychological balance went hand in hand.

"How many lifeless, withered young women make radiant young mothers. How many nervous women with gloomy and melancholic tendencies become serene and balanced mommies!"[107] One illustration shows a robust, smiling young mother, dressed in a Roman-era gown, an infant in her left arm, her right arm around a column, a symbol of balance and pillar of the house of France. During the first pregnancy, "the organism loses the sickly and childish aspect that it very often retains after puberty," whereas "anticonception and abortive methods" made women "old before their time," threatened by "nervousness, despair, psychic and even mental imbalance."[108] Dr. Pierre Merle, who specialized in studying "feminine nature from a physiological and psychological perspective," defined motherhood as a "nervous stabilization," pregnancy often providing "the cure for tenacious problems," and declared that it was the "organic susceptibility" of women that produced "feminine sensitivity."[109] The National Alliance against Depopulation viewed anticonception practices as a danger for the feminine organism, for, as Professor Pinard said, "a woman needs four pregnancies to have normal health," and "*recent research* also tends to prove that the absorption of seminal fluid by the feminine organism stimulates the functioning of her endocrine glands and increases her vitality."[110] For Dr. Carrel, woman held the future of the civilization in her hand, provided that she rediscovered her specific mission, "a mission inscribed for perhaps more than a million years in her genital organs, her glands, her nervous system and her spirit,"[111] namely, motherhood: "But females, at any rate among mammals, seem only to attain their full development after one or more pregnancies. Women who have no children are not so well balanced and become more nervous than the others. In short, the presence of the foetus, whose tissues differ greatly from hers because they are young and are, in part, those of her husband, acts profoundly on the woman. . . . It is therefore absurd to turn women against maternity. The same intellectual and physical training, and the same ambitions, should not be given to young girls as to boys. Educators should pay very close attention to the *organic and mental peculiarities of the male and the female, and to their natural functions.*" [112]

The National Revolution reactivated the old medical stereotypes concerning feminine normality, giving them new vigor and an air of modernity. All these ideas were held by doctors at the beginning of the nineteenth century who themselves mobilized ageless archetypes concerning feminine nature. Thus, there is the archetype of the young virgin, "listless, thin, who can hardly drag herself along," that Virey, who was recognized as an authority in this field for decades,[113] reprised from doctors at the start of the seventeenth century, themselves fed by the medical-philosophical discourses of ancient Greece. Virey's central thesis, which contended that woman remained much like a child because she was deprived of sperm, can be found in the tract of the National Alliance against Depopulation of 1944: "One commonly sees very heavy girls lose their corpulence through marriage as if the *energy* of the sperm imprinted more stiffness and *dryness* in their fibers. . . . It is certain that the male sperm impregnates the woman's organism, that it revives all her functions and *rewarms* them, that she is all the better for it." [114] Energy and weakness, dryness and dampness, hot and cold are the great binary oppositions that attribute positive and negative values to each sex. Françoise Héritier has demonstrated that the medical discourse of the nineteenth century concerning the masculine/feminine opposition was inspired by mythic thought and merely restored the discourse of Aristotle—who himself developed much older archetypes—or that of the Inuits or the Baruya of New Guinea: "These symbolic discourses are built on a system of binary categories, of dualistic pairs, that opposed series like Sun and Moon, high and low, right and left, bright and obscure, light and dark, light and heavy, front and back, hot and cold, dry and wet, masculine and feminine, superior and inferior. Here one recognizes the symbolic armature of Greek philosophic and medical thought as it is found in Aristotle, Anaximander, and Hippocrates, where the balance of the world, like that of the human body or of its humors, is founded on a harmonious mixture of these contraries. Any excess in a field leads to disorder and/or sickness." [115] Vichy's philosophical-medical discourse concerning the biological bases of the sexual division of the social world belonged to the register of mythic thought.

This biological view of the masculine/feminine opposition and the biological views of intelligence and the aptitude for leadership that accompanied it, that it founded and that founded it, all of these processes for naturalizing social constructs developed in an ideological climate obsessed with the return to the corporeal. In a certain way, playing on one of Marshal Pétain's aphorisms concerning the earth, we could say that for the Vichy ideologists, "the body does not lie." If, according to Carrel, the sin of civilization was to separate the physical from the mental, the great error of the French educational system was, according to the officer and educator Pétain, to separate the spirit from the heart and the character, to emphasize the bookish to the detriment of the concrete, to neglect the formation of the body in favor of cramming brains. The National Revolution therefore committed itself to constructing an *order of bodies* that was an entire social philosophy: "To combat the harmful tendencies for which we are paying so dearly at this time, I am taking the liberty of advising mothers to masculinize their sons and feminize their daughters." [116] The moralizing ideologue of the National Revolution joined, perhaps without being aware of this, the calls for masculinity of a press fascinated by Nazi values: "French men, be male. French women, become mothers. And France will once again be saved." [117] *Idées,* the doctrinal review directed by René Vincent, Jean de Fabrègues, and Jean-Pierre Maxence, leading figures among "nonconformist" intellectuals of the 1930s often close to the Action française, who participated in developing the ideology of the National Revolution in the direction of a revolutionary induration specific to creating a new man, proclaimed: "The vitality of the French body is virility: a source of perpetual gushes, an overflow spread by excess, a deeply carnal virility." [118] Even if *Idées* made fun of certain aspects of Vichy's familialism in which it saw only a bland substitute for its appeal to virility,[119] the regime and the period nevertheless obstinately recalled bodies to order. "Sexes have again to be clearly defined," Carrel repeated. "Each individual should be either male or female, and never manifest the sexual tendencies, mental characteristics, and ambitions of the opposite sex."[120]

It is, of course, first in the family, the initial cell of society, which is itself a society, that the language of the body speaks the truth of the social body, hierarchical by nature. The large family is the prime condition for a real apprenticeship of organic solidarities. An only child is always "spoiled"; it is the presence of brothers and sisters that "forms the character"; the "institution of the only child" that gives an "unreasonable place to the child-king" leads to the "degradation of paternal authority that becomes ridiculous for want of an object."[121] The social construction of family roles, of the sexual division of the educational functions, of the relationship between parents and (many) children imposes an initial model of the hierarchical relationship. If children all need to learn and if women always retain something of childhood, men, the "heads of the (large) family" must embody authority. And authority once again finds its divine guarantee: "Domestic authority must be felt by all members of the group; they must know it, understand it, and consent to it; but to be organic, it must be incarnated in one of them and one of them alone. This is the function of the head of the family. . . . At this degree of plenitude, authority then appears to be what it is in reality: a divine reflection, an invitation to perfect order."[122]

In the small family society, it was the *language of the body* that provided the evidence of "natural" command. The review *Éducation* offered the outline of a "living lesson" about the family intended to "strike the sensitive chord" in children, a chord "that loosens if it is not used." This gave rise to a catechism of questions and answers aimed at developing the sense of a family orientation in children: "THE FATHER. He is the head of the family, he commands everyone, he must be obeyed. (A) Is he at home all day long? Where is he? At work. Why? What is the father like? He is tall, strong; he has a deep voice. Describe his clothes. THE MOTHER. (A) Above all, she takes care of the housework and the children. Is she at home all day long? Yes (in principle, but this is not, alas, always the case!). (B) What is the mother like? In general, she is shorter than the father, not as strong, either, but gentler, more affectionate with her children. Is her voice the same as the father's? Describe how she dresses compared to the father." For practical exercises: "Children will like to play family;

either the older ones will be the parents and the younger ones the children, or they will use dolls for more docile children."[123] Refusing to let the "sensitive chord" relax is to educate the gaze concerning bodily difference and, by associating with it a series of hierarchized social roles, to prepare each for his or her "anatomic destiny."

The National Revolution thus provided the opportunity to express explicitly a method of raising the body and learning the difference of bodies that reprised the great mythic oppositions and reinvented a pedagogy of masculinity and femininity. It is an experimental moment to study the direct intervention of the state and of those who placed themselves in the service of its social philosophy concerning sexual differentiation. And the political management of sex—of "genders"—moved through a clarification of the apprenticeships of the youngest, through games and imagination, that framed the path of identification as one definition, imposed as legitimate, by the culture of gender. As I showed earlier, the reeducators of the National Revolution focused feminine education on the early internalization of techniques of the body through a mimetic apprenticeship that imposed the idea of a "natural" association of femininity and corporal care, that of an apprenticeship of mother to daughter of a specific way of listening to the feminine body and of its sole legitimate "vocation," motherhood. The biological view of the feminine is at the heart of this vision of the woman-caregiver, dear to the Church and to the medical profession,[124] that grants women a monopoly over bodily care in the domestic space and subordinates bodily care in the professional space. "Woman is, much more than man, sensitive to the rhythms that dominate all physiological life," said the women's medical specialist who summed up the medical discourse for all ages.[125] She must train her daughter to listen to these rhythms, "monitoring her physically, in the development of her muscles and in her overall health," transmitting to her "the art of caring for people who suffer," an art that one must "begin to learn in the family" and to which "one is never initiated too early."[126]

This specific form of girls' education through the enveloping and continuous pedagogy of the feminine body in the family space constitutes an exemplary mode of symbolic violence, a violence unrecognized as violence because its fundamental and prereflexive suppositions are accepted.[127] With the help of a crisis situation—and immediately following the partial but certain questioning of line domination where the world could no longer be taken evident—the Vichy construction of the "eternal feminine" and clarified these presuppositions. At the same time, it hig⌐ the mechanisms of constraining the body specific to the work of socialization that was carrying out "a progressive somatization of the relations of sexual domination." The social work on the corporal *hexis,* an incorporated policy that legitimized the relation of domination "by inscribing it in a biology that is itself a biologized social construction," acquired, during this period, the status of explicit political work. It was the state itself, through the masculinization of masculine bodies and the feminization of feminine bodies, that intervened in the "somatization of cultural arbitrariness." Assisted by all those whose own interests pushed them to embrace the cause of the return to the "eternal feminine," the state appeared here as the great master of this social psychosomatics consistent with the unconscious schemes and mythic visions of the world. A small feminine corporal education manual summarized what woman should know about her body to put this body in the service of reproduction and family health, the biological moral allowing the declination of a new version of the culture of sacrifice, as this body is, from time immemorial, a body for others. Woman must therefore be attentive to her body, monitor its hygiene, its growth, the regularity of her periods ("Do not say 'That will take care of itself!' Periods are often a sort of health barometer for a woman"), and prepare herself to become the family hygienist: "The home will be what you make it: either the dream location to 'live well' or the worst weapon against the physical and moral health of your family"; "but above all, do not forget that you are woman and that your body must be cultivated for grace, flexibility, and resistance more than for strength. Do not forget that one day you will be a mother"; "this idea must give us a profound respect for our body: we do not have the right to neglect it, for it does not belong to us alone." [128]

If the Vichy cult of gymnastics was a major component of girls' sports education, [129] it did not neglect to redefine the particular limitations of feminine physical education and the feminine specificity of the links among morality, psychology, and the body. In this educational view where the body speaks the essence of being, the discourse concerning sports was always a discourse concerning the virtues specific to each sex. And it was not happenstance if the newspaper published by Uriage, that lofty place for redefining masculine corporal excellence and morality, produced a manifesto in this regard that set the limits straight off: "If we condone the currently accepted definition of masculine sports, intensive muscular exercise aimed at competition, interested in performance, and maintaining the taste for risk, we would have the right to contend categorically that in this form, sports are totally antifeminine. Physiologically first, for woman is built not to fight—which is the privilege of man—but to procreate; nature set the boundaries of her physical possibilities, and it would be dangerous to transgress them. Morally and psychically next, for in her normal role as wife and mother, she would not benefit from a certain 'virilization' of emotions and character!" [130] For "well-balanced," "robust," and "healthy" women, the author wanted women's gymnastics, swimming, and camping, in short, a "just" balance between "outdated biases" and "dangerous exaggerations."

The Commissariat General for Sports sought the same compromise, because the goal was not the same "when this involves men who must be virilized and women who must be made robust, but remain graceful." The Commissariat wanted to put an end to a period of confusion in which women athletes "were much too masculinized" and in which the public authorities had let physical education and feminine sports "develop and degenerate haphazardly": "We submit in principle that from puberty, women's physical and sports education should differ from men's physical and sports education to follow a path that is specific to it, a path traced by taking into consideration the morphological, physiological, and psychic differences that exist between the two sexes." Flexibility more than strength, development of the abdominals, the prohibition against rugby, soccer, cycling, practicing combative sports, the encouragement of rhythmic exercise favorable to nervous coordination, but without going so far as the spectacular exhibition propitious for showing off, will help women remain essentially feminine, wives and mothers worthy to train new generations. [131] In March 1943, the Commissariat General for Sports organized a gala at the large amphitheater of the Sorbonne whose theme was "Woman and Sports." The speaker, a doctor and writer, presented women's physical education as "a great work of natural history that must be introduced into the national history." Women's sports must "give the feminine physiology its balance," "achieve the individual destiny of women and make them capable of playing their role in the destinies of countries, that is, above all if not solely, being capable of perpetuating and beautifying the race." After the age of seven or eight, when physical exercise for both sexes must become distinct, girls will work on flexibility, balance, curves, roundness, with balls, hoops, jump ropes, and, of course, dance. The discourse concerning swimming, "the most feminine of sports," was placed under the protection of "the ancients that peopled the waters with women: sirens, sea nymphs, and nereids."[132] The clarification of possible and impossible masculine and feminine sports, of the territories and limits of women's gymnastics, this limiting of the relation of the female body to space, this framing of the language of the body through the marking out of muscular work, function as recalls to a feminine corporal order. The privileged relationship to the water, to the curve, to roundness, the primacy of flexibility and the opposition of flexibility and strength, the concern for rhythm, all the interdictions included in these gestural prescriptions, all the "values made body," clearly reinscribed the masculine/feminine opposition in mythical logic. The National Revolution made it clear that "the corporal hexis is the political mythology made real."[133]

The Biological Foundations of Domination

The opposition between strength and grace is also an opposition between authority and submission, between reason and intuition, exterior and interior, leader and advisor, as Monsignor Dupanloup put it. The constructions of femininity developed by the Catholic culture and the medical culture where the basic mythic oppositions emerge sustain these infraconscious associations among corporal aptitudes and intellectual aptitudes, psychological penchants, moods, and humors, and gestures that chart the masculine and feminine spaces. This cartography is nothing other than a philosophy of power: "With a more lively imagination and *greater emotivity,* woman, more muscularly weak than man, is more interested in people than in things, in people than in ideas. Man quickly grasps the sense of the entire world and, on the contrary, is more interested in things than in people; he is drawn to science. Man imagines great breakthroughs in the cities. Woman thinks about the charms of the street, of the house." [134] Woman must therefore "second man"; she is a "different and complementary" person. Women administrators, theoreticians, athletes, and intellectuals are "hard and inhuman," experience "tragic maternities," and competition makes them lose "the femininity in their being altogether." [135] Dr. Biot, who placed the legitimacy of medical knowledge at the service of the Catholic definition of femininity and questions concerning "Christian feminism," referred to old theories of temperaments to support the scientific approach to feminine abnormality. The masculine type, who possesses "the best physiological and psychological performance," presents four characters hierarchized as follows: bilious (voluntary motor activity), nervous (reception of impressions), sanguine (vital activity), and lymphatic (power reserve). The ideal feminine constitution has the following hierarchy: nervous, lymphatic, bilious, and sanguine. "Translation," says Biot: "the healthy man is first an energetic leader . . . , woman is a collaborator." Those unfortunate women in whom the four elements are presented in disordered fashion are "*agitated* at cross purposes"; they are often spinsters or divorcées, "protesters," "paradoxical opponents." [136] Alexis Carrel also based the legitimacy of masculine domination on corporal differences: the ovaries and the testicles "impress the male and female characteristics on our tissues, humors, and consciousness. . . . The testicle engenders audacity." The "physiological laws" reduce to nothing the ideas of "promoters of feminism" incapable of accepting that a woman's "organs and, above all, her *nerves*" prohibit women from having "the same powers and the same responsibilities" as men.[137] Thus, "guiding reason" does not have the same characteristics in both parents and is divided at home as in all of social life: "Those that it assumes in men are more related to command, namely, breadth of vision, follow-up, *calm,* impartiality"; in women, "intuition, delicacy, a sense for detail, heart." [138] Heart is what "awakens so fast in the little girl and opens itself wide to the mother's first look"; heart will nourish intuition, the second quality apt for seconding "the positive and constructive side of man." [139]

Reset in the social philosophy of the National Revolution, this biological construction of masculine domination nurtured by the cul-

tural unconscious reactivated during this period of crisis was inseparably a political reflection on the biological foundations of domination and on the predestination to command and obey. If I have
often cited the texts of Alexis Carrel, it is not only because they
offer particularly exemplary expressions of biological legitimization
and therefore of the naturalization of culturally constructed arbitrary oppositions between masculine and feminine "natures." They
also constitute a veritable *system of biological thought about the social world.*
Carrel and the Carrel Foundation not only proposed a banal pronatalist crusade that privileged quantity but also a broader discussion of "biology of lineage," of "biotypology" and "psychophysi-
ology" that was related to quality, heredity, "defects," "mental age,"
"healthy stocks," the products of "crossings" between "biological
groups." Alexis Carrel was a theoretician of "natural" inequality who
saw in "democratic equality" an "error," a dogma "that is now breaking down under the blows of the experience of the nations," a dogma
that did not take into account "the constitution of the body and of
the conscience" because neither individuals nor the sexes are "equal."
"Each is born with different intellectual abilities"; "the tempera-
ment," a mixture of "mental, physiological, and structural" characters, "changes from one individual to another, from one race to
another"; "most civilized men display only a rudimentary form of
conscience"; "soft, emotive, cowardly, lascivious, and violent," "they
have created a vast herd of children whose intelligence remains rudimentary"; finally, we can oppose "the hesitant, the annoying, the impulsive, . . . the weak" to the "reflective," "self-controlled . . . the
well-balanced." To form the strong who are "resistant and hardy," it
takes rough climates, long mountain winters, brutal weather, manly
food, meats, unrefined flours, and alcohol.[140]

Whereas the scientific apparatus of the Carrel Foundation was impressive, the Carrelian vision of the social world had all the characteristics of *an erudite myth.* Primitive images of specifically mythic
oppositions slipped into the anatomic and physiological description
under the cover of the polysemy of words.[141] Views dormant in us and
always ready to awaken, according to the expression of Pierre Gourou,[142] the equation between cold and strength, warmth and weakness, the opposition between men of the North (virility, strength of
body and spirit) and men of the South (relaxed, weak, lacking con-

trol) refer to the principal opposition between masculine and feminine. They boil down to "a generative opposition, that of *master* (of self, therefore of others) and *slave* (of the senses and masters)." Like the work of Montesquieu, the work of Carrel brought about a particular symbolic imposition that resulted from making the projections of social fantasy appear to be a science. The omnipresence of the masculine/feminine opposition in the writings of Carrel contributed largely to producing this effect at the same time that it rearmed the symbolic violence of masculine domination. But the "natural" opposition between "strong" ("balanced") men and "weak" ("impulsive," "emotive") men also justified all the forms of class racism that imbued the ideology of the National Revolution. Rediscovering the right-wing model of historiography forged from the trauma of 1871 and the incorporation of medical language into political discourse, this vision of the masses revived the images of the crowd that associated it with women, the savage, the child.[143] Thus this expression of Tarde, in which we find the agendas of medical feminine culture and the medical-political discourses: "By its routine caprice, its malcontented docility, its credulity, its *edginess,* its abrupt psychological shifts from fury to tenderness, from exasperation to fits of laughter, the crowd is woman, even when it is composed, as always happens, of masculine elements." The opposition between mastered and unmastered nature is one of the major political oppositions between masculine and feminine, a syncretic scheme that psychiatrizes moral and political science. The true elite are on the side of *self-control.* By rejecting "the habits of the herd" they will be able to reconstruct themselves as "an ascetic and mystic minority," capable of rapidly acquiring "an irresistible power over the dissolute and degraded majority."[144]

One of the central objectives the Foundation set for itself in its study of human problems was to reflect scientifically on the quality of "human capital," on "biological classes" and "social classes," on the potentialities of individuals, and on the development of the elite, respecting "individual inequalities" because "the circumstances of development are efficient only within the limits of the hereditary predispositions."[145] The Foundation was therefore concerned with how to make a "mental inventory of the population." It began with children. An assessment of backward children and elite subjects, a systematic study of the symptoms of deficiency, of their organic and mental substratum, and of the causes of superiority were the tasks of the Childhood Development team that initiated impressive quantitative surveys for comparative purposes.[146] Tests, biotypology, and morphopsychology that "confirms certain empirical observations of the old physiognomy of Porta and Lavater," were placed in the service of educators and professional guidance. Thus, once again, the old and new were mixed together. Lavater's doctrine, developed at the end of the eighteenth century, condemned by scientists and criticized by philosophers, owed its fashionable success as a "false science" to the fact that, like the theory of climates, it merely gave a learned form to the social fantasies of the elite of the time. It also contributed to the mythical-learned construction of the masculine/feminine opposition in which one once again finds a rhetoric identical to the Vichy rhetoric: submission, reserve, feeling, but also irritability and fantasy are the lot of women, the "second page of the sheet of humanity," according to Lavater's expression, who do not have a sense of the whole and the depths. Also capable of the worst excesses, woman in revolt is already implicitly associated here with the populace. The submission of the people and the submission of women are subject to the same "natural evidence."[147]

The Foundation firmly applied morphopsychology to the study of young delinquent women placed in a home, La Tutélaire, so that the director could decide with full scientific knowledge whether family placement was desirable or the adolescent needed "firm and impersonal discipline." The major investigations concerning childhood deficiencies would continue to serve as a model during the postwar period[148] and would inspire the developments of professional guidance and the medical psychology of "maladjustment." At the opposite end of the spectrum were those who were not yet called "gifted" but, in the somewhat archaic language of Agathon, "young Frenchmen of quality." An investigation conducted by the biotypology team focused on athletic students, those who stood out against the "lack of virility and bearing" that were so striking when observing youth, according to the experts of the Carrel Foundation, taking up again the tireless Vichy accusation of the carelessness of the youth of cities behind which was outlined the haunting memory of the Popular Front. Questionnaires and tests filled out by the youth of the Chantiers would finally make it possible to reflect on "ascendance-submission" and on the "aptitudes for command." Carrel's *Man, the Unknown* was part of the basic bibliography required for Chantier training courses; graphology and industrial psychology were widely used in the leadership schools established by Vichy.

The Carrel Foundation thus played a leading role in legitimizing and expanding these procedures for measuring aptitudes and unsuitability that escaped the scholastic order. The social philosophy of "natural" inequalities, whose initial model was masculine/feminine inequality, was very favorable to the overproduction of "scientific" theories intended to account for inequalities before the school without taking into consideration or by relativizing socially produced inequalities and their influence on scholastic and social success or failure. As clarified by the Foundation's publication *Les Cahiers* when commenting on these new methods for evaluating children, "The collaboration of teachers, doctors, and morphopsychologists must result in bringing back the importance of exams and competitions to its just proportion." School was not truly for all: "A seasoned observer is able to grasp the significance of the growing characteristics of a child, as well as of a puppy, very early in its life. Developmental conditions cannot transform a weak, apathetic, dispersed, timid, inactive child into an energetic man, a powerful and audacious leader." Now, "the stupid, unintelligent, those who are dispersed, incapable of attention, of effort, have no right to a higher education." Finally, "Today, most of the members of the proletarian class owe their situation to the hereditary weakness of their organs and their mind."[149] In the skirmishes against National Education, Lamirand, the engineer–secretary general for youth, discovered this line of argumentation quite naturally to defend the autonomy of general and sports education: young workers should not be entrusted to vocational education that aims too high, the education departments acting as if all workers were destined to become skilled workers; now, 80 percent of them will be semiskilled workers and will need only "light additional moral, physical, and ideological instruction."[150]

It is in this shift in the educational project toward, as Carrel wanted, replacing exams with "scientific inventories," allowing youth to be classified into categories and making it possible to determine "the position that each is capable of occupying," that professional guidance developed considerably during the National Revolution.

Vichy and the Eternal Feminine ▸ 300

Enlisted in the great investigations of the Carrel Foundation, professional guidance counselors broadened their skills in psychological diagnosis, achieved the creation of "an association" of counselors and the creation of a state diploma in January 1944, and were divided between their loyalty to the school and this historic opportunity to enhance the position and professionalization of the occupation. Counselors were encouraged by the relentless criticism of the Republican educational system that was deployed beginning in the 1940s and by the systematization and the banalization of a sociopolitical theory of natural inequalities, legitimized by what presented itself as the latest state of scientific knowledge. In response, a vast institutional sector for screening and supervising children and "troubled adolescents" was deployed under Vichy. Its historical links to the philanthropic and private rehabilitation sector, which predestined it to this form of competition with National Education, and this exceptional historical situation would allow it to construct a childhood market parallel to the educational market, and to establish the administrative framework of its action that survived long after the war. All this encouraged the final victory of medical and medical-psychological imperialism in this field that imposed the notion of individual "maladjustment" to posit the malfunctions of the relationship between scholastic and social order.[151]

Women and the Defense of the Race

Dr. Carrel at times slipped toward negative eugenism when he reflected on "the preservation of useless and harmful beings" ("defectives," "the abnormal," "criminals") who must be disposed of "more economically" ("conditioning with the whip" for the least dangerous, "euthanasia institutions supplied with the proper gases" for the others).[152] But his central objective, and that of the Foundation he directed, was to improve the "civilized races" through the reproduction of their best elements and to encourage the perpetuation of elites through the development of the "strong" against "the predominance of the weak," by reviving the "ancestral potentialities" of the "noble and energetic strains."[153] Carrel's personal obsessions concerning the sterility of noble stocks were consistent with the demographic thematics of the infertility of the elites deployed during the nineteenth century.[154] His Biology of Lineage team therefore strove first to locate stocks "of good genetic constitution" and then to aid in the propagation of these stocks. For it was pointless to increase the birthrate if the increase was accomplished "as a result of the fertility of defective elements." Nazi racial hygiene had also reactivated the distinction, dear to the German eugenicists of the 1920s, between "mothers of the race" and mothers responsible for "racial degeneration."[155] Like many other thinkers of regeneration engaged in the National Revolution, those at the Foundation did not unconditionally approve of family allowances that rewarded large families and that were "far from encouraging the propagation of the best stocks,"[156] but declared themselves in favor of the prenuptial certificate.

The establishment of a compulsory medical examination before marriage, which had been the subject of numerous discussions during the interwar period,[157] was accomplished by a law of December 31, 1942, that in its turn aroused debate within the medical profession, which was divided concerning its ethical foundations and its real efficacy. In October 1935, a law of the Nazi government regarding the protection of the genetic health of the German people had made the prenuptial examination compulsory.[158] The Foundation supported this measure without reservation, which a social philosophy manual of the regime written for women greeted in these terms: "We do not hesitate to say that marriage must be absolutely forbidden for children who have some profound, incurable defect; this is not only in their interest, but in the otherwise serious interest of the family, of the race, and of society. We know better and better today where mental defects lead. Much fun was made of the movement that, begun in England by Galton, has since been propagated in France in favor of Eugenics. These scoffers are wrong."[159] In its unrestricted support of the new order of the National Revolution, a Catholic review forgot all the Church's reservations concerning this issue to welcome the prenuptial certificate based on a magical theory of heredity: "Just as the characteristics of a race are transmitted from *mother to daughter or from father to son,* certain abnormal characteristics can be transmitted in the family. Young men, young women, go see your family doctor."[160] But Carrel specified that medical exams gave only "the illusion of safety" and that it was necessary to arrive at a "voluntary eugenism" of the elite: "Through appropriate education, we could make young people understand what misfortunes they expose themselves to by marrying into families where there is syphilis, cancer, tuberculosis, nervousness, madness, or weakness of mind. Such families should be considered by them as at least *as undesirable as poor families.*"[161]

Thus, the "positive" eugenics of the Carrel Foundation proposed to replace democracy with what could be called a *biocracy,* in which "hereditarily and biologically gifted beings have a duty to unite only with beings who are also of superior quality."[162] The premier department of the Foundation, the Biology of Population, set as its priority scientific work concerning heredity, genetics, eugenics, and, with the assistance of the General Confederation of Families and the Coordination Center for Family Movements, undertook a "census of the healthy stocks of France, of fertile and professionally gifted families."[163] Here the Foundation provided the "scientific" version of the genealogical concerns that arose under the National Revolution: "Learning to know one's ancestors is good; striving to draw practical conclusions from this knowledge during a tragic era in which each people, each man, must reinvigorate itself is better."[164] In May 1941, the Secretariat of State for Health and the Family envisioned the creation of an Office of French Family Archives that would make an inventory by region with the assistance of knowledgeable locals ("old canons, doctors, notaries who are enthusiasts of local history") and with the assistance of family organizations and folklore societies, of family genealogies. For "only the family . . . can provide us with the elements of a healthy biological doctrine by virtue of blood."[165]

The second task that the Carrel Foundation's department of population biology set for itself was the scientific treatment of immigration: it announced the establishment of documentation concerning foreign immigration in France and the completion of surveys intended to "determine who are the immigrants whose presence may be deemed desirable." The Foundation thus provided the guarantee of its scientific authority to the French State's obsession with restoring the homogeneity of the national organism, weakened as much by the declining birthrate as by degenerating immigration, according to the theoreticians of degeneration who sustained demographic thought during the interwar period.

The biologizing of political thought thus slipped easily from a theory of natural inequalities between the sexes, between classes—

"true" elites and "poor families"—to a vision of inequality among races and a denunciation of the dangers of crossbreeding. In a lecture at the session of the Chantiers de la Jeunesse of Puy in May 1943, Dr. Robert Gessain, secretary general of the Foundation's population team, took up the issue of the "ethnic complex of the French nation." Just as one wanted to triage "healthy stocks" from the others, this involved identifying and distinguishing "assimilable" immigrated groups from the others to base the principles of the immigration policy on physical anthropology:

> Recent progress in the science of human heredity shows that men are genetically unequal at birth. Racial biology teaches us that these geographic groupings of hereditary characters that make up the races are different by their form and their method of physiological and mental functioning. . . . There are human groups of different quality. . . . Whether there was a Saracen or a Jew in the history of the nobility of Languedoc is of no importance, but it is not without importance that, in the demographically anemic France in the middle of the twentieth century, many hundreds of thousands of racially inassimilable immigrants, I mean, for example, due to Mongoloid or Negroid or Judaized racial elements, profoundly modify the hereditary heritage of the nation.[166]

To distinguish "assimilable" groups from the others, the Foundation undertook investigations of the Armenians of Issy-les-Moulineaux and the foreigners of Les Halles neighborhood. "It seeks to know what the products of crossing these foreigners with French men and women are worth," for the presence "of groups of undesirable foreigners from a biological standpoint is a sure danger for the French population."[167]

The Foundation's monthly biographical bulletin, which gives a good idea of the "scientific" reference documentation, abundantly quoted the minor and major ideologues of the National Revolution, the reviews that placed themselves in the service of the regime, and also, without any further reservations, the racist review of Dr. George Montandon, *L'Ethnie française,* and the works of Dr. René Martial, a specialist in crossbreeding.[168] The Foundation also funded a report by Martial in July 1942, and in the lecture cited earlier, Robert Gessain welcomed Montandon's scientific contribution.[169] Director of the Institute for the Study of Jewish and Ethno-Racial Questions, a veritable anti-Jewish academy established in 1943 by the second commissaire general for Jewish Affairs, Darquier de Pellepoix, Montandon made a specialty of the anthropological identification of Jews.[170] A theoretician of "ethnoraciology," in 1941 he founded an openly anti-Semitic and collaborationist monthly review, *L'Ethnie française,* that was interested in "anthroposomatics," "raciology," heredity, eugenics or "racial hygiene," the birthrate, and demography. Its authors constantly called for the renewal of "true French families" and for vigilance concerning the "racial consequences" of immigration. The call for French women to return to the home and for the exhaustive production of statistics on foreigners accounted for in the French population—"in order to measure the gravity of the problem raised by the massive contribution of this foreign blood from a racial standpoint"—went hand in hand.[171]

To return to the true French elite, an anonymous author who signed himself "Pater familias" called for privileging the "biotypology" exam for children to the detriment of scholastic exams that "clearly advantage Jewish children," the well-known precocity of "oriental ethnic groups" (close to feminine precocity) that was in fact a genetic "defect" leading these children to usurp places to which they were not entitled.[172] Georges Mauco provided his assistance to the review to denounce the immigration of "less and less assimilable" elements and in particular condemned the "imposed" immigration of refugees:

All the unfavorable particularities of imposed immigration appear for Jewish refugees. Physical and psychic health, morality, and character are also diminished. . . . Here, again, these are souls fashioned by the lengthy humiliations of a servile state, where repressed hatred is masked by obsequiousness. . . . Do these refugees at least provide an intellectual value in default of moral and physical value? It does not seem so, despite appearances. . . . particularly gifted by their ability and their versatile ingenuity, foreign Jews succeeded easily in a liberal France, where the power of money and intellectualism won out over character and virile strength! . . . Some even attained positions of authority without having any of the qualifications of a leader or knowledge of men. *They thus emasculated authority.*[173]

So this was a false elite among whom "subtlety and ingenuity of mind" won out over "character" (one of the Marshal's magic words), male virtue of the "true" elite, French by descent. Here the author picks up the old anti-Semitic theme of the hermaphrodism of the Jews, effeminate men, that had achieved extreme violence with respect to Léon Blum.[174] For Mauco, it was above all "from a health standpoint" that this immigration was undesirable, "through the contribution of individuals who are physically and mentally diminished" and "through unfortunate mixed marriages and children who are also diminished."[175] As we can see, Carrel's vision of the world was clearly divided, and the thematics of the biological health of the nation were eminently favorable to the liberated expression of racist stereotypes: "Marriages between spouses from different races? While in America, Germany, and Poland these problems have been studied closely since Gobineau, in France we are only in the initial stages of a science in search of itself. I therefore conclude here on only one point: marriages between French and Eastern peoples are not to be encouraged. The people of Israel in particular . . . will infuse in our veins its eternal anxiety and its mournful criticism. It will refine intelligence but . . . we are already declining . . . while during a difficult period the quality that should be overriding is *character*."[176]

Dr. René Martial was a specialist on immigration and on "interracial grafts" and founder of the course on anthropobiology of the races at the Paris school of medicine. He was a member of the steering committee of Darquier de Pellepoix's Institute of Anthroposociology that was to study "the scientific bases of racial selection," a question that "the prewar government kept carefully hidden under a bushel" because "the Jewish-riddled Popular Front has even enacted laws against those who wanted to look into this problem."[177] In agreement with *L'Ethnie française* in thinking that France had become a "human dump," in complete support of revising naturalizations and excluding foreigners and Jews from public service and the medical professions, Martial devoted himself to the question of "half-bloods," of half-breeds, whose characteristics were "vulgarity, facial *asymmetry, poor proportions* of the limbs and trunk, psychic *insta-*

bility or indifference, perverse spontaneity or morbid originality."[178] Like Carrel, he was interested in "healthy" stocks, in the hereditary heritage of the nation, and condemned feminism as a "biological error." He also wanted the Family Code to include the interdiction of mixed marriages, particularly with Jews, "models of instability doubled by anxiety."[179] The Commissariat General for Jewish Affairs was also preoccupied with "half-Jews"—"often more dangerous than pure Jews due to their hybrid nature"—and the absence of this notion in the Jewish Statute. Darquier de Pellepoix would state before the Nazi propaganda service that he had also thought about prohibiting mixed marriages.[180]

It appears very difficult, in light of these texts and their social uses, to distinguish a noble biotypology from a base biotypology. Erudite myth and state racisms interpenetrate. Vichy's obsession with regenerating the hereditary heritage of the nation and restoring the homogeneity of the social body runs from one discourse to the other. Ultimately, the theories and vocabulary of the French Union for the Defense of the Race, the body that organized the propaganda of the Commissariat General for Jewish Affairs from December 1942 (an extension of the Rassemblement antijuif de France founded by Darquier de Pellepoix in 1936),[181] were close to all these "scientific" reflections on human capital. From January 1943 on, this propaganda forum disseminated its theses on the radio on Mondays and Fridays during the dinner hour; a gong began and ended the broadcast punctuating its slogan: "We have lost everything. Our only remaining national treasure is our race."

> All classes of society must understand that all vicious inclinations
> and all chronic illnesses are transmitted by heredity and that, by the
> purity of blood, the entire system of the human body can gradu-
> ally be raised, or, on the contrary, by neglecting this issue of birth,
> gradually degraded until there is as much difference between well-
> born creatures and low-born creatures as there is between a good
> hunting dog and a base mongrel. . . . This amounts to saying that
> anarchical crossbreeding is the direct and principal cause of the
> collapse of empires and families. . . . It is not debatable that this
> crossbreeding was desired and methodically organized in its appar-
> ent anarchy by those very people who had an interest in subjugat-

ing France and in making it the springboard for their domination of the world: I have named the Jews.[182]

The veterinary metaphor continues with purebloods whose race was preserved and improved thanks to the English Stud Book, that "genealogical tree" that was accepted as an authority on breeding: "During this time, what was being done for man? Nothing but stupid anarchy. The Union proposes the creation of an Institute of Social Genealogy and a Department of the French Family whose aim will be to complete the judicious measures that have recently been taken, under the authority of the Marshal, by the Minister of Public Health" (that is, the obligation for a premarital medical examination).[183] As for Martial, the fight against crossbreeding was for the Union the means for "putting the house back in order": "The Jews are predisposed by their very degeneration to madness in all its forms. It is the famous Charcot who affirms this. . . . It is to prevent this scourge that the French Union for the Defense of the Race made part of its program not only the interdiction against interracial marriages but also the measures for protecting against crossbreeds. For, in racial matters, crossbreeds are a border, and borders are always dangerous, it is through borders that invasions are accomplished."[184]

This refocusing on the masculine/feminine opposition was consistent with biotypology, and biotypology with the preservation of the hereditary heritage, with the assimilable and the inassimilable. As we know, for Xavier Vallat, first commissioner general for Jewish Affairs, the Jew was first of all "an inassimilable foreigner." In this social philosophy of withdrawal into oneself and condemnation of the other, the mobilization of French homemakers came to symbolize the homogeneity of the social body. In the regulations for the competition intended to reward the best texts and illustrations celebrating mothers of families organized by *La Revue de la famille* in preparation for Mother's Day 1942, the first article specifies: "A contest is open to all readers of *La Revue de la famille* of *French nationality,* etc."[185] This detail probably served as much to exclude foreign children and adults who might have wanted to send their drawing or poem as to recall, on the occasion of this Mother's Day, that it was a question of national maternity. By specifying that "no Jewish candidates must be approved" among the Ladies of the Social Medical

Services, the women's branch that it established in 1942, the French Legion of Combattants expanded racial exclusion to charity work and granted no exceptions to French Jewish women, while, at least formally, certain Jews could be accepted for acts of war, in the "fighting legionnaires," a less prestigious and active class than the volunteer legionnaires.[186] Here, again, we see that the call for women's participation in the recovery of health went hand in hand with the affirmation of the principle of exclusion. Natalist propaganda, the state construction of femininity based on maternity and legitimately feminine social and sanitary activities, functioned like therapeutic agents that aimed to restore the internal balance of the social body that had to be reborn to purity.

And the best protection against this "dangerous" "border" formed by "crossbreeds" was national feminine sacrifice. "Long live the race, and as a consequence, long live Mothers" was the slogan by which the French Union for the Defense of the Race celebrated Mother's Day 1943:

> Today, we will draw from among the great collective forces, and we will speak to you of Mother's Day. We will exalt this Mother's Day, we will acclaim Mothers themselves, and we will thank the generous, tireless organizers who prepare the annual tribute to mothers that is due them. . . . Your task, young mothers, is not limited to doling out their ration of grape sugar to your young ones. . . . You must also give them the ration for the soul, the nourishment that will make them women and men worthy of this name. Your children, in a healthy body, must have a virile soul, a soul ready for any trial, the soul of France, the soul of the race. And you mothers who have already formed and delivered your child who is already a man to society for the collective good, be thanked for your sacrifice. This multiple sacrifice will undoubtedly be the salvation of our country that so many countryless scoundrels without honor wish to see perish.[187]

Studying the Vichy regime from the perspective of the sexual division of the social world has allowed us to measure both the extraordinary potential for resurgence of the myth of the eternal feminine in a period of crisis and the extent of the strictly political stakes involved in this type of state construction of femininity. The National Revolution teaches as much about the inexhaustible richness of the representations and modes of production of this aspect of the social unconscious that is the "eternal feminine" as the polarization of investments in defense of the myth teaches us about the political and social options of this conservative revolution. This research shows that *the order of bodies is a fundamental dimension of the political order.* The return to the biological foundation of "natural" differences between the sexes and the related idea of an irreducible difference between masculine and feminine "destinies" nurtured, through all sorts of metaphoric slippage, the political ideology and the sociodicy of a regime obsessed with restoring the national homogeneity that should have been destroyed by individualism, egalitarianism, the Declaration of Human Rights, parliamentarianism, and the social clashes of 1936, and that rejected all forms of the "inassimilable." Democratic "lies" were the opposite of the return to the body that "does not lie."

Vichy's construction of the "eternal feminine" is far from being a given. Although it is relatively easy to locate the discourse and the legislation through which the French State celebrated and imposed women's return to the home, exposing the *social and political uses of the women-eternity link* in the symbolic order of the new regime required lengthy research. Nevertheless, it is this dimension that gives real access to the social logics at work in the recurrent production of the myth and in its explosion in 1940. The texts that are the most explicitly devoted to feminine reeducation as per the National Revolution do not convey the entire mythic system. It was therefore necessary to separate ourselves from production that directly concerned women, the family, and women in the family in order to study the way they were summoned and cited as culpable, redemptrices, illustrations, examples, in other spaces of the ideological construction site of the regime. From there, the networks of conscious and more subliminal associations could be drawn and refined. This is what allowed me to produce a new reading of the discourses and the injunctions concerning "the" feminine "nature." Through this spiral approach, this singular historical reconstruction of the "eternal feminine" progressively took on its political, social, and strategic weight.

We know that mythic demons do not fall from the sky. But to trace the paths of their reappearance, it is necessary to undertake a historical sociology of the production of the social representations, which is, by definition, interminable. Approached from this perspective, the subject is necessarily always far from being exhausted; to go further, a detour through comparative reflection would be necessary, for that would make it possible to systematize the logics of questioning already constructed and to restore to them a dynamic force that the violence of banality, both the ultimate object of and the (unconscious?) check to this research, ultimately saps. How, for example, is the "eternal feminine" inscribed in the ideological constellations of the fascist and authoritarian regimes of the period? What interests are its privileged institutional producers defending? What claimed or hidden legacies are invested in it? What are the social mechanisms of its crystallization? How is it inscribed in the philosophy of power?

These are the questions I have raised concerning the National Revolution. They allowed us to identify certain social processes of production of this vision of femininity and to reconstruct the interests of certain of its producers in defending it and amplifying it at a time of restoration and technocratic advances that culminated in the reconquest of influence and sometimes in the creation of new markets. They also led me to pull the historical threads of these interests that are far from being limited to the unanimous imposition of one representation of eternal sexual complementarities. We see clearly here that the struggles for the monopoly over legitimate symbolic violence are caught up in—or associated with—social and political struggles that have a long history, for some an even longer history than the history we were led to explore. Here again, a comparative work, historical this time, would be a means of taking this research further.

It is to the *language of the body* that producers eager for "good" femininity returned in 1940, theorizing in their way the primacy of acquisitions through the body, acquisitions that are never forgotten. As if "true" mothers had been lost along the way—during the 1930s—and it was necessary to teach them everything all over again to absolve some of the national guilt. As if, above all, rearming power involved recentering the masculine/feminine opposition founded on the return to a mimetic order in which the body functions as a reminder of sexual identity. The French State thus supplied a politically based theory for the corporal education of femininity: this involved anchoring in the body those lessons of "moral gymnastics" that teach young girls forever and for always to forget themselves to exist legitimately. To take up the path of selflessness once again. To forget oneself and, being forgotten, to exist only in a rich silence, alongside, in the margins of history and the world, withdrawn and retired. To prepare oneself from childhood, without words, by miming the eternal gestures of the all-powerful mother-educator. To listen in oneself to the corporal awakening of the only destiny to come. To resemble oneself in advance, agelessly, inscribed forever in repetition.

This political vision that returns to the biological foundation was the occasion for the state to develop a logic of the body that made the corporal *hexis* the ultimate truth of individuals, and made the memory of gestures the privileged medium of the only apprenticeships useful for occupying the place to which each is predestined. If I have cited at length Vichy texts concerning women, it is in part to give a sense of how much this state discourse concerning the body was conscious of the effects of internalization of these forms of apprenticeship through mimicry, of this channeling of movement that in its eyes characterized the necessary and sufficient education of girls. Here, the state explicitly spoke the political truth of this bodily supervision and management of childhood that are at the origin of sexual identities. The National Revolution and its epigones produced and delivered a political sociology of the construction of the image of the body.

If to speak of women and to women is to speak of the body, to bring them back to the body, to the inequality "that results from their body," by the same token, the catalogue of positive and negative feminine virtues takes on a particular charge of symbolic violence, for it no longer seems to have any historical, social, or cultural limits. And the public expression of the intimate, of domestic corporal apprenticeships of the feminine "vocation" seemed ready to become state discourse that says the "unsayable," which usually does not need to be said. During this period of national reeducation, which claimed to be the opportunity for awareness of the reasons for the disaster and of the means to exorcise it, the primary function of the political exhumation of the old priority granted to the body in constructing the eternal feminine identity was perhaps to make it possible to escape history, to forget history.

Vichy discourse concerning the "eternal feminine" can thus present itself as an eternal discourse concerning the eternity of things. It denies any notion of the cultural construction of sexual difference, incessantly returning to the body and to the difference between bodies. It biologizes the social relations of the genders all the more as it tends to biologize all the social failures, finding the secret of the vitality of peoples in "millenary balances" and "cosmic continuities." It nationalizes the female body by reference to the carnal anchoring of Barrèsian nationalism. It inscribes itself in the myth of eternal return, making women the guardians of tradition, of fires, and of country cemeteries that give dynamic vitality to the soil, making them intermediaries of harmony with the eternity of the world against all the intrusions of history, dressing them in folkloric costumes that make them the embodiments of "living folklore": Mistral's young Arlesian girls colonized by the National Revolution; heroines of Mother's Day responsible for the apparently ageless heritage of maternal virtues. Associating women with peasants — "feminine realism" with the "instinct" of countryfolk — it makes them the intercessors of the "return to the real."

It is the weft of the *völkisch* ideology and also of Salazarism that sought to sustain "the little Portuguese house" "habitually" against all doctrines that dismiss nature and tradition.[1] Folklorizing, a false history that fixes, is one of the tools of amnesia, an eternally political arm. By pulling this thread, it would be possible to construct a comparative sociology of the processes of *folklorizing femininity,* and to reveal the consistencies and variations in its political and social functions. By questioning the political meaning of this conscious and justified return to what nurtures the sociocultural unconscious of femininity and its apprenticeships, the identification of women with the nature of their body and, through this, with nature,[2] it would be possible, case by case, to historicize the social processes of reproduction of this form of symbolic violence that is so difficult to question, it often eludes consciousness.

One way of historicizing the "eternal feminine" spoken by the National Revolution, and therefore of grasping certain processes for producing the categories it mobilized immediately and enshrined as "obvious," was to construct the constitutive elements of the subculture of femininity that blossomed under the French State and to name this subculture. Identifying and defining what I called the culture of sacrifice allowed me to escape the vicious circle of repetition while still questioning this repetition by identifying the central agendas of this culture, its privileged producers, its literary, religious, medical, and political expressions, the invariants of these expressions, and the singular methods of association (conscious and unconscious) that characterized its use in this historical context. I was therefore able to inventory the cultural and symbolic legacies that were still active in this representation of femininity and the masculine/feminine opposition. Thus I identified the means of combating this policy of forgetting that allowed the National Revolution, with the support of its high priests, to present as the return to the eternity of things what was in fact the product of a long history.

The regime used this culture to call France to a collective mea culpa, and that is where I began to delineate its social and historical bases. Approaching the culture of sacrifice through the denunciation of feminine culpability revealed the extraordinary kinship of the analyses of the defeats of 1940 and 1870: in both cases, conservative tradition situated the fault of women at the heart of the social errors that had caused the debacle. The political stakes of the culture of sacrifice were explicitly revealed in the parallel condemnations of the Commune and the Popular Front. The complaints concerning paid vacations, tandem bicycles, permanents (cause of the rural exodus), and family allowances (cause of workers' laxity) won out over the accusation of middle-class egotism and frivolity.

By delivering his seminal message concerning the opposition between the spirit of pleasure and the spirit of sacrifice, Pétain gave those who were ready to seize it a magic formula. This "astrology of history" conducive to metaphoric bidding permitted all the associations and word games of social agents defending their own interests—material, institutional, ethical, and symbolic.

This "invention" of the culture of sacrifice illuminates to some extent the partial prior "inventions" of the requirement that women be selfless that already carried, each in itself, this entire symbolic universe. If, when drawing "the lesson from lost battles," Marshal Pétain had not formally opposed the spirit of sacrifice to the spirit of pleasure as early as June 20, 1940, and if all the supporters of the "eternal feminine" had not recognized themselves in his little phrase, it may have been impossible to gain such extensive access to this consummate state of a subculture of gender that merely borrows the pieces of the puzzle from learned sources and common sense. All the elements were already there, sustaining this culture that until then was invisible, or less visible, and that could not be named until it became one of the very foundations of power. *Explicitly politicizing the feminine culture of sacrifice is what truly gives it its full sense* and its public visibility, causing it to escape the intimist banalization of withdrawal to the private sphere.

Through a historical sociology of the feminine incarnations of and investments in the culture of sacrifice, it was possible to bring to light certain individual and collective processes of appropriation and internalization of this symbolics of femininity in their relationship to the specifically political anchorings of constructions of feminine identity that were historically close. The analysis of women's defense of this vision of their place in the social order that triumphs with the National Revolution thus constituted a sort of psychoanalysis of the social consciousness that revealed itself at the same time inseparably to be a history of the politicization of constructions of women's presence in the social world and in the public space.

To account for this adherence that met the expectations of the regime, we had to go back to the identity-related acquisitions of a culture of femininity that could only be read in 1940 as a culture of dispossession and as the exaltation of a world of privation. By defending the mother-at-home agenda, the leaders of Catholic women's action defended the Catholic feminine culture that had succeeded over time in constructing and renewing protected feminine spaces that it would be absurd to consider only as spaces of exclusion. These spaces were also modes of access to knowledge, to instruction, to participation in public life, to professionalization, to new forms of feminine existence in the city that were ensured by and developed in them. The inscription of this "baggage" in a symbolic world that reinforced in constantly renewed fashion the idea of an "eternal feminine" and of the eternal masculine/feminine complementarity contributed at the same time to perpetuating submission and to paradoxical forms of emancipation, experienced as such in the shelter of the symbolic barriers of a tolerated and tolerable self-image. It suffices to take note of the limits imposed on the socially acceptable expression of lay feminism to see that this model greatly exceeded its restricted space of production and was recognized by society as a whole.

This sociology of the internalization of Catholic feminine culture of sacrifice and selflessness ultimately culminated in the observation of the age-old nature of the processes of politicization in which feminine action and the feminist movements were caught up, a phenomenon that allowed us to view them together. To those women who, since the start of the century and during the interwar period, defended stay-at-home mothers without remaining at home themselves, the National Revolution appears all the more a symbolic victory because it was a political victory. The victory of the old anti-Dreyfus feminine action leagues, of the suffragist movements of the right, of Christian feminism of the 1930s that competed with "red" unionism are all political and politically annexed forms of the feminine defense of a conservative social order. In this sphere of the sociohistorical construction of femininity that seemed at the beginning to belong to a study of symbolic forms, the pregnancy of the political struggles could not be forgotten. In response to the Dreyfus affair, women first supported the social milieu to which they belonged, and the suffragist battles demonstrated that they were first, as far as politicians were concerned, a clientele that needed to be either encouraged to fight against the Republic or harnessed to fight against the Church.

It is undoubtedly in part this political polarization of the field of feminine and feminist action, which subjects the constructions of feminine identity to the logic of the political field and leaves the masculine political monopoly untouched, that is at the source of the structural and symbolic weaknesses of the movements of feminine "emancipation" from the end of the nineteenth century. Through the mandatory political affiliations that led them to slip into a system of oppositions external to their feminine/feminist concerns and subjected them to the masculine political order, the women's movements never ceased giving their masculine supporters symbolic pledges of proper feminine cooperation. Identification with the masculine political struggles through this form of subordinated, shifted, withdrawn participation in the play for power, indispensable for leaving the ghetto of private speech, also carried with it the recognition/misappreciation of masculine domination. And if, up until the 1930s, the struggles between a conservative-Catholic pole and a lay-Republican pole engaged in the revolutionary project of academic and professional coeducation were violent, the struggles on the front of symbolic violence were still feeble, often embodied by pariahs sentenced to social death. The representations of the social world specific to the myth of the eternal feminine that are systematized in the culture of sacrifice can thus even more easily inspire a National Revolution culture of femininity that returns to silence and oblivion the symbolic content of earlier political battles (those concerning the notion of head of the family, for example, or women's right to work following the fallout of the crisis of 1929).

With the help of the crisis, at a time when all the "astrologies of history" (of which the "eternal feminine" is not the least uncanny) were triumphing, the partial, institutional, and strategic expressions of previous periods come into conjunction, thereby sweeping away the very idea of different constructions of femininity, throwing them into the oubliettes of history and forgetting them. However, the 1930s was a decisive period for the educational and professional advancement of women and, in 1945, they would obtain the right to vote, then, rapidly, completely coeducational schooling and broad access to a whole professional space that they had started to invest before the war. So, was Vichy a parenthesis? Can moments of social regression be understood as unavoidable stages whose effects are ultimately of little importance with respect to the historical evolution viewed over a longer period?

This would be to forget that such moments of reaction can always reappear suddenly, and that the myth can always be resurrected because legitimate feminine identity is constantly an issue of struggles that mobilize, for diverse reasons, antagonistic social groups, institutions with diverging interests, and agents committed to defending opposing worldviews whose vision of the feminine is central: it is always a subject of conflict, and the conflict is not limited to periods of violence. Behind the explosion of the myth in 1940 was a lengthy project of symbolic cartography carried out in diversified professional and institutional spaces, articulated in the political battles of successive decades, and that also borrowed images of "the" feminine "nature" from ageless historical funds, from heritages of "erudite myths." In 1939, the competing expressions of feminine identity were still weak, respectful of what was socially acceptable, limited by the ferocious and immediate sanction of transgression; the social bases of the construction of a new feminine relationship to the world was still fragile and threatened. Through this research, we see clearly that the vision of femininity and the sexual order mobilized by the National Revolution largely preexisted it. And it would be too easy to forget that the factions of the political left had contributed arguments that enclosed women in the private space, excluding them from public life and even denying them, although belatedly, the right to vote. Political misogyny does not belong to the political right alone, and is still the question of the day.

Male producers of the "eternal feminine" who saw the National Revolution as a "divine surprise" each took part in constructing the culture of sacrifice in the defense of diversified material, symbolic, ethical, and aesthetic interests for which the defense of this vision of femininity is both a condition and *an encompassing symbolic expression*. The continuous work that tends to perpetuate the relationship of sexual domination appears to be a divided work: it sometimes obeys the logics of maintenance and conquest, sometimes the logics of defending institutional vitalities, and sometimes the logics of national political struggles. The most productive periods for this multiform work are always the opportunity for ideological re-creations of the "eternal feminine" that draw from the relatively archaic available cultural stocks, enriching them with new expressions and new legitimations. The "eternal feminine" is a continuing creation, never completed, always renewed, that owes its apparently atemporal and ahistorical character to the fact that the oldest schemes are transformed without being transformed in order to buttress new social (political, cultural, institutional) uses of feminine submission. I have privileged the study of ecclesiastical, academic, and medical institutions, institutions that traditionally produce masculine/feminine classifications, not only because their authorized spokesmen supported and anticipated the National Revolution in its enterprise of reeducating women, giving it an invaluable kind of "apolitical" guarantee, but even more so because in 1940 they are privileged sites for studying the strategic uses of the resurgence of the myth, uses that are less clearly readable in the ordinary course of its specific reactivations.

A time of reconquest of France, the eldest daughter of the Church, for the hierarchy and the majority of the Catholic institutions, the National Revolution was the opportunity to recall the decisive place of women in the vitality of religious vocations and in the defense of "free" education. The ancient Catholic feminine culture would thus be redeployed in all its subtlety to mobilize this form of feminine identity whose triumph and submission were both confirmed by the new regime, which denied it the paradoxical potentialities of liberation it had carried within it, particularly in the field of education. The ideologues of private Catholic education, who supplied the Legion française des Combattants with its odes to the family, would be the staunchest defenders of limiting girls' education, going so far as to deny them access to theoretical learning in order to enclose them in familial and domestic education that can be learned only in the family. Their message resonated in harmony with the message of conservative ideologues who had been fighting against the Republican school since the turn of the century and who rejected all forms of democratizing education: in support of the elitist educational policy of Vichy, they united in their suspicion of all newcomers to secondary education, those students whose accelerated "avidity" and "intoxication" recalled the excesses of the "bacchantes of knowledge."

Defending the old image of the family doctor, the French medicine of the old medical lineages that made it possible to escape the threats of the plethora and civil statism, the proponents of a doctors association saw its ultimate creation in 1940, and put their knowledge of the feminine body and its most secret physical and psychic balances to work for the state. To encourage women to be mothers, at home, private auxiliaries of medical legitimacy, the medical profession in turn mobilized inexhaustible funds from medical constructions of femininity, whose prescriptions the Carrel Foundation would attempt to make technical to ensure its place in the new market of mothers and children.

Familialists and natalists, jurists and demographers found the opportunity for a broader audience in 1940, as Marshal Pétain himself placed the declining birthrate at the head of the causes of the defeat. These new advisors to the prince wanted to make statistics a political science in the same way that doctors used and abused the biologization of the rhetoric of the culture of crisis to impose their skills with respect to political philosophy and would make feminine submission to the demographic order the lever of their conquering activity, condemning cases of nonsubmission as crimes with the help of specialized courts.

The return to the order of bodies and the control of feminine bodies and spaces is consistent with the *defense of the body*. When the ecclesiastical or medical institutions reactivate the mother-at-home agenda, they speak of themselves, of their difficulties maintaining a former state of recruiting and clientele, of institutional force and vitality to reconquer in the face of disaffection and infidelity. When the conservative ideologues of the school enclose girls in domestic apprenticeships, they are defending an educational system devalorized by "massification." The large medical family who believes that medicine can be transmitted only through the family, the activists for religious vocations who see in mothers of large families the source of the Church's survival, the propagandists for closure of the educational system who see in female lycée students the threatening embodiment of all *outsiders,* agree to make returning women to maternity and keeping women at home one of the means of defending their body of belongingness against all forms of decline.

Because it authorized and encouraged such a total expression of schemes that usually exist in dispersed state and because it inscribed this cultural arbitrary that is the "eternal feminine" at the core of its political philosophy, the National Revolution makes more accessible both the social and political logics of diversified institutions and the sociodicy that are at work in this construction of femininity. However, this collective reconstruction of "the" feminine "nature" and of the place of women in the city tends to impose the idea that, for women, myth and history are the same thing, that they overlap in the eternal reproduction of the same: for the ideologues of the regime, the "eternal feminine" is always already there. And we can sufficiently measure the force, the longevity, and the internalization of the schemes they mobilized to agree with them at first. "The troubling strangeness," or rather, "the troubling familiarity" — "a sort of fright that attaches itself to things always familiar" — that can be experienced by immersing oneself in this asphyxiating literature compels one to remain there.

By taking the 1940s as our subject, are we merely grasping an eternally present defense of the "eternal feminine" that would in this circumstance simply find the opportunity for a fuller expression, freed from censure, of its vision of the sexual division of the social world? In other words, was Vichy simply a point of culmination, or did the inauguration of the French State produce a break? Did it produce something new? To answer no is merely to consider the masculine and feminine discourse concerning "good" femininity that multiplied under the French State to be an "ordinary" expression of this social unconscious. This led us to question more profoundly its overall political stakes: the crisis and the monopoly produced an unprecedented situation in an exceptional sociohistorical climate that was both imaginable and unimaginable several years before. The inauguration of the new regime was the opportunity for *complex processes of ideological conjunction and crystallization* propitious for the numerous bids and rigidifications on which I have tried to focus.

Something new was invented during the National Revolution in the relation between the political and ideological uses of the myth by the French State and the strategic uses of its privileged producers. The corporatist logics, the market conquests, the unrealized or less fully realized prophetic vocations, the political payback—all the forms of competition that inspire forward movement fed the steady escalation of immediate investments in a political philosophy of feminine submission. The ambiguity of the regime[3] that combined traditionalists and modernists, paternalistic social ethics of local notables and technocratic logics that bear new forms of state intervention, old familiast modes of propaganda and modern forms of mobilization of—and legitimization by—"public opinion" can only give a new momentum to old vocations and give rise to new vocations in an ideological construction site that sometimes takes on the overtones of a call for proposals. In this work site, the defense of the "eternal feminine" is also an integrating element that brings consensus, a commonplace that encourages these neutral sites in which contradictions that separate the various factions of the dominant class find appeasement, even if the confrontations between statism and the desire for direct rule of the conservative elites retained all their violence.[4] This historical method of constructing femininity seems to sweep away accepted cleavages and periodizations. To support the "eternal feminine" Vichy joined forces, before and after the "ill wind" of August 1941, before and after the second Laval government, with nearly all factions: traditionalists and modernists; provincial notables and the technocrats of the Commissariat for the Family and the Carrel Foundation; familialists and natalists; Catholic and lay ministers of national education and those from the avant-garde for private education who mobilized the educational model embodied by the Les Roches School and the psychological advances of the École des parents; old pioneers of the Action Française such as René Benjamin and close collaborators of *Je suis partout* such as Abel Bonnard. The consummate state of the culture of sacrifice results from the conjunction of these interests that ultimately defined the social landscape of adherence to the values of the regime, though not necessarily to its politics in the strict sense.

Vichy was the revenge of conservative forces, a counterrevolution that combined both faces of the opposition to the Republic: the old opposition to 1789, to Human Rights, to the feeless, lay, and mandatory school, and the more recent opposition to the Popular Front, to all the forms of "massification" of the 1930s (the école unique, the rural exodus that overpopulated the cities, large concentrations of workers, paid vacations that led to the invasion of the countryside and polluted the lovely month of May), and to the immigration of "inassimilable" refugees.[5] Paradoxically, on this "apolitical" construction site of femininity during the National Revolution, this revenge found expression, and returning women to maternity and keeping mothers at home functioned like political metaphors of a return to "before": before the rehabilitation of Dreyfus, before the "invasion" of medicine by métèques, before the social laws of 1936, before the masses were encouraged to pursue "the spirit of pleasure."

But it was time neither for muted nostalgia nor for parliamentary debates: it was time for action, to move to action. And the return to the myth of the eternal feminine, infiltrated by all these political aversions, ultimately made it possible to justify the worst: the return to a France rid of racial impurities. In this sense it aided an antidemocratic and antimodernist vision of the world that justified repression, class racism, and state anti-Semitism through the return to an eternal order of things and beings. The most innocuous of the Vichy texts on returning mothers to the home is a condemnation of individualism and of the principles of Human Rights. *The political philosophy of the eternal feminine* thus produced an amalgamation between sexual submission and social submission and, by celebrating national maternities, imposed its obsessions concerning the "inassimilable." French women, or rather, "the" French woman, were inscribed by the power in its racist rhetoric. Maternity is always national, and the declining birthrate leads to "savage" immigration. Feminists, like Jews, are "inassimilable." And the inscription of women as guilty parties in this catastrophic vision and this apocalyptic apprehension of the facts that, according to Colette Guillaumin, always bear in them racist presuppositions[6] marked women in their turn with the sign of threat and exclusion. Returning mothers to the home was part of the national cure of purity. At the end of this work, we might think that the processes of immediate and prereflexive adherence to the National Revolution, borne by this identification with the prophetic message that celebrated French mothers, had their share of responsibility in the belated blindness to the racist stakes of the regime even though these were announced from the start. The political imposition that required women to withdraw to the home, the private, the ahistorical, is not unrelated to the fantasy of virilizing elites, itself caught up in the fascination of totalitarian regimes, in the "magnetic field" of fascisms.[7]

NOTES

INTRODUCTION

1 Robert O. Paxton, *Vichy France: Old Guard and New Order, 1940–1944* (New York: Norton, 1972), 20. For the subsequent citations, see pp. 136, 33; emphasis added.

2 Joan Scott proposes to undertake comparative sociohistorical analyses of these historical processes of establishing a point of view as the dominant point of view; see "Gender, a Useful Category of Historical Analysis," *American Historical Review* 5 (December 1986); also available in *Gender and the Politics of History* (New York: Columbia University Press, 1988).

3 Philippe Pétain, "Appel du 20 juin 40," in *La France nouvelle: Principes de la communauté. Appels et Messages* (Paris: Fasquelle, 1941), 18.

4 Pierre Bourdieu, "Une interprétation de la théorie de la religion selon Max Weber," *Archives européennes de sociologie* 12 (1971): 12–15.

5 Sigmund Freud, "Traitement d'âme" (1890), in *Résultats, Idées, Problèmes,* vol. 1, *1890–1920* (Paris: PUF, 1984), 8–9.

6 Marc Bloch, *L'Etrange Défaite* (1946; Paris: Gallimard, "Folio history," 1990), 202. Available in English as *Strange Defeat,* trans. Gerald Hopkins (New York: Octagon Books, 1968). However, this note is not translated in the English edition. Unless otherwise noted, all subsequent references are to the English edition.

7 Yves Durand, *Vichy 1940–44* (Paris: Bordas, "Connaissance," 1972), 66. It is interesting to note that Pétain accorded prisoners of war a central role in this scheme of redemption through suffering, because captivity appeared to be a situation propitious for examining one's conscience; see Yves Durand, *La captivité, histoire des prisonniers de guerre français* (Paris: FNSP, 1980).

8 See Yonina Talmon, "Millenarianism," *International Encylopaedia of Social Sciences* (New York; Macmillan, 1968), 10: 351–53.

9 The return of sexual inequality as the initial inequality that founds the structure of the mythic, ritual, and social universe was fundamental in the construction of the millenary movement in Brazil; see Francine Muel-

Dreyfus and Arakcy Martins-Rodrigues, "Réincarnations," *Actes de la recherche en sciences sociales* 62–63 (1986).

10 Geneviève Fraisse, "La différence des sexes, une différence historique," in *L'Exercice du savoir et la Différence des sexes,* ed. G. Fraisse et al. (Paris: L'Harmattan, 1991), 25.

11 Bloch, *Strange Defeat,* 165–66.

12 Richard Griffiths, *Pétain et les Français, 1941–1951* (Paris: Calmann-Lévy, 1974), 213.

13 On the opposition between the established and the outsiders, see Norbert Elias and John L. Scotson, *The Established and the Outsiders: A Sociological Enquiry into Community Problems* (Thousand Oaks, CA: Sage, 1994).

14 Sigmund Freud, "The Uncanny," in *Studies in Parapsychology* (New York: Collier Books, 1977). In his semantic analysis of the term *unheimliche,* Freud writes: "The 'uncanny' is that class of the terrifying which leads back to something long known to us, once very familiar" (20).

15 Paxton, *Vichy France,* 168.

I. WRITERS OF THE DEFEAT IN SEARCH OF ETERNITY

1 Bloch, *Strange Defeat,* 148.

2 See George L. Mosse, *The Crisis of German Ideology: Intellectual Origins of the Third Reich* (New York: Schocken, 1981).

3 "La France maintenue en ordre," *L'Espoir français* (1 March 1941).

4 Robert O. Paxton, *Parades and Politics at Vichy: The French Officer Corps under Marshal Pétain* (Princeton: Princeton University Press, 1966), 10.

5 See Gérard Loiseaux, *La littérature de la défaite et de la collaboration* (Paris: Publications de la Sorbonne, Série France XIXe-XXe, 1984), 351–60.

6 Charles Maurras, *La Seule France* (Lyon: Lardanchet, 1941).

7 Roger Bonnard [dean of the law school in Bordeaux], *Revue du droit public* (October 1941); quoted in Danièle Lochak, "La doctrine sous Vichy ou les mésaventures du positivisme," in *Les Usages sociaux du droit* (Centre universitaire de recherches administratives et politiques de Picardie: PUF, 1989), 253–85.

8 Georges Bernanos, *Lettre aux Anglais;* quoted in Loiseaux, *La littérature de la défaite et de la collaboration,* 361.

9 Michel Mohrt, *Les Intellectuels devant la défaite, 1870* (1941; Paris: Corrêa, 1942). The citations that follow are on pp. 190–96, 140, and 62–67.

10 Renan had played a decisive role in the birth of literary nationalism at the end of the nineteenth century, and Barrès acknowledged his role in these terms: "I would have to say that he is one of those rare men who go to work immediately. What work? The work that we never cease to indicate with all our strength: the restoration of France through the knowledge of the causes of its decline" (*Scènes et Doctrines du nationalisme,* quoted in Loiseaux, *La Littérature de la défaite et de la collaboration,* 370).

11 Henry de Montherlant, "La France et la morale de midinette," in

L'Équinoxe de septembre (1938) (Paris: Gallimard, 1976). For an analysis of the image of women in Montherlant, see Simone de Beauvoir, *Le Deuxième Sexe* (Paris: Gallimard, "Folio essais," 1949) 1: 320–41.

12   Gustave Thibon, "Réalisme de la terre," chapter 1 in *Retour au réel, nouveaux diagnostics* (Lyon: Lardanchet, 1943), 3, 5.

13   Daniel Halévy, *Trois Épreuves 1814, 1871, 1940* (Paris: Plon, "L'Abeille No. 3," 1941). The citations that follow are on pp. 133, 166–73. It is interesting to note that his father, the academician Ludovic Halévy, had published *Notes et Souvenirs 1871–72* (Paris: Calmann-Lévy, n.d.) after the Commune, in which he reflected on the necessity of a more enlightened training for the elite. See Paul Lidsky, *Les Écrivains contre la Commune* (Paris: Maspero, "Cahiers libres," 1970), 87.

14   Raymond Aron, "Remarques sur quelques préjugés politiques," *La France libre* 36 (1943); quoted in Sébastian Laurent, *Daniel Halévy face à l'histoire et à la politique* (DEA in history under the direction of Serge Berstein; Paris: Institut d'études politiques de Paris, 1993), 120.

15   See Alain Silvera, *Daniel Halévy and His Time: A Gentleman-commoner in the Third Republic* (Ithaca, NY: Cornell University Press, 1966).

16   Henry Bordeaux, *Les murs sont bons: Nos erreurs et nos espérances* (Paris: Librairie Arthème Fayard, 1940), 20. The citations that follow are on pp. 163–64, 123–28, 248. Henry Bordeaux, a member of the Académie française, always defended conservative political and religious positions; with this book, he became one of the ideologues of the National Revolution. In 1941 he published *Images du Maréchal Pétain* and, in the collection "Forces nouvelles" *Médecins et Curés de campagne,* these inexhaustible literary heroes of regeneration.

17   Maurice Barrès, *Scènes et Doctrines du nationalisme;* quoted in Zeev Sternhell, *Maurice Barrès et le nationalisme français* (Brussels: Complexe, 1985), 288.

18   Philippe Pétain, "Individualisme et nation," *La Revue universelle* (1 January 1941); emphasis added.

19   Gustave Thibon, "L'inégalité, facteur d'harmonie," in *Diagnostics, essai de physiologie sociale* (Paris: Librairie de Médicis, 1940), 98–99, 109.

20   Paxton, *Vichy France,* 215, 242; Pascal Ory and Jean-François Sirinelli, *Les Intellectuels en France de l'affaire Dreyfus à nos jours* (Paris: Armand Colin, 1986), 128.

21   Henri Massis, *Maurras et notre temps* (Geneva: La Palatine, 1951), 2: 170–76; emphasis and quotation marks in original.

22   Eugen Weber, *Action française* (Stanford, CA: Stanford University Press, 1962), 501–503; Michèle Cointet, *Le Conseil national de Vichy, 1940–1944* (Paris: Aux amateurs de livres, 1989), 89–95.

23   Thibon, *Retour au réel,* 240, 168, 64–65.

24   Ibid., 84.

25   Ibid., 66.

26   Thibon, "De l'esprit d'économie," in *Diagnostics,* 21–23.

27 Philippe Pétain, "Allocution de Capoulet-Junac," quoted in Gérard Miller, *Les Pousse-au-jouir du Maréchal Pétain* (Paris: Seuil, 1975), 135.

28 Thibon, *Retour au réel*; emphasis added.

29 Émile Zola, *La Débâcle*, quoted in Lidsky, *Les Écrivains contre la Commune*, 19. For the development of this theme, see 98–121.

30 Zola, *La Débâcle*, quoted in Lidsky, 119.

31 Bordeaux, *Les murs sont bons*, 105.

32 Mohrt, *Les intellectuels devant la défaite*, 66–67.

33 See Anne-Marie Thiesse, *Écrire la France: Le mouvement littéraire régionaliste de langue française entre la Belle Époque et la Libération* (Paris: PUF, 1991), 48–51.

34 Daniel Halévy, "Paris, la terre, les croyances," in *La France de l'esprit 1940–1943: Enquête sur les nouveaux destins de l'intelligence française* (Paris: Sequana, 1943) 42–45. Opening with a text by Maurras, this collective call to a cultural revolution brings together contributions from Gustave Thibon, Albert Rivaud, Thierry Maulnier, Bernard Faÿ, Alexis Carrel, Jacques Copeau, and Maximilien Vox. Its conclusion returns to René Benjamin.

35 *L'Écho des provinces* [journal of the Comité edited in Nice with the assistance of the Médecin family] (October 1941); quoted in Christian Faure, *Le Projet culturel de Vichy*, CNRS (Lyon: Presses universitaires de Lyon, 1989), 73. To the young Arlesian girls in regional costume Marshal Pétain would give the honor of sponsoring their club, la Capello d'Arles, created on the day of the Marshal's visit, December 3, 1940.

36 See Philippe Martet, "La revendication occitane entre les deux guerres: Aspects politiques," in *Du provincialisme au régionalisme, XVIIIᵉ–XXᵉ siècle* (Actes du Festival d'histoire de Montbrison, Montbrison, 1989).

37 I am referring here to Thiesse, "Régionalisme et Révolution nationale," chapter 8 in *Écrire la France*.

38 Pierre Barral, "Idéal et pratique du régionalisme dans le régime de Vichy," *Revue française de sciences politiques* 5 (October 1974).

39 René Farnier, *Régionalisme et Folklore*, Legion brochure, n.d. Farnier was félibre majoral (one of fifty members of the governing committee of the Félibrige), provincial president of the National Folklore Committee, and technical consultant for regionalism to the French Legion of Combatants.

40 Cointet, *Le Conseil national de Vichy*, 84.

41 Joseph de Pesquidoux, *Pour la Terre* (Toulouse: Éd. du Clocher, 1942), 11–12, 14, 71, 78, 25, 76; emphasis added.

42 See Thiesse, *Écrire la France*, 271–73.

43 Henri Pourrat, *Vent de mars* (Paris: Gallimard, 1941), 50, 133; capitalization in the text.

44 In the collective work celebrating the new regime, *France 41: La révolution nationale constructive, un bilan et un programme*, ed. Raymond Postal (Paris: Éditions Alsatia, n.d.), Pourrat, who wrote the chapter "La question paysanne," gives a social philosophy course through cooking advice: "In the Velay, Mario Versepuy used to tell me, everything would be fine if

people were taught how to cultivate the garden, to have vegetables, to prepare real meals. Perhaps housewives have too much to do these days, so much work wears them out: so they get rid of dinner in fifteen minutes"; finally, it is "to escape dismal maternal cooking" that children go to the city (425).

45 Henri Pourrat, *Le Chef français* (Paris: Robert Laffont, 1942), 29, 101. In this book, Pourrat describes and comments on a visit of the Marshal that he organized in Ambert in October 1941.

46 George L. Mosse, *Nationalism and Sexuality: Respectability and Abnormal Sexuality in Modern Europe* (New York: Howard Fertig, 1985), 97–98.

47 Colette Capitan Peter, *Charles Maurras et l'idéologie d'Action française* (Paris: Seuil "Esprit," 1972). For what follows I refer to pages 44–45, 96, 102–3, 120–21.

48 *L'Action française* (28 November 1910), quoted in ibid., 121.

49 Denis Peschanski, "Le Régime de Vichy a existé: Gouvernants et gouvernés dans la France de Vichy: juillet 1940–avril 1942," in *Vichy 1940–1944: Archives de guerre d'Angelo Tasca* (Paris: CNRS, 1986), 10–11.

50 Henry Rousso, "Qu'est-ce que la Révolution nationale?" *L'Histoire* 129 (January 1990).

51 Weber, *Action française,* 446.

52 *Le Petit Marseillais* (9 February 1941); quoted in French in ibid., 447.

53 See Weber, *L'Action française;* Silvera, *Daniel Halévy and His Time;* Gisèle Sapiro, *La guerre des écrivains 1940–1953* (Paris: Fayard, 1999), 273–81.

54 Weber, *Action française,* 443.

55 Robert Havard de la Montagne, "Chronique de la quinzaine," *La Revue universelle* (9–10 May 1941; 11 June 1941).

56 See, in particular, the pioneering study by Stanley Hoffmann, "Aspects du régime de Vichy," *Revue française de sciences politiques* (March 1956); available in English as "The Vichy Circle of French Conservatives," trans. Robert E. Herzstein, in *Decline or Renewal? France since the 1930s* (New York: Viking, 1974), chap. 1.

57 Ory and Sirinelli, *Les Intellectuels en France de l'affaire Dreyfus à nos jours,* 93–112; Weber, *Action française,* chaps. 18, 19, 20, 23; and Gisèle Sapiro, "Texte et Histoire litteraire," *Texte* 12 (1992).

58 Albert Bayet, article in *La Lumière* (30 July 1937); quoted in Weber, *Action française,* 395.

59 Paxton, *Vichy France,* 21.

60 In her study of the ideology of the Action française, *Charles Maurras et l'idéologie d'Action française* (122–24), Capitan Peter analyzes the fascination/repulsion for the moral depravity one ascribes to others, taking pleasure through reprobates in what one attributes to them and what one does not authorize for oneself. This analysis is similar to that of Norbert Elias concerning the condemnation of the "minority of the worst"; see Elias and Scotson, *The Established and the Outsiders.*

61 René Gillouin, "Responsabilité des écrivains et des artistes," *Journal de Genève* 8–9 (February 1942). Close to the Action française and a member of the Fustel-de-Coulanges circle, Gillouin, a philosopher and literary critic, was introduced by Alibert at Vichy, where he proposed to Pétain a highly appreciated report on education: "Evils of Individualism, of Rationalism, of Optimism, and of an Absurd Confidence in the Virtue of Instruction for Forming the Person." See J. A. D. Long, *The French Right and Education: The Theory and Practice of Vichy Education Policy, 1940–44* (Ph.D. thesis, Oxford, St. Antony's College, 1976), 81. A regular contributor to *La Revue universelle,* Gillouin was a member of the Marshal's cabinet (for whom he wrote several speeches) until April 1942 (Paxton, *Vichy France,* 258).

62 "Doctrine de l'État français," *La Revue universelle* (14 July 1941; 15 August 1941).

63 "Vérités et rêveries sur l'éducation," *La Revue universelle* (12 June 1941). René Benjamin had received the prix Goncourt in 1915 for *Gaspard,* the first war novel that had a printing of 150,000 copies. We will return later to Benjamin's career as a pamphleteer who specialized at the Action français in denouncing the Republican school and the "primary peril" and militated during the National Revolution against the instruction of women. He wrote three works celebrating Pétain: *Le Maréchal et son peuple, Les Sept Étoiles de France, Le Grand Homme seul* (Paris: Plon, 1941, 1942, 1943).

64 *La Revue universelle* (9 May 1941).

65 Weber, *Action française,* 565–71.

66 Ibid., 506–7, 551.

67 André Corthis, "Le marxisme est l'ennemi de la femme et du foyer," *Candide* (15 October 1941). Novelist of women and of Spain, close to Morand, Corthis had won the grand prix for the novel awarded by the Académie française in 1924 for *Le Pauvre Amour de Doña Balbine* (Paris: Flammarion).

2. THE CHURCH AND FEMININE CONTRITION

1 Jacques Chevalier, a Catholic philosopher, mystic, and traditionalist and a professor at the University of Grenoble, godson of Pétain, and minister of national education from December 1940 to February 1941, had reestablished the "duties toward God" in public schools and granted multiple advantages to private education. His successor, Jérôme Carcopino, was more concerned with not targeting public education, but would nevertheless grant private Catholic education an annual subsidy of 400 million francs. The Catholic institutes were recognized as having public utility. Mounier considered at the time that these measures continued to foster anticlerical sentiment. See Jacques Duquesne, *Les Catholiques français sous l'occupation* (Paris: Grasset, 1966), 87–105. During a discussion at the colloquium of Lyon in 1978, Pastor Casalis pointed out that Vichy's education policy contributed to pushing Protestants into the opposition and making

them "rediscover their old reflexes from the time of persecution," while all the Catholic clergy of the Vendée "were collaborators for the simple reason that the subsidies given to the private school had never reached this level" (*Églises et Chrétiens dans la IIe Guerre mondiale*, vol. 2 *La France,* ed. Xavier de Montclos, Monique Luirard, François Delpech, and Pierre Bolle [Lyon: Presses universitaires de Lyon, 1982], 154).

2   Quoted in Renée Bédarida, "La hiérarchie catholique," in *Le Régime de Vichy et les Français,* ed. Jean-Pierre Azéma and François Bédarida (Paris: Fayard, 1992), 449.

3   Pierre Laborie, *Résistants, Vichyssois et autres: L'évolution de l'opinion et des comportements dans le Lot de 1939 à 1944* (Paris: CNRS, 1980), 206.

4   Claude Langlois, "Le régime de Vichy et le clergé d'après les Semaines religieuses des diocèses de la zone libre," *Revue française de sciences politiques* (August 1972).

5   *Semaine religieuse* (28 February 1941).

6   *Semaine d'Annecy,* the bishop's sermon for the Legion's anniversary mass, 21 August 1941; quoted in Langlois, "Le régime de Vichy et le clergé"; emphasis added.

7   Monique Luirard, "La Révolution nationale: Adhésions, réticences et refus (fin 40–avril 42)," in *Églises et Chrétiens dans la IIe Guerre mondiale,* 167.

8   Duquesne, *Les Catholiques français sous l'occupation,* 67.

9   Ibid., 78–79.

10   Langlois, "Le régime de Vichy et le clergé."

11   Quoted in Duquesne, *Les Catholiques français sous l'occupation,* 54.

12   See ibid. (151–58), for the founding of the *Cahiers du Témoignage chrétien*. Its first issue published a text written by Father Fessard, *France prends garde de perdre ton âme,* denouncing Nazism; a description of the "great gathering of bishops around the casket of Philippe Henriot" (350–53); and the confrontation between de Gaulle and the Archbishop of Paris (414–20).

13   This connection is made by Marie-Geneviève Massiani, "*La Croix* sous Vichy," in *Cent Ans d'histoire de "La Croix" 1883–1983,* ed. René Rémond and Émile Poulat (Paris: Le Centurion, 1988), 301–21.

14   A. Latreille, E. Delaruelle, J.-R. Palanque, and R. Rémond, *Histoire du catholicisme en France* (Paris: Spes, 1962).

15   Jacqueline Freyssinet-Dominjon, *Les Manuels d'histoire de l'école libre, 1882–1959, FNSP* (Paris: Armand Colin, 1969).

16   Loiseaux, *La Littérature de la défaite et de la collaboration,* 73.

17   See Long, *The French Right and Education,* 203. René Jeanneret was an elementary school teacher who before the war belonged to the École française, a conservative focus group for elementary education.

18   Faure, *Le Projet culturel de Vichy,* 156–70.

19   It evokes the history of the political construction of the sanctuary of Fatima in Portugal and its officialization by the New State in 1929. The

visions, dating from 1917, had given rise until then only to a local popular cult. See Silas Cerqueira, "L'Église catholique et la dictature corporatiste portugaise," *Revue française de sciences politiques* 3 (June 1973).

20 Theodore Zeldin, *Anxiété et Hypocrisie*, vol. 5 in *Histoire des passions françaises, 1848–1945* (Paris: Seuil, "Points Histoire," 1979), 284. In favor of Catholic secondary education, the Assumptionists also founded the weekly *Le Pèlerin* in 1873 and the daily *La Croix* in 1883, whose offensive anti-Semitism played an important role in the development of the Dreyfus affair. See the article "Assomptionnistes" in the *Encylopaedia Universalis* (Thesaurus), 18: 120.

21 Duquesne, *Les Catholiques français sous l'occupation,* 104.

22 In Pau, Marshal Pétain had said: "In the new France, no one will be saved if he has not first worked to reform himself" (quoted in Durand, *Vichy 1940–1944,* 65).

23 Robert Havard de la Montagne, "Chronique de la quinzaine," *La Revue universelle* (25 May 1941). Such texts are astounding, for religious piety was never recognized as one of Pétain's particular virtues. Pierre Barral (in *Églises et Chrétiens dans la IIᵉ Guerre mondiale,* vol. 2, *La France,* 246) says that Pétain was "emancipated from the Church, even if in 1940 he went to mass at Saint-Louis de Vichy." Gérard Miller (*Les Pousse-au-jouir du maréchal Pétain,* 159) reports this remark by de Gaulle about Pétain the man: "Family! What a joke. He never wanted children. He is an old roué."

24 H. Roux, "Marie," and A. Duval, "Église catholique," in *Encyclopaedia Universalis,* 10: 525–26, and 5: 994–1005.

25 Commentary of the photo agency concerning a photo of Le Vernet pilgrimage; Museum of Contemporary History, Bibliothèque de documentation internationale contemporaine (hereafter, BDIC), Hôtel national des Invalides; emphasis added.

26 Quoted in Duquesne, *Les Catholiques français sous l'occupation,* 29.

27 Once again, it is Marshal Pétain who is speaking through the mouth of the priest.

28 Quoted in "Les grands jours du Puy," in *Le Pèlerinage de la jeunesse française, 15 août 1942, et son anniversaire, 15 août 1943* (Le Puy: Imprimerie Jeanne-d'Arc, n.d.), 33–34.

29 Serge Laury, "Aspects de la vie religieuse pendant la Seconde Guerre mondiale dans le Nord-Pas-de-Calais," *Revue du Nord* (University Lille-III, April–June 1978), 372–73; emphasis added.

30 See Zeldin, *Anxiété et Hypocrisie,* 5: 304.

31 Jean Delumeau, *La Peur en Occident (XIVᵉ–XVIIIᵉ siècle)* (Paris: Fayard, 1978), 260–80, 356–88, 398–449.

32 Duquesne, *Les Catholiques français sous l'occupation,* 34–35.

33 Quoted in Ibid., 33.

34 Ibid., 158–62, 249–54.

35 Quoted in Wilfred D. Halls, *Les Jeunes et la Politique de Vichy* (Paris: Syros/

Alternatives, 1988); originally published in English as *The Youth of Vichy France* (Oxford: Clarendon Press, 1981), 166; emphasis added. All citations are to the English edition.

36 Quoted in Lidsky, *Les Écrivains contre la Commune,* 64.

37 Ernst Cassirer, *The Myth of the State* (Paris: Gallimard, 1993), 281–83.

38 Jean-Marie Mayeur, "Les évêques dans l'avant-guerre," in *Églises et Chrétiens dans la IIe Guerre mondiale,* 12–14.

39 Ibid.

40 Robert Talmy, *Histoire du mouvement familial en France, 1896–1930* (Paris: UNCAF, 1962), 2: 225. This pontifical document came five months after the conference of the Anglican Church that had adopted a resolution authorizing contraceptive practices in marriage provided that they were inspired by high moral considerations, such as providing a better education to one's children.

41 M. S. Gillet, *Réveil de l'âme française* (Paris: Flammarion, 1942), 134. Subsequent quotations are on pp. 102, 45, 125. Father Gillet remained faithful to the National Revolution to the end. In 1943, he sent Pétain a message from Rome to assure him of his devotion and to indicate to him that the attitude of Father Carrière in Algiers, a Dominican and vice president of the Provisional Dissident Assembly, was not approved of by the general of the order (Duquesne, *Les Catholiques français sous l'occupation,* 334). One sees clearly here that the Church was riddled with political rifts to the extent that they broke out within the same religious order. Father Gillet wrote many works of theology and morality whose titles are evocative of the social order he wished to see established: *L'Église et la Famille; Population, Dépopulation, Repopulation; La Virilité chrétienne; La Peur de l'effort intellectuel; Culture latine et Ordre social.*

42 In November 1940, the cardinal expressed himself through the Inter-France agency: "All of this could lead to a civil war even more formidable than the one in 1871, a more durable revolution than that of the Commune." He supported the anti-Bolshevik Légion française. See Yves Marchasson, "Autour du cardinal Baudrillart," in *Églises et Chrétiens dans la IIe Guerre mondiale,* vol. 2, 227–28.

43 A work of classification and cartography of the pilgrimages of France that succeeded in "conserving its ancestral, sometime millenary, traditions": "Since 1940, we had reached 1,400 saints' pilgrimages. During 1942, once a month we will devote one article per month to one of these pilgrimage areas" ("Les Pèlerinages en France, leurs origines, leurs traditions, leur folklore," *Voix françaises* [9 January 1942]).

44 *Voix françaises* (15 June 1944).

45 Father Sertillanges, "Rénovation morale de la France," *Voix françaises* 1 (17 January 1941); "La famille française et le divorce" (7 February 1941); "Rôle de la femme française" (18 April 1941); "Les nationalités et les races" (20 June 1941); emphasis added.

46 *Cité nouvelle* (10 January 1941); emphasis added.

47 *Renouveaux* (1 October 1940). Capitalization in the text; emphasis added.

48 Paul Droulers, "Catholiques sociaux et révolution nationale (été 40-avril 42)," in *Eglises et Chrétiens dans la IIe Guerre mondiale*, 213–23; Duquesne, *Les Catholiques français sous l'occupation*, 66–67, 145, 156; Bernard Comte, "Conscience catholique et persécution antisémite: L'engagement de théologiens lyonnais en 1941–42," *Annales, Présence du passé, lenteur de l'histoire, Vichy, l'occupation, les juifs* 3 (May–June 1993): 653–54.

49 F. Sertillanges, "La maison, c'est le monde," *Nos mères* (Paris: Spes, France vivante, 1942).

50 Gustave Thibon, who made the biological metaphor into a political arm of war, also used this image to denounce the "prodigious diminishing of the world" produced by "technical progress" and "democratic exhibitionism": "It is worse than a wound: it is the tendency toward hemophilia. Our blood flowed for a long time, drop by drop, without our attending to it, in this false euphoria that precedes catastrophes; it still flows every time we neglect a duty or we delude ourselves with a lie" (*Retour au réel*, 52).

51 Marthe Oullé, "Propos sur la jeunesse" [lecture given at the Grand Théâtre of Toulon in December 1940], *Cité nouvelle* (10 April 1941). A bit ahead of her time, Oullé could easily appear among the targets of Susan Faludi, who hunts down the myth of reformed "superwomen" in America during the 1980s; see Faludi, *Backlash: The Undeclared War against American Women* (New York: Crown, 1991).

52 Delumeau, *La Peur en Occident*, 400.

53 Zeldin, *Anxiété et Hypocrisie*, 5: 261.

54 F. Sertillanges, "Maternité sociale," *Voix françaises* (25 April 1941).

55 F. Desbuquois, "France neuve, vérités retrouvées," *Cité nouvelle* (10 janvier 1941); emphasis added.

56 Charles Suaud, "L'imposition de la vocation sacerdotale," *Actes de la recherche en sciences sociales* 3 (May 1975).

57 Laury, "Aspects de la vie religieuse pendant la Second Guerre mondiale dans le Nord-Pas-de-Calais."

58 "La Vierge dans la cité" *Renouveaux* (1 May 1942).

59 Paul Doncoeur, "La femme d'aujourd'hui," in *La Femme d'aujourd'hui* (Paris: Éd. de l'Orante, 1943); emphasis added. This work is made up of a series of subscription brochures in 1941 by the same publisher under the collection title "La relève." Another contradiction within the Church: Father Doncoeur, a former collaborator of *Études* and in that capacity coeditor of *Cité nouvelle*, and who was also abundantly cited in *Renouveaux*, published *Péguy, la révolution et le sacré*, in 1942 with the Éditions de l'Orante and preached a "new" world under the Marshal's leadership. Presented at the theological college of Fourvières, the book got a cool reception from two hundred Jesuit priests, but had a large readership among the youth movements.

1   Jean-Pierre Azéma, *De Munich à la Libération 1938–1944* (Paris: Seuil, "Points Histoire," 1979), 70.

2   Henri Dubief, *Le Déclin de la IIIe République, 1929–1938* (Paris: Seuil, "Points Histoire," 1990), 82, 106.

3   Paxton, *Vichy France,* 12.

4   *La Vie en fleur* was a brochure published by the Office de publicité générale, Commissariat générale à la famille (n.d; BDIC, reserve Gr. fol. 126–1). It contains articles from physicians and midwives and anonymous texts, aphorisms, and calls to order.

5   Michel Foucault, *An Introduction,* vol. 1 of *The History of Sexuality,* trans. Robert Hurley (New York: Pantheon, 1978), 25–26; originally published as *La Volonté de Savoir,* vol. 1 of *Histoire de la sexualité* (Paris: Gallimard, Bibliothèque des histoires, 1976).

6   ". . . an economic socialization via all the incitements and restrictions, the 'social' and fiscal measures brought to bear on the fertility of couples; a political socialization achieved through the 'responsibilization' of couples with regard to the social body as a whole (which had to be limited or on the contrary reinvigorated), and a medical socialization carried out by attributing a pathogenic value—for the individual and the species—to birth-control practices" (ibid.,104–5).

7   Francis Ronsin, *La Grève des ventres: Propagande néo-malthusienne et baisse de la natalité française (XIXe–XXe siècle)* (Paris: Aubier-Montaigne, 1980), 15, 17. For what follows, see chaps. 6 and 7, 12 and 13.

8   V. Magnan and M. Legrain, *Les Dégénérés: État mental et syndrome épisodique* (Paris: Ruef, 1895).

9   Alain Corbin, *Les Filles de noce: Misère sexuelle et prostitution (XIXe siècle)* (Paris: Flammarion, "Champs," 1982), 36–53, 436–52.

10 Quoted in Lidsky, *Les Écrivains contre la Commune,* 65.

11 For the following remarks, I refer to William Schneider, "Toward the Improvement of the Human Race: The History of Eugenics in France," *Journal of Modern History* 54 (June 1982).

12 Ronsin, *La Grève des ventres,* 137–47.

13 Yvonne Kniebiehler and Catherine Fouquet, *Histoire des mères* (Paris: Montalba, 1980), 311.

14 See Françoise Thébaud, "Maternité et famille entre les deux guerres: Idéologie et politique familiale," in *Femmes et Fascismes,* ed. Rita Thalmann (Paris: Éd. Tierce, "Femmes et sociétés," 1986), 85–98.

15 On the family policy resulting from the transformation of the social bases of familialism and on the symbolic constructions of the family that it induces, see Rémi Lenoir, "Transformations du familialisme et reconversions morales," *Actes de la recherche en sciences sociales* 59 (September 1985).

16 Robert A. Nye, *Crime, Madness and Politics in Modern France: The Medical Con-*

cept of National Decline (Princeton: Princeton University Press, 1984), particularly chap. 5, "Metaphors of Pathology in the 'Belle Époque': The Rise of a Medical Model of Cultural Crisis," 132–70.

17 Quoted in Rita Thalmann, "Le service maternel," chap. 3 of *Être femme sous le IIIe Reich* (Paris: Robert Laffont, 1982), 99–137.

18 On the notion of commonplaces and their capacity for letting mythic roots play, see Pierre Bourdieu, *Distinction* (Cambridge, MA: Harvard University Press, 1984), 468–69.

19 Cassirer, *The Myth of the State,* 291.

20 Alain Girard, *L'Institut national d'études démographiques: Histoire et développement* (Paris: INED, 1986), 41. Unless otherwise indicated, subsequent quotations concerning the demographic decline of France are taken from this work.

21 Drieu La Rochelle, *Mesure de la France* (Paris: Grasset, 1922); quoted in Halévy, *Trois Épreuves,* 124–25. In *Gilles,* La Rochelle takes up his theme of the "decadence" born of depopulation and associates it with the search for a golden age: return to the earth, to village churches, and to a mythical Middle Ages. His obsession with the national health founds a defense of fascist values, and his eschatological vision fuels his anti-Semitism. See Michel Winock, "Une parabole fasciste: *Gilles* de Drieu La Rochelle," in *Nationalisme, Antisémitisme et Fascisme en France* (Paris: Seuil, "Points Histoire," 1990), 346–73.

22 Gilles Nadeau, *Les Années fractures,* documentary, November 1993, Arte.

23 Alain Drouard, *Une inconnue des sciences sociales: La fondation Alexis-Carrel. 1941–1945* (Paris: INED/MSH, 1992), 110–19.

24 Pierre Bourdieu, "Le Nord et le Midi, contribution à une analyse de l'effet Montesquieu," *Actes de la recherche en sciences sociales* 35 (November 1980).

25 Alexis Carrel, letter, 23 September 1942, Archives nationales, 2 AG 78, Dr. Ménétrel, dossiers on various medical questions; emphasis added.

26 Alexis Carrel, letter to his brother-in-law, 12 April 1938, quoted in Drouard, *Une inconnue des sciences sociales,* 100.

27 Alexis Carrel, *L'Homme, cet inconnu* (Paris: Plon, 1935), II, VI. Available in English as *Man, the Unknown* (New York: Harper and Brothers, 1935), iv–xiii.

28 "Quelques extraits de *L'Homme, cet inconnu* du Dr. Carrel," appended to *L'Éducation des filles: Quelques principes directeurs* (Limoges: Association des parents d'élèves de l'enseignement libre, APEL, 1941); emphasis added. Carrel's work, which obeys the logic of the "erudite myth," lends itself particularly well to this method of brief quotations in the form of aphorisms that were all the rage during the National Revolution.

29 Editorial, *La Famille dans l'État, nouvelles dispositions juridiques, principes d'action, réalisations pratiques, Les Documents français* (July 1942); the subtitle of this monthly published from January 1941 in Clermont-Ferrand is *Revue des hautes études politiques, sociales, économiques et financières.* It offered profiles of the great Vichy ministers and the legislative reforms they carried out.

30 Office of general publicity, 1942; BDIC, reserve, Gr. fol. 126–18.

31 Philippe Renaudin, *La Famille dans la nation*, lecture given on 16 June 1943 at the Sorbonne, published by the Commissariat général à la famille; BDIC, reserve, Gr. fol. 126–2.

32 Aline Coutrot, "La politique familiale," in *Le Gouvernement de Vichy, 1940–1942,* ed. René Rémond (Paris: Armand Colin, 1972), 245–63.

33 Commissariat général de la famille, *La Commune rempart de la famille* [brochure] (Paris Commissariat général à la famille, Office de publicité générale, n.d); BDIC, reserve Gr. fol. 126–7.

34 Pierre Bourdieu and Luc Boltanski, "La production de l'idéologie dominante, lieux neutres et lieux communs," *Actes de la recherche en sciences sociales* 2–3 (1976).

35 This commentary concerning a photo of a Coop-Élévage henhouse overcrowded with chicks is an example of this ordinary violence: "The declining birthrate has not yet, thank God, reached the farmyards of France" (10 June 1943; reproduced in *La Propagande sous Vichy,* ed. Laurent Gervereau and Denis Peschanski [Nanterre: BDIC, 1990], 19). The comparison made by the propagandist to raising chickens can be related to the following text by Goebbels: "Woman's duty is to be beautiful and to bear children. The female bird adorns herself for her mate and hatches eggs for him" (quoted in Thalmann, *Être femme sous le IIIe Reich,* 101).

36 Lenoir, "Transformations du familialisme et reconversions morales," 24; Cointet, *Le Conseil national de Vichy,* 104, 147.

37 Georges Pernot, *Note sur la politique familiale,* 29 July 1940; BDIC, reserve, Dossier z2, "Jeunesse, famille."

38 Fernand Boverat, *L'Enseignement de la démographie et la morale familiale: La révision des manuels scolaires* (Lyon: Alliance nationale contre la dépopulation, délégation générale en zone non occupée, n.d.), BDIC, reserve, Q document 3998.

39 Ronsin, *La Grève des ventres,* 145.

40 Françoise Thébaud, *Quand nos grand-mères donnaient la vie: La maternité en France dans l'entre-deux-guerres* (Lyon: Presses universitaires de Lyon, 1986), 222.

41 Fernand Boverat, letter, 27 October 1941, to M. Lavagne d'Ortigue, chef du cabinet civil of Marchal Pétain; Archives Nationales, 2 AG 497, "Family," Fernand Boverat folder.

42 G. Jeannin, "Démographie européenne," *L'Actualité sociale* 166 (October 1941).

43 At the Conseil national, as well, Gaston Lacoin, an attorney, a Catholic, and president of La plus grande famille, vice president of the Federation of Large Families (Cointet, *Le Conseil national de Vichy,* 97, 147).

44 "Retour à la famille," *La Revue de la famille* 208 (September 1940).

45 G.-M. Bonvoisin, "La politique familiale du Maréchal," *L'Actualité sociale* 169 (January 1942).

46 On these themes, see Miller, *Les Pousse-au-jouir du maréchal Pétain,* 52–54, and Gervereau and Peschanski, *La Propagande sous Vichy,* 122–35.

47 Gustave Bonvoisin, "Revive la France!," *La Revue de la famille* (January 1943); emphasis added.

48 Lenoir, "Transformations du familialisme et reconversions morales"; Hervé Le Bras, "Histoire secrète de la fécondité," *Le Débat* (8 January 1981).

49 Girard, *L'Institut national d'études démographiques,* 32.

50 Renée Duc, interview, *Berliner Lokalanzeiger* (February 1937); quoted in Thalmann, *Être femme sous le IIIe Reich,* 119; emphasis added.

51 Renaudin, *La Famille dans la nation,* 20.

52 *Françaises que ferons-nous?* (Saint-Amand: R. Bussière impr., 1943), "France plus belle."

53 Azéma, *De Munich à la Libération,* 93.

54 Raymond Postal, "Le Chef, la Nation, les Hommes," in *France 41: La Révolution nationale constructive, un bilan et un programme,* 15.

55 Maurras, "Restauration de l'État," chap. 7 in *La Seule France.*

56 Quoted in Jacques de Launay, *Le Dossier de Vichy* (Paris: Julliard, "Archives," 1967, 264); the emphasis is Weygand's.

57 Presentation of the motives for the law concerning the Jewish Statute of October 3, 1940, *Journal officiel* (18 October 1940); quoted in Jean Thouvenin, *Une année d'histoire de la France, 1940–1941* (Paris: Sequana, 1942), 257. Thouvenin, editor of the collection "La France nouvelle" at Sequana, welcomed the antiforeigner and anti-Semitic laws: "It seems legitimate that we wish to bear our suffering among ourselves, between real Frenchmen" (254–55).

58 Marshal Pétain, address, 10 October 1940; quoted in ibid., 216.

59 Fifteen thousand citizens, including some six thousand Jews, would thus lose their French nationality. See Michaël R. Marrus and Robert O. Paxton, *Vichy France and the Jews* (New York: Basic Books, 1981), 4; originally published as *Vichy et les juifs* (Paris: Calmann-Lévy, 1981). Unless indicated otherwise, all references for the following are to this work, particularly chap. 2, "The Roots of Vichy Antisemitism."

60 The second Jewish Statute of June 2, 1941, extended professional exclusion and imposed the *numerus clausus* at the university, the detailed census of all Jews in the Unoccupied Zone and of their possessions, and the Aryanization of Jewish property and enterprises; all the measures applied to French as well as foreign Jews. On December 11, 1942, the French State required that the personal documents, identity card, and ration card of French and foreign Jews residing in the Free Zone bear the notation "Jew."

61 Quoted in Ralph Schor, *L'Opinion française et les Étrangers, 1919–1939* (Paris: Publications de la Sorbonne, 1985), 639.

62 Quoted in Weber, *L'Action française,* 552.

63 Reproduced in Schor, *L'Opinion française et les Étrangers,* 624.

64 Pierre-Étienne Flandin, "Risques de guerre et chances de paix," *Revue politique et parlementaire* (10 April 1939).

65 Georges Mauco, *Les Étrangers en France: Leur rôle dans l'activité économique* (Paris: Armand Colin, 1932), 490.

66 Jean Giraudoux, *Pleins Pouvoirs* (Paris: Gallimard, 1939), 56–66; emphasis added.

67 Ibid., 62.

68 Marrus and Paxton, *Vichy France and the Jews,* 366.

69 Citing the feminist claims of the 1930s in order to condemn them, André Rouast, a Catholic jurist and ardent defender of the National Revolution, takes as his target precisely the right of a foreign woman married to a Frenchman to keep her nationality: "From 1927, the campaign to emancipate woman led to allowing her to keep her own nationality when she married at the risk of creating moral dissension between spouses who each retain a distinct nationality" (*La Famille dans la nation* [Paris: PUF, "Bibliothèque du Peuple," 1941], 20).

70 Quoted in Christine Bard, *Les Filles de Marianne: Histoire des féminismes, 1914–1940* (Paris: Fayard, 1995), 406.

71 Ibid., 409. In *Le Journal* in 1933, the same Clément Vautel led a campaign against welcoming German Jewish refugees "who call themselves victims of Hitler's regime" (quoted in Schor, *L'Opinion française et les Étrangers,* 625).

72 Marrus and Paxton, *Vichy France and the Jews,* 367.

73 William Garcin, *L'Individualisme: Cahiers de formation politique,* Vichy, n.d., Bibliothèque de documents internationale contemporaine (BDIC) first part, Cahier 1, 10.

74 Boverat, *L'Enseignement de la démographie et de la morale familiale.*

75 Georges Pelorson, "Jeunesse 1941," in *France 41: La Révolution nationale constructive,* 223–25; emphasis in the original.

76 "Famille d'abord!" *La Revue de la famille* 224 (January 1942).

77 Le Bras, "Histoire secrète de la fécondité," 94.

78 Renaudin, *La Famille dans la nation,* 8–9.

79 Commissariat général à la famille, *L'Université devant la famille* [brochure] (Paris: Commissariat général à la famille, Office de publicité générale, 1942); BDIC, reserve, Gr. fol. 126–19.

4. VIOLENCE AND STATE PROPAGANDA

1 Anne-Marie Sohn, "Entre deux guerres, les rôles féminins en France et en Angleterre," in *Le XXe, Siècle,* vol. 5 of *Histoire des femmes en Occident,* ed. Françoise Thébaud (Paris: Plon, 1992), 95.

2 For an analysis of the representations of the political economy of the nineteenth century concerning women working in industry and, particularly, of their conceptual limitations that impose the idea that work and family belong to two separate worlds, see Joan Scott, "L'ouvrière, mot impie, sordide," in *Gender and the Politics of History* (New York: Columbia University Press, 1988).

3 Rose-Marie Lagrave, "Une émancipation sous tutelle: Éducation et travail des femmes au XXe siècle," in Thébaud, *Histoire des femmes en Occident*, 438.

4 Antoine Prost, *L'Enseignement en France, 1800–1967* (Paris: Armand Colin, 1968), 103–4.

5 Ibid.; I calculated these percentages using the statistical tables reproduced on p. 346.

6 "This is not a key, it is a rattle," Mme. Crouzet-Ben Aben wrote about this diploma in "La clientèle secondaire féminine et ses besoins," in *Revue universitaire,* 2 (1911).

7 See Françoise Mayeur, *L'Enseignement secondaire des jeunes filles sous la IIIe République* (Paris: Presses de la FNSP, 1977).

8 Robert Viala, "Comment fut créé l'enseignement secondaire de jeunes filles," *Le Sexe des élites, Les Amis de Sèvres* 126 (1987).

9 Edmée Charrier, *L'Évolution intellectuelle féminine* (Paris: Éd. Albert Mechelink, 1931). I refer to this work for the following data.

10 The first female recipient of a bachelor degree in literature was Julie Daubié (school of Paris, October 8, 1871), who had already been the first woman to receive a baccalaureate degree from the School of Lyon in 1862. Daubié was thus not that young, as she had published a book in 1866 entitled *La Femme pauvre au XIXe siècle,* a collection of texts that had already won a competition organized by the educational district of Lyon in 1859, "What Means of Subsistence Do Women Have?" As we can see, Daubié was more interested in sociology and economics than in literature. Contrary to Jules Simon (*L'Ouvrière,* 1860), who saw a solution for the poverty of female workers only in keeping women at home, she demanded equality before the law, in drafting these laws, in access to training and to apprenticeships, and in salaries. On this debate, see Scott, "L'ouvrière, mot impie, sordide."

11 Thus, in January 1918, the senior president of the Chambre des députés, Jules Siegfried, called for recognition of women's right to vote to honor their participation in the national defense: "It will be necessary for the sacred union to subsist throughout the entire country, just as in this chamber, and that in the upcoming elections, by a gesture of justice and recognition, women be given a voting ballot for their admirable behavior during the war" (quoted in Joseph Barthélemy, *Le Vote des femmes* [Paris: Félix Alcan, 1920], 132).

12 See Michèle Bordeaux, "Femmes hors d'État français," in *Femmes et Fascismes,* 141–43. Few studies exist on the Vichy policy toward women, and only women have been interested in it. Other than the work of Bordeaux, which discusses the theme of female antiheroes of history and faithful spouses of heroes and analyzes the laws regarding women's work and divorce, and the work of Hélène Eck, "Les Françaises sous Vichy, femmes du désastre, citoyennes par le désastre?" (in Thébaud, *Histoire des femmes en Occident,* 185–211), which studies the reinforcement of the family institution,

the ambiguities of the "social," and women's work, Miranda Pollard has published "Women and the National Revolution," in *Vichy France and the Resistance,* ed. Roderick Kedward and Robert Austin (Totowa, NJ: Barnes and Noble Books, 1985), 36–47, which analyzes "gender" in the ideology of the regime, and "La politique du travail féminin," in *Le Régime de Vichy et les Français,* ed. Jean-Pierre Azéma and François Bédarida, 242–50. In this same work, Dominique Veillon studies "La vie quotidienne des femmes" (629–39). One of the significant effects of symbolic violence created by the apparent banality of Vichy discourse concerning women was that it prevented this question from being constructed as a legitimate object of the historical research that is now so abundant concerning this period.

13 Archives nationales, 2 AG 497.

14 Madeleine Cazin, *Le Travail féminin* (law thesis, Rennes, 1943); quoted in Bordeaux, "Femmes hors d'État français."

15 The Church was firmly opposed to enrolling women in the STO. It maintained that these call-ups were going to place women in moral danger (Halls, *The Youth of Vichy France,* 369).

16 Eck, "Les Françaises sous Vichy: Femmes du désastre, citoyennes par le désastre?"

17 See Thalmann, *Être femme sous le IIIe Reich,* 144–61.

18 I wish to thank Margaret Maruani for providing me with the unpublished research project "Crise économique et droit à l'emploi des femmes" that she presented at the Centre National des Arts et Métiers CNAM in 1983.

19 Charles Richet, "Travail et famille," *Revue des deux mondes* (10 October 1940).

20 Pétain, *La France nouvelle,* 60–62.

21 Poster reproduced in *La Propagande sous Vichy, 1940–1944,* 25.

22 Ibid. Laurent Gervereau, "Y a-t-il un style de Vichy?," 110–47.

23 Quoted in Thébaud, "Maternité et famille entre les deux guerres"; emphasis added.

24 *L'Instituteur et son rôle dans la restauration de la famille française,* by an elementary schoolteacher, preface by Paul Haury (Paris: Commissariat générale à la famille, Office de publicité générale, n.d.), BDIC, 0 document 22715. This form of corporatist anonymity is completely in keeping with the regime. It is likely that Inspector Haury inspired and corrected the exercise.

25 Archives nationales, 2 AG 498.

26 Haury, *L'Université devant la famille,* preface by Gilbert Gidel, rector of the educational district of Paris.

27 Preface by M. Hardouin, secretary general for social workers (Paris: Commissariat général à la famille, Office de publicité générale, n.d.), BDIC, reserve Gr. fol. 126-4.

28 Published by the Office of General Propaganda with the assistance of *Votre Beauté* (n.d.), BDIC, reserve Gr. fol. 126-3.

29 Archives nationales, 2 AG 498.

30 *La Famille dans l'État, Les Documents français.*

31 Jean Bergeaud [lecturer for the Commissariat General for the Family], "L'exposition de la famille française," *La Revue de la famille* (July 1943).

32 Erving Goffman, "La ritualisation de la féminité," *Actes de la recherche en sciences sociales* 14 (1977).

33 See Denis Peschanski, "Vichy au singulier, Vichy au pluriel: Une tentative avortée d'encadrement de la société (1941–1942)," *Annales* (May–June 1988); *La Propagande sous Vichy, 1940–1944.*

34 G. de Korff, "La jeunesse en Italie," and "La jeunesse allemande," *Bulletin des jeunes* 28 (August 1942) and 33 (November 1942). In the *Bulletin de France,* the Amicale cites Bonald, for whom the French Revolution produced the only child; develops an unsurprising defense of the family and the birthrate, supported by the writings of Boverat; and regularly ridicules the "simpleton" who is for Jews, Freemasonry, and Americans. In issue 10 of 10 August 1941, we find a letter from a "Frenchwoman devoted to her country," the feminine incarnation of the "elite propagandists" brought together by the Amicale: "We plan, several women and I, to fight permissiveness, to restore honor to sobriety and correct dress. . . . I believe that for a movement of good taste to succeed, it must be launched by women who have great influence arising from their fortune and their family. There will never be too many of us to stamp out permissiveness and vulgarity." A particularly sinister expression of the National Revolution, the Amicale de France, which claimed sixty thousand subscribers to the *Bulletin* in June 1941, worked for a strong-arm realignment using intimidation and denouncement. To my knowledge, there is no detailed study of this movement, but perhaps the archives do not make this possible. Claude Lévy and Dominique Veillon stress the importance of this private association that placed itself in the service of state propaganda; see "Propagande et modelage des esprits," in *Le Régime de Vichy et les Français,* 186.

35 "Rôle de la jeunesse féminine dans la jeunesse française," *Bulletin des jeunes* (15 December 1941).

36 The expression comes from Émile Faguet in *Le Gaulois* (4 June 1915); quoted in Kniebiehler and Fouquet, *Histoires des mères.* The following information is taken from this text, 302–10.

37 Mathilde Dubesset, Françoise Thébaud, and Catherine Vincent, "Les munitionettes de la Seine," in *1914–1918: L'autre front,* Cahier du Mouvement social no. 2, ed. Patrick Fridenson (Paris: Éditions ouvrières, 1977), 189–219.

38 G. A. Doleris and J. Boucastel, *Maternité et Féminisme: Éducation sexuelle* (Paris, 1918); quoted in ibid., 208.

39 Kniebiehler and Fouquet, *Histoire des mères.* For the familialist offensive of the national reconstruction period in the face of the persistence of married working women during the 1920s, see Lagrave, "Une émancipation sous tutelle: Éducation et travail des femmes au XXe siècle," 432–62.

40 Talmy, *Histoire du mouvement familial en France*, 2: 217–20.

41 Thalmann, *Être femme sous le IIIe Reich*, 112–13.

42 Mosse, *Nationalism and Sexuality*, 95, 161.

43 Maurice Crubelier, *Histoire culturelle de la France, XIXe–XXe siècle* (Paris: Armand Colin, "U," 1974), 61–62.

44 Abel Bonnard, *Éloge de l'ignorance* (Paris: Hachette, 1926), 21.

45 "La journée des mères 1941," *L'Actualité sociale* (June–July 1941).

46 Paxton, *Vichy France*, 222.

47 Jean Guéhenno, *Journal des années noires* (1947; Paris: Livre de Poche, 1966), 313; quoted in ibid., 222.

48 Archives nationales, F 41921, French State, Chantiers de la jeunesse, note related to Mother's Day, 12 May 1941.

49 Long, *The French Right and Education*, 203.

50 Archives nationales, F 41291.

51 Reproduced in *La Propagande sous Vichy*, 119.

52 Archives nationales, F 41291.

53 Ibid.

54 Jérôme Carcopino, *Souvenirs de sept ans, 1937–1944* (Paris: Flammarion, 1953), 434.

55 *L'Actualité sociale* (June–July 1941).

56 *Cité nouvelle* (25 June 1941).

57 *La Propagande sous Vichy*, 119.

58 Duquesne, *Les Catholiques français sous l'occupation*, 63.

59 See Scott, "Gender, a Useful Category of Historical Analysis."

60 Maurice Jacquemont, *Petit Guide de la journée des mères* (Paris: Édition sociale française, 1943); preface by Georges Hourdin, secretary general of the National Center for the Coordination and Activities of Family Movements.

61 Pierre Bourdieu, "Les rites commes actes d'institution," *Actes de la recherche en sciences sociales* 43 (1982). I refer to this article for the discussion that follows.

62 *La Revue de la famille* (May 1942).

63 Thérèse's "little way" was constructed by the exegetes and critics who brought about her canonization as a popularized form of sainthood that perfectly embodies the official ideology of the Church concerning the feminine mystic at the end of the nineteenth century. As Veuillot says in *L'Univers* in 1906, the young, "humble," "modest," and "obedient" Carmelite "had simply served God, with confident and assiduous faithfulness, in the smallest things"; see Rubert Muller-Rensmann, *Trois Grands Pôles du miracle en France: La médaille miraculeuse, Lourdes, Thérèse de Lisieux* (3d cycle thesis directed by Jacques Maître, Ecole des Hautes Etudes en Sciences Sociales [EHESS], 1983), 335–36.

64 Gabriel Robinot Marcy, "Aux chantiers de jeunesse: Pour la fête des mères," *Cité nouvelle* (10 October 1941).

65 Archives nationales, F 41291; emphasis in the original.

66 *La Revue de la famille* (June 1942).

67 Archives nationales, F 41291, propaganda brochure for Mother's Day intended for the regional delegates to the family, April 1942.

5. THE HERITAGE AND INCARNATION OF
CATHOLIC FEMININE CULTURE

1 Henri Rollet, *L'Action sociale des catholiques en France 1871–1914* (Paris: Desclée de Brouwer, 1958), 2: 34.

2 Durand, *Vichy 1940–1944*, 81.

3 "France nouvelle, Plan 3: Communauté familiale et ordre nouveau," *Renouveaux* (1 January 1941); emphasis added. The date of the "survey," October 1940, demonstrates the speed of the commitment of the women of Catholic action. Sociohistorical work needs to be done concerning the developments that the notion of "public opinion" underwent under Vichy and concerning its concrete uses both in the state bodies and in the broad sector of private initiative that mobilized for social reconstruction; in light of what was happening in the women and family sector, a traditionalist sector if ever there was one, we note an important turn toward this *modern* form of government and imposition of political representations. At times, the National Revolution takes on the bizarre appearance of a constant public opinion poll.

4 "La femme et la maison," *Chronique sociale de France* (May–June 1943).

5 "Un problème familial, à propos de la réglementation du travail des femmes," *Renouveaux* (1 December 1940).

6 I am referring to Muller-Rensmann, *Trois Grands Pôles du miracle en France,* and to Latreille et al., *Histoire du catholicisme en France,* vol. 3.

7 Claude Langlois, *Le Catholicisme au féminin: Les congrégations françaises à supérieure générale au XIXe siècle* (Paris: Cerf, 1984).

8 Quoted in ibid., 307–9.

9 This antimodernism would predominate during the interwar period in the influential Thomist current; the insignia of the Fédération nationale catholique (FNC), presided over by General de Castelnau, who during the 1920s led a veritable league action against the Cartel des gauches, is a steel-clad knight armed from head to toe. The myth of the Middle Ages flowered under Vichy. See Latreille et al., *Histoire du catholicisme en France,* vol. 3, 581–83, and Serge Berstein, *La France des années 30* (Paris: Armand Colin, 1988), 62.

10 On the banalization of the figure of Mary and her cult, see Jean-Marie Aubert, *L'Exil féminin: Antiféminisme et modernisme* (Paris: Cerf, 1988), 135.

11 Jacques Maître, "Entre femmes, notes sur une filière du mysticisme catholique," *Archives de sciences sociales des religions* (January–March 1983): 105; emphasis added. I refer to this text for what follows. See also by the same author "Idéologie religieuse, conversion mystique and symbiose mère-

enfant, le cas de Thérèse Martin (1873–1897)," *Archives de sciences sociales des religions* (January–March 1981), and "L'adolescence d'une grande mystique: Thérèse Martin (sainte Thérèse de l'Enfant-Jésus)," *Recherches et Documents du Centre Thomas-More* (September 1984).

12 Carlo Ginzburg, *Les Batailles nocturnes* (Paris: Flammarion, 1984).

13 Langlois, *Le Catholicisme au féminin*, 601.

14 Ibid., 645.

15 Prost, *L'Enseignement en France*, 183.

16 Aubert, *L'Exil féminin*, 96.

17 Odile Arnold, *Le Corps et l'Ame: La vie des religieuses au XIXe siècle* (Paris: Seuil, 1984).

18 See Francine Muel-Dreyfus, *Le Métier d'éducateur: Les instituteurs de 1900, les éducateurs spécialisés de 1968* (Paris: Minuit, "Le sens commun," 1983), 65–73.

19 Jacques Gadille and Jean Godel, "L'héritage d'une pensée en matière d'éducation des femmes," in *Éducation et Images de la femme chrétienne en France au début du XXe siècle*, ed. Françoise Mayeur and Jacques Gadille (Lyon: University Jean-Moulin, L'Hermès, 1980), 21.

20 Claude Langlois, "Aux origines de l'enseignement secondaire catholique de jeunes filles, jalons pour un enquête, 1896–1914," in Mayeur and Gadille, *Éducation et Images de la femme chrétienne en France au début du XXe siecle,* 88–89.

21 Prost, *L'Enseignement en France*, 204, 207–8, 218.

22 Mayeur, *L'Enseignement secondaire des jeunes filles sous la IIIe République,* 1.

23 Ibid., 389–92.

24 For information concerning the feminist movements during the years 1870–1914, I refer to Laurence Klejman and Florence Rochefort, *L'Égalité en marche: Le féminisme sous la IIIe République, 1868–1914* (Paris: Des femmes/ Presses de la FNSP, 1989), and for the years 1914–1940, to Bard, *Les filles de Marianne.*

25 "La France aux Français" was the slogan invented by the anti-Semite Édouard Drumont (Exhibit "L'affaire Dreyfus et le tournant du siècle, 1894–1910," BDIC, Museum of Contemporary History, Hôtel des Invalides, April–June 1994).

26 For the information concerning this movement, I refer to Anne-Marie Sohn, "Les femmes catholiques et la vie publique: L'exemple de la Ligue patriotique des Françaises," in *Stratégies des femmes* (Paris: Tierce, 1984), 97–119.

27 Henri Rollet, *Andrée Butillard et le féminisme chrétien* (Paris: Spes, 1960), 63.

28 See Rollet, *L'Action sociale des catholiques en France, 1871–1914,* 35; Jeannine Verdès-Leroux, "Pouvoir et assistance: Cinquante ans de service social," *Actes de recherche en sciences sociale,* 2–3 (1976); R.-H. Guerrand and M.-A. Rupp, *Brève histoire du service social en France, 1896–1976* (Paris: Privat, 1978).

29 The sociocultural environment of the leading circles of these movements merged with that of the Dreyfus family, its allies and Dreyfus supporters belonging to the elites of the Republic; see Michael Burns, *Dreyfus, a*

Family Affair: From the French Revolution to the Holocaust (New York: Harper-Collins, 1991).

30 Christophe Charle, Naissance des "intellectuels," 1880–1900 (Paris: Minuit, "Le sens commun", 1990), 93.

31 Sohn, "Les femmes catholiques et la vie publique: L'exemple de la Ligue patriotique des Françaises," 98; Bard, Les Filles de Marianne, 43.

32 Barthélemy, Le Vote des femmes, 598, 605.

33 Conseil national des femmes françaises, Cinquante années d'activité 1901–1951: La célébration du cinquantenaire (11 January 1952): 28–29.

34 Paxton, Vichy France, 155, 161.

35 Quoted in Bard, Les Filles de Marianne, 231.

36 See Claude Barbizet, Blanche Edwards-Pilliet: Femme et médecin, 1858–1941 (Le Mans: Cénomane, 1988), and Christine Bard, ed., Madeleine Pelletier (1874–1939): Logique et infortunes d'un combat pour l'égalité (Paris: Côté-Femmes, 1992).

37 Mary Douglas, De la souillure (Paris: François Maspero, 1981), 119, 128. Available in English as Purity and Danger: An Analysis of Concepts of Pollution and Taboo (London: Routledge and Keegan Paul, 1966).

38 George L. Mosse showed the existence, everywhere in Europe, of this concern for "respectability" of the feminist and feminine action movements and their adoption of the dominant stereotypes of femininity; see Nationalism and Sexuality, 110–13.

39 Latreille et al., Histoire du catholicisme en France, 3: 544; Suaud, "L'imposition de la vocation sacerdotale."

40 Bard, Les Filles de Marianne, 268.

41 Langlois, Le Catholicisme au féminin, 634.

42 Between 1920 and 1940, however, one notes a significant resumption in female religious recruiting, almost comparable to the maximum of 1855–1880. The reasons for this resumption can be seen in the demographic imbalance of the postwar period, which imposed stringent female celibacy and also worked strengthening communities and toward idealizing Christian marriage; the lasting success of the Jeunesse Agricole Chrétienne (JAC) in the countryside and the Jeunesse Etudiante Chrétienne (JEC) in urban areas would ultimately contribute to drying up the sources of community recruiting; see ibid., 524, 633.

43 Jean-Louis Loubet del Bayle, Les Non-Conformistes des années 30: Une tentative de renouvellement de la pensée politique française (Paris: Seuil, 1969), 290.

44 For this information, I refer to Latreille et al., Histoire du catholicisme en France, 3: 578.

45 Guerrand and Rupp, Brève histoire du service social en France, 56.

46 Ibid., 64–65, 90.

47 In 1920, at the instigation of the family leagues, a Comité d'études familiales [to study the problem of depopulation and find a means for defending large families — Trans.] was created and attracted numerous northern industrialists who worked for large families and the family vote. In 1927, the

powerful Fédération des Unions de familles nombreuses du Nord, also founded in 1920, united four hundred groups and 180,000 people. In 1930, the congress of the Fédération nationale des familles nombreuse, held in Lille, was the occasion for profamily members to clearly affirm their objective and thus to distinguish themselves from the National Alliance against Depopulation: to save religion through the family and the family through religion. See Talmy, *Histoire du mouvement familial en France,* 1: 221, 2: 107–13.

48 Quoted in Rollet, *Andrée Butillard et le féminisme chrétien,* 74–75, 85.

49 From its foundation, the École normale sociale was interested in training Catholic militants for union activity. In 1925, it published a practical guide for union training: the "social apostolate" of the "unionized apostle," defined by the UFCS, would greatly inspire the feminine trade unionism of the Conféderation Française des Travailleurs Chrétiens (CFTC) from the 1920s to the war; see Joceline Chabot, "Les syndicats féminins chrétiens et la formation militante de 1913 à 1936," *Le Mouvement social* 165 (1993).

50 Semaines sociales de France, Nancy, XIXe session, 1927, *La Femme dans la société* (Lyon: Chroniques sociales de France, 1928).

51 Gillet, "L'unité de la morale pour les deux sexes," in ibid., 110–11.

52 R. P. Albert Valensin [professor of the school of theology of Lyon], "Le christianisme et la femme, ce qu'il pense d'elle, ce qu'il a fait d'elle," in Semaines sociales de France, *La Femme dans la société,* 159. On the idealization of woman as a means of distancing her from public life, see Aubert, *L'Exil féminin,* 135–41.

53 Léontine Zanta, "Le féminisme: Ses manifestations variées à travers les faits, les institutions, les tendances, les mouvements d'opinion," in Semaines sociales de France, *La Femme dans la société,* 69, 71, 79. The first French woman doctor of philosophy, one of the few female intellectual university graduates from the current of Christian feminism, Zanta thus defines, with perhaps unintentional humor, the expectations of the Semaines sociales: "Woman's place is effectively at home, in the family, and all the efforts of this Semaine, if I have clearly understood the thought of those who organized it, is to leave it there, but by making it more stable and better" (68).

54 "Lettre du cardinal Gasparri, écrivant au nom de Sa Sainteté Pie XI, à l'École normale sociale, le 9 november 1925," in Semaines sociales de France, *La Femme dans la société,* 163.

55 Bard, *Les Filles de Marianne,* 178–83.

56 Durand, *Vichy 1940–1944,* 163.

57 *La Française* (15 February 1936).

58 Rollet, *Andrée Butillard et le féminisme chrétien,* 101–17.

59 *La Française* (20 February, 10 April, 17 April 1937).

60 Antonin Sertillanges, *Féminisme et Christianisme* (Paris: Gabalda, 1908), 337.

61 Rollet, *Andrée Butillard et le féminisme chrétien,* 78–79.

62 See *L'École des parents* 3 (1957), and 10 (1959); Rollet, *Andrée Butillard et le*

féminisme chrétien, 83–84; André Isambert, *L'Éducation des parents* (Paris: PUF, "Paideia," 1960), 30–36. I am referring primarily to the handwritten reports of the first board meetings and to the press clippings from the years 1930–1935 kept in the archives of the École des parents. I wish to thank Christine Michel, who helped me collect the documentation on the history of this foundation.

63 Mme Vérine, speech, in *Le Noviciat du mariage* [collection of lectures of the École des parents] (Paris: Spes, 1932), 16–17; capitalization in original.

64 "A propos de l'École des parents, ce que nous dit Mme Vérine," *La Française* (19 September 1931).

65 Mme Gernez, "Comment on prépare la jeune fille au mariage," in École des parents, *Le Noviciat du mariage.*

66 Mme de Martrin-Donos, "Le rôle de la famille dans la formation de la personnalité," in *De la personnalité, formation et conquête* [published by the École des parents] (Paris: Spes, 1933), 267; emphasis in original.

67 Vérine, "La Famille," in *France 41,* 197; emphasis in original. In 1942, Vérine made familial unanimity, a rampart against "sectarianism" and "partisan passions," an explicitly political arm given the context: "As for the political perspective, there should never be any division in families in this regard; suffering must be a school of energy and there is only one outcome for unhappiness: to draw closer around the leader who represents the Country and for us parents to give the example of loyalty, discipline, obedience, and patience" (Vérine, "Climat familial 42," in *Les Devoirs présents des éducateurs,* ed. G. Bertier et al. [Paris: Édition sociale française, 1942]).

68 "From the Vichy Information and Propaganda Center, women's section, questionnaires were sent to the central secretariate of the UFCS with the request to pass them on to our supporters. . . . It was thus an excellent opportunity to provide our modest cooperation to the Information Center and thus to the government by telling our thoughts as women, concerned with seeing the country become more and more committed to the path of true recovery" ("Ce que pensent les femmes françaises," *La Femme dans la vie sociale* 138 [May 1941]).

69 "The family group must survive any change in regime, any social upheaval, because it is of a natural order, and because it is strictly irreplaceable" ("Personne humaine et cadres sociaux," *La Femme dans la vie sociale* 144 [January 1942]).

70 Summarizing, in June 1941, the social doctrine of their movement formulated in 1925 by Reverend Verdier, who later became a cardinal, they broke it down into three new subheadings: Family, Work, Nation.

71 "Let us continue to reread the titles of the feature articles. How clearly they speak! 'Renovation' . . . is the issue from 1941? No: this article is from January 1939" ("Notre journal et sa carrière," *La Femme dans la vie sociale* 147 [April 1942]).

72   "Comment la LMF se développe," *La Mère au foyer, ouvrière de progrès humain* (Ligue de la mère au foyer, May 1941).

73   In the introduction to its brochure, the LMF cites the speech of April 1941 given by Cardinal Suhard, Archbishop of Paris, about Mother's Day: "If we want France to live, let us then give France real mothers of families. . . . A mother knows that nothing great is made here below except through suffering. Mothers must remind everyone of the fecundity of sacrifice."

74   *La Femme dans la vie sociale* 138 (May 1941) and 153 (November 1942).

75   Of 1.3 million French men who were prisoners in Germany, 767,000 were married men and fathers of families; the poverty of their wives was extreme. See Veillon, "La vie quotidienne des femmes," 629–39.

76   A. Butillard, "Licenciement des femmes," *Chronique sociale de France* (November-December 1940). Against certain articles that "persist in not wanting to open their eyes," *Renouveaux* recalled that what this law did was "necessary but entirely insufficient" because it was necessary to eliminate "all that impedes in souls the spirit of duty and sacrifice, which are at the basis of the family institution" and that "woman's natural role, her social role par excellence, is to be the guardian of the home and the educator of her children" ("A propos de la réglementation du travail des femmes," *Renouveaux* [1 December 1940]).

77   Bourdieu, *Distinction,* 471.

78   *La Mère au foyer,* 49.

79   "Notre journal et sa carrière."

80   "Andrée Butillard, l'unité nécessaire," *La Femme dans la vie sociale* 146 (March 1942); emphasis added.

81   Marie-Aline Barrachina, "La section féminine de la Phalange espagnole: L'exclusion du politique comme aboutissement d'un discours survalorisant," in Thalmann, *Femmes et Fascismes,* 119–33.

82   When the Nazi Party decided to exclude women from all its management bodies, the decision was approved by the few militant women present whose authorized political action would then be called "Service of sacrifice" (Thalmann, *Être femme sous le IIIe Reich,* 66).

6. FAMILY IMPERIALISM AND FEMININE SUBJECTION

1   Paxton, *Vichy France,* 137.

2   Durand, *Vichy, 1940–1944,* 27.

3   Émile Durkheim, *L'Évolution pédagogique en France* [course given from 1904 to the war of 1914] (1938; Paris: PUF, "Quadrige," 1990), 18–19.

4   See in particular Coutrot, "La politique familiale," 245–63, and Michèle Cointet-Labrousse, "Le gouvernement de Vichy et les familles," *Informations sociales* 4–5 (1980): 26–30. Although she clearly disassociates the action of the Commissariat General for the Family from the organicist political ideology of the regime, Coutrot nevertheless cites a "discontinuity" in

the family policy, taken overall, among Vichy, the Third, and the Fourth Republics, but this does not change the direction of her analysis.

5   *Revue des deux mondes* (15 September 1940), reprinted in Pétain, *La France nouvelle, principes de la communauté,* 60–62. *Le Temps* also links the return to the family, "strongest column of the new State that we wish to establish," to a battle against the "deracinated" individual and against "the freedom of the individual that was only an illusion, a mirage, a fiction" ("La famille dans l'État," *Le Temps* [10 August 1940]).

6   "Individualisme et nation," *La Revue universelle* 1 (January 1941), reprinted in *La France nouvelle,* 112, 116.

7   *La France nouvelle,* 155.

8   Gillouin, "Pétain," opening text of *France 41: La Révolution nationale constructive,* 79–80.

9   Here, Garcin gives a more explicitly political turn to the recurring condemnation of legal individualism that is accused of perverting the Civil Code, a condemnation that borrows ceaselessly from Renan. Thus Gustave Bonvoisin writes in "Revive la France!": "It is too difficult to raise children? Why? Why because, in our contemporary France, everything, as Renan used to say, seems to have been planned for an isolated man who was born a foundling and dies unmarried."

10 William Garcin, in *La Famille, étude de la communauté familiale,* "Cahiers de formation politique" 6 (Vichy, n.d.), 6, 13, 22.

11 Archives nationales, 2 AG 645, reprinted in Cointet, *Le Conseil national de Vichy,* 411; emphasis added.

12 Renaudin, *La Famille dans la nation,* 5.

13 Bonvoisin, "La politique familiale du Maréchal." The article opens with a reminder of the "Words of the Chief" and repeats, on his behalf, the condemnation of individualism—"the Head of State boldly denounces individualism as the great error that corrupted the education of the French people"—thus incorporating it without any objectivity into the new celebration of the family.

14 Garcin, *L'Individualisme,* 8–9.

15 See Paxton, *Vichy France,* 167; Bordeaux, "Femmes hors d'État français, 1940–1941," 145–47; André Desqueyrat, "La nouvelle loi sur le divorce," *Cité nouvelle* (10 May 1941).

16 Jean Dauvillier, in *Le Divorce,* "Cahiers de formation politique" 16 (Vichy, n.d.), 33.

17 Pierre Birnbaum, *Un mythe politique: La "République juive"* (Paris: Fayard, 1988), 219–24.

18 Quoted in Michèle Cotta, *La Collaboration 1940–44* (Paris: Armand Colin, 1964), 66.

19 Jean Guibal, *La Famille dans la révolution nationale* (Paris: Éd. Fernand Sorlot, "Cahiers français," 1940).

20 Marrus and Paxton, *Vichy France and the Jews,* 143.

21 Quoted in Bordeaux, "Femmes hors d'État français, 1940–1944."

22 Franck Alengry, *Principes généraux de la philosophie sociale du Maréchal Pétain* (Limoges: Lavauzelle, "La grande lignée française," 1943), 27. Professor of constitutional law at the Faculty of Paris and at the School of Political Science, Joseph Barthélemy had been beaten in the elections of 1936 and was vehemently opposed to the Popular Front. He was minister of justice from February 1941 to March 1943 and says in his *Mémoires* that "if in France there was a necessary Pétainist cult, he was, happily, a high priest." See Paxton, *Vichy France,* 167; Cointet, *Le Conseil national de Vichy,* 64.

23 Quoted in Marrus and Paxton, *Vichy France and the Jews,* 99.

24 Henri Solus [professor at the Faculty of Law of Paris], "La réforme du divorce," *L'Actualité sociale* (June–July 1941).

25 *Françaises que ferons-nous?,* 48.

26 Dauvillier, *Le Divorce.* The author is referring to Paul Bourget (*Un divorce,* 1904), for whom the principle of the "sacrifice of the individual interest to the general interest" imposes the indissolubility of marriage.

27 Alfred Coste-Floret [law school lecturer], "La réforme du divorce," *Cité nouvelle* (25 February 1941).

28 "Un frein au divorce," *La Femme dans la vie sociale* 138 (May 1941).

29 Georges Desmottes [doctor of law, attorney to the Court of Appeal of Caen, representative of the Commissariat General for the Family], "L'abandon de famille," *L'Actualité sociale* (November 1942).

30 Lochak, "La doctrine sous Vichy ou les mésaventures du positivisme," 253–85.

31 Laborie, *Résistants, Vichyssois et Autres,* 197–205.

32 Étienne Videcoq, "Les droits et les devoirs des époux" and "Qui doit diriger la famille?," *La Revue de la famille* (January and February 1943); emphasis added.

33 Commentary on the law in the special issue of *L'Espoir français,* "Le Maréchal protège la famille" (August 1943), special printing for the Ministry of Information that offers an illustrated panorama of all the measures of the regime in favor of the family.

34 Rouast, *La Famille dans la nation,* 21, 43, 46.

35 "Le congrès familial de Lourdes," *L'Actualité sociale* 185 (October 1943); "La famille à l'honneur au 70ᵉ pèlerinage national de Lourdes," *La Revue de la famille* 243 (October 1943). In 1943, the term "partisan" had political resonance for everyone.

36 Georgette Varenne, *La Femme dans la France nouvelle* (Clermont-Ferrand: Imprimerie Mont-Louis, 1940), 5. The author wrote two other catechisms on work and country, the latter being devoted, through "the" woman, to the family. I refer to pages 38, 6, 10, 28, 20, 58, and 55.

37 Dr. P. Merle, "La nature féminine, sa singularité dans l'universel humain," in *La Femme et sa mission* (Paris: Plon, "Présences," 1941); emphasis added. This work of "experts," abundantly cited, for example, in the special issue

of *Votre Beauté, Femme, Famille, France* of October 1941, ends with an overview by Daniel-Rops: "A new regime cannot establish itself in France without defining with much precision the place it intends to accord to woman and the role it wants her to play."

38 René d'Argentan, "Le respect de la femme," *La Légion* (15 April 1942).

39 *L'Instituteur et son rôle dans la restauration de la famille française,* by an elementary school teacher, 26–27.

40 Varenne, *La Femme dans la France nouvelle*, 62; emphasis added.

41 Nicole Loraux, *Les Enfants d'Athéna: Idées athéniennes sur la citoyenneté et la division des sexes* (1981; Paris: Seuil, "Points Sciences humaines," 1990), 107–9.

42 Quoted in Dominique Veillon, *La Mode sous l'Occupation: Débrouillardise et coquetterie dans la France en guerre, 1939–45* (Paris: Payot, "Histoire," 1990), 224–26.

43 Varenne, *La Femme dans la France nouvelle*, 57.

44 Paule-Marie Weyd, "La femme à la campagne," *Cité nouvelle* 13 (10 July 1941).

45 A. du Palais, *Pour la refaire* (Paris-Avignon: Les Livres nouveaux, 1940); emphasis added. "This task of recovery is not reserved solely for our great leader; we are all called to it, and I repeat, with emphasis, especially *all women!* For to rebuild the country, we must above all rebuild the family; that is essentially our work" (8).

46 Vice Admiral de Penfentenyo, *Manuel du père de famille* (Paris: Flammarion, 1941), with a preface letter from Marshal Pétain, who wanted it to be "distributed as widely as possible," 34–35, 38, 113; emphasis added.

47 Arnold, *Le Corps et l'Ame: La vie des religieuses au XIXe siècle,* 85–88.

48 E. Biancani and H. Biancani, *La Communauté familiale* (Paris: Plon, "Présence," 1942), 20, 27.

49 Ibid., 179.

50 *Équipes et Cadres de la France nouvelle,* mouvement de formation de cadres spirituels, civiques et nationaux, Vichy, 2 rue de l'Église, BDIC, Tract 5-A-1, "Appui mutuel des époux," and Tract 25-A-7, "Rôle civique de la femme et de la jeune fille"; emphasis added. This association, formed in February 1941 and approved in October 1942, was typical of the propaganda groups that served the regime. Founded by former DRAC, members of the Ligue des Droits du religieux ancien combattant, created in 1924 to resist the secular politics of the Cartel, its aim was to train "cadres" (leaders) in all milieux by providing them "work plans" concerning the "data essential for reconstructing the country," in order to disseminate "healthy ideas from a civic standpoint." For the foundation and the activity of the DRAC movement, which counted thirty-five thousand members in 1930, see Antoine Prost, *Les Anciens Combattants et la Société française, 1914–1939* (Paris: Presses de la FNSP, 1977), 1: 98, 3: 155; available in English as *In the Wake of War: Les anciens combattants and French Society,* trans. Helen McPhail (Providence, RI: Berg, 1992), 41, 101.

51 I am borrowing this expression from the title of an article in *La Femme dans*

la vie sociale ("Figures de non mariées" 144 [January 1942]) that, in its pleas for "old maids," constitutes a striking formulation of this vision of the world in which childless women were pariahs: "Those women who never married because the country or the very ideal of marriage required this renunciation, far from being pushed to the margins of the family movement, provide it an example of this spirit of sacrifice, without which there is no solid, fecund family. It is entirely possible, moreover, that their unused desire for maternity inclines them to be temporary replacement mothers and for families, these outside helpers we will speak of in other articles."

52 "Les moyens d'action," in *La Famille dans l'État, Les Documents français,* 9.

53 Renaudin, "La famille réalité sociale," in *La Famille dans l'État,* 5.

54 Marcel Peyrouton, minister of the interior from 1940 to April 1942, quoted in French in Paxton, *Vichy France,* 196. *La Mairie rurale* (1 November 1941) printed a handwritten letter from Dr. Serge Huard, secretary of state for family and health: "The commune is the initial assembly of family cells; it is the *little nation* that, in all hearts, is associated with the big nation. Thus, its principal magistrate, the Mayor, appears in the family State like a sort of *Patriarch* who knows, advises, guides and protects" (emphasis added).

55 In the Stéphanoise region, the municipal councils, the majority of whose members were members also of the Popular Front, were suspended as soon as the French State was established. The reform of municipal councils that began in January 1941 appeared to be the revenge of the vanquished of 1936. See Monique Luirard, *La Région stéphanoise dans la guerre et dans la paix (1936–1951)* (Paris: Centre d'études foréziennes, Centre interdisciplinaire d'études et de recherches sur les structures régionales, 1980), 307–15. In the Paris region, numerous communist and socialist councilors were replaced. A mother of eight children, president of the Union des patronages, succeeded Henri de Kerillis in Neuilly. Henri Sellier was replaced by an engineer who was the father of ten; see Cointet, *Le Conseil national de Vichy,* 256.

56 "L'UFCS et les conseillères municipales," *La Femme dans la vie sociale* 141 (September–October 1941).

57 *Ecole et liberté,* Free Zone, 6 (September–October–November 1940) and 7 (July–August 1941).

58 "Ce qu'apporteront les femmes au conseil municipal," *La Femme dans la vie sociale* 139 (June 1941); "L'UFCS et les conseillères muncipales"; emphasis added.

59 Barthélemy, *Le Vote des femmes,* 605–8, 594.

60 See "L'installation des conseillères de Louviers" and "Les conseillères municipales nommées par les municipalités," *La Française,* 20 February 1937 and 28 February 1937.

61 "Organization des Dames SMS," and "Recrutement des Dames SMS," *La Légion* (15 November 1942) and (1 December 1942).

62 Charles Trochu [chairman of the municipal council of Paris], preface to *La Commune rempart de la famille* [brochure] (Paris: Commissariat général à la famille, office de publicité générale, 1962); BDIC, Réserve, 126–27.

63 Ibid., 6.

64 Emmanuel Gounot, attorney in Lyon, professor at the free faculty of law, and chairman of the Ligue des familles nombreuses of Lyon and of the Rhône, prepared the initial draft of this law in the commission responsible for studying the status of family associations.

65 Georges Hourdin, "La loi Gounot et ses caractéristiques," *L'Actualité sociale* 179 (March–April 1943).

66 Quoted in Henri David, "Vers une organisation de la famille française," *La Légion* 19 (15 November 1941).

67 G.-M. Bonvoisin, "Bâtir sur la famille," *L'Actualité sociale* 178 (February 1943).

68 William Garcin, *Révolution sociale par la famille,* Fédération française des associations de familles (Vichy: Éd. du Secrétariat général à l'information, n.d.), 36.

69 Guibal, *La Famille dans la Révolution nationale,* 25.

70 P.-A. Chevrier, "Les Associations de familles, leur rôle et leur mission," *L'Actualité sociale* 181 (June 1943).

71 Cooperative bulletin from the Commissariat General for the Family to the regional delegates 9 (15 March 1943) that bears the note "Strictly personal and confidential, copy number two" (Archives nationales, 2 AG 497).

72 "L'application de la loi Gounot: Une conférence sur la mise en oeuvre de la loi Gounot," *L'Actualité sociale* 188 (February 1944).

73 Chevrier, "Les Associations de familles, leur rôle et leur mission."

74 The order of April 12, 1945, amended the law regarding divorce of April 2, 1941, by eliminating the three-year period during which divorce was forbidden following marriage. The natalist concern would, on the other hand, inspire the regime's improvement of the Medal of the French Family in 1947 and the re-creation of Mother's Day in 1950.

75 Lenoir, "Transformations du familialisme et reconversions morales"; Michel Chauvière, "Du code de la famille à la Libération," *Cahiers du GRMF* 1 (August 1983), and "L'action familiale ouvrière et la politique de Vichy," *Cahiers du GRMF* 3 (1985), which contains extremely interesting debates among the players of the Popular Family Movement during the war.

76 Antoine Prost, "L'évolution de la politique familiale en France de 1938 à 1981," *Le Mouvement social* 129 (October–December 1984).

77 "L'action familiale ouvrière de la politique de Vichy," *Cahiers du GRMF* 3 (1985): 95.

78 Paul Leclercq, delegate general of the National Coordination and Action Center for Family Movements (Occupied Zone), "L'intégration de la famille dans la constitution du nouvel État Français," typed report, 8 Au-

gust 1941, Archives nationales, 2 AG 497. The report of the proceedings of the National Coordination Center specifies that the Center, after having examined the Leclercq report, proposed it to the commission of the National Council responsible for developing the new constitution (Archives nationales, 2 AG 497).

79 "Pour que la famille ait dans la constitution la place qui lui revient," National Coordination and Action Center for Family Movements for the Occupied Zone, Archives nationales, 2 AG 605.

80 Documents sent by William Garcin to Commander Sautriau on 28 July 1941, Archives nationales, 2 AG 605.

81 Garcin, "La famille, unité politique," in *Révolution sociale par la famille,* 35; emphasis added.

82 Circular from the Ministry of Justice dated 25 March 1942; Paxton, *Vichy France,* 167. This measure is clearly in the image of the massive adherence of magistrates to the regime as this was reconstructed in the works presented at a conference organized by the École nationale de la magistrature, held in Bordeaux on December 1, 1993; see "Les juges sous Vichy," *Le Monde* (31 December 1993).

83 Michèle Cointet-Labrousse points out that only the legitimate family offered this model of apprenticeship; see "Le gouvernement de Vichy et les familles."

84 Haury, *L'Université devant la famille.*

85 Quoted in *École et Liberté* (April 1943); the review by APEL was pleased that at the school for militia cadres, instruction followed the principle that "the political system must be based on the family."

86 Gustave Thibon, "Considérations actuelles," *La Revue universelle* (10 October 1941).

87 See Françoise Blum, "Question sociale, question des femmes?," in *Le Social aux prises avec l'histoire,* "Cahiers de la recherche sur le travail social," vol. 3, *La Question sociale* (May–June 1991).

88 Thus the "family homes" (modeled after Lauzun's institution) that were organized in 1941 into the National Union of Rural Homes of France to "give peasant families the means of ensuring the integral training of their daughters and their sons" (Secrétariat général à la jeunesse, *Bulletin de presse* 41 [19 December 1941]).

89 Weyd, "La femme à la campagne"; emphasis added.

90 On the middle-class perception of "the respectable poor," and of the working-class crowds of the Popular Front, see Bloch, *Strange Defeat,* 164–69.

91 1 Cor. 14; quoted in Delumeau, *La Peur en Occident,* 405.

92 On this point, see Mosse, "What Kind of Woman," chap. 5 in *Nationalism and Sexuality,* especially 110–12.

93 Handwritten letter dated 7 February 1941, Archives nationales, 2 AG 605.

1 The French Information Office, the new name of the Havas Agency transformed into a state agency and into an instrument of propaganda, justified
its unconditional submission to the new regime in a letter to its department
heads only, by referring to the examples of Spain, Italy, and Germany:
"It is self-evident that at a time when circumstances command that everything be done to help with the national recovery, the directors of the Havas
Agency could only support the government of Marshal Pétain in its efforts
for the disciplined renewal of French thought." See Jacques Polonski, *La
Presse, la Propagande et l'Opinion publique sous l'Occupation* (Paris: Ed. du CDJC,
1946), 57–58.

2 Taine, *Essais de critique et d'histoire;* quoted in Sternhell, *Maurice Barrès et le
nationalisme français,* 294.

3 Anne-Marie Sohn, *"La Garçonne* face à l'opinion publique: Type littéraire
ou type social des années 20," *Le Mouvement social* 80 (1972). According to
the author, 12 percent to 25 percent of the adult population read this book.

4 In the many novels that followed, more peacefully, in the vein of *La Garçonne,* there are numerous typists, doctors, lawyers, and "businesswomen,"
and education figures prominently: for example, *Quand je serai bachelière,
Les Deux Étudiantes* (ibid.)

5 Paul Bourget, preface to *Psychologie du féminisme* by Léontine Zanta (Paris:
Plon-Nourrit, 1922), x; emphasis added.

6 I am referring here to John E. Talbott, *The Politics of Educational Reforms in
France, 1918–1940* (Princeton: Princeton University Press, 1969).

7 A lawyer in Orléans, Jean Zay aroused the mistrust of the university institution. In 1939, he volunteered as an officer in the Reserves. He was one
of the group of deputies that attempted to reach North Africa aboard the
Massilia in June 1940. While imprisoned by the Vichy government for desertion, he wrote his memoirs, *Souvenirs et Solitude,* published in 1946. During
his transfer to another prison, he was assassinated by the militia in June
1944. Zay, one of the major figures held responsible for the defeat, because
the school served as a scapegoat beginning in the 1940s, was also a favor-
ite target of anti-Semites. In 1942, Philippe Henriot, the radio voice of the
collaboration, wrote a pamphlet, *Les Carnet secrets de Jean Zay,* and Céline
had adopted the habit of writing "je vous Zay" for "je vous hais" (I hate
you). See Talbott, *The Politics of Educational Reforms in France,* 210; Paxton,
Vichy France, 153; Marrus and Paxton, *Vichy and the Jews,* 38n.

8 See Prost, *L'Enseignement en France, 1800–1967.*

9 *Le Temps* (14 November 1929). In its issue the day after, the newspaper congratulated these women for their strong line; quoted in Talbott, *The Politics
of Educational Reforms in France,* 156.

10 *École et Liberté* (April 1938).

11 Talbott, *The Politics of Educational Reforms in France,* 62, 144, 223.

12 Ibid., 178–204, 218–44.

13 Duquesne, *Les Catholiques français sous l'occupation*, 89–90.

14 On this topic, see François Bonvin, "Une seconde famille, un collège d'enseignement privé," *Actes de la recherche en sciences sociales* 30 (1979).

15 See Rémy Handourtzel, "La politique scolaire, les instituteurs (1940–1944)," *Les Cahiers de l'animation, INEP* 49–50 (1985).

16 Cited in Paxton, *Vichy France*, 153. It is also possible that this massive and brutal condemnation of primary education and of the educational system of the prewar period and the particular condemnation of Jean Zay contributed to making the anti-Semitic purge of education a commonplace. For a description of this purge and its bureaucratic triteness, see Claude Singer, *Vichy, l'Université et les juifs: Les silences et la mémoire* (Paris: Les Belles-Lettres, 1992).

17 The annexation of this historian, who died in 1889, by the Action française took place in 1905, the seventy-fifth anniversary of his birth. Although he had been neither a monarchist nor a practicing Catholic, the new royalists elected him as a precursor of their nationalist anti-Germanic vision with the permission of his widow. A committee was formed that excluded all academics with the slightest link to the pro-Dreyfus party. A scandal erupted that led to several resignations, but the annexation was finally completed, and Fustel de Coulanges would appear prominently in the Vichy pantheon (Weber, *Action française*, 36–37).

18 Henri Boegner, "Une expérience d'un quart de siècle," *Cahiers du Cercle Fustel-de-Coulanges*, n.s., 1st year, 1 (December 1953).

19 Ibid.; Weber, *Action française*, 264.

20 In 1936, Serge Jeanneret was secretary general of the Union corporative des instituteurs, a right-wing professional organization that fought the Syndicat National des Instituteurs (SNI). In 1941, he published *La Vérité sur les instituteurs*, in which he castigated primary education and called for its purification. He ended up joining Doriot.

21 Long, *The French Right and Education*, 34; Henri Boegner, "Le Cercle de Fustel de 1939 à 1952," *Cahiers du Cercle Fustel-de-Coulanges*, n.s., 3–4 (December 1955).

22 Agathon, *Les Jeunes Gens d'aujourd'hui: Le goût de l'action, la foi patriotique, une renaissance catholique* (Paris: Plon, 1913).

23 Ibid., 59.

24 Ibid., 60–64. In 1914, a lycée teacher, Amélie Gayraud, published *Les Jeunes Filles d'aujourd'hui*, a survey of elite female lycée students. Catholicism was less militant than among the young people surveyed by Agathon, and they rejected the "lamentable" fate of "young marriageable girls," because having a profession allowed them to "choose the man of our dreams calmly," while agreeing "to give priority to the work necessary to the family: husband and children first! But almost all wished for a possible reconciliation" (quoted in Crubelier, *Histoire culturelle de la France*, 289–90).

The least that can be said is that the survey of young girls would not have the posterity of Agathon's survey, because its interest did not appear to be political, and it took all of Maurice Crubelier's curiosity for its existence to be made known to us.

25 On this point and on the symbolic and practical gulf between primary and secondary education as constructed in the political debates between Republicans and conservatives concerning the educational obligation during the years 1880–1914, see Muel-Dreyfus, *Le Métier d'éducateur*, 17–89.

26 Quoted in French in Weber, *Action française*, 264–65.

27 "Intelligence et démocratie," *Cahiers du Cercle Fustel-de-Coulanges* 2 (December 1928).

28 P. Dufrenne [a primary inspector of peasant origins who converted to Catholicism, and one of the founders of the Cercle], "L'école unique," *Cahiers du Cercle Fustel-de-Coulanges*, 5 (May 1929).

29 A. Debailleul, "La formation de l'élite," *Cahiers du Cercle Fustel-de-Coulanges*, 6 (July 1929).

30 Boegner, "Le cercle Fustel de 1939 à 1952." On the positions of Pétain and Weygand concerning education in 1935, see Long, *The French Right and Education*, 57–59.

31 Quoted in Griffiths, *Marshal Pétain*, 162.

32 Lyautey had anonymously published an article in the *Revue des deux mondes* in March 1891 that became one of the bibles of right-wing thought concerning the school, "Le rôle social de l'officier dans le service militaire universel," in which he expanded the supervisory functions of the army to all training of young people and described a new type of leader.

33 Paxton, "The Officers Turned Schoolmasters," chap. 6 in *Parades and Politics at Vichy*.

34 General Weygand, *Comment élever nos fils?* (Paris: Flammarion, 1937), 40, 42; emphasis added.

35 Long, *The French Right and Education*, 36.

36 Boegner, "Le cercle Fustel de 1939 à 1952," 165, 167.

37 Handourtzel, "La politique scolaire et les instituteurs." It is not my intention here to go into the details of Vichy educational policy, but simply to identify its pertinent elements for the development of my thesis concerning the political functions of the reproduction of the "eternal feminine" in the field of education. The most complete work on the subject is the thesis of Long, *The French Right and Education*, whose publication in French would be invaluable.

38 Pétain, *La France nouvelle, principes de la communauté*, 45–54; emphasis added.

39 "Le mot d'ordre du maréchal Pétain: Rassemblement national, entretien avec Jean Martet," *Le Journal* (30 April 1936), quoted in Griffiths, *Marshal Pétain*, 184.

40 On the disciplinary measures taken beginning in 1940, see *Les Documents français, La Réforme de l'enseignement* (January 1941).

41 The expression is Pierre Pucheu's, quoted in Paxton, *Vichy France,* 157.

42 The comments of the minister clearly reveal these stakes: free education is for him a "fatal myth," fruit of a "demagogic legislation," the return to the fee-paying secondary system allowing that "the lessons of the teacher, instead of being lost in the anarchy of overpopulated classes, recover their effectiveness in the healthy atmosphere of a normally balanced educational setting" (Jérôme Carcopino, radio speech, 3 September 1941; reprinted in *Le Temps* [5 September 1941]). The scholarships were awarded to students who earned an average of 12/20; students who did not receive scholarships could enter the second cycle with an average of 10/20.

43 "La réforme de l'enseignement, historique," *Le Temps* (11 September 1941); emphasis added.

44 Ibid.

45 Gustave Thibon, "Christianisme et démocratie," *La Revue universelle* (10 July 1941); emphasis in original.

46 René Benjamin, *Vérités et Rêveries sur l'éducation* (Paris: Plon, 1941), 185–87; emphasis in original.

47 Ibid., 188. For once, René Benjamin is not in agreement with Marshal Pétain, who, while inaugurating new university buildings in Montpellier in 1941, was offered a bouquet of flowers by a female student. "What are you studying, miss?" her asked her. "Chemistry, M. Pétain." "Ah, very good! That comes the closest to cooking!" (personal memory reported in Kniebiehler and Fouquet, *Histoire des mères,* 325).

48 Évelyne Sullerot, "La condition féminine dans la France de Vichy," in *Les Années 40,* Taillandier/Hachette, 34 (16 May 1979): 945.

49 F. Brunetière, "Éducation et instruction," *Revue des deux mondes* (15 February 1895); emphasis added.

50 He reports that in Loches, where the police combed the streets on the occasion of his arrival, the young men of the Action française threw out the unionized schoolmasters: "They advanced five men for every lay teacher. The crowd was silent and watched. Each lay teacher was grabbed, raised from his seat, turned over, held with his feet in the air, and taken out in this position, in silence, without a single other gesture, amidst admiration. There was such quickness, such assurance, such dignity! Only the undertaker can remove bodies with this noble mastery." But things did not always happen with as much "dignity." In Épinal, workers and schoolmasters mobilized against his arrival, booed him in the street, and struck the windows of his car. In the Chamber, his articles in *L'Avenir* on the convention of schoolmasters of Strasbourg provoked a debate. See René Benjamin, *Aliborons et Démagogues* (Paris: Arthème Fayard, 1927), 182, 168, 154.

51 Ibid., 84.

52 Bonnard, *Éloge de l'ignorance,* 9–15, 40–42; emphasis added.

53 Abel Bonnard, *Pensées dans l'action* (1941); quoted in J. Mièvre, "L'évolution

politique d'Abel Bonnard (Jusqu'au printemps 1942)," *Revue d'histoire de la Deuxième Guerre mondiale* 108 (October 1977).

54 Ministerial circular published in *Information universitaire* (16 May 1942); quoted in Long, *The French Right and Education,* 249. Coming from an unmarried man whose homosexual relations were scandalous, the circular probably left teachers puzzled.

55 Bonnard, *Éloge de l'ignorance,* 44.

56 Quoted in E. Maillard, "La réforme de l'enseignement," *Revue d'histoire de la Deuxième Guerre mondiale,* special issue, *Vichy et la jeunesse* 56 (1964): 47.

57 Quoted in Griffiths, *Marshal Pétain,* 251.

58 André Rousseaux, "Le ministère de la rééducation nationale," *Le Temps* (29 June 1940).

59 Léontine Zanta, "La femme française d'ajourd'hui," *Voix françaises* (12 September 1941).

60 *Journal officiel* (2 September 1941): 3698–710.

61 Law of August 15, 1941, related to the general organization of public education, *La Réforme de l'enseignement, Les Documents français,* September 1941.

62 *Le Temps* (4 September 1941). I have found no trace of this measure in the *Journal officiel;* It is likely that *Le Temps* is here mistaking desire for reality, which in no way lessens the impact of its formulation. The abolition of "scientific equality," which until then obligated students in terminal classes to take the same number of hours of mathematics, regardless of the section, apparently involved both sexes. Carcopino saw in scientific equality a "pedagogical overloading" and especially "an unacceptable privilege conferred on the sciences" to the detriment of Latin-Greek (Carcopino, *Souvenirs de sept ans,* 419).

63 *Journal officiel* (2 September 1941), 3710–716.

64 Circular of 12 September 1941; quoted in Long, *The French Right and Education,* 224.

65 The fact that in Paris in 1942 a much larger percentage of girls than boys earned the diploma of preparatory primary studies (DEPP), the precursor of the sixth-level entrance exam established by Carcopino, was a sign of the strength of the female presence in the secondary system that probably caused the lawmaker of times of crisis to draw back (Halls, *The Youth of Vichy France,* 28).

66 Carcopino, *Souvenirs de sept ans,* 420; emphasis added. Earlier, in August 1940, Carcopino wrote that the first measure he would take as new director of the École normale supérieure of the rue d'Ulm — "to put the house I knew there back in order" — was to exclude women, who had been pursuing their education there since the interwar period, and send them to Sèvres (179).

67 The surveys of *Le Temps,* "Le bachelier au seuil des carrières. xv: Pour les jeunes filles," *Le Temps* (12 September 1941).

68 Ernest Charles, "Ces bachelières . . . ," *Le Temps* (20 October 1940).

69 See Duquesne, "Problème scolaire and politique religieuse," chap. 4 in *Les Catholiques français sous l'occupation.*

70 "To fathers, to mothers, falls the great duty of seeking a vocation for their sons and daughters. Under the proconsulate of M. Jean Zay, of Masonic memory, we saw attempts at professional orientation monopolized and controlled by the State. We denounced them at the time. It was the era when one claimed to make all public primary school teachers great dictators of orientation" (Henri David, "L'orientation professionelle et la famille," *École et Liberté* [organ of family educational duties published under the direction of the APEL] [May 1943]).

71 *École et Liberté* (June–July–August 1940); emphasis added. In the editorial "L'éclatante leçon des faits," the newspaper claims "the immense advantage" of "knowing what we want and of being able to propose to the country a program to be applied without a single hour's delay if it does not want to perish." Its support for the political agendas of the regime would not falter, and in March 1943, on behalf of the struggle against Bolshevism, an article justified the STO in the following manner: "The work of French men in Germany is not a consequence of the defeat. It is France's collaboration for the edification of the new Europe and the defense of civilization."

72 *École et Liberté* (September–October–November 1940).

73 "Le point de vue des APEL sur une réforme de l'enseignement, note présentée à Monsieur le Secrétaire d'État à l'Instruction publique," *École et Liberté* (March 1941).

74 Associations des parents de l'enseignement libre [APEL], *L'Éducation des filles,* Limoges, 1941. Henri David, delegate for propaganda of the Union nationale des APEL, also contributed regularly to *La Légion* on all subjects concerning the family. In 1928, as a professor at the Catholic faculty of Lille, he was senior editor of *La Voix des familles,* an organ of the powerful Fédération des unions des familles nombreuses du nord de la France. In 1931, he was responsible for launching the review *École et Liberté,* published *La Liberté d'éducation dans la famille* in 1932, and stated in 1934 that he was in favor of the family vote (Talmy, *Histoire du mouvement familial en France,* vol. 2).

75 As early as October 1940, the APELs had sent a note to the Ministry concerning the reform of female educational programs in which they announced their survey and saw that the "time had come" and the "necessity of moving very quickly": "We are on the site. Let's build" ("Culture féminine: L'éducation des filles," *École et Liberté* [January 1941]). The impact of this militant volunteerism was no doubt significant at the Ministry of National Education, which needed to rally all good will to the new regime.

76 APEL, *L'Éducation des filles,* 9; emphasis in original.

77 Ibid., 17. The phrase could have appeared on the poster for the film *Le Voile*

bleu by Jean Stelli, released in 1942, which was a great commercial success in French cinema under the Occupation; See Jacques Siclier, *La France de Pétain et son cinéma* (Paris: Henri Veyrier, 1981), 99–103. Gaby Morlay plays the governess of middle-class families whose husbands were killed at the Front in 1914. Devoting her life to the education of other people's children, she makes this substitute maternity a ministry and, during a reunion that evokes Mother's Day, all "her children," now adults, provide their support during her old age. Although the evocation of a feminine situation of solitude, linked to the two wars, won this film, in which many women recognized their destiny, a very wide audience, its success was also a result of the exaltation of this feminine form of sublimation that was encouraged by the regime.

78 Henri David, "Esquisse d'une pédagogie féminine," *Cité nouvelle* (25 September 1941).

79 Georges Bertier, who had been president of the Fédération des associations d'éclaireurs de France from 1920 to 1936, supported Vichy's educational project and was an educational advisor of the Alexis Carrel Foundation. His son-in-law and colleague at the Les Roches School, Louis Garrone, was one of the prime movers of the youth policy in the southern zone as director of youth training to the secretary general for youth; see Bernard Comte, *Une utopie combattante: L'école des cadres d'Uriage, 1940–42* (Paris: Fayard, 1991),158, 336.

80 "Objectifs," *Éducation* 1 (January 1935).

81 "La femme française n'est pas exclue du nouvel ordre national," *Éducation* (December 1940).

82 "Les perspectives nouvelles de l'orientation professionnelle," *Éducation* (February 1941).

83 "L'enseignement ménager va devenir obligatoire," *La Revue de la famille* 227 (April 1942).

84 "La loi sur l'enseignement ménager," *La Femme dans la vie sociale* 150 (July 1942).

85 *École et Liberté* (June 1943).

86 "Réunion de complément de formation des cadres des Écoles féminines de cadres," Secrétariat général à la jeunesse, *Cahier d'information* 3 (January 1942).

87 Stanislas de Lestapis, "Réhabilitation de l'éducation familiale et ménagère," *Cité nouvelle* (10 May 1941).

88 *Une belle mission des travailleuses sociales,* brochure published by the Commissariat General for the Family, Office de publicité général, BDIC, 126–27.

89 Hyacinthe Dubreuil, *A l'image de la mère, essai sur la mission de l'assistante sociale* (Paris: Édition sociale française, 1941); emphasis added. The author wrote works against the industrial revolution that killed the family and in 1936 was part of the Study Center for Human Problems, one of the founding ancestors of the Carrel Foundation.

90   Marcel Mauss, "Les techniques du corps," in *Sociologie et Anthropologie* (Paris: PUF, 1960), 369.

91   *Une belle mission des travailleuses sociales.*

92   *Les Chantiers de la jeunesse, premières expériences, perspectives d'avenir,* Châtelguyon, 14 March 1941, Roneo; BDIC, reserve, dossier Z2, Youth, Family.

93   They were also proportionally less numerous: one national leadership school for women (Écully) and two for men (Uriage and La Chapelle-en-Serval); two regional schools for women (and two projected) compared to ten for men (Halls, *The Youth of Vichy France,* 308).

94   Quoted in Coutrot, "La politique familiale."

95   "Note sur la politique familiale," typed, Archives nationales, 2 AG 605.

96   Gabriel Robinot Marcy, "Les centres de jeunes travailleuses, pour préparer la femme de demain," *Cité nouvelle* (25 October 1941). I myself searched without success for information on the Écully school in the departmental archives. Its trace has literally vanished.

97   Anne-Marie Hussenot, "La mission de la femme française,"*Jeunesse . . . France!* (8 May 1941).

98   "Expériences éducatives, comment s'y prend une mère de dix enfants," *Éducation* (March 1941).

99   Lina Fontègue, *Le Rôle de la femme devant les devoirs présents,* lecture given at the University Center of Caen, 23 November 1941 (Caen: Imp. Ozanne, n.d.).

100   *École et Liberté* (November–December 1942).

101   Paul Crouzet, *La Vraie Révolution nationale dans l'instruction publique,* "Cahiers violets," number 1 (Toulouse: Privat-Didier, 1941). Inspector General Crouzet was the editor of this collection "for spiritual renewal."

102   Benjamin, *Aliborons et Démagogues,* 265.

103   Henri Boegner, "Le patriotisme dans l'enseignement de la philosophie," and Paul Dufrenne, "L'école unique," *Cahiers du Cercle Fustel-de-Coulanges* 1–2 (October 1929) and (4 March 1930).

104   Albert Rivaud, "L'enseignement de la philosophie," *Revue des deux mondes* (1 November 1943). Rivaud, a philosopher and Germanist, a professor at the Sorbonne, at the École des science politiques, and at the École supérieure de guerre, and member of the Académie des sciences morales et politiques, was minister of national education for three weeks in June–July 1940.

105   Vérine, "La famille," 195.

106   The correspondence concerning this project is kept in the Archives nationales, 2 AG 497, "Family"; emphasis added.

107   Bourdieu, *La Distinction,* 469.

108   Marc Bloch, "Un philosophe de bonne compagnie," text published in January 1944 in *Les Cahiers politiques,* reprinted in *L'Étrange Défaite,* 240–65. This text does not appear in the English edition.

109   Pétain, message of 11 October 1940, in *La France nouvelle, principes de la communauté,* 78.

110 Thibon, "Christianisme et démocratie"; emphasis in original.

111 Gillet, *Réveil de l'âme française,* 45.

112 Jérôme Carcopino, presentation of grounds for the law of August 15, 1941, *Éducation* (December 1941).

113 Thibon, *Diagnostics, essais de physiologie sociale,* 98, 23, 109.

114 On the culture of notables, see the French edition of Bloch's *L'Étrange Défaite,* 196–97, and Durand, "Les notables," in *Le Régime de Vichy et les Français,* 371–85.

115 Haury, *L'Université devant la famille;* emphasis added.

116 "Health is a necessary condition, but not sufficient for *virility.* And there, however, is the master quality of a strong people, the quality par excellence that the Chantiers can give to young Frenchmen. . . . The Chantiers do even more to help everyone surpass himself; they are not content to work to make complete men: they spread among them—among the best—the emulation to become Leaders; they produce from the mass '*true elites,*' sole guarantors of a true *moral resurrection*" (*Les Chantiers de la jeunesse,* Châtel-guyon, 14 March 1941; emphasis in original).

117 Loubet del Bayle, *Les Non-Conformistes des années 30,* 298–301.

118 Republished in a book in 1935 with a preface by General Weygand, Lyautey's article on "Le rôle social de l'officier" was reread in light of the events of 1936 as a manual of social peace. Georges Lamirand, an engineer and militant Catholic of the Équipes sociales, was inspired by this article to define the nature of the "good" commander of engineers in enterprises in *Le Rôle social de l'ingénieur,* published in 1932 with a preface by Lyautey himself. On the triumph of the notion of cadres and the celebration of the engineer under Vichy, a "competent and disciplined leader," "officer of the labor army," who must "gaze into the depths of the eyes of his men" "to give the impression of physical superiority" and to express his virile qualities right down to his clothes, according to Lamirand's expressions, see Luc Boltanski, *The Making of a Class: Cadres in French Society,* trans. Arthur Goldhammer (Cambridge, England: Cambridge University Press, 1987), 79.

119 Georges Bertier, "Une mystique pour les jeunes Français," *Éducation* (March–June 1942).

120 See Nye, "Sport, Regeneration and National Revival," chap. 9 in *Crime, Madness and Politics in Modern France, the Medical Concept of National Decline,* 310–29. Pierre de Coubertin, whose tireless efforts to restore the Olympic Games ended successfully in 1896, wrote in his *Essais de psychologie sportive* in 1913: "Very often, psychoneuroses are characterized by a sort of disappearance of virile sensitivity, and only sports can restore and affirm it. It is the art of virilizing bodies and souls."

121 "Les disciplines nouvelles: La tenue," *Le Bulletin de France* 35 (15 May 1941).

122 J. Jaouen, "Une jeunesse plus virile," in G. Bertier et al., *Les Devoirs présents des éducateurs,* 35.

123 Comte, *Une utopie combattante: L'École des cadres d'Uriage, 1940–1942,* 50, 54–55.

124 P. Dunoyer de Segonzac, "Intellectuels," *Jeunesse . . . France!* (8 March 1941).

125 Jean-Jacques Chevallier [professor of public law at the University of Grenoble and director of general education for the Commissariat for General Education and Sports], introduction to *L'Ordre viril et l'Efficacité dans l'action,* "Le Chef et ses jeunes," 7, École nationale des cadres d'Uriage, BDIC.

126 Ibid., 8–9, 20, 37, 39; emphasis in original.

8. CONTROL OF BODIES

1 I wish to thank Claire Givry, who helped me compile the voluminous documentation concerning the medical field and the familialist movement, and who shared with me certain difficult moments of the lengthy collection process for the material required by this research.

2 Anonymous typed letter, n.d.; Archives nationales, 2 AG 605, "Family" file.

3 Archives nationales, 2 AG 78, Dr. Ménétrel, files on various medical issues; capitalization in original.

4 Henri Michel, *Vichy année 40* (Paris: Robert Laffont, 1966), 116.

5 R. Descouens, *La Vie du Maréchal Pétain racontée aux enfants de France* (Nice: Éd. de la Vraie France, 1941); quoted in Azéma, *De Munich à la Libération,* 104. In a German newspaper of 1935, a photo of Hitler, paternal and smiling, bent toward a little blond girl whose two hands he holds, illustrates an article entitled "Adolf Hitler, Doctor of the German People"; reproduced in Robert Proctor, *Racial Hygiene: Medicine under the Nazis* (Cambridge, MA: Harvard University Press, 1988), 50.

6 Thibon, "Réalisme civique," chap. 2 of *Retour au réel,* 51.

7 Ibid., 7, 53; emphasis added.

8 "La politique sociale de l'avenir," *Revue des deux mondes* (15 August 1940); quoted in "Vichy et la crise de la conscience française," in Azéma and Bédarida, *Le Régime de Vichy et les Français,* 82. Bédarida stresses how much the Vichy conception of national identity included exclusion.

9 See Nye, *Crime, Madness and Politics in Modern France,* 132–70, 330–39.

10 Concerning the relationship between sanitary prophylaxis and social prophylaxis at the turn of the century, see the articles collected in "L'haleine des faubourgs," *Recherches* 29 (December 1977).

11 Zeev Sternhell, "Déterminisme, racisme et nationalisme," chap. 3 of *La Droite révolutionnaire, les origines françaises du fascisme, 1885–1914* (Paris: Seuil, "Points Histoire," 1978), 146–76.

12 Postal, introduction to *France 41,* 14, 22.

13 In March 1943, the meeting of the Standing Commission on Medical Studies of the Legion was entirely devoted to the undernourishment of adults and children, to the syndrome of this deficiency, and to relations with medical-social centers (Commissariat légionnaire à l'action sociale, Service hygiène et santé; BDIC, Q document 4258).

14 "Pourquoi ce journal?," *Le "Médecin français"* 1 (March 1941). This was a clan-

destine publication of the medical committee of the National Front beginning in 1943 that ensured "the link between the various medical centers,
civil organizations, or maquis" that would result in the creation of the Comité de Résistance médicale. See Robert Debré, "La Résistance médicale,"
in *La Résistance intellectuelle,* texts and testimonies collected and presented
by Jacques Debû-Bridel (Paris: Julliard, 1970).

15 Paul Milliez, *Médecin de la liberté,* interviews with Igor Barrère (Paris: Seuil,
1980).

16 Thibon, *Diagnostics, essai de physiologie sociale,* 134.

17 Dr. Huard, a surgeon and former intern of the Laennec Hospital and
former international rugby star, was presented this way by a journalist of
Candide (20 August 1941), who also disclosed the qualities of the trusted
physician, including, of course, that of being father of a large family:
"He has divided his life between sports, his family (he has 4 children), the
Boucicaut Hospital, where he used to operate in the morning. Appointed
General Secretary of Health a year ago, he attacked all those who, under
the cover of the title of physician, indulged in deplorable abuses."

18 Serge Huard, preface to *L'Éducation et la Santé,* by P. Delore (Paris: Flammarion, 1941), 9.

19 P. Delore, *Tendances de la médecine contemporaine, la médecine à la croisée des chemins*
(Paris: Masson, 1936), xiii, 207, 214.

20 Professor Leriche, a surgeon who practiced in Lyon and Strasbourg, a
professor at the Collège de France who wrote that he only half-heartedly
agreed to become president of the Association, totally supported the
policy of the secretary of state for health; his ignorance of medical trade
union circles of the prewar period and his tag-along attitude earned him
criticism from a large portion of the medical profession that favored the
creation of the Association. "We do not know the issues to be discussed or
the men with whom we discuss them," he stated in his memoires: *Souvenir
de ma vie morte* (Paris: Seuil, 1956), 94.

21 René Leriche, "Médecine 41, tendances et devoirs," in *France 41,* 344.

22 Jean Mignon, "Débats sur le corporatisme," *Le Concours médical* 49–50
(December 1942).

23 Émile Sergent, *La Formation intellectuelle et morale des élites* (Paris: Société
d'Éditions économiques et sociales, 1943), 10, 23, 90. The comparison of
the medical "chief" with the Marshal is also made by Professor Castaigne,
who states that all the professor's students (he himself had once been his
intern) have "fallen into the habit of calling him the Marshal of Medicine,
and this title, which now takes on a more considerable meaning, is truly
deserved" (Castaigne, "Les médecins de France," *Les Documents français* 4
[April 1941]).

24 Georges Lafitte, *Le Médecin, sa formation, son rôle dans la société moderne* (Paris:
Delmas, 1936), 794, 799.

25 Carrel, *Man, the Unknown,* 283–84.

26 Carrel, "La science de l'Homme," in *La France de l'esprit 1940–1943,* 112. Elsewhere, Carrel is less optimistic. He writes to his brother-in-law in June 1943: "After the Rockefeller Institute, it is intolerable and ridiculous to be at the head of a French administration. The stupidity and the impotence of our compatriots are truly infinite. Never, unless one lives with them, could one understand their lapse" (quoted in Drouard, *Une inconnue des sciences sociales, la fondation Alexis-Carrel 1941–1945,* 148). It is likely that Dr. Carrel, despite his great intelligence, did not understand that the National Revolution was far from representing the entire country and that the historical situation of the Occupation could disturb minds to some extent.

27 In 1928, the Confederation of French Medical Unions was created by combining the Union des syndicats médicaux de France and the Fédération nationale des syndicats médicaux. Founded in 1884 to resist—already—the "excessive requirements of the Mutuality and of the State," the Union would impose the principle of the physician's free choice in reaction to the laws concerning free medical assistance of 1893 and work accidents of 1898. In 1928, the Confederation claimed approximately twenty thousand physicians, that is, four-fifths of the physicians practicing in France. See Paul Cibrié, "Les communautés médicales," in *Médecine et Communauté* (Paris: Librairie Médicis, 1943), 22–44. Dr. Cibrié, secretary general of the Confederation in 1929, was vice president of the second Higher Council of the Doctors Association in 1942; then in 1945, he was again president of the Confederation, which was reestablished on this date after having been dissolved, like all unions, by Vichy.

28 Paul Cibrié, *L'Ordre des médecins,* preface by Moro Giafferri, Esq. (Paris: Laboratoire Midy, 1935).

29 Sergent, *La Formation intellectuelle et morale des élites,* 217–19.

30 See Christophe Charle, *La République des universitaires, 1870–1940* (Paris: Seuil, 1994), 315–16.

31 Cibrié, *L'Ordre des médecins,* 39.

32 A. Oudin [doctor of law], *L'Ordre des médecins* (Paris: Les Éditions de la nouvelle France, 1941), 28.

33 Jean Lanos, "Le malaise médical," *Le Médecin* (15 November 1926); emphasis in original.

34 Paul Delaunay, "La profession médicale en France," in *Histoire générale de la médecine,* ed. Prof. Laignel-Lavastine (Paris: Albin Michel, 1949), 3: 732. The fact that this text, written before the war, according to its references, can appear as is in a very official work of medicine on medicine published in 1949 clearly shows the force and banality of these explanatory systems for the crisis in influential medical circles.

35 Proctor, *Racial Hygiene: Medicine under the Nazis,* 65–70, 145–66.

36 Konrad Jarausch, *The Unfree Professions: German Laywers, Teachers and Engineers, 1900–1950* (Oxford: Oxford University Press, 1990).

37 Reproduced in Maurice Beauchamp, *Pour la Rénovation française: Bases*

(Famille, profession, région, nation) (Paris: G. Durassié et C_{ie}, 1941), 95; this work was crowned by the Académie française on July 10, 1941. The French Renovation, a movement founded by Beauchamp before the First World War under the patronage of Barrès, appeared to its promoter in 1940 as a premonition of the National Revolution.

38 Lafitte, *Le Médecin, sa formation, son rôle dans la société moderne,* 787.

39 Cibrié, "Les communautés médicales," 36.

40 Quoted in Ernest Desmarest, *L'Ordre des médecins* (Paris: Masson, 1941), 18.

41 Schor, *L'Opinion française et les Étrangers,* 608–10.

42 Oudin, *L'Ordre des médecins,* 62–63.

43 Ibid., 63–64.

44 Desmarest, *L'Ordre des médecins,* 18–21.

45 Marrus and Paxton, *Vichy France and the Jews,* 160. It is quite obvious that all these legislative measures authorized the most extreme reflexes of corporatist defense. Thus this example given by the medical resistance newspaper: "*L'Heure bretonne,* a German newspaper translated for Bretons, recently published an article of a colleague. This colleague, analyzing the distribution of physicians in Brittany, counts one for every 3,000 inhabitants. According to him, this is way too many. There is a plethora, it is necessary to act. Yes, but unfortunately in Brittany there are no Jewish or foreign doctors. Never mind that: our distinguished colleague proposes to withdraw the right to practice from all non-Breton doctors" ("De mieux en mieux: Pléthore," *Le "Médecin français"* 8 [September–October 1941]).

46 "Certain departmental boards fear that the prohibition orders issued against foreign doctors will have only a theoretical effect. In truth, it is their job to use the powers currently conferred upon them by the law, and they must not hesitate to indicate to the Administrative Authorities doctors who are not taking note of the notification of their prohibition. Several departmental boards have resolutely taken this path. We can cite by way of encouraging example the case of a foreigner who, continuing to practice medicine despite the interdiction against this, was recently sentenced by the Prefect to administrative internment in a camp of the region" ("Les médecins étrangers," *Bulletin de l'Ordre des médecins* 3 [August 1941]: 124).

47 Joseph Billig, *Le Commissariat général aux questions juives* (Paris: CDJC, 1960), 3: 28–34.

48 Speech given on January 25, 1942, during the meeting of departmental boards of the Occupied Zone in Paris and approved by the representatives of thirty departmental boards of the Doctors Association; this text was sent to Professor Leriche, the very controversial president of the Higher Council of the Association (Archives nationales, 2 AG 78).

49 André Braun, *L'Ordre des médecins* (Paris: Librairie du Recueil Sirey, 1941), 48.

50 Cibrié, *L'Ordre des médecins,* 16.

51 Cibrié, "Les communautés médicale," 38, 42.

52 Quoted in R. Grasset, *Au service de la médecine: Chronique de la Santé publique durant les saisons amères (1942–1944)* (Clermont-Ferrand: Imp. de Bussac, 1956), 15.

53 Report of the convention published in *Le Concours médical* 38 (September 1942).

54 "Speech given by Dr. Grasset at the time the powers of the Higher Council were conferred upon the National Board of the Association," *Bulletin de l'Ordre des médecins* 3 (1943).

55 Henri Hatzfeld, *Le Grand Tournant de la médecine libérale* (Paris: Les Éditions ouvrières, 1963), 46–48.

56 Archives nationales, 2 AG 78.

57 Hoffmann, "The Vichy Circle of French Conservatives."

58 Concerning the history of the nostalgic construction of the medical image of the family doctor and its metamorphoses during the 1970s, see Francine Muel-Dreyfus, "Le fantôme du médecin de famille," *Actes de la recherche en sciences sociales* 54 (1984).

59 "Understanding must reign among the members of the medical profession, and doctors must make up a large family," writes Dr. Laffite in his plea for the "renovation" of medicine (*Le Médecin de France, son rôle dans la société moderne,* 789).

60 Dr. Cibrié, "Les médecins étrangers en France," *Le Médecin de France* (15 April 1930).

61 Oudin, *L'Ordre des médecins,* 23.

62 Desmarest, *L'Ordre des médecins,* 28.

63 Sergent, *La Formation intellectuelle et morale des élites,* 63–64.

64 *Bulletin de l'Ordre des médecins* 4 (1942).

65 See Yvonne Knibiehler, "Idéologies et politiques familiales," *Informations sociales* 4–5 (1980).

66 "Une loi de protection" [the law of 16 August 1940], *Le Temps* (22 August 1940). In *La Seule France,* Maurras reprises this article in full, saluting both this recognition of the principle of professional heredity and the elimination of the "métèque-king" from the medical profession.

67 "Serment d'Hippocrate, A l'adresse des Femmes de Médecins, La vraie femme du médecin, Texte ancien retrouvé et traduit du grec en novembre 1934," certified true copy, Dr. Jean Halle, Honorary doctor of the Hospitals, *Cahiers Laennec* 1 (January 36).

68 "Madame Pasteur, un modèle de femme française," *Candide* (31 December 1941).

69 J. Castaigne, "Le professeur Sergent et les élites médicales," *Revue des deux mondes* (15 November 1943).

70 In the homage to Sergent after his death in 1943, Professor Castaigne cited the speech given by Professor Sergent when he left the presidency of the Academy of Medicine in January 1942: "Professor Sergent gave another bit

of advice, particularly valuable at a time when too many French have a tendency to trust their health and that of their children to so-called specialists with only a degree and to abandon the sound tradition of the family doctor whose professional and moral worth they know" (ibid.). Elsewhere, Professor Castaigne states: "In big cities, some doctors, particularly foreigners, it must be said, called themselves specialists without having completed any special studies in the sense that they claim to have a special competence. How much more worth the old system had. Families had their single doctor who had known them for years" ("Les Médecins de France").

71 Dr. Charles Fiessinger, *Souvenirs d'un médecin de campagne,* ed. Alexis Redier (Paris: Librairie de la Revue française, 1933), 114. Fiessinger provided articles for the newspaper of the Action française, *Le Médecin.*

72 Delore, *L'Éducation et la Santé,* 63–64, 83, 88, 127; emphasis added. Dr. Delore was founding director of the Regional Health Education Center of Lyon.

73 Biancani and Biancani, *La Communauté familiale,* 148.

74 Vérine, *Le Noviciat du mariage,* 11, 17.

75 Laffite, *Le Médecin, sa formation, son rôle dans la société moderne,* 161–65.

76 "Pour celles qui veulent se dévouer, les Écoles de la Croix-Rouge," *Éducation* 59 (February 1941).

77 See Veillon, "La vie quotidienne des femmes," 629–39.

78 Dr. Hélène Lesterlin de Bellet, *Joie de vivre: Petit manuel de vie saine à l'usage des jeunes filles de France* (Paris: R. Bussière in Saint-Armand du Cher, 1943, [disseminated by the Secretariat General for Youth]), 3–5; emphasis in original.

79 Quoted in Sergent, *La Formation intellectuelle et morale des élites,* 62. It was Professor Sergent himself, undoubtedly more assured of his own total adherence than that of his own colleagues, who drafted the critique of this grandiose opuscule in *La Presse médicale* in September 1942.

80 See Castaigne, "Le professeur Sergent et les élites médicale."

81 Thalmann, *Être femme sous le IIIe Reich,* 104.

82 Professor G. A. Wagner, in charge of women's services for the Charity Hospital in Berlin, director of the Gynecology Archives, declared "the nation's stock of ovaries a national resource and property of the German State" (quoted in Proctor, *Racial Hygiene; Medicine under the Nazis,* 125).

83 de Penfentenyo, *Manuel du père de famille,* 112.

84 See Thébaud, *Quand nos grand-mères donnaient la vie,* 19–22.

85 C. Watson, "Birth Control and Abortion in France since 1939," *Population Studies* 5 (1952).

86 *Revue de l'Alliance nationale contre la dépopulation,* 1939; reprinted in Thébaud, *Quand nos grand-mères donnaient la vie,* 17.

87 Garcin, *Révolution sociale par la famille,* 17–18.

88 Fernand Boverat, *Le Massacre des innocents,* new ed. 1944; Archives nationales, F 41291. In his report on the birthrate, with the team he directed

at the Carrel Foundation, Boverat would say that doctor-patient privilege must not protect criminals: "Now the woman whose life is endangered by an abortionist is a criminal, like a mother who wounds herself with her knife while cutting the throat of her newborn" (French Foundation for the Study of Human Problems, Projects, Department I, *Une doctrine de natalité* [Paris: Librairie de Médicis, 1943]), 37.

89 Pierre l'Ermite, "Les femmes qui tuent," *Voix françaises familiales* (January 1944).

90 René d'Argentan, "Le massacre des innocents," *La Légion* (15 February 1942).

91 Louis Portes, "A propos de l'avortement criminel," in *Dangers et Risques de l'avortement,* brochure of the Commissariat General for the Family, confidential, n.d.; BDIC, reserve, Gr. fol. 126–6.

92 Watson, "Birth Control and Abortion in France since 1939."

93 *L'Oeuvre* (7 March 1942). The newspaper thus introduced Dr. Huard's press conference: "Almost a year ago, *L'Oeuvre* drew the attention of the Public Authorities to one of the most serious plagues slyly attacking the French population in its power of renewal and in the quality of its procreators: abortion. We demanded a ruthless, repressive law that was to deliver a fatal blow to the industry of certain quacks, foreign for the most part, and certain 'specialized' midwives."

94 Thalmann, *Être femme sous le IIIe Reich,* 120, 134.

95 Watson, "Birth Control and Abortion in France since 1939."

96 Ibid., 286; Guerrand and Rupp, *Brève Histoire du service social en France,* 84.

97 *Bulletin de liaison* (15 March 1943).

98 Dr. Roy, "Le fléau de l'avortement," *L'Actualité sociale* 180 (May 1943).

99 *Cahiers de la Fondation française pour l'étude des problèmes humains* 2 (October 1944): 22.

100 Alexis Carrel, *Réflexions sur la conduite de la vie* (1950; Paris: Presses Pocket, 1981), 77. This posthumous work was finished by Carrel's wife from his notes.

101 See Alain Brossat, *Les Tondues, un carnaval moche* (Paris: Éd. Manya, 1993).

102 Watson, "Birth Control and Abortion in France since 1939."

103 Henri Minot, "L'Informe," *Le Médecin* (15 June 1927).

104 Carrel, *Man, the Unknown,* 27, 319, 321.

105 Ibid., 24.

106 *Cahiers de la Fondation française pour l'étude des problèmes humains* 1 (1943); 2 (1944); unless otherwise indicated, I am referring to these two publications and to the "Rapport au Chef de l'État sur l'activité de la Fondation en 1942," Archives nationales, 2 AG 78.

107 "La maternité donne à la femme son équilibre," in Commissariat General for the Family, *La Vie en fleur,* 108.

108 "La maternité embellit la femme," in ibid.

109 Summary of *La Femme et sa mission,* in "Femme, Famille, France," *Votre*

Beauté (October 1941), and "La maternité donne santé et beauté," in *La Plus Belle Femme au monde,* Office of general propaganda with the assistance of *Votre Beauté* (n.d.).

110 "Les dangers des pratiques anticonceptionelle," February 1944; "This tract is not for children"; Archives nationales, F 41 291; emphasis added.

111 Carrel, *Réflexions sur la conduite de la vie,* 117.

112 Carrel, *Man, the Unkown,* 92; emphasis added.

113 Julien-Joseph Virey wrote, among others, the articles "Man," "Woman," and "Girl" for the *Dictionnaire des sciences médicales* published by Panckoucke in sixty-seven volumes from 1812 to 1822; he also published thirty-seven works, including *Histoire naturelle du genre humain,* published in 1801 and republished in 1825, and *De la femme sous ses rapports physiologique, moral et littéraire,* published in 1823, which for a long time would impose itself as a reference work on feminine nature; see Yvonne Knibiehler and Catherine Fouquet, *La Femme et les Médecins* (Paris: Hachette, 1983), 88. On the medical representation of the "feminine continent," see also Jean-Pierre Peter, "Les médecins et les femmes," in *Misérable et Glorieuse: La femme du XIXe siècle,* ed. Jean-Paul Aron (1980; Brussels: Complexe, 1984), and "Entre femmes et médecins," *Ethnologie française* 3–4 (1976).

114 Quoted in Knibiehler and Fouquet, *La Femme et les Médecins,* 96.

115 Françoise Héritier, "Le sang du guerrier et le sang des femmes: Notes anthropologiques sur le rapport des sexes," *Les Cahiers du GRIF* 29 (winter 1984–1985): 12–13.

116 Varenne, *La Femme dans la France nouvelle,* 23.

117 Henri Vibert, "Êtes-vous des hommes?" *Le Réveil du peuple* (17 December 1940); quoted in Cotta, *La Collaboration, 1940–44,* 217.

118 Quoted in Bordeaux, "Femmes hors d'Etat français," 137.

119 "The revolution is underway. In cadenced step, family men, male cohorts, are going toward their prime on the altars of the grateful country, from the hands of sturdy young women in ancient headdresses" (Jacques Bostan, "Prélude à heurter," *Idées* 10–11 [September 1942]).

120 Carrel, *Man, the Unknown,* 314–55.

121 *L'Instituteur et son rôle dans la restauration de la famille française* and *La Commune rempart de la famille.*

122 E. Coeurdevey, "L'autorité du chef de famille," *Éducation* 70 (March 1942).

123 A. Brandt-Mieg, "La famille, centre d'interêt," *Éducation* 78 (March 1943).

124 On the Catholic tradition of women caregivers nurtured by the culture of sacrifice and its influence on the medical field, see Jacques Léonard, "Femmes, religion et médecine: Les religieuses qui soignent en France au XIXe siècle," *Annales* (September–October 1977).

125 Biot, "Biologie et nature de la femme," in *La Femme dans la société,* 134.

126 Varenne, *La Femme dans la France nouvelle,* 42, 44.

127 See Pierre Bourdieu, *Réponses: Pour une anthropologie réflexive* (Paris: Seuil, 1992), to which I refer for what follows; 142–43, 146–47.

128 Lesterlin de Bellet, *Joie de vivre: Petit manuel de vie saine à l'usage des jeunes filles de France,* 21, 50, 63, 14.

129 See Jean-Louis Gay-Lescot, *Sport et Éducation sous Vichy* (Lyon: Presses universitaires de Lyon, 1991), 60–61, 80–81.

130 "Le sport et la femme," *Jeunesse . . . France!* (8 May 1941). In the same way, the fascist Italian regime long prohibited feminine participation in Olympic competitions—dangerous for the reproductive capability of woman—as it prohibited the feminine sections of fascist university groups from competing in the sparring matches of the *littoriali* of culture and art, because these sparring matches required a power of synthesis "that does not seem to be proper to woman's mentality" and involved "discussions that were often lively and fiery that would not be appropriate to feminine delicacy." See Denise Detragiache, "De la 'mamma' à la nouvelle Italienne: La presse des femmes fascistes de 1930 à 1942," in *La Tentation nationaliste, 1914–1945,* Rita Thalmann (Paris: Éd. Deuxtemps/Tierce, 1990), 162–63. This exclusion from the world of competition in its most spectacular form once again inscribes the feminine world in the "reserved" sphere of the private space and self-restraint on the pediment of feminine virtues.

131 Marie-Thérèse Eyquem, "La doctrine nationale dans les associations sportives féminines," and "Éducation physique et sportive féminine," *Éducation générale et Sports* [review of the Commissariat General for General Education and Sports] 17 (October 1943) and 1 (January–February–March–April 1942).

132 "La femme et le sport," *Éducation générale et Sports* (April–May–June 1943).

133 Pierre Bourdieu, *Le Sens pratique* (Paris: Minuit, "Le sens commun," 1980), 117.

134 "La femme et la solidité du lien conjugal," *La Femme dans la vie sociale* 164 (December 1943); emphasis added.

135 Mme du Peloux de Saint-Romain, "La femme et la maison," *Chronique sociale de France* (May–June 1943).

136 René Biot, "Biologie et nature de la femme," 129–30; emphasis added.

137 Carrel, *Man, the Unknown,* 89–90; emphasis added.

138 R. P. Sertillanges, "La maison, le père," *Voix françaises* (23 January 1942); emphasis added.

139 Varenne, *La Femme dans la France nouvelle,* 57, 60.

140 Carrel, *Man, the Unknown,* 271, 121, 127, 139, 243, 304.

141 Bourdieu, "Le Nord et le Midi, contribution à une analyse de l'effet Montesquieu."

142 Pierre Gourou, "Le déterminisme physique dans 'L'Esprit des lois,'" *L'Homme* (September–December 1963).

143 See Suzanna Barrows, *Miroirs déformants: Réflexions sur la foule en France à la fin du XIXe siècle* (1981; Paris: Aubier, 1990); the quotation that follows is taken from this work (48; emphasis added).

144 Carrel, *Man, the Unknown,* 295–96.

145 Ibid., 299, 271, 255.

146 *Cahiers de la Fondation pour l'étude des problèmes humains* 1 and 2; unless otherwise indicated, I refer to these two brochures for the description of the surveys conducted by the Foundation.

147 See Martine Dumont, "Le succès mondain d'une fausse science: La physiognomonie de Johann Kaspar Lavater," *Actes de la recherche en sciences sociales* 54 (September 1984).

148 Laurent Thévenot has shown that the reflection on "eugenic social value" developed in part at the Carrel Foundation made the Institut National des Etudes Démographiques's (INED) reputation for statistics during the period from 1950 to 1960 ("La politique des statistiques: Les origines sociales des enquêtes de mobilité sociale," *Annales* [November–December 1990]).

149 Carrel, *Man, the Unknown*, 255, 271, 298.

150 Quoted in Michèle Cointet, *Le Conseil national de Vichy: Vie politique et réforme de l'État en régime autoritaire, 1940–44* (Ph.D. diss., Paris-X, 1984), 877–78.

151 See Michel Chauvière, *Enfance inadaptée: L'héritage de Vichy* (Paris: Les Éditions ouvrières, 1980); Francine Muel-Dreyfus, "L'initiative privée: Le 'terrain' de l'éducation spécialisée," *Actes de recherche en sciences sociales* 32–33 (1980).

152 Carrel, *Man, the Unknown*, 318–19.

153 Ibid., 300, 296, 276–77.

154 See Le Bras, "Histoire secrète de la fécondité," 85–87.

155 See Gisela Bock, "Racism and Sexism in Nazi Germany: Motherhood, Compulsory Sterilization and the State," *Signs* 3 (spring 1983).

156 *Cahiers de la Foundation pour l'étude des problèmes humains* 1: 21. One finds this portrait of "bad stocks" in *La Revue de la famille* 230 (July 1942): "these swaggering fathers who are always armed with some human right" who "as family allowances increase feel their thirst grow," "these vicious protesters who drape themselves in their family like a flag."

157 Schneider, "Towards the Improvement of the Human Race: The History of Eugenics in France."

158 Proctor, *Racial Hygiene: Medicine under the Nazis*, 132.

159 Varenne, *La Femme dans la France nouvelle*, 64.

160 "Causerie du docteur," *Voix françaises familiales* (May 1942); emphasis added.

161 Carrel, *Man, the Unknown*, 364; emphasis added.

162 Félix-André Missenard [vice regent of the Foundation and director of the department of the Biology of Population], "Note sur le redressement de la natalité française"; quoted in Drouard, *Une inconnue des sciences sociales, la fondation Alexis-Carrel*, 223, 224. In the same note, he proposed rejecting "excessive studies for women," eliminating the "professional opportunities that he found inappropriate (lawyer, engineer)," fighting against the "attraction of worldly and sports pleasures that divert from having children," and creating a rosette for pregnant women and mothers of large families.

163 "Rapport au Chef de l'État sur l'activité de la Fondation en 1942," Archives nationales, 2 AG 78.

164 André de Maricourt, "Connaître ses aïeux est un devoir à remplir," *Voix françaises* 37 (26 September 1941).

165 "Note sur la création d'un Office des archives de la famille française"; archives of the CDJC, CCXXXVIII-34.

166 Quoted in Drouard, *Une inconnue des sciences sociales, la fondation Alexis-Carrel,* 231.

167 *Cahiers de la Fondation française pour l'étude des problèmes humains,* 2:21.

168 The collection of the monthly *Bibliographical Bulletin of the Foundation,* whose first issue dates from October 1942, is kept at the BDIC, 4°P 3917.

169 Drouard, *Une inconnue des sciences sociales, la fondation Alexis-Carrel,* 230. It is surprising that in his work devoted to demonstrating that only anodyne and banal conceptions of social hygiene inspired the work of Carrel and his Foundation, Drouard does not deem it useful to clarify for his readers the role played by Montandon and Martial in the anti-Semitic propaganda of Vichy.

170 On the sinister career of Montandon, see Marrus and Paxton, *Vichy France and the Jews,* 300–301; Billig, *Le Commissariat général aux questions juives,* 2: 310–15; Pierre Birnbaum, *La France aux Français: Histoire des haines nationalistes* (Paris: Seuil, 1993), 187–98. One could add to these biographies that Montandon, an obscure Swiss doctor and self-taught theoretician of physical anthropology, could also figure (like René Martial) in the gallery of dominated intellectuals maintaining a shaky relationship with the university whose "scientific" production and audience on the eve of the French Revolution are analyzed by Robert Darnton, *La Fin des Lumières* (Paris: Librairie académique Perrin, 1984).

171 For example, Dr. Henri Briand, "Les vraies familles françaises doivent revivre," *L'Ethnie française* 1 (1941).

172 "Place pour nos enfants," *L'Ethnie française* 1 (1941).

173 Georges Mauco, "L'immigration étrangère en France et le problème des réfugiés," *L'Ethnie française* 6 (1942); emphasis added.

174 See Birnbaum, "Hermaphrodisme et perversions sexuelles," chap. 7 in *Un mythe politique: La "République juive."*

175 This text has been totally forgotten. At the liberation, Georges Mauco was appointed secretary general of the High Committee of Population and Family (where one would find Fernand Boverad and the profamily supporters) and occupied this position until 1970. Interested in psychopedagogy and psychoanalysis, in 1945 he founded the first psychopedagogical consultation at the lycée Claude-Bernard.

176 de Maricourt, "Connaître ses aïeux est un devoir à remplir"; emphasis in original.

177 *Le Matin* (22 December 1942); quoted in Polonski, *La Presse, la Propagande et l'Opinion publique sous l'Occupation,* 145.

178 René Martial, *Les Métis: Nouvelle étude sur les migrations, le mélange des races, le métissage, la retrempe de la race française et la révision du Code de la famille* (Paris: Flammarion, 1942), 179, 44; emphasis added. On the psychiatric construction of a specifically Jewish psychic instability, see Sander L. Gilman, "Jews and Mental Illness: Medical Metaphors, Anti-Semitism, and the Jewish Response," *Journal of the History of Behavioral Sciences* 20 (April 1984).

179 Martial, *Les Métis,* chap. 9, particularly 215, 219, 225.

180 See Marrus and Paxton, *Vichy France and the Jews,* 283–310; Billig, *Le Commissariat général aux questions juives,* 2: 170–73.

181 Billig, *Le Commissariat général aux questions juives,* 2: 316.

182 Union française pour la défense de la race, broadcast of 5 February 1943, 12 P.M.; the transcription of these broadcasts is kept in the archives of the CDJC, LXI-105, 18.

183 Union française pour la défense de la race, broadcast of 8 February 1943, 12 P.M.; CDJC, LXI-105, 22.

184 Union française pour la défense de la race, broadcasts of 12 February and 1 February 1943; CDJC, LXI-105, 25, 14.

185 *Revue de la famille* 225 (February 1942); emphasis added.

186 "Recrutement des Dames SMS," *La Légion* 32 (15 December 1942); "Instructions sur le recrutement de la Légion," *La Légion* 19 (15 November 1941).

187 Union française pour la défense de la race, *La Fête des Mères* by Paule Marguy, broadcast of 17 May 1943; capitalization in the transcription; CDJC, LXI-105, 79.

CONCLUSION

1 The doctrine of Salazar and the unending philosophical-political developments of this "habitually" "focal-word where all the rays of thought converge," are presented by Henri Massis in *Chefs* (Paris: Plon, 1939), 99–103, in which he collects the amazing conversations that he had with Mussolini, Salazar, and Franco just before the war.

2 See Nicole-Claude Mathieu, *L'Anatomie politique: Catégorisation et idéologie de sexe* (Paris: Côté-Femmes, 1992), particularly chap. 2, "Homme-culture et femme-nature?"

3 See Paxton, *Vichy France,* 139–45.

4 See Hoffman, "Aspects du régime de Vichy."

5 See Jean-Pierre Azéma, "Vichy," in *Histoire de l'extrême droite en France,* ed. Michel Winock (Paris: Seuil, "Points Histoire," 1994), 191.

6 Colette Guillaumin, *L'Ideologie raciste: Genèse et langage actuel* (Paris-La Haye: Mouton, 1972), 50–51.

7 Philippe Burrin, "La France dans le champ magnétique des fascismes," *Le Débat* 32 (November 1984).

Dunoyer de Segonzac, Pierre, 200, 253
Dupanloup, Monsignor, 186, 295
Duquesne, Jacques, 49
Durand, Marguerite, 135; Yves, 3, 109, 125
Durkheim, Émile, 172, 216, 217, 224, 246, 247
Duthoit, Eugène, 56, 61, 157
Dutoit, Monsignor, 48

Eck, Hélène, 102, 342 n.12
École des parents, 157, 164–166, 213, 239, 248, 277, 323
École et Famille, 211
École et Liberté (APEL), 213, 357 n.85, 363 nn.70, 74
École normale sociale, 136, 156, 158, 349 n.49
École supérieure de cadres féminins d'Écully, 244, 365 n.93
École supérieure de cadres masculins d'Uriage, 244, 251, 253, 254, 294, 365 n.93
Éducation, 79, 238, 239, 240, 244, 248, 251, 291
Éducation, L', 239
Edwards-Pilliet, Dr. Blanche, 138
Elias, Norbert, 331 n.60
Equipes et cadres de la France nouvelle, 202
Espoir français, L', 178
Ésprit, 155, 214
Ethnie française, L', 304–306
Études, 55, 336 n.59

Fabrègues, Jean de, 155, 290
Farnier, René, 330 n.39
Faÿ, Bernard, 216
Federation of Associations of Parents of Lycée and Collège Students, 213
Fédération française des étudiants catholiques, 154
Federation of French Families, 175, 194

Fédération internationale des femmes médecins, 159
Fédération nationale des associations de familles nombreuses, 76
Fédération nationale catholique (FNC), 160
Fédération nationale des syndicats médicaux, 369 n.27
Fédération protestante de France, 165
Fédération des Unions de familles nombreuses du Nord, 349 n.47
Félibrige, 28
Feminine Civic and Social Union (UFCS), 126
Féminisme chrétien, Le, 125, 135
Feminist University Federation, 134
Femme contemporaine, La, 135
Femme dans la vie sociale, La (UFCS), 165, 167, 241
Ferry, Jules, 98
Fessard, Father, 41, 56, 333 n.12
Fèvre, Henri, 65
Figaro, Le, 7
Flandin, Pierre-Étienne, 86
Flaubert, Gustave, 18, 27
Fondation française pour l'étude des problèmes humains. *See* French Foundation for the Study of Human Problems
Forestier, Father, 47, 48
Foucault, Michel, 65
Française, La, 134, 183
Française d'aujourd'hui, La, 110, 336 n.59
France-Family (France-Famille) (radio broadcast of the Commissariat General for the Family), 109, 253
France 41: La Révolution nationale constructive, un bilan et an programme, 164
Franco, General, 24, 378 n.1
François, Lucien, 107
Fraternal Union of Women, 135
French Eugenics Society, 67
French Foundation for the Study of Human Problems, 72, 264, 373 n.88

French League Of Women's Right (LFDF), 134

French Legion of Combatants, 282, 309. *See also* Légion française des combattants

French Union for the Defense of the Race, 307, 309

French Union for Women's Suffrage (UFSF), 134–138, 155, 160

French Women's Patriotic League, 135

Freud, Sigmund, 3, 328 n.14

Fronde, La, 135

Fustel de Coulanges, 22, 176, 359 n.17

Fustel-de-Coulanges Circle (Cercle Fustel-de-Coulanges), 33, 215, 217, 218, 220, 224, 227, 246, 247

Galton, Sir Francis, 302

Gambetta, Léon, 18, 27

Ganay, Father Maurice de, 57

Garcin, William, 175, 176, 195, 281, 352 n.9, 357 n.80

Garrone, Louis, 364 n.79

Gaulle, Charles de, 43, 333 n.12

Gayraud, Amélie, 359 n.24

General Confederation of Families, 303

Gérando, Joseph-Marie, baron de, 22

Gerbe, La, 135

Gerlier, Cardinal, 41, 116, 230

Gessain, Dr. Robert, 304

Gide, André, 36, 247

Gillet, Father, 52, 60, 158, 250, 335 n.41

Gillouin, René, 36, 175, 179, 191, 216, 332 n.61, 334 n.23

Ginzburg, Carlo, 129

Giraudoux, Jean, 87–89, 106

Gobineau, Arthur de, 17, 66, 306

Goebbels, Joseph, 339 n.35

Goffman, Erving, 109

Gounot, Emmanuel, 194, 195, 356 n.64

Gourou, Pierre, 297

Goyau, Georges, 35, 136

Grasset, Dr. Raymond, 270, 271, 274

Grimaud, Abbé, 156

Gringoire, La, 85

Guéhenno, Jean, 114

Guibal, Jean, 179, 195

Guillaumin, Colette, 324

Guillaumin, Emile, 28

Guitton, Jean, 83

Guizot, François, 233

Halévy, Daniel, 19, 20, 21, 24, 28, 33, 216

Halévy, Ludovic, 329 n.13

Haury, Paul, 91, 104, 105, 108, 247, 344 n.24

Haut comité de la population et de la famille, 68, 76, 77. *See also* High Committee of Population and Family

Henriot, Philippe, 43, 160, 333 n.12, 358 n.7

Heritier, Françoise, 289

Herriot, Édouard, 212

High Committee of Population and Family, 377 n.175. *See also* Haut comité de la population et de la famille

High Council for Natality, 111

Higher Council of the Doctors Association, 262, 269, 272

Hitler, Adolf, 7, 112, 267, 280, 367 n.5

Hoffmann, Stanley, 272

Hourdin, Georges, 345 n.60

Huard, Dr. Serge, 104, 108, 261, 275, 283, 355 n.54, 368 n.17, 373 n.93

Hugo, Victor, 134

Huntziger, General, 16

Idées, 290

Institute of Anthroposociology, 306

Institute of Social Geneology, 308

International Scientific Union on Population, 87

Service du travail obligatoire (STO),
101, 343 n.15
Siegfried, André, 70, 137, 153
Siegfried, Jules, 342 n.11
Siegfried, Mme Jules, 134, 137
Simon, Jules, 342 n.11
Simonot, Dr., 66
Société des agrégées, 159
Société des gens de lettres, 210
Solanges, Father Bruno de, 50
Sorel, Georges, 20
Soury, Jules, 258
Spengler, Oswald, 69
Stelli, Jean, 364 n.77
Sternhell, Zeev, 258
Study Center for Human Problems,
364 n.89
Study Commission for Youth of the
Conseil National, 216
Suhard, Cardinal, 41, 43, 351 n.73
Sullerot, Évelyne, 226
Supervielle, Jules, 82

Taine, Hippolyte, 17, 22, 24, 209
Tarde, Alfred de, 216
Temple, Shirley, 187
Temps, Le, 1, 86, 87, 213, 214, 222, 230,
232, 234, 274, 352 n.5, 361 n.42, 362
n.62
Thalmann, Rita, 112
Thérèse of Lisieux, 24, 35, 121, 128,
129, 130, 155
Thévenot, Laurent, 376 n.148
Thibon, Gustave, 18, 23, 24, 28, 33, 83,
200, 223, 229, 250, 251, 256, 287

Union for the Defense of the Race,
308
Union libérale israélite, 165
Union nationale des avocates, 159
Union des syndicats médicaux de
France, 369 n.27

Vacher de Lapouge, Georges, 258
Vallat, Xavier, 308
Varenne, Georgette, 353 n.36
Vaugeois, Henri, 32
Vautel, Clément, 88, 89, 341 n.71
Veillon, Dominique, 343 n.12, 344
n.34
Verdier, Cardinal, 49, 51, 156
Vérine (pseudonym of Marguerite
Lebrun), 165, 166, 239, 248, 277
Vérone, Maria, 226
Victoire, La, 7
Vie en fleur, La, 64, 91, 278
Vie intellectuelle, La, 214
Vincent, René, 290
Viollet, Abbé, 165, 239, 248
Viot, Marcel, 197
Virey, Julien-Joseph, 374 n.113
Voix françaises, 53
Voix françaises familiales, 53, 281
Votre Beauté, 107, 108, 188, 354 n.37
Vu, 7

Wagner, G. A., 372 n.82
Weber, Eugen, 33, 37; Max, 3, 70
Weygand, General, 84, 216, 218, 219,
366 n.118
Witt-Schlumberger, Mme de, 134
Women's Civic and Social Union
(UFCS), 156–161, 165, 167–169, 184,
182
Women's Social Action, 136
World Conference on Population, 82

Ybarnégaray, Jean, 137, 215
Young Christian Women Workers
(JOCF), 244

Zanta, Léontine, 231
Zay, Jean, 179, 212, 214, 236, 358 n.7,
359 n.16, 363 n.70
Zola, Émile, 27

Francine Muel-Dreyfus is Directrice d'études at
l'École des Hautes Études en Sciences Sociales in Paris.
She is the author of *Le Métier d'éducateur: Les Instituteurs
de 1900, les Éducateurs Spécialisés de 1968* (1983).

Kathleen Johnson holds a Ph.D. in French from the
University of California, Irvine. She has published
articles on the novels of Jorge Semprun.

Library of Congress Cataloging-in-Publication Data
Muel-Dreyfus, Francine
[Vichy et l'éternel féminin. English]
Vichy and the eternal feminine : a contribution
to a political sociology of gender / Francine
Muel-Dreyfus ; translated by Kathleen A. Johnson.
p. cm.   Includes index.
ISBN 0-8223-2777-5 (cloth : alk. paper)
ISBN 0-8223-2774-0 (pbk. : alk. paper)
1. Vichy (France)—Politics and government.
2. France—History—German occupation, 1940–
1945. 3. National socialism and women—France—
Vichy. 4. Women—France—Social conditions.
I. Johnson, Kathleen A. II. Title.
DC397 .M7413 2001   705.42′0944′09044—dc21   2001033656